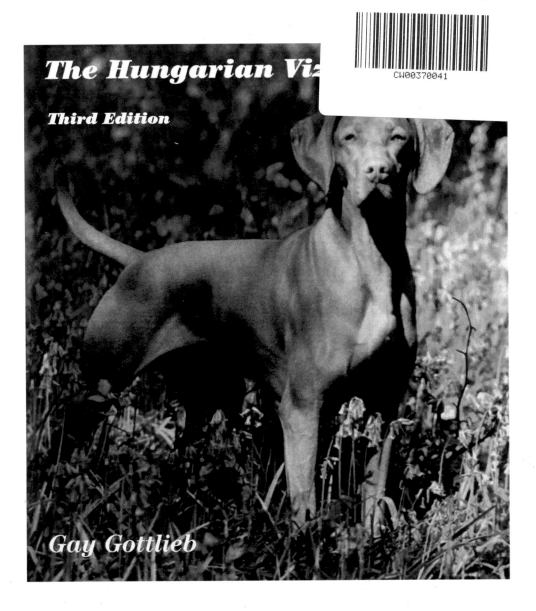

The Hungarian Viz...

Third Edition

Gay Gottlieb

Front cover: Armstrong's Happy Hero. Photo: Kevill Armstrong.

Title page: White's Russetmantle Admiral of Arunszvar.

Appendices photographs: Zara Hart.

© 2011 Russetmantle Books England. All rights reserved.

Published by: Russetmantle Books.

ISBN: 978-0-9569497-0-7

Reprinted in 2011 by: CMP (uk) Limited • www.cmp-uk.com

Preface to the Third Edition of The Hungarian Vizsla

It was a great shock to all in the Vizsla world when Gay Gottlieb passed away in October 2009. She was 78 years old yet still full of energy and in the prime of life, continuing to breed, show and work her Russetmantles, and planning the third edition of this popular book. Only a few months previously she had been honoured by the Lifetime Achievement Award of the Hungarian Vizsla Society. The huge demand for another edition of The Hungarian Vizsla has been met by her son Peter Gottlieb. Nobody can improve upon Gay's depth of knowledge of the breed, her inimitable style and the love and joy that shine from every page, and not a single word has been altered beyond this preface.

In her second edition Gay acknowledged the help of Barbara Douglas-Redding, Sharon Seward, Sue Millson, Sue Harris, Louise Petrie-Hay and Jackie Perkins.

In addition to her original dedication, this edition is dedicated to the memory of Gay Gottlieb by her children, Sue, Peter, Max, Jim and Mark.

Dedication

To Sydney and our children.

Introduction

I wrote the major part of this piece for the first edition of the book and it appeared in the chapter on Standards. Since then my appreciation and love for the breed has grown, so the chapter grew too! However, it seems to say it all about the breed so here is my introduction to the Hungarian Vizsla.

From the first moment I saw a Hungarian Vizsla I was captivated by the breed and I am still. To this day, the breed does not cease to enchant, captivate and arrest me. I appreciate his manifest devotion, his loving and emotional sensitivity, the nature which craves approval and a loving touch. I admire his ability to switch to the wildness of his animal world which he does not relinquish for one moment, and which lurks there as part of his very being. This is the essence of him, and I love being responsive and responsible for nurturing his natural instincts as a gundog.

To me he remains the proud creature that I met nearly 30 years ago standing in the sunlight, his russet-gold coat rich against the spring green. He was alone in a field, alert and agile, every muscle tense, head held high, nose twitching, aware of nothing else but the sights and senses in his dog world. He relaxed and threw himself on the ground and rolled, pressing his shoulders deep in the grass, pushing his muzzle forward into the daisies. Finally he lay still on his back, his legs in the air while he gazed at the passing clouds. This joy and zest for living culminated in one last ecstatic fling before he sprang to his feet effortlessly and stood proudly as before. He caught sight of us laughing at him. He ran towards us wagging his tail with delight. I never cease to appreciate this breed's ability to move me and then reduce me to laughter by its ridiculous antics.

Months later, I saw more Hungarian Vizslas at a field trial. It was a cold, wet, foggy day. The rain poured relentlessly, soaking dogs and handlers through to the skin. I had driven through the countryside since dawn, anticipating a glorious, clear autumn day, expecting all the excitement of a shoot with the added thrill of watching Hungarian Vizslas competing - nothing could have been further from my imaginings. There was no game to be seen, visibility was nil, small groups of sodden competitors huddled gloomily under the scant shelter provided by the bare trees. But as the green-clad figures trudged from field to field hoping for sight, sound or scent of pheasant, the Vizslas trotted by their sepulchral side, ever alert and ready to work. No sodden mud or lack of game could suppress their eagerness, nor rain or wind halt them. I watched a small Vizsla bitch work through a field of kale so high there was no sign of a russet-gold coat but, as she quartered back and forth the foliage bent, indicating her methodical search for game. Another Vizsla, on point, could not be distracted. He knew there was game in the hedge, and there was. While he stood rigid, raindrops fell from his ears, nose and belly. The pheasant shot, on command he bounded off into the fog to retrieve it and returned with his prize, carrying it gently to hand, shivering with cold and excitement. (Steadiness is not included in the Standard, but it is vital in this breed, as it is in any gundog.)

This breed is a pleasure to own if his temperament suits you and yours suits him. He needs to be part of your life and your world. He loves to feel he is one of the family. Whether he is in the house or out walking with you, he is not a dog that remains out of sight for long. He rarely wanders far and his eyes seek you out wherever you are. He may appear to be asleep by the fire but, if you move, he will be wide awake, prepared to go where you will. His idea of comfort and relaxation may not fit in with his owners' plans for him, for it is difficult not to spoil him. He expects to sit by you on the settee, his brown eyes gazing at you in rapture as he rests his head on your shoulder. If you ask him to remove himself, he cannot believe you mean it and will stubbornly hide his head under your arm or beneath a cushion. He is happy to sleep in your bedroom, kitchen or the kennel, but happiest of all to have company at all times.

His faithfulness is never questioned; such is his devotion to his family and his territory, it can lead to over-possessiveness. He is a creature of contrariness and fancies, his sensitivity and stubbornness difficult to understand and deal with. It can affect his behaviour in every aspect, be he pet or gundog. He can cringe if spoken to harshly whilst firmly persisting on having his own way until you have asserted yourself in a particular manner which he finds acceptable. But woe betide you if you do it by force. He can fold up completely as his stubbornness increases and it can undo months of effective training. He can be terrified by a fly, he may hide behind your chair at the sight of a curtain billowing in the breeze, the smallest kitten can dominate him, but he will guard your property, and the fiercest of meter ladies will flinch if she dares to approach your car.

He finds it difficult to accept that not everyone likes to have their wrist held in his mouth, however gently, a habit all Vizslas seem to have. Some Vizslas can become too persistent, insisting on asserting themselves to a point where they can get out of hand. He needs discipline and, if not corrected, his assertion can lead to aggression. From early on, he must know who is 'boss'. Once that is established he accepts totally and would rarely challenge it except in fun.

At his best, he should be well-muscled and well-covered but not fat. Nothing is hidden on this short-coated breed. Every fault and blemish can be seen. He should be an agile dog, lithe and speedy. He can jump and leap like a deer, using his powerful quarters. His sure-footedness can be alarming - watch him leap from rock to rock or racing up and down sheer cliffs without a slip. Working the Vizsla through woodland, not a footfall is heard such is his sensitivity to silence and the need for stealth. This breed can work all day, never seeming to tire. He is a strong swimmer and should love the water.

He has a delightful, whimsical side to his nature. He can stalk a butterfly or a bee, pointing as it settles on a flower then, discerning it as an insect and not game, will tiptoe past! What pleasure it is to watch puppies stalking and pointing summer moths as they flutter in the light shed from the lamp. He will sit quietly watching a water wagtail darting backwards and forwards, or a house martin building its nest. He can merge with the stillness of the trout by the weed awaiting its passing nymphs. He can move through reeds and rushes with almost no sound, lowering himself into the water with hardly a ripple, swimming so skillfully along the water's edge that even a moorhen will not know he has passed by.

I remember walking six adult Vizslas through the woods after a thaw, the drips as they fell sounding loud on the autumn leaves, the mist lurking about the trees. The silence and loneliness made twelve dark eyes dart from side to side. I was glad of their company and they of mine as we crept out of the wood and walked quickly home for tea.

Most people who own a Hungarian Vizsla would agree that he is not for those who have never owned a dog before. He needs a good deal of understanding and tolerance and he will stretch your patience beyond its limits sometimes. Roar at him in a temper, he will creep towards you as if beaten and will take time to forgive you, but he will never forget.

A good Vizsla will work for you in any capacity. He needs to use his brain. He is highly intelligent at his best; his awareness and alertness, his responsiveness to command and the ease with which he can learn allows him a varied range of activities - hunting, working trials, trialling, showing, agility or whatever you wish. However none of these is possible unless you can come to terms with his temperament. His desire to please and his longing to hear his owner praise him, his intense wish to be involved with whoever is handling him can be the key in early training. A compromise can often be the trick, instead of direct confrontation, as long as he respects you. Over-handling and too much discipline without giving him a chance to succeed in any direction can augment a certain stubbornness that is part of his nature. Reward by hand and voice will get you everywhere; severe treatment, nowhere.

He will learn a lesson very quickly and as quickly become bored if pressed to repeat it over and over again. If this is understood many a confrontation can be avoided. Little and often suits his nature rather than long spells of discipline, or he will start to flout authority and use his clowning antics to amuse himself and you. His enthusiasm is irresistible and will constantly extricate him from unmentionable misdemeanors.

It is these qualities that are so admirable in the breed and so complicated to deal with; self-willed, stubborn, so independent, so electric. These traits, coupled with his endearing, unbounded affection, can at times cause the strongest and most experienced of handlers to clench his fist. A certain resistance sets in. At this point, a pattern of behaviour familiar to many will continue unless we are willing to accept it and deal with it in a less conventional manner. At times it is almost whimsical; one moment 'he won't', the next moment 'he will'.

It is my belief that, when put under pressure (any form of competition and, as likely as not, the added ingredients of the handler's tension and anxiety), the Vizsla's response will reflect this tension and his ability to perform will be impaired.

Thus the breed does not suit everyone by any means. It does not necessarily make the ideal gundog for those who wish to perform in the formality of competition in the field. But for those who have found the key; perhaps to their own nature as well as the dog's, a good Vizsla in the field cannot be equalled: his speed, his keenness and persistence in finding game, his ability to face cover, his great nose, and his willingness to work for his owner are second to none.

The Hungarian Vizsla is a gundog first and foremost. To work should be his natural instinct. His complicated personality is best suited to this purpose. If he is not worked, it is very necessary that his owners provide him with a varied and full life as an alternative.

It is a fact that the Hungarian Vizsla in Britain has changed little in appearance and temperament since the day he was first imported. He maintains the ability to work and to comply to the Standard. The breed is not split; there is every expectation that the handsome, winning dog in the ring can be out filling the game bag the following day.

Because of the ease with which he learns, too much pressure can be put on him too early and this can cause him to become over-anxious and excited. If his wish to do his best for you continues without being recognised you can cause him to develop into a dreadful fawning, clinging, insecure animal who will be useless to himself and you and a nuisance to all. Firmness, calmness, gentleness, and a soft voice taking him step by step from one lesson to the next, never allowing ambition to push the pace, getting him to feel the joy of your pleasure, knowing he has done well, will pay such dividends as he gets older that he will be ready for more and so will you.

As an amateur it is not easy to undertake the task of training any of the hunt, point and retrieve breeds, for the whole exercise is quite complicated from the handler's point of view as well as the dogs! But training classes are available in various parts of the country and there are now several good books on how to train the hunt, point and retrieve breeds.

Some owners have discovered the shyness and feyness of the Vizsla is not for them, but for those who have been able to understand and enjoy all his ways, he can be the most affectionate, lively and fascinating of companions.

Early Origins

The origins of the Hungarian Vizsla are very difficult to trace but his history probably began in the 9th century when the warring Magyar tribes migrated from the Steppes of Asia. They led a nomadic life until eventually they settled in the Carpathian basin, now know as Hungary. It is thought that by tradition the Magyars, when not occupied with cattle breeding, hunted a great deal. On their travels they were accompanied by their horses, sheep, cattle and camels as well as their hunting and herding dogs. It is believed that, through the centuries, the Hungarian herding breeds we see today evolved from these early Magyar herding dogs. It is thought that the modern Vizsla is descended from the hunting dogs which had been crossed first with

Part of a Gothic panel (15th century) from Christian museum in Esztergom (Hungary) showing dog believed to be Vizsla.

other native dogs, then with the Turkish 'yellow dog' when the Turks invaded and occupied Hungary during the 16th and 17th centuries.

The Turks' occupation lasted for 15 years. During this time the Vizsla is mentioned in the correspondence of the day and, by the end of the 16th century, the name 'Vizsla' had become generally accepted, replacing the name 'yellow pointer'.

Vizsla (the plural being Vizslak, not Vizslas), means 'to seek' in Turkish and it could be supposed that the name also originates from a hamlet in the Danube Valley that bore the same name in the 12th century. The Hungarian pronunciation of the 'i' in Vizsla is like the 'e' in 'event'. The 'zs' is pronounced as the 's' in 'pleasure' or 'measure'.

Falconry with dog believed to be Vizsla.

Hungarian scholars believe that the progenitor of the breed can be seen in some of the illuminations depicting hunting scenes in the 12th and 13th century, illustrated in the *Viennese Chronicle* written by the Carmelite Friars in 1357. This manuscript is the recognised illustrated record of Hungarian culture and it mentions the Vizsla by name.

Early Sporting Dogs

For centuries the breed was owned by the sporting nobility of Hungary who used their dogs to scent and search for birds which were either netted or caught by falcons. Letters reported to be in the Hungarian National Record Office in Budapest include one written by Michael Komlossy in 1515, requesting a Vizsla *suitable to net quails*. Another written in 1563 by Kirstoff Bathyani requested a dog (Vizsla) with *a good nose, a retriever for quail*.

In the 1700s, when firearms were introduced, the Zay family of Zaycegroe were known for their skill in breeding and training their dogs for hunting and working with the gun, and their strain was much sought after by the aristocracy who valued the Vizsla for his pointing and retrieving ability. It is believed that our modern prototype was evolved by the selective breeding by the Zays to satisfy the needs of the sporting nobility of the day.

Development of the Standard Type Dog

Toward the end of the century, various breeds were brought into Hungary and were purposely bred to the Hungarian Vizsla. It was the fashion for the aristocracy to bring in 'English gamekeepers'. They brought their retrievers with them and inevitably they were used on the native bird dogs.

Karoly Thuroczy with his Vizsla 'Trick'.

Hungary: a retrieve in the snow.

In 1880 Zoltan Hamvay imported the English Setter and Julius Barczy de Barczihaza brought in the Irish Setter. These dogs were bred to the Vizsla. It is also suggested that as well as other pointing breeds (the English Pointer for instance), some hound breeds were also used such as the Bloodhound, German Vorstehund, Balkan Beagle, the ancient Foxhound, Pannonion Hound and the Rumanian Copie. Later research indicates that the Sloughi was among the common ancestors. There is no evidence that the German Short-Haired Pointer or the Weimaraner were used at any time in this breed's history. The outcrossing was not done 'under the blanket', but purposely to increase the hunting quality, thus strengthening the characteristics of the native Vizsla. It is believed that the first stud book was kept by these two breeders and, around this time, the first Field Trial for the Hungarian Vizsla was held.

Thus the breed existed approximately in its present form in the 18th century, then selective breeding in the 19th century improved its good properties, finally resulting in the present day Vizsla.

The Aim – A Multi-Purpose Dog

The Vizsla had always been owned by the nobility. He had been bred in the private kennels of the powerful barons. Until 1946, when it became a republic, Hungary was a feudal state and the distinctive feature of the rural economy was the large number of big estates owned by the feudal lords, a class who had ruled the land arrogantly for centuries. The countryside differed widely from one district to another and some of the terrain the dogs had to work was the best shooting ground in Europe, well known for the abundance and variety of game it held. Thus a multi-purpose dog was required who would work fur and feather, and the versatile Vizsla could fulfil these requirements. He needed to be fast, with the sort of nose that would permit him to find game in the thick cover of crops or high grasslands or in the vast plains of corn. He was called upon to find the giant hare, often hidden in the high tufts of grass on the open Putza of the central Hungarian plain, and to drive the hare towards the waiting guns.

This same dog hunted out deer in the dense forests, driving them into the clearing towards the guns. In the woods and thickets he had to point woodcock and pheasant, and on the banks of the lakes and rivers and in the marshland he must flush waterfowl, wild duck, goose and quail. He was also required to hunt and hold at bay wild boar and wolf – this was done with several dogs working together. The Vizsla flourished under these conditions and his natural retrieving ability on land and in the water added to his valuable qualities.

The 20th Century

The Austro–Hungarian Empire had extended its influence over a large area for many years, but with frequent border changes two-thirds of Hungary's pre-war 1914–1918 territory was annexed by the neighbouring states. As a consequence, a considerable number of Hungarians (over 3,000 000) now lived in those countries, so many Vizsla owners suddenly found themselves part of Czechoslovakia, Rumania, Italy, Germany, Poland or Russia. In addition, a succession of wars and agricultural crises led to the emigration of about 1,500 000 Hungarians, the majority of whom eventually reached North America.

Two world wars and the Russian occupation almost spelled doom for the Vizsla. Following World War I, numbers had declined and it was felt that the breed had lost

'Hanved' (Nimrod magazine 1917).
Note the white markings.

'Witti' in 1918, owned
by Gyula Popovich.

9

its identity due to too much outcrossing with too many foreign breeds. A dedicated few searched far and wide for bird dogs resembling the old Vizsla. After this monumental task, some dozen dogs became the foundation stock of all registered Vizslas in Hungary.

The First Vizsla Club in Hungary

The first Vizsla Club in Hungary was formed in 1924 with Dr Kalman Polgar as the president. It had always been his dream to restore the breed. Another founder member was Captain Karoly Baba. He published a book on training, breeding and the care of the Vizsla. Other founding members and officers were:

Hon President	Count Lazslo Esterhazy
Treasurer	Mr Petocz
Registrar	Josef Stifft
Genealogists	Professor Balazs Otvos
	Professor Endre Felix
National Judge	Dr Elmer Markus
Supplies	Dr Janos Wirker

All the members owned Vizslas and all were devoted to restoring the breed. An initial standard was worked out and efforts were made to establish a strain and type. Through a very controlled breeding programme, it became possible to breed out the colour variations and extensive white markings on the chest and feet which had begun to appear.

A great boost to the breed at this time was the win achieved by Captain Baba's champion Vegvari Betyar, who took first place over several prize-winning English and German Short-Haired Pointers at the incredible age of 13 years. Her record was only surpassed by the National Champion Kati, owned by Dr Polgar, who earned the greatest number of awards and was best working Vizsla at 13 years old. She bore 73 puppies in her lifetime.

Effects of War on the Breed

In 1935 the Fédération Cynologique Internationale recognised the Hungarian Vizsla as a separate breed and the Standard was also revised. By 1944, 5000 Vizslas had been registered and the breed seemed to have established itself again, only to find that hardly a decade later 80–90% had been sadly affected by the ravages of World War II and the Russian occupation of Eastern Europe between 1956 and 1958.

A piece called *My Hunting Pals* by Lorant de Bastyai describes vividly his homecoming after the World War II:

> *When I left the Hungarian Army and reached our country home, I found the empty house in an untidy condition, the furniture half broken lying huddled together, and my books were torn and slung around the room. There was no sign of my dear hawks and my Hungarian pointer dog was also missing. After learning from my friends in the neighbouring houses that they had given my birds their freedom and there was such a shortage of meat, I asked 'How about my dog?' The answer was, 'Perhaps retrieving pheasants and partridges on the Russian plains, perhaps in the German woods.' Every*

normal human being, after tidying up the house would start to get new furniture, new curtains and so on. But not me. After I had put the broken furniture on the bonfire in our garden and half broken items which I could repair later back in the rooms with the remains of my books, my main thought was to get the hawks and the dog again.

Later he describes how he acquired his future Vizsla:

I did not have to wait long for my future dog. One early summer afternoon, I was sitting in my drawing room with war-damaged furniture still around, reading the daily post and Lurak, my hawk, was on my fist. Suddenly the bird started behaving in an unusual way, giving a high pitched warning call: 'Pitt – pitt – fitch!' All the doors and windows were open in the warm summer weather and through one of these open doors the 'strange thing' walked in, holding in its mouth a piece of meat longer than the head of this five-month-old Hungarian pointer puppy. She came in as if this had always been her home, and on the other end of the lead was one of my friends.

This little Vizsla – Pacal – became his devoted companion.

The Russian Occupation

In the era of the Russian occupation from 1956–1958, over 188 000 Hungarians sought homes elsewhere, many taking their dogs with them. The old Hungarian families established themselves in European countries and thus the breed was dispersed widely. It is believed that some of the best stock left the country in this manner. If we look at any of our extended pedigrees, all common ancestors come from Hungary or Czechoslovakia. From photographs of the breed in these two countries it is noticeable how, although the type remains the same, the conformation differs considerably. The Hungarian dogs appear to be lighter in bone and smaller than the Czechoslovakian dogs which appear heavier and to have more substance. This difference was quite noticeable in our basic English stock but it would seem today that we are producing Vizslas which do combine both quality and substance.

Among the many who fled the country after the Russian occupation, was Colonel Jeno Dus, director of the Magyar Vizsla Club. He managed to mimeograph the stud books and the minutes of all the club meetings. He buried these original documents near the Austrian border and escaped to freedom.

In these confused times many Vizslas were lost or went astray. (Some people lost their lives as did their Vizslas trying to get across the border.) In 1956, when Michael Kende was appointed the new director of the Magyar Dog Breeders' Association, it was decided that those Vizslas which were of unknown origin should be registered if they were thought to be 'very good' in appearance and showed 'a good nose'. These in turn should be bred with Vizslas having two or three generation pedigrees. The progeny could once more be bred to another one of unknown origin. All puppies were inspected closely. If it were agreed that their standard was good enough, they were registered and the parents entered in the stud book.

I should like to quote an extract from an interesting article written by Group Captain David, who left Hungary in 1958:

I was HBM Air Attaché in Hungary from May 1956–Sept 1958 and was invited by the Military Protocol Department in Budapest to attend a boar shoot in the Bakonyi forest in August 1956. The jaegermaester who accompanied me had a wonderful Vizsla bitch with him. The Vizsla's fame as a hunting dog is well known behind the Iron Curtain.

Winners of a 1978 Field Trial in Hungary.

Their bravery is second to none. They are one of the few breeds who will face up to a wild boar to protect their masters.

Captain David bought one of this bitch's puppies. He continued:

I named him Betyar because the Robin Hood-like tribe of rascals (Betyars) used to operate from the Bakonyi forest.

The puppy was about five weeks old and easily rested in my right hand at the time we came together. He is now nearly 13 years old and has been a wonderful friend to have for all these years. His life has been adventurous. He was with me in Budapest throughout the Hungarian uprisings and the dreadful aftermath. He escaped from my house during curfew time and was shot by a Russian sentry who was guarding a gun post outside. The sentry was only doing his duty – shooting at something making a noise. The poor puppy managed to

Hungarian show dog. Note the undocked tail.

crawl back to my house and I found him nearly dead on the doorstep. Luckily the bullet had gone right through him and missed all the vital organs. He responded bravely to nursing and in two weeks was his old self again. He avoided any soldier in brown or khaki uniform after that. Indeed, on one memorable occasion he chased three Russian soldiers down our road. He meant business. The Russians were scared and the local Hungarians highly delighted.

The Magyar Vizsla.

The Present Day

Hungary was a socialist state. At the time of bringing this book up to date, there have been further political and social changes; Hungary is now a democratic republic state. A number of private breeders are scattered throughout the country and a few of the state-operated farms have kennels as a sideline. It is not an unusual sight in Budapest to see a Vizsla out shopping with his owner, which means that he has adapted to the flat dwelling life. Although the very rich varieties of water fowl once found in the marshy regions and lakes now mostly survive in nature reserves, there is still ample opportunity for the Vizsla to work. Shooting remains a popular sport and the forests of Hungary still harbour abundant numbers of red deer and wild pig, and the lowlands contain rodents, hares, partridge and

A young male admired by the author during a trip to Hungary in the 1990s.

13

pheasants. Hunters' associations are led by the National Association of Hungarian Hunters. The organ of the association, the *Nimrod*, contributes to the education and training of hunters to a great extent.

In August 1982, the Second World Congress of Breeders of Hungarian Breeds was held in Budapest. Those attending had the opportunity to visit Hortobagy National Park, a reserve holding herds of horses, cattle and sheep. Later they visited Lake Balaton, the largest lake in the European continent, where they met Miklós Farkasházi, then secretary of the Hungarian Vizsla Club. He had arranged a demonstration of the dogs working in a nearby field. The first exercise was to quarter, the second was three retrieves of planted seen game (two pheasants and a hare), and in the third demonstration the dogs had to track a hare that had been dragged along the ground. This they appeared to do with skill, retrieving the hare to hand. They moved on to the water demonstration and here had to retrieve live and dead ducks; some achieved the live retrieves more successfully than others, and it was felt that some dogs did not have enough drive. The last exercise was to test steadiness; all the dogs had to be steady to shot. They all sat collectively and only one Vizsla broke, but this was this dog's second 'failure' that day. It was felt that he had a temperament problem and Miklós Farkasházi explained that, due to this, the dog would have to be eliminated from any breed programme. It was noted that many dogs in the demonstration had long tails; fewer dogs are docked now that the 1981 Standard does not ask for a docked tail.

Angela Boys went over to Hungary in September 1972 to a show held in the International Fairground. One hundred and thirty-nine Vizslas were catalogued. There were two judges, one was M Galazs (Karoly) and the other none other than M Dravenka (Istvan) who proudly told her that it was he who had sent the first Vizslas over to England. Angela reported:

> *Judging and showing is done in a very relaxed way with the judges walking about with a cup of coffee, stopping for a word with a spectator, kissing a hand, then back to the dogs. Each judge has a table and chairs under a striped umbrella, where he dictates his criticism of each dog to his assistant and then gives a copy to the exhibitor.*

The placed dogs were good and Angela Boys admired two bitches who she would have bought if she could! She reports that though many were put down for being slab-sided, racy and oversized, colour was good – a rich dark gold being much appreciated – and the pale colours were put out. She writes:

> *It is easy for one to criticise but I saw loose feet, loose elbows, cow hocks, roach backs, weak quarters with no second thigh and hawk eyes, yellow green.*

Miklós Farkasházi was to have judged the breed in 1982 in England. His appointment was anticipated with great interest and he had a very good entry but, sadly, he was unable to leave Hungary. It was not to be until 1998 when the breed was judged by Dr Jakkel from Hungary that we could say our Hungarian Vizslas have been judged by someone from their 'Country of Origin'.

chapter 2

Early Imports (1953–1969)

According to Kennel Club records, the first registration of Vizslas was in 1953, although it has been reported that there were a pair of dogs in Hay-on-Wye before 1939. At the beginning of the war, a Mr Talgarth was offered a dog and bitch of Hungarian Retriever breed to save them from being put down. Owing to conditions at the time, he accepted the bitch only – there were no papers – but her wonderful nose and general keenness were commented on and there is little doubt that this was a Vizsla.

Agnes and Ernest (Mrs J Wyndham-Harris)

In August 1953, Agnes and Ernest were imported from Hungary by Mrs J Wyndham-Harris. Born in 1948 (Puschi ex Vlada), they were a brother and sister bred by M Dravenka (Istvan). Mr Wyndham-Harris was in the Diplomatic Service, first living in Budapest, then in Paris. When the family returned to England, they brought these two dogs back with them as companions and gun dogs. The brother and sister were mated three times. In 1953 there were six puppies, three dogs and three bitches: Boldro Apollo, Boldrogrange Ann, Boldroville Adonis, Intrepid Anthony, Resourceful Annabelle and Wyndham Aldexandra. In 1954 there were five puppies, four dogs and one bitch: Boldrowood Prince, Boldrowood Bountiful, Boldrowood Brigard, Brilliant Buda and Boldrowood Princess. Three of the dogs and the bitch were exported to America to Mr Charles Hunt. Major R H Petty (Strawbridge) bought the bitch Boldrogrange Ann and in May 1955 Ernest and Agnes were transferred to his ownership. In 1955 two dog puppies were born: Strawbridge Ficko and Strawbridge Pete. Pete was later exported to America.

Petrie-Hay's Strawbridge Czinka, one of the Waidman foundation bitches.

Adalyn von Hunt (Major R G Petty)

Major Petty was to play a significant role in the breeding of the early Vizslas. In August 1956 he imported Adalyn von Hunt from America. She was bred by Mr and Mrs C F Hunt and born in 1955 (Morho z Povazio ex Asta v Povazio). Adalyn was mated three times. In 1957, she had eight puppies by Strawbridge Ficko, five dogs and three bitches: Strawbridge Amos, Angy, Alka, Antal, Apro, Arany, Arpad and Attila. From this litter three were exported to America. In 1958 she was mated again to Ficko, this time producing seven puppies, three bitches and four dogs. These were Strawbridge Barna, Bella, Bruce, Ben, Boske, Buda and Rhett Butler. Rhett Butler was exported to America. In 1960 Adalyn was mated to her son Strawbridge Barna from which came four dogs and four bitches: Strawbridge Ceda, Cigany, Chiktosh, Cilla, Csana, Csibeza, Czinka and Csillag. Czinka was sold to Mr and Mrs Hilbre-Smith, who previously had bought two puppies from Mrs Wyndham Harris, and later she was transferred to Mrs Louise Petrie-Hay of the Waidman prefix. In 1965 Czinka represented the breed at the Game Fair and was also

featured in *The Field*. She was a typical Vizsla, both in conformation and character. In the house she was very affectionate and quiet and in the field had the tireless enthusiasm and energy so well known to Vizsla owners. She died at 13 years of age.

These two imported bitches, Agnes and Adalyn, produced 36 puppies between them, and all were registered at The Kennel Club. Nine were exported to America and Strawbridge Barna went to Germany in 1967. Unfortunately, there are no records or photographs to be found so it is not known whether these early Vizslas would fit the standard of today.

Tardosi Gyongyi (Alec MacRae)

Early in 1960 Mr Alec MacRae imported Tardosi Gyongyi from Hungary. She was bred by Mr Lajos Dudas of Budapest in 1959 (Betyar ex Csiklsikoi Ari Nora). Alec MacRae had bought his first Vizsla in 1956 from Major Petty. He saw the litter advertised in *The Field* and went to see these 'new' dogs. He says that from the first he was attracted by their appearance, friendly disposition and history. He bought Strawbridge Buda and became the first Vizsla owner in Scotland. He imported two Vizslas from Hungary, thus bringing in the new blood so badly needed by this time. He trained and worked his dogs up in Scotland on grouse, pheasant and wild fowl. He also field trialled his dogs, proving a great stalwart of the breed. He is spoken of with affection by all who knew him. Mrs Lyndesay-Smith writes in the breed notes in 1967 that '*Mr MacRae of Strathyre deserves all credit for the efforts he is making to popularise the breed.*'

Top: History in the making. L to r, Petrie-Hay's Waidman Bor, Tardosi Gyongyi, Strawbridge Czinka, Waidman Zigi. Above: Shian, 14 year old lady.

Tardosi Gyongyi was called Shian. Alec MacRae mated her first to Strawbridge Buda and later to his second import. The puppies carried his prefix Creagan which can be seen in many of the early pedigrees. When Shian was six years old, Alec was over-dogged and he insisted on giving her to Louise Petrie-Hay. He drove down from Scotland with her, arriving at teatime. She did not appear to be worried when he left, had a meal and settled in with the other dogs. However, for the next month, each time the front door was open she would sit in the drive waiting for his return, and every car that came had to be checked in case it was her master. In time she accepted the situation, but her faithfulness to her master always remained.

Shian met her old master two years later at the Game Fair and was ecstatic with joy. Although not a hard man, Alec showed no great affection, but she would not leave his side until they parted at the end of the day.

She was an excellent guard, both of the home and the car, a trait many Vizsla owners will recognise. She had tremendous drive and ability, would work every type of country, face cover and could swim like an otter. Only her over-keenness prevented her from becoming a field trial winner. She was an excellent brood bitch and would let no one near her puppies for the first 10 days. Although no beauty, being short on the leg and long in the back, she had a great heart and character, plenty of bone and a very typical head. She certainly left her stamp on the breed.

Mrs Virginia Phillips of the Kinford prefix bought her first Vizsla, Creagan Anya, from Alec MacRae. Later Anya was trialled successfully.

Sibriktelpi Tigi (Alec MacRae)

In April 1962 Alec MacRae imported his second dog from Hungary. This was Sibriktelpi Tigi, a dog bred by Mr J Farkas and born in 1961 (Eden Kerti Csibesz ex Sibriktelepi Maca). The following year, Alec field trialled him and he became the first Vizsla to win an award in a trial.

Virginia Phillips recalls that he was a charming dog and she liked him immensely. He was a super worker, tall, elegant and strong. He had a poor front and slack feet, but a noble head, excellent temperament and a good rich colour. He was mated to her Creagan Anya and the progeny included Kinford Ficko, Lidi and Rica.

Lidi was sold first to Mrs Joan Matuszewka of Monroe Weimaraners, and later transferred to Miss Pauline Rankin of the Zelten prefix. Rica became one of Mrs Barbara Douglas-Redding's foundation bitches: Wolfox Kinford Rica. Rica died of leukaemia in 1970 aged 6½ years. Barbara writes that:

Rica was my constant companion and slept in an armchair at the foot of my bed. Strangely enough no-one else of all the ginger girls fancy adopting that vacancy and I am haunted by a chestnut ghost on its empty seat.

From Anya's second mating to Tigi came Kinford Vlada, one of Louise Petrie-Hay's foundation bitches. Vlada went Best of Breed at the City of Birmingham Championship Show in 1968 and won first prize in the Any Other Variety open bitch class at Crufts in 1969. She was the dam of the first two show champions in the breed: Mr W Foster's Kinford Zsuzsi and my own Waidman Remus. Waidman Ficko was Zsuzsi's sire and Waidman Fules was Remus'.

Joram de la Creste.
Photo: Sally Ann Thompson

Joram de la Creste
(Mrs J Matuszewska)

The next recorded import was in 1963. Joram de la Creste was imported from France by Mr Winter, an American serviceman. This dog was bred by Countess de la Celle la Creste; born in 1962 he was by Schan Von Trutzhoff ex Kobra Z Povazia. Shortly after coming to this country, his owner had to return to the United States and the dog was given to an elderly couple living near Hastings. Louise Petrie-Hay saw an advertisement for his sale in *Dog World* under 'Bracque Hongroise'. She travelled down to see him and found him tied up in the garage by a heavy chain. She bought him and arranged that Joan Matuszewska should look after him, as she was unable to do so at the time. In 1964 The Kennel Club records his transfer from Mr Winter to Mrs Matuszewska. Joram was a handsome dog – this can been seen from his photographs, and those who knew him remember his great quality and style. He gave a sense of nobility, power and elegance. His length of neck, straight topline and strong quarters, as well as his rich colour, can be seen in some of our Vizslas today. He is in most of our Vizsla pedigrees.

Mrs Barbara Douglas-Redding writes in her breed notes on 9 July 1965 that at the Three Counties Show Joram de la Creste was second in Any Variety Graduate Gundog. Later she writes:

> *Southampton Championship Show gave us our first breed classes in the south. Joram went Best of Breed. Thirteen entries in the two classes were not too bad for a start. Our judge Mr L C James (deceased) was very interested and said kind things about our British dogs. We have a long way to go but interest is growing all the time.*

Joram turned out to be a very complex character. He was not excitable nor fizzy, but his unpredictability became more and more evident. Virginia Phillips recalls that warnings not to touch him were displayed on the benches. Louise Petrie-Hay tells me that he would become aggressive at fairly regular intervals; that one had warning of this but, as time went on, it became more frequent. From evidence from those who knew him, it is agreed that he had suffered much deprivation in his early life and his experience of manwork had affected him. Many tests were carried out by different vets, but there is no conclusive evidence pointing to either epilepsy or brain damage, given the absence of objective data. An aura of vagueness and myth remains about him to this day.

This handsome dog was used at stud seven times. In 1964 he was mated to Strawbridge Czinka. This produced the first Waidman litter which included Fules,

Ficko and Flook. Fules worked well and looked good. In 1966 at the City of Birmingham Show he won the novice class; in 1967 he won the Any Variety Novice Class at Crufts and in 1968 he won the Gamekeeper Class at Crufts. When his training was finished, he was sold to Wing Commander Stamford-Tuck of Battle of Britain fame. In 1966 he was mated to Wolfox Kinford Rica. From this mating Wolfox Tallulah was

Douglas-Redding's Sh Ch Wolfox Fabia. Photo: Pearce

successfully shown by Barbara Douglas-Redding and Wolfox Topaz by Dr Capel-Edwards who wrote various articles on the breed. Topaz represented the breed on television.

In December 1966, Joram was mated to Creagan Agnes belonging to Mr Evan Young, a very early owner and worker of the breed in Scotland with the prefix Tintohill. Two dog puppies in this letter, Tintohill Buda and Betyar, will be seen in many of our pedigrees.

In 1967 Virginia Phillips used Joram on Creagan Anya. From the litter, Kinford Nora was to become the foundation bitch of Mrs W Foster's Gamelands prefix. In this year Joram also served Kathleen Auchterlonie's Tintohill Astra. Astra was Kathleen's foundation bitch on which she built her successful working and showing kennel. A dog from this litter, Saline Attila was sold to Barbara Douglas-Redding and, when mated to Kinford Rica, produced Sh Ch Wolfox Fabia, Sh Ch Wolfax Flora and Flavia. The last two went to Mrs Sheila Gray to become the foundation bitches of her Abbeystag kennels. Saline Achilles was worked by Kathleen Auchterlonie and became well known in the field trial world. Saline Ayesha, a bitch, was bought by Mrs Jackson to become the foundation bitch of the Starleypoint Vizslas in Scotland.

In 1967 Joram was mated to Kinford Lidi owned by Pauline Rankin and this litter produced Atlanta Lass of Zelten and Sh Ch Artic of Zelten. Artic won many tickets and on many occasions Pauline and I stood side by side in the Open Dog Classes. One day Artic would win and on another it would be the turn of Remus. We both enjoyed the amicable contest.

Pauline's dog had had an unfortunate accident when he was a puppy, and lost an eye playing with his litter mates. In spite of this handicap Bill Foster, the all-round judge, put him up and gave him his first CC. Pauline had to publicly produce the vet's letter for the judge to verify the reason for his loss. Other judges followed suit and he was made up. All credit to the judges, for he was a very fine dog in every respect.

Late in 1967 Joan Matuszewska decided that Joram should be put to sleep as he was becoming unmanageable, but Kathleen Auchterlonie persuaded her to let him be transferred to her care in Scotland. Sadly, after eight months Kathleen had to have him put down. Joram's last mating was in 1968 to Tor Uaine Bracken up in Scotland. This bitch was owned by Mrs Morrison and produced Fruin Ransom and Reward.

I have questioned many breeders and no-one recollects that any of Joram de la Creste's known offspring has reproduced his alarming behaviour pattern. Given the small numbers of the breed in this country and the high integrity of the relevant breeders, this data is to be relied upon. In my view his behaviour would seem

Auchterlonie's Saline Szeppataki Csaba (Dani) aged 13 months.

attributable to environment and physical considerations. It is said that he was trained to do 'manwork' in France and this could have had an effect on his behaviour. As there is no evidence of his progeny inheriting his behaviour pattern, no one could conclude that it was not genetic. Even after considerable research I have not been able to produce documentary evidence of the early training, but his owners believed this to be true.

Szeppataki Csaba (Mrs K Auchterlonie)

Another import arrived in 1969. Szeppataki Csaba was bred by M J Zelton in 1968 and imported from Hungary by Mrs K Auchterlonie. His sire was Kisufalui Dani and his great dam was Arkoparti Erzsok Ledi. It is interesting to note that his great-grandfather was Sibriktelepi, Tigi's great-great-grandfather. Kathleen Auchterlonie's beloved Dani, as he became known, was shown, worked and field trialled. He was a medium-sized dog, good-looking, heavier-boned than some and a different type altogether than later imports from Hungary who were smaller in every respect. All who knew Dani were caught by his attractive personality. He enjoyed life and loved to work. Kathleen's only complaint was that she could not get him out of the water. He loved to dive deep down and would alarm her by remaining below too long. Barbara Douglas-Redding wrote in her notes:

> Dani is a very strongly coupled up, short-backed dog, plus well angulated with a splendid muscled up second thigh. He is already working well.

All the puppies from Dani's first litter to Tintohill Astra went to working homes. From his second mating to Astra, the bitch Saline Coire became one of Miss Angela Boys' foundation bitches, establishing her Galfrid prefix. This bitch was mated to Sh Ch Waidman Remus, the first Russetmantle Vizsla. Out of the litter Sh Ch Galfrid Sofia of Russetmantle became one of this kennel's foundation bitches. Another well-known and loved Vizsla, Mrs Heather McCabe's Sh Ch Chantilly Jester, was sired by Dani when mated to Saffron Flora in 1972. It is interesting to note that Saffron Flora had the same sire on both sides and was outcrossed to Dani.

Further Imports (1970–1979)

Warhorse Lwow
(Mrs B Henderson)

In 1970 there were four imports. The first was Warhorse Lwow, or Horse for short. He was bred in America (Am Ch Warhorse O'Jay ex Warhorse Bella) by Messrs Warhol and Minde, born in 1966 and imported by Mrs B Henderson. The Henderson family lived briefly in England and then moved to Ireland. Horse was a gentle, good tempered dog. In the States he did well in the show ring and also won his companion dog certificate. Unfortunately he was crippled severely by a motor accident and was in plaster for weeks. He went to Barbara Douglas-Redding as the Hendersons were travelling between England and Ireland at this time. Barbara wrote:

Henderson's Warhorse Lwow CD.

> *I took this poor old cripple in after a bad motor accident. He had had to cope with two quarantines plus hook worm in Hawaii. A super dog. I loved him. The dear old sweetie naturally was a bit disoriented to start with but we soon got over that.*

Horse adored life at Maison Redding, and all the ginger girls! It is said that he would have worked and probably would have done well in the show ring over here but after his accident he could not even exercise. However, none of these trials and tribulations affected his sweet nature. He sired two

Gottlieb's Ch Russetmantle Troy, one of the first five champions in the breed.

Petrie-Hay's Bingo & Bella vom Wurmbrandpark. Centre, judge L Page. Photo: Cooke

litters. In 1970 he was mated to Mrs Henderson's Wolfox Editha. From this litter Starbeater Phoenix was to become another of Miss Angela Boys' foundation bitches for the Galfrid prefix. A daughter from this bitch, Galfrid Leda, became a foundation bitch for the Russetmantle Kennel and she produced Ch Russetmantle Troy, one of the first five champions out of the 18 we have in the breed to date (1997).

Horse's second mating in 1971 was to Abbeystag Wolfox Flavia, Sheila Gray's bitch.

Out of this litter, three pups were exported to Norway.

Bingo and Bella vom Wurmbrandpark
(Lord Ashcombe/Louise Petrie-Hay)

The next imports to arrive were brother and sister, Bingo and Bella vom Wurmbrandpark. They were bred by Gunther Wanivenhaus and imported from Austria by Lord Ashcombe. They were born in 1969 (Bodo Von Der Dopplehutte ex Tormaspustai Zsa Zsa), and were a year old when they came out of quarantine and went to live on Lord Ashcombe's estate outside Guildford. Whilst in quarantine Bingo mated Bella but the resultant pups were destroyed. A year later they were sent to Louise Petrie-Hay for training but, unfortunately, the freedom they had enjoyed on the estate where game, including deer, abounded made it impossible to produce reliable, steady dogs suitable for the sort of shooting which they would get.

Lord Ashcombe decided they they should stay at the Waidman Kennels and they were transferred accordingly. They were shown two or three times and won the dog and bitch ticket at the National Gundog Championship Show in 1972, Bingo gaining the Best of Breed (BOB) award. Judge Ivan Swedrup's critique of Bella at Birmingham Championship Show describes her as strongly built, of good size and type with good legs and feet. All who knew her found her to have a sweet temperament. Many comment that she was an elegant bitch and a rich russet gold.

Bingo was a handsome dog. Mr Swedrup's comments perhaps do not do him justice: 'Strong, big, well shaped dog of good type'. Barbara writes: 'I had a pre-conceived idea that Austrian Vizslas were rather larger and coarser than their Hungarian counterparts. This is certainly not the case with these two. They are elegant and aristocratic to a degree, with beautiful conformation.'

Bella's progeny

Bella had only one litter; her heats were irregular and she never came into season again. She was mated to Waidman Nagy (by Waidman Kosikin ex Tardosi Gyongyi). Waidman Brok, a dog puppy from this litter, features in

Louise Petrie-Hay in 1979 with Waidman Brok (right) and his daughter Waidman Crumpet.

many pedigrees and sired many of the forerunners of today's working and showing Vizslas. He was regularly worked and successfully trialled. When put to Sh Ch Sanside Czarina the litter produced Sh Ch Swanside Czorna, one of the top-winning bitches in her day – sadly she produced no progeny. Brok was the first Vizsla to gain the highest place in a field trial open to all the hunt, point and retrieve breeds. This was in January 1975 in a novice stake.

Rice's Sh Ch Swanside Czorna. Photo: Pearce

I spent many happy days picking up with Louise Petrie-Hay with our Vizslas. Although an old man (sadly he died in 1984), Brok would work solidly all day and was absolutely trustworthy – if he said a bird was there, it was. He would veer off down a hedge, working on his own, pretending his deaf old ears could not hear the whistle. Young Troy (eight years old) and Brok's sons and daughters, respecting his grey hairs, would never dream of picking up a bird that was Brok's. From early morning until nightfall his old legs would not falter. No-one could resist his old grey face and his pleading eyes to come for a day's shooting. His litter brother, Waidman Buda, went to Virginia Phillips. Waidman Bogar was sold to Mr M Farmer who, in his first year of field trials, entered him in four and saw him placed in all of them.

Mills de Hoog's Sh Ch Swanside Miklos.

Bingo's progeny

Bingo was mated seven times. Many of his progeny were seen in the ring and the field. When mated to Roger Simkin's lovely bitch Sh Ch Swanside Czarina (foundation bitch of the Swanside Vizslas) two show champions were produced: Swanside Zsigmund and Swanside Miklos. Miklos went to Major George Wilkinson's Andesheim Kennels to be trained for a while, and Ziggy was sold to Richard Houghton of the Peckers prefix.

Swanside Zsigmund gained his title in no time at all. When put to Ch Galfrid Tara, Ch Peckers Perchance was a bitch from the first mating and Sh Ch Peckers Parody from the second.

23

Houghton's Sh Ch Swanside Zsigmund.

Swanside Miklos later went to the well-known GSP Wittekind Kennels owned by Mrs Minecke Mills de Hoog. He gained his title and became the only Vizsla to go through to Reserve Best in Show (RBIS). This he did at the the National Gundog Championship Show in 1975. Miklos died in his third year. He was mated twice, first to Galfrid Leda of Russetmantle and then to Sh Ch Galfrid Sofia of Russetmantle. This mating produced Russetmantle Kushba, owned by Mrs Heather McCabe. Kushba gained her Junior Warrant and title by the age of 15 months. Dearly loved by Heather, her short life came to an end at 15 months when she was run over.

Another of Bingo's matings was to Elia Amira (by Sh Ch Futaki Lazsla ex Saline Caroline) and a bitch from this litter, Golden Claret, became the foundation bitch for the Swindells and their Czassa prefix. She was mated to her brother and produced Sh Ch Czassa Calista.

Sadly, Bingo died of leukaemia in 1976. Having been his constant companion for seven years of their lives, Bella was quite unable to understand or accept his absence. Her unhappiness was unbearable and Louise Petrie-Hay had her put to sleep shortly afterwards.

Starleypoint Komlosreti Arok (Mrs Jackson)

The fourth import in 1970 from Hungary, Starleypoint Komlosreti Arok, was brought in by Mrs Jackson in Scotland. He was bred by Kelner Janosonn and was born in 1969 (Kevei Arom Csimbi ex Hubertus Marcisz). This dog suffered badly in quarantine as no other import appears to have hitherto. He lost weight appallingly and his hind action was severely affected. He was used for stud seven times.

In 1971 Saline Ayesha, Mrs Jackson's foundation bitch, was mated to Kisufalui Dani. Miss Boys had a puppy, Starleypoint Vilmos; she also had a puppy, Galfrid Fecske from his mating with Brockbanks Braewater Heidi. Fecske was exported to Australia where she became a show champion. Later sold, Vilmos lived his life in the lap of luxury in Monaco. He was renowned for his reputation as an escapologist.

Starleypoint Kati also came from this litter. She was shown by Mrs Jackson at Crufts in 1972 and 1973. Arok was mated to Kati in 1972 and from this litter a dog, Starleypoint Ulles, was sold to Mr Maitland-Smith who worked and trialled him successfully. He was placed third in the first Hungarian Vizsla Society Field Trial in 1973. Mr Maitland-Smith moved to Canada, taking Ulles with him. From a repeat mating in 1975 a bitch, Starleypoint Victoria, became Mr and Mrs Farquhar's first Vizsla for the prefix Istvan.

Futaki Lazslo
(Mrs S Gray)

In 1972 Mr and Mrs Gray imported Futaki Lazslo from America. He was bred by Bela Hadik and born in 1971 (Dual Ch/Ft Ch Janos v.w. Come Lately ex Ft Ch Futak Lenke). Barbara Douglas-Redding writes:

Gray's Sh Ch Futaki Lazslo. Photo: Pearce

> I don't know whether the name Bela Hadik means much to Vizsla folk over there. It certainly does to some of us who have owned and bred for some years. He was of course extremely well known in the USA as a prominent breeder of show and working stock. Born in Budapest in 1905 he left Hungary in 1945 after serving in the Hungarian Cavalry in World War II. It was he who produced the breed's first Dual Champion, Futaki Daraz, in America. His Futaki line has since then produced bench champions, field champions and three of the four dual champions over there. He died in New Hampshire February 16th 1971.

Lazslo came from this very illustrious kennel and was a useful addition to Sheila Gray's Abbeystag line. He had much to contribute to the breed. He came from a Hip Dysplasia-clear line and had a breeder's letter himself. He was a medium sized dog and a very good type who did well in the field and in the show ring, gaining his show champion title. He passed on his good qualities. He sired two champions, Ch Abbeystag Bruna (dam Abbeystag Wolfox Flora)

Gray's Ch Abbeystag Emilio. Photo: Fall

and Ch Abbeystag Emilio (dam Sh Ch Abbeystag Wolfox Flavia). All credit to Sheila Gray who trained her dogs herself – no mean feat! Barbara Douglas-Redding's Sh Ch Abbeystag Claudia of Wolfox was also by Lazslo. She recalls seeing Lazslo for the first time just after he had come out of quarantine, saying that he was in splendid condition both physically and mentally: 'He is a very smart show boy and a lovely colour.'

It is interesting to note that he had great similarity in type and size to American Warhorse Lwow CD. Sadly he died in 1980, which was a great blow to Sheila Gray.

The Hungarian dog Matai Lurko. His son Galfrid Gaspar features in many British pedigrees.

He was greatly missed for he was part of her family of Vizslas and was a sweet-tempered, friendly dog, as were all the dogs from this kennel.

Matai Sari of Galfrid (Miss A Boys)

In 1971 Angela Boys imported Matai Sari of Galfrid who was born in 1970 (Matai Bitang Tucsok ex Matai Boske). Angela went over to Hungary to look at the Vizslas in their country of origin. She was introduced to many breeders and she especially like the Matai Vizslas owned by Miklós Farkasházi, chairman of the Hungarian Kennel Club and a well-known judge and authority of the breed in Hungary and abroad.

Angela bought two bitches. They were mated in Hungary and whelped in quarantine over here. Sari was the first to arrive. She produced seven puppies by Matai Lurko, CACIB and trial winner. All the pups were healthy and Sari handled the state of affairs without turning a hair. Her temperament was excellent, she was very sweet natured and a good gundog. She had been partly trained in Hungary and after she came out of quarantine she went to Major George Wilkinson's Andersheim kennels where her training was finished. She returned to Angela Boys and, although not possessing the qualities to go to the top as a show dog, she was entered in one or two shows and was placed. She was in the Crufts' 'personality parade' in 1975. She was trialled a few times and won a Certificate of Merit. She worked regularly until eventually she was lent to Mr and Mrs Slim whose old Vizsla had died at the beginning of the season. Sadly she was with them only five months before she died of cancer of the liver at the age of seven. Sari was loved by all who knew her. She was a great ratter and Angela Boys describes how many a time she would dive into a nearby trout stream and retrieve a fish to hand. Her name is in many of our modern pedigrees, and she contributed much to the breed.

Boys' Galfrid Gaspar & his daughter Sh Ch Galfrid Jade. Photo: Pearce

Sari had five litters, one in Hungary, one in quarantine and the other three while with

Angela Boys. From the litter born in quarantine, three were to feature in field trials: Galfrid Gaspar, Galfrid Gelert and Galfrid Gerda. Gaspar's name appears in many pedigrees, siring progeny who worked and showed. He gained his Junior Warrant. He was consistently in the cards when shown but never gained his title. He sired Sh Ch Galfrid Jade when put to his mother Sari. When put to Saline Coire of Galfrid, Sh Ch Galfrid Mia was one of his offspring. Three puppies from the mating with Sh Ch Windover Ondine of Galfrid went abroad,

Boys' Galfrid Odo & Sh Ch Galfrid Mia.
Photo: Pearce

one to South Africa, another to France and a third to Malaya. A small bitch out of this litter, Galfrid Otis,was given to Major George Wilkinson as a present and became the 'apple of his eye'. There was an occasion when this little Sari grand-daughter was entered in one of the Society's Field Trials. A part of the Judges' report for the day states:

> Otis worked well despite her size and the fact that the heather was making a right mess of her undercarriage which was red and sore. Later on Otis was going over to retrieve a snipe that had been shot. An obviously wounded hare got up and went off across the heather and down along a narrow ditch out of sight. George Wilkinson was told to send his bitch for this hare as it obviously had priority over the dead snipe. He was a little bothered as he did not think Otis could carry a hare. 'Try her' was all the sympathy he got. She was put on the line and followed it well. The last we saw of her she was way down the hill going toward a bit of woodland. A long pause. George Wilkinson sensibly refrained from calling her as the wind was far too strong. In the distance, the little Vizsla could be seen carrying the hare, head high and trying not to trip up over its tangled legs. A very proud handler went to meet her and relieve her of her burden. It was an excellent bit of tracking and showed courage and determination.

Owing to such bad conditions it was not possible to get a result. It was felt that the dogs and handlers had acquitted themselves so well the Vizsla Society placed first, second and third, and the final placing at the end of the day was a win for Galfrid Otis.

Houghton's Ch Galfrid Tara. Photo: Pearce

27

George Wilkinson wrote in the 1979 Vizsla Society newsletter:

> *It is with the deepest regret that I have to report the death by accident of my Hungarian Vizsla Galfrid Otis. She was in all a great character and the cause of her death was, to my deepest sorrow, through her devotion to me and my own absent-mindedness. In addition to her prowess in the field, she was my constant companion and guard. No one dare enter my car without my being present. She was gentle and sweet natured with my small grandchildren. She was just reaching the peak of her form and one looked forward to many years of shooting and trialling with her.*

Her litter brother Galfrid Gelert was sold to Trevor West and trained by George Wilkinson. Trevor West became a familiar figure at field trials, gaining many wins with his Vizslas. Galfrid Gerda was sold to me and was my first brood bitch. She was trialled a few times, winning a certificate of merit at one. She was mated once to Sh Ch Waidman Remus and produced four puppies. One bitch went to Holland. Another,

Houghton's Ch Peckers Perchance. Photo: Dalton

Flax, was trained by George Wilkinson and was sold to a working home, as was Gerda eventually.

From Sari's mating to Galfrid Pej, Galfrid Tara went to the Russetmantle kennels. Later she was sold to Richard Houghton of the Peckers prefix and he made her up and later qualified her. When Tara was put to Sh Ch Swanside Zsigmund, she produced Ch Peckers Perchance in her first litter and Sh Ch Peckers Parody in her second.

Faradpusztai Charlott of Galfrid (Miss Angela Boys)

The second bitch to join the Galfrid kennels in 1972 was Hungarian import Faradpusztai Charlott of Galfrid, bred by Sarley Janosne and born in 1969 (Matai Legeny ex Allatkerti Dorka). Chitri, as she was called, was a disappointment to Angela Boys who, to this day, is convinced that this bitch was not the one she was expecting to arrive in England. Chitri had three litters. She was in whelp by Matai Bitang Tucsok and had her seven puppies in quarantine without any trouble. One of the dog puppies was Galfrid Hugo who was to go to Mrs Doraine Larner of the Yelrehta prefix. He was campaigned in the show ring by Doraine and by Eddie Bundy and later on by the professional handler under Mr D Page. When put to Halstock Fair Maid of Yelrehta a bitch from that litter, Yelrehta Gemini, also gained her title. Another bitch, Yelrethta Maria, went to Mr and Mrs J Swindell of the Czassa prefix.

From Chitri's mating with Sh Ch Waidman Remus, Galfrid Imro went to Spain where he was shown and worked successfully. Another litter brother, Galfrid Imre, went to Holland where he gained his title.

Chitri and Sari were both small bitches but Chitri did not have the style nor the warmth or working ability of Sari although she was another excellent ratter! Her coat was light and she had a rather broad ribcage. She became grey very early in her life.

Matai Vica and Matai Pirok (Mr Alan Heyman/Mr John Parke)

Two more bitches were imported from the Matai kennels in Hungary. Mr Alan Heyman visited Mikos Farkashazi and bought Matai Vica and Matai Pirok. Vica was born in 1973 (Helvecia Alfa ex Matai Gerle) and she was the first to arrive in England. Six months later Pirok (Matai Lurko ex Matai Panni II), who was six months younger than Vica, arrived.

Vica was trained by Mr John Parke, friend and shooting companion of Alan Heyman. John described Vica as an exceptional worker. He trained her in four months. He was given Pirok, or Heidi as she was known, and she took a little longer to train – 18 months! Both Vizslas were shot over and trialled very successfully. These two bitches were also small, very much the same type as Angela Boys' two imports.

Vica was mated to Futaki Laslo when she was 2½ years old. She had eight puppies but there are no recorded registrations of these pups. John Parke had a bitch from this litter and was over the moon with her working ability. He found her very easy to train and he worked her regularly.

He did not breed from Heidi. He described her as a *'funny little thing'*. He felt she had been mistreated in quarantine, which resulted in her deep distrust of anyone but him. Nevertheless this 'funny little thing' managed to win field trials!

In the 1974 October edition of the Hungarian Vizsla Society newsletter reporting the results of the field trial on the Marshland Estate (the ground kindly offered by Alan Heyman for the trial), Mr J Parke's Matai Pirok was first, Alan Heyman's Matai Vica was second and Trevor West's Galfrid Gelert was third. It is reported that Pirok was beautifully handled; she ranged freely but was under complete control and all the time was working to find game. John Parke was to be doubly congratulated as the day before he won the Weimaraner Club's novice stake running against German Shorthaired Pointers, Weimars and a large Munsterlander. This was the first time that a Vizsla had been placed first in a stake for all breeds which hunt, point and retrieve. Heidi won another field trial in 1977.

Mocsarkereso Vac of Galfrid (Miss Angela Boys)

Mocsarkereso Vac of Galfrid (Matai Vadasz ex Morcos Pushtai Bori), bred by Istvan Kass in 1976, was imported from Hungary by Miss Angela Boys in 1977. She

Boys' Mocsarkereso Vac of Galfrid. Photo: Pearce

Gottlieb's Sh Ch Galfrid Sofia of Russetmantle.
Photo: Pearce

gained many RCCs and 2CCs, and was a gentle, companionable, bitch. She had a good front and shoulders, beautifully proportioned head, being a medium-sized Vizsla with a lot of scope. She brought a new line to the Galfrid kennel. She was mated to Galfrid Gaspar in 1977 and twice to Galfrid Odo (1979 and 1981). From the first litter Galfrid Fergus, a very handsome dog, was always in the cards. He was exported to South Africa in 1981 and became a champion soon after. In 1982 Vac was mated to Galfrid Sean (brother to Sh Ch Galfrid Sofia of Russetmantle). Galfrid Rudi won the dog CC at Leeds Championship Show at the age of 14 months, and his litter sister Rosa gained her first championship certificate at Crufts in 1984 and gained her title later in the same year. Vac's fifth litter was by Galfrid Job in 1983.

Imports in the 1980s

Prins (Mrs Kwieschke)

In 1981, Dutch, Lux and Swiss Sh Ch Prins was imported from Holland by Mrs Kwieschke and Mr R Finch. Born in 1975 and bred by S Middleton, his sire was Kamp Milo-cinnamon Magyar VD, Beulaker and his dam Luizza. Prins came out of quarantine in fine fettle. He was first shown at Manchester Championship Show and won the RCC under Richard Houghton. He then went on to gain his Show Champion title in a matter of months, handled by Dick Finch, eminent judge and breeder and exhibitor of the Hansom Weimaraners. Prins also won high placings in the veteran stakes in 1982. He was a very handsome and elegant dog, different in type to our present Vizslas, of which few could hold their own at his age. He had a noble bearing, fine head and well proportioned body, very showy, and covered the ground with a beautiful stride. Prins was mated to Mr M Elliott's Russetmantle Pepper in 1983; there were nine puppies in the litter, six dogs and three bitches. From a mating with Hookside Dusk of Pipwell came Sh Ch Pipwell Golden October, who gained five CCs.

Cool Hand Luke (Mrs Anna Coombes and Miss J Coombes)

In 1984 Cool Hand Luke was imported from the United States by Mrs Anna Coombes and Miss J Coombes. Born in 1983 and bred by Mrs P Hartman, his sire was Am Ch Sarcos Melto Mariner and his dam Am Ch Firebrands Ziggy Stardust.

In 1986, Anna also imported from the United States Penlees Red Alert at Castlefield, bred by Mrs B Anderson and born in 1983 (Am Ch Dirigo Camblers

Marker ex Am Ch Firebrands Constant Comment). Both these dogs were seen in the ring. Red Alert was striking with a rich, russet gold coat. He moved with great power. He sired three litters, producing some longhairs. The Castlefield Kennel went on to produce Sh Ch Rhapsody in Blue when Russetmantle Jan was put to Ch Abbeystag Emilio. Out of this litter came Fandango in the Sun at Hookside, owned by Martyn Elliott, who

Kleinman's Ch Valleyhunter Special Envoy.

became a full champion. Rhapsody in Blue had a successful show career, gaining 15 CCs. When mated to Sh Ch Captain Quincey two show champions were produced: Henseys Castlefield Mill Lane (7 CCs) and Castlefield Windmill Girl.

Valleyhunter Little Dream and Valleyhunter Matai Countess (Ms Stephanie Kleinman)

In 1989 Valleyhunter Little Dream (Dirigo Marker PD-N-Full ex Valley Hunter's Legend), bred by Mrs J Assaf, was imported from the United States by Ms Stephanie Kleinman. Stephanie also brought over a bitch, Valleyhunter Matai Countess, who was in whelp to Matai Zsivany Hung Ch (mated in the United States). She gave birth in quarantine before returning to Jean Assaf. Jean Assaf resided in Israel with her Vizslas before moving to America. From this litter, Ch Valleyhunter

Lambert's Sh Ch Gryffe Opal. Photo: Pearce

Special Envoy influenced the breed, providing pace and drive to many of his offspring. He was shown and trialled with much success by his owner. When put to Little Dream, she produced Stephanie's second full champion Valleyhunters Valhalla. In the late 1990s, Stephanie Kleinman left Britain to live in the United States, taking her Vizslas with her.

Lambert's Sh Ch Mystical Megan of Gesztenye.
Photo: Butler

Middle: Knight's Alcsi Orsi.
Above: Three generations on holiday. L to r: Knight's
Alcsi Orsi, Szolnoki Asvanviz, S. Pitypalatty, S. Kincs.

Imports in the 1990s

Dade and Derby of Kirbydeene (Mr and Mrs R Downing)

In 1990, two brothers, Dade and Derby of Kirbydeene were imported from France by Mr and Mrs R Downing. Born in 1988, they were bred by Mr Cathelain and sired by Verocei Asa ex Vixie. These handsome boys were shown and their temperaments were excellent. Dade was mated to Ch Gardenway Charlotte. From that litter Gardenway La Valliere of Shalback gained a CC. His son by Gryffe Cumulus of Gesztenye, Cryffe Rittia, gained two CCs. Gryffe Rittia was bred by Mrs Plunkett and has done well for the Lamberts as their foundation bitch. When mated to Gardenway Master Mariner she made up Gryffe Opal and when mated to Ch Cuzco Laski she made up Mystical Megan of Gesztenye.

Alcsi Orsi (Mr and Mrs O Knight)

In 1990 an import came in from Hungary who was to figure in the gene pool. Mr and Mrs O Knight brought back a bitch, Alcsi Orsi (Csatarkai Cudar ex Alcsi Gizi), bred by Mrs J Kiss. She was to become the foundation bitch for the Knight's Szolnoki prefix.

When mated to Pitswarren Zacchaeus three from the

resulting litter were to do well in the ring. Sh Ch Szolnoki Zacasher (4 CCs and 4 RCCs) and Sh Ch Szolnoki Zacanyja (6 CCs) gained their titles. Both have the Pitswarren affix and are owned and shown by the Harpers. Ann Knight kept a bitch puppy, Szolnoki Asvanviz, handling her to win two CCs and four RCCs.

When Alcsi Orsi was mated to Ch Alsziv Pasque, Mrs S Millson bought a dog puppy, Szolnoki Konyak at Lutra. He proved himself in the field at the very end of the 1997–1998 season. He won third place in a Novice Trial. Sue trains and handles her dogs but this was her first trial. Her prefix is always in the cards in the ring and she has two homebred bitches waiting for a third ticket, Lutra Mayfly and Lutra Atlantic Breeze. Both are from a second mating (Gardenway Master Mariner ex Lutra Golden Mystery).

Sue works tirelessly for the breed. Her records, first kept by hand and now on computer, are an invaluable contribution to the breed.

Kilato Teri Furge Molany of Hemlake (Mrs K Le Mare)

In 1994 another import from Hungary arrived who has also contributed to the gene pool. Int and Hun Ch Kilato Teri Furge Molany of Hemlake (Int and Hun Ch Vadaszfar Kozak ex Kavai Pompas) was brought in by Mrs K Le Mare. He was bred by Mr R Jozefine. He was first shown under Pam Play *(Dog World)*. It was written at the time: '*This is the first time out for this handsome boy and of course great interest was shown. It is good to have new blood come into the breed. He has a very impressive pedigree.*'

Millson's Szolnoki Konyak at Lutra. Photo: Kent

Le Mare's Int. Hung. Ch Kilato Teri Furge Molkany of Helmlake. Photo: Dalton

Perkins' Sh Ch Gardenway Dawn Breeze. Photo: Perkins

Breeders have taken advantage of his bloodlines. When put to Ch Gardenway Dawn Run, two offspring kept by Jackie Perkins proved themselves in the ring: Gardenway Dawn Breeze (4 CCs) and her brother, Gardenway Dramatist, who was to gain his title in the late 1990s. This handsome dog, handled by owner Karina Le Mare, won his first CC appropriately enough at the National Gundog Championship Show. He was to gain his title in the late 1990s.

Vermillion Villarsia (Mr and Mrs Nigel Cox)

In 1996 Mr and Mrs Nigel Cox imported Vermillion Villarsia (Mr Bean) from Holland (Peleli Dori Bela ex Vallota Vermilion, bred by Mr A Poz-Boxtart). Nigel trained his dog, featuring in the 1997 Spring Pointing Tests. He is an exciting, fast Vizsla to watch. On his first time out he won a puppy working test. He won a Certificate of Merit at the GSPA Field Trial and the Novice Trial held by the Weimaraner Club of Great Britain This clever youngster is one to watch.

The Hungarian Vizsla in Competition

November 1973 saw the first field trial for the breed. It was a Novice Stake organised by the Hungarian Vizsla Society and took place in Northumberland. Windover Ripp, owned and handled by Mr F W Berry, gained a first. Saline Caroline, owned and handled by Mr E Greig, got second place and Starleypoint Ulles, Major Maitland-Smith's dog, came third.

I especially remember a field trial on the Marshland Estate in 1975. It was beautiful land and a fine day for once. We all started off with such high hopes as always but handling dogs and, in this case Vizslas, is an activity that can be a great leveller. Apart from the first three placings, there were no others.

Angela Boys wrote in the breed notes reporting the field trial:

> Sheila Gray had come over from Dorset with her home bred Sh Ch Abbeystag Bruna who unfortunately met one of the many hares, as did George Wilkinson's Galfrid Otis, and so did Virginia Phillips' goodlooking Waidman Buda. Louise Petrie-Hay stopped Waidman Brok on another but he played with his retrieve. Gay Gottlieb's Galfrid Gerda failed on the water test as did my own Matai Sari, both of them keen water dogs. Why do they do this to us? Having gotten my own Gaspar through the day without a runner on which he usually runs in, at the very end he failed on his retrieve – a dead cock pheasant – at which he took one look and walked away. We all have the 'should have been here last week' Joyce Grenfell situations. 'Never done that before,' we say weakly, but there is always another day and everyone enjoyed it. One by one we were eliminated that day but, as each disappointed handler joined the waiting group, all were able to sympathize.

In the 1977 Society Newsletter, Louise Petrie-Hay wrote:

> Congratulations to Michael Farmer. Not only was the field trial at Loton the first of our trials he had ever attended but it was also the first time he and Bogor (Waidman Brok's brother) had run in a trial – he was placed second. Then he went up to Ford in Northumberland and was lucky enough to get a run in the novice stake run by the GSP Club where competition was very hot and the card filled with GSP trial at Burton le Coggles and although 5th reserve on the card was fortunate to get a run owing to a number of withdrawals. This time he won. Not bad for the first season! And I am delighted to report that he intends to continue next year. His example should give heart

and encouragement to many Vizsla owners who have really good working dogs but just not the bravery of Mr Farmer to have a go in trials.

In order to encourage the novice to 'have a go', the Hungarian Society held its first 'get together' in 1977. It was conceived by the Society to encourage and help all those Vizsla owners who wished to work their dogs, a day together with other nervous novices and some not-so-novice, organised and planned to encourage everyone to attempt the basic exercises of hunt, point, and retrieve.

The 'get together' is constructed in such a way that there is no competition. Every handler is given every opportunity to do his best in the most relaxed, friendly atmosphere. During the course of the day the Vizslas are released from any discipline or the pressures of performing and join in the 'race'. Owners and dogs alike throw inhibition to the wind. It is a most delightful and comic occasion – 40

The Vizslas' idea of a get together!
Photo: Dr S Gottlieb

Bradbrooke's Sh Ch Russetmantle Bee.

Vizslas romping through the high summer grass; somehow the amusement it affords still allows us to admire our lovely breed.

1977 also saw the first demonstration at the Game Fair by breeds which hunt, point, and retrieve. The Vizsla has been well represented every year since then, the Club and the Society providing information for interested visitors at the breed stand.

In 1979 the Hungarian Vizsla Society was granted a Kennel Club licence to run its first open qualifying field trial.

The Society also ran their first working test and 13 Vizslas entered. John Churchill's Laser Duite (by Waidman Brok ex Calversam Amber) was best overall winner, gaining the Marion Trophy. Mary Bradbrook also won a working test with Russetmantle Bee (by Russetmantle Crisp ex Russetmantle Ash) at 10 months old.

The Hungarian Vizsla Club held their first Open Show in the spring of 1983 and it was a very well-organised, happy event, well supported by many Vizsla enthusiasts. The judge, David Layton (Midlander) well respected as judge, trainer, and breeder of the German Short-haired Pointer, had a good entry of 55 to go over. He made Mrs Bugden's Russetmantle Glade of Duncarreg (by Ch Russetmantle Troy and Sh Ch Galfrid Sofia of Russetmantle) Best In Show and still not out of puppy!

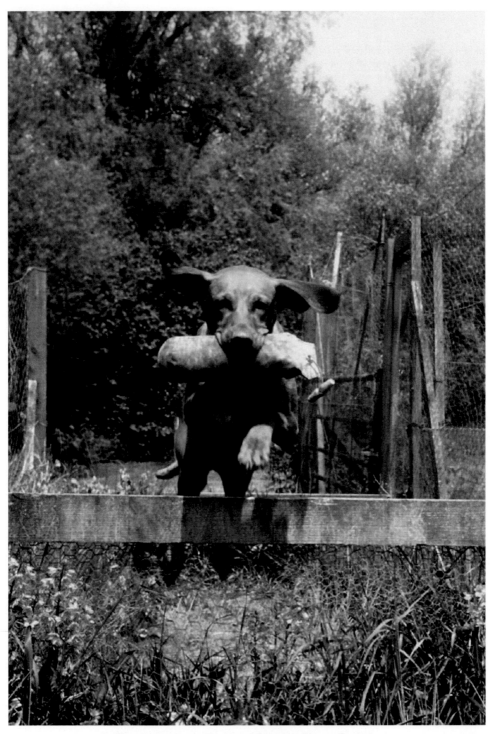

Harris' Perdita's Puzzle of Szajani. Photo: Carlisle

1983 seemed to consolidate the earlier efforts of many to encourage everyone to get their Vizslas working; those who had tried working tests the year before had a go at field trialling this year. Sue Cowburn's Peckers Penny, bred by Richard Houghton (by Swanside Little Trooper ex Ch Peckers Perchance) had been shown successfully. She had also been picking-up for a couple of seasons. Penny gained Certificate of Merit at her first trial, and she won the second at the Hungarian Vizsla Society All-Aged Stake held at Sansaw. What an achievement – trained and handled by Sue. I think many of us who witnessed her receiving the award had tears in our eye.

Sue Harris, who also shows her Vizslas successfully, won the Novice Stake at Apley Park with her Perdita's Puzzle of Szajani (by Waidman Brok ex Starleypoint Victoria) for the second time, and her young puppy Szajani Csipke (Czassa Camboge ex Perditas Puzzle of Szajani) gained a Certificate of Merit and Best Puppy award. Richard Houghton trialled his Sh Ch Peckers Perchance for the first time, and she won a Certificate of Merit, making 'Stella' his first champion to be made up in a trial. My Ch Russetmantle Troy won his second Certificate of Merit at this trial, which was held by the Large Munsterland Club at Westerham.

Sylvia and Nigel Cox were also to be congratulated, as their young Viszony of Vallota won the All-Aged Stake run by the German Shorthaired Pointer Club in Norfolk and, in 1984, made history by winning an Open Qualifying Stake.

Three show champions made up this year became champions: Perkins' Sh Ch Russetmantle Grebe of Gardenway, Sh Ch Gardenway Bula, and Neill's Sh Ch Saline Judi.

By the end of 1983 there were 38 show champions in the breed in Britain. Five of those were champions, two dogs and three bitches.

In 1986, the *Dog World* breed notes commented:

> On October 10 1986 the Club held its first Championship Show, judged by Angela Boys (Galfrid). There was a gentle, friendly atmosphere about the day; those seated round the ring outside had the pleasure of watching a marvellous entry of Vizslas. Angela was very thorough, judging with much knowledge of the breed. Winter's Sh Ch Captain Quincey of Glendun won the gigantic silver cup for BIS. Fairlies' Russetmantle Quire gained her first CC and she was made up soon after. She proved to be the Fairlies' foundation bitch for their prefix, Tasairgid. When mated to Sh Ch Galfrid Whig she produced two show champions, Sh Ch Tasairgid Designer Genes and Sh Ch Tasairgid Pure Genius at Dravhamor.

Mary Bradbrook and Russetmantle Bee won

Perkins' Ch Russetmantle Grebe of Gardenway.

Fairlie's Sh Ch Tasairgid Designer Genes.

Winter's Sh Ch Captain Quincey of Glendun.

McCabe's Sh Ch Chantilly Jester of Oroshaza.
Photo: Pearce

Gottlieb's Sh Ch Russetmantle Paris.
Photo: Dr S Gottlieb

the bitch Championship Certificate and Best of Breed under Mr Braddon at Leicester Championship Show and then went on to be pulled out in the last four in the Gundog group. Bee gained her title and won the Gundog group at SKC – the first Vizsla ever to achieve this honour – in 1984.

Generally the mid-1980s was an exciting time. In the ring Paddy and Jean Winter's Sh Ch Captain Quincey of Glendun gained his title and was to become a great ambassador for the breed, winning 23 CCs. Bred by pet owner Mrs M Marlow, by Oroshaza Phara (a working Vizsla) ex Russetmantle Posy, his pedigree is of interest. Phara's sire was Heather McCabe's Sh Ch Chantilly Jester of Oroshaza, one of the top winning Vizslas (20 CCs) in the 1970s. Posy's brother and sister were Sh Ch Russetmantle Paris and Poppy. I have to say I always had a soft spot for this handsome, typical Vizsla. Quincey always made me smile. When being judged, he would eye the judge, following every move. His appeal was his gentle nature. Tragically, fire destroyed the Winter's kennels one night in April 1990. Quincey and his kennel mates were consumed by smoke. The breed was smitten. We held a memorial services prior to being judged at WELKS Championship Show. We all assembled in the ring to pay tribute – it was a sad occasion.

In the ring in the mid-1980s, Jackie Perkins' Ch Gardenway Charlotte was totting up the CCs (20, only to be outdone by

Gardenway Dawn Run, achieving the bitch record of 23 CCs). Both bitches were from the same breeding, Ch Russetmantle Grebe (16 CCs) ex Ch Galfrid Bula (4 CCs). At the same time, Sh Ch Russetmantle Paris gained 18 CCs. Ch Russetmantle Quiver gained his title and went on to succeed in the field and in the ring, collecting 20 CCs. He died tragically of cancer of the spleen at six years old.

In *Dog World* a small piece was written after Quiver had won BOB under judge Dr Arrowsmith:

Perkins' Ch Gardenway Charlotte. Photo: Pearce

> It was not the first time Mrs D Arrowsmith had awarded Quiver as she had given him an award at the Large Munsterlanders Club Field Trial the year before. How many judges have been able to put up the same dog in both field and the show ring?

> In 1985 a Vizsla proved it was possible to go to the top in the field. The bitch who made history in the breed was FT Ch Viszony of Vallota, owned, bred, trained and handled by Sylvia and Nigel Cox. She was by Waidman Brok ex Calversham Amber. She was shown as a youngster but it was in the field and trialling that she came into her own. It should be appreciated that to win her title she was competing in Open Stakes, open to all breeds. Sylvia writes:

Perkins' Ch Gardenway Dawn Run.

> The August before her first birthday we had a working holiday in Scotland; it was here on the grouse that we first had stars in our eyes for her. She showed terrific pace, style and stamina, but it was the 'hungry want' of every bird on the moor that showed the most.

Viszony retired with 35 Field Trial Awards to her name.

Gottlieb's Ch Russetmantle Quiver.

Harper's Pitswarren Zacchaeus (aged 14 months).

Harper's Sh Ch Gardenway Rica of Pitswarren (aged 18 months).

Harper's Sh Ch Pitswarren Levi. To date, the top winning Vizsla - 37 CCs. Photo: Dalton

The Hungarian Vizsla Society held their first Championship Show on 23 October 1987. F G Waring had an entry of 69 Vizslas. Hows' Sh Ch Pipwell Golden October won Best Bitch and Ch Russetmantle Quiver won BIS. It was thrilling, and a word of encouragement to all slow starters. Many a time Quiver was beaten as a youngster and his immaturity and lack of concentration and co-ordination left me in despair but, as he grew on mentally and physically, he was able to control his limbs!

Jackie Perkins' Ch Gardenway Dawn Run won two gundog groups in 1989 at National Gundog and Birmingham National. These group wins seemed to be the beginning of the Hungarian Vizsla holding his own in competition with other gundog breeds in the ring. As we will see in the 1990s, there were to be many successes in the big ring and it was not unusual to see the Vizsla in the last line up.

Also by 1989 the Harper's Sh Ch Pitswarren Levi started his career as a puppy. He was to become the top-winning Vizsla in the breed, gaining his title in the 1990s. He won 37 CCs and 15 Reserve CCs. In 1993 he won at the Manchester Society Res Gundog Group, East of England, the Gundog Group and RBIS show at Leeds that year and in 1994 he repeated this win. This great dog never put a foot wrong in the big ring; he seemed to revel in the atmosphere. Peter handled him to perfection and it will be many years before his record is overtaken. Bred by the Harpers from Pitswarren Zacchaeus ex Sh Ch Gardenway Rica of Pitswarren, this mating also produced a second show champion, Pitswarren Leila. Levi himself sired Sh Ch Pitswarren Tanzie ex Russetmantle Dream of P.

The 1990s

Sh Ch Pitswarren Levi was not the only Vizsla to feature in group wins in the 1990s. In 1993 Mrs Lynsey Townend's Rainscote Risky Business (Mouse) won the Gundog Group at Blackpool. Homebred (Sh Ch Galfrid Kipps ex Hookside Damson), Mouse sadly died of cancer at a young age having gained 2 CCs and 5 RCCS. Lynsey is one of the stalwarts of the breed, working tirelessly in the Breed Rescue.

Wilks' Sh Ch Russetmantle Ember. "Leasel" produced winning stock for the 'Nicael' affix.

To cap the end of the year, Ch Alsziv Pasque won the Gundog Group at LKA. He had gained his second ticket and BOB at this show. He went on to win another Gundog Group at Manchester in 1994. Pasque (11 CCs and 11 RCCs) became the Digby's first homebred champion (Sh Ch Szappanos Szeivacs of Abbeystag ex S Ch Hookside Sounds of Silence at

Digby's Ch Nicael Russe at Alsziv. Photo: Dalton

Alsziv). He proved a useful stud dog for this prefix, siring their second champion, Nicael Russe of Alsziv. At the end of the 1997–98 season, Russe gained his full title by winning a Certificate of Merit and then gained a 4th in the JVC novice trial. He is handled by Ann Digby. Russe also won BOB and Group 3 Crufts 1998.

When Pasque was put to Wilke's bitch Sh Ch Russetmantle Ember (Ch Abbeystag Emilio ex Sh Ch Russetmantle Poppy), one of the top-winning bitches (16 CCs, 16 RCCs), her first and second matings produced winning stock that dominated the show ring. From the first mating came Sh Ch Nicael Polestar of Streamhawk (6 CCs, 9 RCCs) and from the second Russe' brother Nicael Rully who was made up in the late 1990s. Nicael Roboso is maturing into another force to be reckoned with (1 CC).

Larry Wilks' foundation bitch was Sh Ch Russetmantle October (4 CCs), the same breeding as Ember. When put to Sh Ch Russetmantle Paris (18 CCs, 9 RCCs), the mating produced Sh Ch Russetmantle Finch of Gunalt (13 CCs, 11 RCCs). He and his brother Russetmantle Fennel, owned and trained by Larry, worked consistently in the field.

In 1994 Cootes Sh Ch Stregaya Fleet (Stregaya Echo ex Sh Ch Glendun Dollar of

Steele's Sh Ch Nicael Polestar at Streamhawk.
Photo: Buller

Wilks' Sh Ch Russetmantle October.
Photo: Dr S Gottlieb

Gottlieb's Sh Ch Russetmantle Finch of Gunalt.
Photo: Dr S Gottlieb

Stregaya) won RBIS at National Gundog. He repeated this prestigious win at Richmond in 1995. Fleet had given us all a thrill back in 1992 when he gained his first CC and BOB and then was pulled out in the Group. This prefix has had consistent winners over the years in the ring and in the field. Echo did well for the Cootes, being placed in two trials, as did another of their breeding, Stregaya Highlander, who won a first and a second in 1996. Sally handles her dogs in both the show ring and the field.

Also in 1995 Legett's Sh Ch Swallow Sunset (Sh Ch Russetmantle Finch of Gunalt ex Castelfield Midnight Blue) took Reserve in the Gundog Group at Birmingham City. Also from this mating Osprey Moon, owned by K Dimon, won the HVS Novice Trial. He also had success trialling Midnight Blue who gained a second and a third in All Age Stakes.

In 1996 the Upton's Sh Ch Wicked Lady of Tragus (Gardenway Red Admiral of Tragus ex Glendun Pippa) won RBIG at Midland Counties. The Winter's Glendun prefix has contributed to both the Stregaya and Tragus successful kennels. Wicked Lady has proved her worth as a foundation bitch as well as dominating the ring (17 CCs, 9 RCCs), handled impeccably by Peter Upton.

Finally, in 1997 Bicknell's Sh Ch Pitswarren Isaac of Szentendre (Ch Fandango in the Sun at Hookside ex Sh Ch Pitswarren Leila) won RBIG at SKC. Isaac had given many of us great pleasure in 1996 after winning the CC and BOB at Crufts

Cootes' Sh Ch Stregaya Fleet. Photo: Paul

Upton's Sh Ch Wicked Lady of Tragus.
Photo: Russell Fine Art

Barbara Douglas-Redding;
expert handler & elder statesman of the breed.

when we saw him pulled out in the last eight in the Group. He also won the HVC Championship Show that same year. Karen's Sh Ch Kencombe Delius cannot be ignored (Sh Ch Szappanos Szeivacs of Abbeystag ex Sondek Duchess). Max held the record of five BIS plus numerous group wins before he was retired from the open show circuit.

Barbara Douglas-Redding Dies

Barbara Douglas-Redding died at the beginning of the 1990s, aged 82. One of the early pioneers of the breed, she became known as the elder statesman and her Wolfox prefix is scattered throughout our pedigrees. She was an excellent handler. We novices owe much to her kindness and immense knowledge of dogs and especially our breed. She rarely judged, preferring to show her beloved Vizslas. She made up Wolfox Fabia and Abbeystag Claudia of Wolfox.

Her *Dog World* breed notes entertained us endlessly. She gave us an intimate peep into her world. One of my favourite 'peeps' was apropos a remark someone made: 'absolute rhubarb, were I not such a sweet refined OAP I'd put it in plainer language'. She expressed in her breed notes so vividly how she felt on showing her Vizsla for the first time. Her talent was that we could all relate so closely with her own experiences.

The first time I exhibited was donkeys years ago. Two days before the show my Vizsla bitch produced a poorly eye. Panic stations for a completely novice mum. I sat with her for two days in a darkened room, eye improved, and after all that trauma I had no clue what to do on arriving at Olympia in a complete tizz wazz. However, we got the 'flavour' so to speak, and made many lasting friendships.

The Hungarian Vizsla Club and the Hungarian Vizsla Society

In 24 June 1968, the first AGM of the Hungarian Vizsla Club was held in Worcester. Twenty-five founder members had applied to The Kennel Club and they were duly issued with a licence. Thirteen members were present at the AGM. Virginia Phillips was elected secretary, Mr Trist was treasurer and Louise Petrie-Hay was elected chairman.

Objectives

The objectives of the club were:

- To encourage high standards in breeding for working ability and conformation; to promote interest in training the Vizsla for field trials, as gundog, for obedience show and personal companion.
- To work actively to protect and advance the interests of the breed by encouraging sportsmanlike competition at field trials, breed shows and competitive obedience events.
- To urge members to breed only fully registered dogs that were within the Vizsla standard.
- To support research and educational work to reduce and/or eliminate undesirable or detrimental congenital traits from the breed.
- To conduct field trials, breed shows and obedience trials and training courses.
- To encourage owners and/or handlers to attend working gun dog classes and obedience training classes.

1970–1971 were unhappy years for the Club. Disharmony had reached the stage where the original members felt the club was not carrying on the spirit in which it was originally founded, which was to give advice and assistance to owners of working Vizslas. Therefore, on 29 November 1972, the Hungarian Vizsla Society was approved and registered under that name. Jim Gray - Sheila Gray (Abbeystag)'s husband - was an active supporter and secretary from 1976 to the early 80s. So it came about that the small band who originated the Club resigned and started up the Society, leaving the Club in the hands of newcomers to the breed. In spite of attempted reconciliations over the years, as yet, the two remain firmly separate although many Vizsla owners are members of both.

In 1973 members of the Hungarian Vizsla Club received notices of resignation from the chairman, Bill Foster, and the secretary, Margaret Foster. The reason for the resignations was 'owing to certain actions by some members of the club to which we cannot remain impartial'. Thus, there was yet another change in the Club's history. Major J L Houghton was elected chairman and Roger Simkin (Swanside) became secretary. A year later Major George Wilkinson took on the job of chairman since Major Houghton wished to retire. The new treasurer was Mr Lambert. George Wilkinson, keen on working and trialling his dogs, energetically fostered and provided the means for further working trials and, until 1980–1981, the Club and Society held at least two field trials each a year. All who were interested in trialling their Vizslas supported both. In spite of this, frequently there were not enough entries to fill the card of 12 running, so GSP, Weimar, and Great Munsterlander owners would be invited to join us.

Marshall's Sh Ch Vaternish Bronze Star at Lowerdon. Photo: Rayner

In 1980 the Hungarian Vizsla Club changed hands again. Major George Wilkinson felt he should retire and the secretary, Mrs Dorothea Hunt, joined him. Mr Richard Houghton was elected chairman and Mrs Sharon Seward became secretary.

During the 1990s, the development of the breed has been fostered by the Hungarian Vizsla Club and the Hungarian Vizsla Society, whose aim is to provide information, support and guidance for members in order to promote responsible ownership, Both now have a voluntary Code of Ethics. Both have a healthy membership which

L to r: Sylvia Cox, judge Rob E Hart & the author in Holland, 1989.

increases year by year as the breed grows. Today the committees work enthusiastically and with dedication, providing not only Field Trials and shows but fun days and training, as well as working tests.

Brian Chisolm (Vaternish), as Secretary of the Society, had significant influence in his term of office (1992–1996). He judges the breed at Championship level and believes sincerely in fostering the working and showing Vizsla, as does his wife, Wendy. He made his first Vizsla, Shooting Star of Vaternish, into a champion. She gained seven CCs, winning her first at under eight months of age. When mated to Sh Ch Galfrid Whig, she produced Sh Ch Vaternish Bronze Star at Lowerdon.

Brian working Shooting Star all her life, mainly on the grouse moor. She was a dearly loved companion. As she neared her last days, Brian and Windy knew there was not long for her, and Brian decided to take her pigeon shooting for the last time as she loved nothing more than being his shooting companion. Treasured memories, and the essence of the Vizsla.

Spring Pointing Tests in Holland

In May 1989, a group of HPR field trial judges were invited to attend and some to judge some spring pointing tests in Holland. There were four or five car loads of us and we were entertained royally. Sylvia Cox and I had the honour to be invited to walk up with the Dutch judge judging the junior class.

All the entrants were young Vizslas, some had only been in training for three months. We were horrified to see groups of great hares romping about on the land. We were impressed by the speed and distance the Vizslas quartered with head held high. Our experienced judge was delighted when a youngster showed initiative including running in up to three or four fields away – chasing a hare! He explained: 'The dog must gain confidence, once he has self assurance he will work for us!' Sylvia and I were a bit rattled. In Britain we place such store on steadiness we were shocked to see a Vizsla allowed to run in.

However, we all saw adult Vizslas working during our stay and steadiness did not appear to be a problem. Thus we had food for thought.

Development of the Breed in Great Britain

During the 1960s, a strong band of Vizsla enthusiasts both north and south of the border were breeding, working and enjoying their dogs. In 1964 there were 27 Kennel Club registrations and in 1965 there were about 300 Vizslas in the country. Total Kennel Club registrations from 1954 to 1981 amounted to 1385. Few dogs were shown, and the breed was still classified as a rare breed until 1971. At that time Barbara Douglas-Redding wrote:

> What a thrill, now that we have our own column alphabetically in Dog World breed notes, instead of being a Rare Breed for so many years.'

She went on to say:

> We have a lot to learn, especially about colour, conformation and working ability from our somewhat limited resources.

In 1967, Barbara Douglas-Redding wrote that the breed would have three representatives at Crufts: Kinford Nora, Wolfox Kinford Rica and Wolfox Topaz. At Crufts 1968, eight Vizslas were entered in Any Variety sporting classes. Forty-three registrations were recorded that year at The Kennel Club. Until 1971, Hungarian Vizslas could only enter in Rare Breed or Any Variety classes. There were very few actual breed classes. Those who did show at that time found it very disheartening as Barbara wrote:

> *This qualifying business for Crufts is almost a dead duck, trying your chances in the Any Variety classes provided by a few championship shows that are stuffed with the cream of established breeds.*

Therefore, 1971 was a memorable year for the breed. In 1970 Barbara wrote in her breed notes: '*Well, here it is, with Crufts 1971 catalogue in my left hand, I write that there are four breed classes for us with challenge certificates, to be judged by Mrs Violet Yates.* She continues:

> *This has been achieved by sheer slog and the loyalty of a handful of owners who have bred, registered and supported in every possible way over the last few years. Now we must never let this wonderful breed get into the doldrums from idleness in accepting them but doing nothing constructive towards their future in the field, shows and as companions. It's up to every one of us. Don't forget they have been here since 1953.*

I would like to add that Barbara Douglas-Redding herself contributed more than most. She always had a 'good one' and she bred good ones repeatedly. She did a lot of winning but was always ready to encourage newcomers in the breed. It was a hard slog in those days. I remember standing endlessly in those enormous Any Variety classes at Open Shows. Rarely was my Remus pulled out, but one or two good wins somehow kept one going. Margaret Foster's Kinford Zsuzsi was rarely beaten. She won an enormous Any Variety Not Classified class in 1970, making her eligible for the Big Ring in the gundog group and she was pulled out fourth. Barbara wrote to me in 1982: 'My old dears, like me, are ancient. Fabia 12½ years, Aquila 11½ and terribly white. The puppies? Beren and Claudia rising 10 years. Time flies on and I get less delicious daily.'

In 1971, Hungarian Vizslas were awarded six sets of Challenge Certificates for the first time in England at Crufts, WELKS, SKC, Birmingham National, Leeds and LKA. Crufts had 14 entries that year. Margaret Foster, who was contributing to the breed notes at this time, wrote: '*A great deal of interest was shown in our breed at Crufts. A delighted Mrs Gottlieb won the dog Challenge Certificate with Waidman Remus, and Kinford Zsuzsi won the bitch ticket and BOB. Zsuzsi was again in the final six in the gundog group.*'

These two Vizslas were to be the first dog and bitch show champions in the breed over here. Kinford Zsuzsi, bred by Louise Petrie-Hay, was by Waidman Ficko and Kinford Vlada. Waidman Remus, also bred by Louise Petrie-Hay, was by Waidman Fules and Kinford Vlada. Sh Ch Kinford Zsuzsi and Sh Ch Waidman Remus were mated in 1972 and from this litter a bitch and a dog were exported to Australia where they became show champions. Another dog from this litter, Gamelands Zorro, belonged to Margaret Rice. He gained his title and was campaigned in Scotland and England.

Gottlieb's Sh Ch Waidman Remus; the first male Sh Ch in the breed. Photo: Pearce

Foster's Sh Ch Kinford Zsuzsi; the first Sh Ch in the breed.

One hundred and fifty-three registrations were recorded in 1980. One hundred and seventy-three registrations were recorded in 1982, showing that by this time the breed had gathered an increasing number of enthusiasts, both in the field and in the show ring. Entries had reached up to 45–50 at some championship shows. Crufts 1973 had seven exhibitors; in 1983 there were 27! Sheila Gray wrote in her report in the Hungarian Vizsla Society newsletter on Crufts 1982:

Our steward Mr J Lamb called the first class together, both he and the judge Mr R Finch were looking smart complete with bowler hats!

She also commented on the excellent entry awaiting Mr Miklós Farkasházi at Ardingly show ground at the Hammersmith Gold Medal Show:

Imagine how we felt on arrival to find that Mr Farkashazi had not been allowed to leave Hungary; most of us came many miles for a true Hungarian breeder's opinion.

Breed Type

On Size

In 1972 and 1973 breeders were particularly concerned over height and size in the breed because the recent imports and their progeny were smaller than most of the stock already in this country.

I remember standing next to Angela Boys in the ring, she with Gaspar and I with Remus. Both were within the Standard, but Gaspar was at the bottom and Remus at the top of the scale. The late Arthur Westlake was judging. He stood in front of us with his cowboy hat to one side: 'Now that's the Hungarian type – smaller, and that's the large English type.' I felt as if I were handling an elephant! Gaspar won the class as the judge explained '*I am judging to the Hungarian standard*'!

Barbara Douglas-Redding writes:

Size is a subject that is looming up. Every now and again, oversized and too-tall Vizslas are cropping up from the same bloodlines that produce specimens of the correct size. It will take more years to sort these faults out considering the progeny from stock imported in the last three years. My mind boggles as to how it can be coped with.

Well, I would say we are still attempting and we are still having problems. An uneven litter is not unusual. For example, four puppies at seven weeks weighed as follows: one dog was 6.6kg (14.6lb), a second was 5.8kg (13lb), one bitch was 6kg (13.4lb) and a second was 7.7kg (12.6lb).

In the Hungarian Society Newsletter of October 1975, Virginia Phillips writes in an article called 'Food for Thought':

There has been much written recently in the national press on the subject of dog foods and suggestions made that, in some households, the dogs are fed on better and more balanced fare than the children. Old established breeders in this country are rather disturbed about the conflicting impressions gained by British visitors to Hungary about the size and stamp of present-day Vizslas. A few years ago our stock recently imported from Hungary appeared to fulfil their requirements on size, shape colour etc and be fitted to perform the all-round job for which they were intended. Nowadays, size varies considerably, heightwise and in the amount of bone and the shapes of the heads show wide discrepancies.

One can appreciate that there are likely to be differences between American-bred dogs and ours and obviously different methods of feeding and rearing as well as preferences for certain characteristics would influence their lines. It is interesting to note that a Hungarian author reported that the wartime breeds were still feeling the effects of widespread undernourishment experienced during the Second World War, and that pups were frequently weaned on Semolina and thereafter did not have the benefit of our carefully prepared and balanced foods with their mineral and vitamin additives. Could the present smaller size of some of those Hungarian imports be attributed to their rearing or is it a result of a deliberate breeding policy?

Barbara Douglas-Redding wrote in 1974:

Last week I measured Beren. He's just about 25", the top male limit. I forbade him to think of growing another hair's breadth. At Birmingham National 1974, Dr Esther Rickards, the judge, had some difficult classes to judge which she herself admitted was because of the size variations. She looked at my Beren and said, 'He's biggish isn't he?' I replied, 'He's just up to the top limit the last time I measured him and I've not dared since.' Her charming reply was, 'Don't dear, don't.

Margaret Foster in her breed notes wrote in 1974:

I think all judges of our breed should bear in mind the standard which is now official. This states the lowest height for bitches is 21" and the highest for dogs 25". I am told there is a dog now winning in the ring who is 3" below the standard. Someone remarked to her 'I see you are getting miniatures in the ring now!

On Colour

There are some interesting comments on colour. In 1972 Barbara Douglas-Redding wrote:

Here are a few translations on the colour theme to occupy you. They are taken at random, mostly from Hungarian sources. In this country we register Vizslas as 'Russet-

gold', but the following give food for thought: dark sandy, yellow with gold sheen, dark tan, dark yellow, sedge yellow, rather dark sandy yellow in several different shades – dark brown and pale yellow are objectionable – chestnut, like a chestnut horse, roast bun, bread roll and crust of bread!

In 1968 an article in *Country Life* called 'A Gundog from Hungary – the Magyar Vizsla', written by M S Lampton, comments on colour:

The colour is officially described as yellow, this is not as we know it in Labrador Retrievers but a deeper shade reddish golden or bracken colour. Brown or pale fawn are unacceptable colours.

At WELKS 1972 Mr Udvardy of Hungary, an FCI judge of all Hungarian breeds, visited our benches. He commented that he wanted a fairly rich russet colour free from paler shoulder flashes as he saw in the United States,. Returning to the question of size he felt that many of the Vizslas he saw at Welks were oversized, too tall to fit in with the Hungarian standard, also there were too many with straight shoulders. He thought some of the exhibits he saw were somewhat light in bone for real fieldwork.

Barbara Douglas-Redding comments:

Well, over here in our shooting world they are used as what the Americans term 'bird dogs', and really nothing larger than a hare is their expected lot in Great Britain as opposed to coping with bigger game in other parts of the world.

On Eye Colour

At one of the Birmingham championship shows in 1972 Mrs De Casembroot was worried by the number of pale-eyed exhibits present. Barbara Douglas-Redding felt that the light eye fault which had been increasingly noticeable in some of the youngsters over the last 18 months was a thing we should try to correct somehow. From all accounts, this was not just incidental to Great Britain but was popping up in the Vizsla world everywhere, including the country of origin. She also came to the conclusion that the pattern of lightness was not always settled in the change from the early blue to what should become a nice warm sherry, fitting in harmoniously with the coat colour by the time the pups have left home, so it is only the show stock seen in the ring who give indications of this trend.

In 1980, Angela Boys records in her breed notes that Mr Froggat had a large entry of 47 Vizslas at LKA and that, 'There were a lot of young puppies out winning'. Mr Froggat said he noticed a lot of light eyes. 'Dare I point out,' Angela commented, 'that many puppies have light eyes until they reach maturity. The eye that will darken has a dark rim to the iris and is totally different to the staring hawk eye, a serious fault and fortunately rare in the breed in England.'

S M Lampson, in his article in The Field commented on the eye: *The eyes of the Vizsla, unlike those of most more familiar breeds, may be pale yellow although if dark they are quite in order!*

Barbara Douglas-Redding wrote:

One of Sheila Gray's pups by the Late Warhorse Lwow CD is now just over a year old. To start with, she had one green eye and one brown. This lasted ages. Now both eyes are the correct colour, so live and learn and refrain from making snap judgements at an early age. Let us not get too worried about heads and colours yet, but concentrate on trying to get our conformation and movement right plus, of course, keeping correct working *temperament well to the fore. Colour fanatics in other breeds in the past have done great disservice to their breeds in the long run.*

She also quoted American Professor Phil Wright, a well-known breeder of Vizslas, as saying:

I was fortunate enough to see [in Hungary] at a hunting training session, the top winning show Vizslas and a goodly number of dogs which both show and hunt extensively. There is not a shadow of doubt in my mind that the Vizsla in Hungary is primarily a hunting dog. I did not see a large Vizsla in Hungary. The dogs I saw in several towns and villages as well as in Budapest were almost entirely of the golden rust colour, reddish or rust-tint, yes, but Irish Setter red, no! I also say that many show dogs are veering away from the real type of the breed, tall dogs, straight shoulders, poor feet, funny gait and rosy red colour are becoming common in shows. They could not back it up in the field.

Barbara Douglas-Redding commented:

I found this all very interesting reading. Although we have quite a variation in sizes over here in Britain, I do think that conformation generally has improved out of all recognition in the past 20 years. Most of you will not have seen the early imports or their progeny.

Breed Type Today

In 1997 *Dog World* invited prominent breeders and breed judges of the day to contribute their comments in a forum. One of the questions was 'How has breed type altered over the years?"

Sheila Gray (Abbeystag)

Typical Vizslas in the 70s were elegant, lively, well boned and, with a few exceptions, larger than today's dogs. Heads were gaunt, noble and distinguished. Type today is sounder in depth, particularly fronts and elbows, and there are not so many Queen Anne fronts, and distinction in heads can be found but are not typical today.

Angela Boys (Galfrid)

The winning dogs of today appear to be better boned with better conformation. Some of the stock shown is well up to size – some over the Standard. At the other end of the scale, there are a lot of very finely boned, spindly dogs about.

Jackie Perkins (Gardenway)

When I came into the breed in the late 70s, the breed was smaller in height generally than some today. We see Vizslas winning who are clearly over the Standard whilst others lack substance.

We also seem to have come full circle with fronts which were pretty poor 20 years ago, and improved tremendously until the early 90s.

Peter and Liz Harper (Pitswarren)

When we first came into the breed the dogs were medium sized, medium boned animals, with a reputation for wide fronts, loose elbows and poor movement. Whilst fronts and movement have greatly improved, it could be considered to have been achieved by producing a diversity of type and losing that degree of moderation so specific to the Standard. Areas of particular note are size, colour, broad skulls with short muzzles, exaggerated angulation and an increasing tendency to hound-like appearance as opposed to the medium-sized, elegant dog we should be producing.

Paddy and Jean Winter (Glendun)

Unfortunately, our breed has altered in size and type. We are losing sight of the Standard and not putting enough thought into our breeding lines.

Brian and Wendy Chisholm (Vaternish)

Poor fronts which were once a failing in the breed have now been largely bred out. However, the lean and noble expression appears to be less common. There are too many scent hound-type heads in evidence or animals with too little sculpting on the face resulting in a blank expression.

Sylvia Cox (Vallota)

The greatest alterations have been very good and very bad. Fronts and rears are mostly good. Noble heads? There are too many short, square muzzles. It is serious. What has happened to prominent breast bones? And where is that length of loin (moderate to long) which allows our breed to gallop fast?

Gay Gottlieb

In 1983, I was asked to comment on the breed in an article for the *Society Newsletter*, and these were my comments:

Question: Do I think the breed has improved over the last decade?

Answer: *I don't think fronts have changed at all. They were bad and they are bad overall. We still have an uphill task. We are still at sixes and sevens over height, some too big, some too small and light in bone but, on the other hand, top lines are firm and straight and hind action is good. Many Vizslas can power round the ring with a strong, elegant action and most are in such muscular condition they could certainly do a day's work. I do feel that overall type has improved. A Vizsla looks like 'The Standard Vizsla', proud, lively, of distinguished appearance, head gaunt and noble. Temperaments have improved beyond measure; at one time a ring full of Vizslas could look a poor shy lot, backs hunched, tails clamped, ears back, many unhappy to be gone over by the judge. It is a rare sight now to see a shy Vizsla. To me this is the most important improvement of all. No point in having a beautiful dog who cannot be touched.*

Back in the forum 1997 I wrote: I believe the breed has altered in correcting fronts – it was unusual to find tight feet and pasterns, tight elbows and good shoulder angulation ten years ago or so. The breed rarely featured in the Gundog Group. Today it is not unusual for us to be pulled out in the last line-up and a few have now won the Group. I do worry about size and type.

In Conclusion

Inevitably breeds will have a diversity in type and will go through the doldrums as the Vizsla has done. I tend to agree with Sylvia Cox. Answering the question in the forum: 'What are your hopes and fears for the breed's future?' she replied: *That the breed can return to what some of the dogs used to look like, without the faults!*

Sheila Gray in answer to this same question said: *That the very qualities in make, shape and temperament which are unique to the Vizsla are not lost in the effort to make them successful, show or working dogs. Knowing the Vizsla's sense of humour and fun and its charming way of making a fool of itself and us, it may never happen!*

Stop press:

McCullough's Sh Ch Vereker Sparrowhawk was top winning dog in 1998; he also went BIS Gundog Society of Wales and was Group 1 Blackpool Championship Show 1998.

McCullough's Sh Ch Vereker Sparrowhawk. Photo: Carol Ann Johnson

chapter 3

All drawings in this chapter kindly supplied by Jackie Perkins (Gardenway).

The Standard outlines the necessary features of a particular breed - although the functional principles of the dog remain the same, each breed is unique in its appearance. The Standard provides the blueprint and it is to this prototype that all breeders should refer. Thus, an image of the Hungarian Vizsla is provided as a fundamental reference for all who wish to advance the breed. Many breeders will have their own idea of their 'ideal' Vizsla, but does it fit the Standard? The Standard must be studied and learned in order that the breeder understands how the structure of a dog suits its function. The judge must also know how to interpret the Standard, for it is he who judges the physical and mental attributes of the dogs in the ring and their level of excellence in the field.

Viewing the dog as a whole, the parts should fuse together in unity, and to understand the uniqueness of any breed it is important to know how each element works correctly in relationship with the others. A breeder cannot hope to breed a good dog without knowing the points that make it a good dog; a judge cannot judge a dog without knowledge of the points that deserve appraisal.

Some basic features must be considered, such as type, balance, conformation, style, soundness and temperament. To understand more of the breed essentials and characteristics, it is important to examine the Standard in great detail. This should give a deeper appreciation of the particular features of the Hungarian Vizsla.

The Kennel Club Standard
for the Hungarian Vizsla

The Breed Standard of the Hungarian Vizsla was approved in April 1973 by The Kennel Club and revised in 1975. In 1983 The Kennel Club instructed that all Breed Standards must conform in specific wording, titles and headings. Thus the British Standard was rephrased and shortened.

My Comments on the 1975 and 1983 Standard

Characteristics
The Hungarian Vizsla should be lively and intelligent, obedient but sensitive, very affectionate and easily trained. It was bred for hunting, for fur and feather on open ground or in thick cover, pointing and retrieving from both land and water.

Although there are more Vizslas in the show ring today than ten years ago, we have not reached the point at which the breed has a show type and a working type, as has happened in some gundog breeds. It is difficult to maintain these two aspects, one reason being time, another that to keep a show dog in top condition needs particular exercise and feeding; if he is working as well he will inevitably lose some condition and weight and can be overmuscled. Above all, a gundog needs to have an early training pattern; too much physical strain on soft bone can create faults in the dog's conformation. The basic reason for a bad front is bad breeding but the condition can be aggravated by working a dog too early.

Vizsla owners who work and show their dogs are to be commended, since it is they who will not allow the natural conformation of the dog to change. If we do not deviate we may not have the supreme champion or the greatest field trial dog, but the beautiful Golden Pointer will remain a 'many sided hunting dog' or a 'many sided dog'.

General appearance

A medium sized dog of distinguished appearance, robust but lightly boned.

We can breed robust and heavy dogs, slight and very light boned dogs, some like Whippets and some like Bloodhounds, but the correct type is 'robust and not too heavily boned'. A light boned Vizsla could be a weedy one. When compared to the Weimaraner and German Shorthaired Pointer, it should be understood that there are substantial differences, one being this particular aspect of his conformation.

Head and skull

The head should be gaunt and noble. The skull should be moderately wide between the ears with a median line down the forehead and a moderate stop. The muzzle should be a little longer than the skull and, although tapering, should be well squared at the end. The nostrils should be well developed, broad and wide. The jaw strong and powerful. The lips should cover the jaws completely and should be neither loose nor pendulous. The nose should be brown.

The word 'gaunt' has been deleted from the English Standard now, and 'lean' has replaced it. 'Gaunt' in the Oxford English Dictionary is defined as 'famished, slim and haggard', which does seem rather harsh. We have many types of head in the breed. In particular, one type is narrow with little stop, the eyes are close together and small, the muzzle tends towards snipeyness with little lip. Another type conforms nearer to the Standard, but can easily tend toward a heavy head, the skull being too wide with an exaggerated stop, a muzzle too short and blunt, too much lip and throatiness giving a Bloodhound look.

The muzzle measurement in the 1975 Standard was an incorrect translation and has now been corrected in the revised Standard to read, 'the muzzle is a little shorter than the skull'. I have noticed that the nose can turn a dark brown when the bitch has puppies but it soon reverts to its natural pigmentation when the pups are weaned. The description of the lips can be misleading for they must not be tight and should be generous – a very important characteristic of the breed since this is important to retrieving gently to hand. The Vizsla must have a soft mouth.

Eyes

Neither deep nor prominent, of medium size, being a shade darker in colour than the coat. The shape of the eyes should be slightly oval and the eyelids should fit tightly. A yellow or black eye is objectionable.

Eyes are the feature one's attention ultimately settles on when looking at this dog. The Vizsla eye can show his gentleness and devotion, the boldness, strength and softness of character that should be part of his nature. He can look straight into your heart, but beware of a cold, steely-eyed expression, giving the impression that 'there is no-one at home'. The size of the eye when correct gives the open, honest expression necessary in this breed. If the eyes are too small, too round or too close together, this

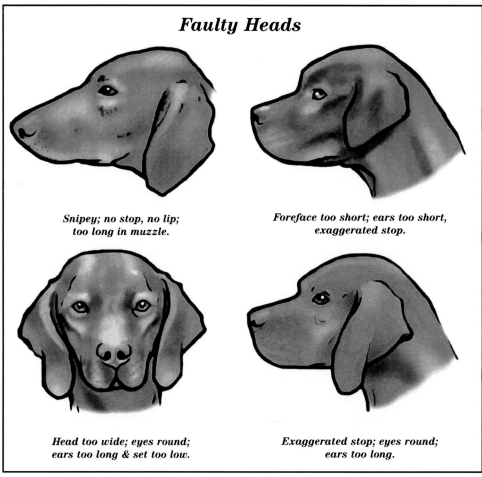

Faulty Heads

Snipey; no stop, no lip;
too long in muzzle.

Foreface too short; ears too short,
exaggerated stop.

Head too wide; eyes round;
ears too long & set too low.

Exaggerated stop; eyes round;
ears too long.

characteristic is lost. Pale eyes are a fault, but often this is no longer a problem by the time the dog is two years old. We have judges who complain 'What is happening to the breed, the eyes are too light' and often this means that the judge does not know the breed intimately, never having bred a litter or owned a puppy, so may not know that the Vizsla puppy eye goes through various colour changes, from blue when born, to green, to yellow or light brown to hazel, then to a shade darker than the coat. It can take up to two years to reach the correct colour. Thus we have many youngsters in the ring who will not have the correct eye colour on the day but will, no doubt, change as they mature.

Ears

The ears should be moderately low set, proportionately long with a thin skin and hanging down close to the cheeks, should be rounded 'V' shaped not fleshy.

What a wealth of feeling ears can express in this breed. When the Vizsla is standing alert and interested they give the head a frank aspect. When he is seeking or giving affection the ears can fold close to his head giving him a simple look, especially if he is one of those who is able to smile! If he is worried by a noise behind him and listening intently he can raise his ears while wrinkling the brow, the ears still hanging limp. When the ears hang correctly they should frame the head, and should not fold outwards or inwards. An important feature is the thinness of the ear; if it is too thick, it does not hang correctly.

The ears should reach to the corner of the mouth easily. A puppy's ears can meet in front of the muzzle! If they do not reach the corners of the mouth very early on they probably will not grow to the correct length. Ears always seem to grow shorter, not longer! It is often found that the shorter ear goes with a narrower head.

Mouth

Sound white teeth meeting in a scissor bite, full dentition is desirable.

A bad mouth is rare in the breed so far. There should be 42 teeth in a dog's jaw, 20 in the top jaw and 22 in the lower.

When puppies are 3–4 months old, their mouths can look a mess. Some teeth are loose, some stick out, some have already fallen out, the gums look swollen, the mouth looks awry. As all the milk teeth fall out and the new ones take their place, the mouth usually corrects itself in a very short time. It can be worrying if one has no knowledge of this. In some cases a puppy may not lose all his milk teeth. As the second teeth appear, the puppy can have a double tooth or several double teeth. It is best to leave them in for a short while as, in time, the problem usually corrects itself. However, if not dealt with at all, malformation of the teeth can occur. It is said that an over-shot mouth will never be corrected but an undershot can, if it is not too exaggerated.

Forequarters

Shoulders should be well laid and muscular, elbow straight pointing neither in nor out, the forearm should be long.

The revised Standard asks for elbows close to the body, which is a good point, but I am still not sure that straight elbow is correct. Surely it would seem more appropriate to say 'the forearm should be long and straight'. 'Pasterns upright' in the new version I believe needs to be qualified by 'with spring', but at least they are mentioned now. Sadly, the humerus is still not mentioned. Thus I believe Tom Horner's comments are vital (see below).

In common with the other hunt, point and retrieve breeds we have a problem with fronts. No sooner do they seem to improve than the faults appear again. Looking at photographs of Vizslas in Hungary and America, especially in Hungary, their shoulders seem no better than ours. It is not for the want for trying to improve this point. It may be a result of lack of experience and knowledge of conformation in this country, but frequently the Vizsla which has the better front does not conform to the type that we all strive for. He is often the narrow, tucked-up sort that is not typical, nor should be, of the breed.

One wonders whether well laid and muscular shoulders do not cancel each other out. In many cases, a muscular shoulder can also create a loaded shoulder. We can increase the outside muscles without damaging the structure but, since the muscles beneath the blade run hand in hand, if they are increased and thickened the blade will be pushed out at the top, which will either widen the front or rotate the blade on the curve of the ribs, bringing the point in and turning the elbows out. Thus we have not one problem but a complex set of inherited faults to correct while at the same time trying to breed to type.

Tom Horner, in an article called 'It Seems to Me' in *Dog World*, wrote that:

> *In sharp contrast to the long legged Terrier, the conformation of the forehand in Spaniels, Setters, Pointers and Retrievers is such that in each of these breeds the dog stands with his forelegs much more under them than do the Terriers. Both groups require the long sloping shoulder blades to enable them to carry their heads correctly but the great difference lies in the length and placement of the humerus or upper arm, that little bone which joins the bottom end of the shoulder blade to the elbow and about which too many breed standards have little or nothing to say. In the long-legged Terriers the upper arm is short and steep, in the gundogs it is much longer and more sloping so that the angle between it and the shoulder is much smaller than in the Terriers and Pointers, and the elbow is placed much further back on the ribcage than in the case of the Terriers.*

The advantage of a strong erect pastern is that a straight leg will bear more weight and also some of the work is taken off the muscles. The slight 'give' in the joint absorbs the shock of the foot striking the ground. Sloping or slack pasterns are not desirable as the dog will tire quickly. Often flat feet and slack pasterns occur together. If these are due to lack of muscle then they can be corrected by regular exercise on a hard surface. In many cases, the cause is due to the front assemblance being incorrect. If this is so the dog could have a 'fiddle front'. No amount of muscle formation could correct this fundamental fault.

A final quote from Tom Horner:

> *Few points add more to quality in a gundog or any other breed than a really well-placed pair of shoulders. Even a really big ribbed dog can have a good forehand provided his shoulders and upper arms are of the right length and in the right place. Very few dogs have real quality unless their shoulders are about right, so that good shoulders and upper arms are points well worth striving for in any breed programme. Well sprung ribs well carried back and reaching down to the elbow are a must in all gundogs.*

The neck

This has now been included in the revised Standard. A muscled neck enables the Vizsla to give a well-balanced appearance. However muscled he is throughout, until he is mature enough to hold his head up at the correct height, he will have too much weight on his forehand. He needs to spread the load evenly over the hindquarters in order to take as much weight as possible on the front end. Otherwise he would be very good at handstands but not quite so good at driving his body forward from the quarters! Thus we have the term 'well balanced' or 'unbalanced'.

The line of the neck should slope gracefully over the wither so that there is no definite line of demarcation. In most cases a long neck goes with a good shoulder, whereas a short neck goes with an upright shoulder.

Body

Back should be level, short well muscled, withers high. The chest should be moderately broad and deep with prominent breastbone. The distance from the withers to the lowest part of the chest should be equal to the distance from the chest to the

Faulty Forequarters

Shoulder angulation.
Left: Correct; well laid. Right: Incorrect. Upper arm short & steep.
Upright shoulder blade.

Left: Toeing in. Right: Loose elbows.

Left: Narrow front. Centre: Wide front. Right: Feet pointing east & west.

Body Faults

Too much tuck-up.

Roach back.

No tuck-up. Too deep.

Slab sided.

Barrel chested.

The Hungarian Standard states that the trunk is slightly longer than in the quadratic breeds, AB-CE. The distance from the withers to the lowest part of the chest should be equal to the distance from the chest to the ground, CD-DE.

ground. The ribs should be well sprung and the belly should be tight with a slight tuck-up beneath the loin. The croup should be well muscled and almost parallel.

The Hungarian Standard states that the trunk is slightly longer than in the quadratic breeds (square). It is my belief that this omission in our Standard could lead to a fundamental change in the anatomy of the Vizsla. At the official International Conference of the Breeders of Hungarian Breeds in 1982, Miklós Farksházi went over the Vizsla Standard and he stated:

> The Vizsla is not a square but slightly longer in the body than in height. The dog should not look like a pointer, nor should be become as strong and as fast a dog as the Pointer. The difference should be maintained.

In the main, toplines in the breed are not a problem although there are one or two dippy ones and some roached, frequently indicating a shy temperament and not a structural fault. If the shoulder placement is incorrect, the elegant smooth topline from occiput to the tip of the horizontal tail is lost, and the topline will be broken as the dog stands, walks or trots.

If a puppy does not start off with a good deep chest (or a good depth of brisket) which reaches well down to the elbow tip when viewed from the side, and if the breastbone is not fairly prominent, as likely as not the chest will never be deep enough or 'drop' as far as it should and the dog will look shelley. That is, he will have a narrow and shallow chest, deep enough but with too much tuck-up giving a leggy look to the dog. A gundog needs plenty of heart room, the ribs being neither too barrelled nor slab sided. He needs plenty of 'body' if he is to do a good day's work. It is preferable that his proportions be too generous than too slight.

Hindquarters

Should be straight when viewed from the rear, the thighs should be well developed with moderate angulation, the hocks well let down.

Surely this should read, 'thighs should be well developed, stifles with moderate angulation'. The thighs need to be well developed. Without good muscle no dog could work for long nor could he find the drive to give impulsion to the rest of his body. It is a poor dog who has no thigh and probably a weedy one too. Too high on the hock and too little angulation gives a straight leg; this dog could sprint well and pull but could not pushwith efficiency. The Vizsla needs to send his body forward with plenty of impetus. As quoted from *The Dog in Action* by McDowell Lyon, *"'longuns' for early speed, 'shortuns' to keep going"*.

Cow hocks are not necessarily a problem in the breed; they are certainly a fault since the back will lose efficiency in the loss of the straight forward line because the leg is crooked. A close mover is also faulted; again because of the interference of the drive forward due to the weakness of the pastern, as weight is applied the pastern will turn inward.

Feet

Feet tight, compact, well rounded with strong full pads.

The difference between a cat foot and a hare foot is purely in the length of the third digital bone. In the hare foot the third digital bone is longer than the same bone in the cat foot. The hare foot allows increased leverage action and, therefore, speed since the

Vizsla does not need speed (unlike the Greyhound), so much as endurance in the field. The cat foot is the most effective: the shorter, more compact foot is less subject to injuries and its reduced leverage action lessens the strain on the ligaments.

Pads are very important in a good foot. If the heel pad is thick and well built up (which it should be), the legs will receive much less shock from rough or hard going and will increase endurance by shortening the leverage action.

Splay feet are a very bad fault, although they may be improved by good road work. However, in any breeding programme it is inadvisable to include an animal with this fault. Since endurance is so vital in this breed, good feet should be considered one of the most important points of all.

Dew claws should be removed as damage can be caused by catching them on an obstacle and a very painful injury can result. Aesthetically, the leg looks much cleaner without these unsightly appendages sticking out.

Gait

Graceful and elegant with a lively trot and a ground covering gallop.

This is the most graceful and elegant golden dog if the conformation is correct and fits the Standard. The dog will move with a lively trot, daisy clipping as he goes. The gallop can look both flowing and effortless. Watching a Vizsla quartering ground using his nose, searching at a gallop, the quickness of his turns gives the sense of power and endless energy that his well-built body affords.

McDowell Lyon's *The Dog in Action* is an essential book to read for those who are truly interested in movement. He writes 21 pages just on the gait.

R H Smythe in his book, *Judging Dogs*, confirms the need for an open mind and fascination for more and more facts:

> There is a general belief held even by a few judges that, if a dog is sound in conformation, has a good shoulder, elbows and front, and has sound hips, and stifles and sound hocks, it cannot help but travel sound. Unfortunately this is not always the case. Moreover, a few dogs with quite poor conformation may occasionally travel sound, or at

Faulty Hindquarters

Straight (ie parallel).   *Cow hocks.*

Faulty Back Legs

Straight stifle.   *Sickle hocked.*

least much better than certain other dogs which on grounds of conformation, one would expect to go better than they actually do. There is a reason for this, and it lies not in the anatomical layout but in the dog's nervous system. The fault lies in lack of, or faulty synchronisation of, the muscles of the body and particularly of those controlling the limbs.

Added to this, a dog may have perfect conformation and impeccable synchronisation of the muscles of the body but still not move correctly. This fault may be due to the dog's temperament. He can be inhibited in every way by his lack of initiative, drive and character. If psychologically he is insecure and unhappy, he is not likely to allow his body the freedom it needs to move correctly.

Faulty Feet

Cat feet.   *Flat feet.*

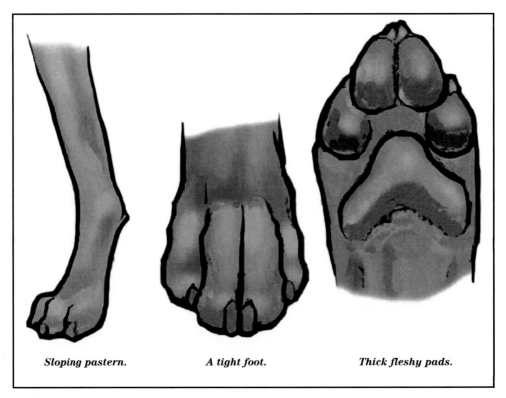

Sloping pastern.   *A tight foot.*   *Thick fleshy pads.*

Tail

Should be of moderate thickness, rather low set, with one third docked off. Whilst moving should be held horizontally.

A good set of tail with correct dock, gives the Vizsla a well-balanced look. In the American book *Your Vizsla* by Stauss and Cunningham, it reads:

Tail length was once a serious problem because the breeders and veterinarians did not check the standard's one third off stipulation. Tails are now uniform with the gently curving arch upward so necessary for seeing the dog in the field in tall grass!

We would agree with C Bede Maxwell in her book *The Truth About Sporting Dogs* (also an American book) which states that:

Many Vizslas are ring posed with boxer-pegged tails, but one notes some drop to the proper position in gaiting. It is one of the several troubles for handlers that while American field trial fashion wants tails up, the natural construction of purebreds favours the straight or the down as per the Breed Standards. My hope is that Vizslas with that in-built protection against 'selective breeding' may escape any alteration in the anatomical construction of their hinderparts. My own practice in the rings is to ask the handler to correctly position the tail of any mishandled dog.

Docking tails is a very controversial subject. Mutilation (for that is the word) for the sake of aesthetics is offensive to many. Most in the breed would agree that the dock give the dog a smarter outline but those dogs that are seen with long tails (though docked, some tails do grow on) do not appear particularly out of place.

For those who regularly work their dogs, docking is another matter and necessary; a badly damaged tail can be very painful and takes a long time to heal, often opening up the following season. Thus opinion in the working fraternity runs high when anti-docking suggestions are posed.

Coat

Should be short and straight, dense and coarse and feel greasy to the touch.

The present Standard adds 'smooth and shiny', giving us more facts to go on and is a much more appropriate description. The Vizsla coat must be one of the easiest coats to manage, needing little or no brushing, except when moulting, since the fur is so short there is very little mess. The sheen on the coat is attained by good food and good exercise. It is a single coat and, although it appears thin and sparse on the underside of the dog, it is surprisingly thick when correct. When a Vizsla is as keen as he should be, he will not be deterred by any type of cover. Many will not believe this until they have witnessed a dog disappear into low blackthorn or brambles and come out unscathed, in spite of a thorn or two stuck in him.

Due to the density and greasiness of the coat, water rolls off as it does off a duck's back, unless the coat is soaked. Even then it dries quickly. The Vizsla seems acutely sensitive to the touch, he loves nothing better than being stroked. It fills him with delight. His coat is a pleasure to feel and, though it is greasy, it does not seem so.

Colour

Russet gold. Small white marks on chest and feet, though acceptable, are not desirable.

As always, colour is in the eye of the beholder. To describe a colour is nigh impossible. Our Vizslas do vary in colour. We have some almost too dark, some definitely too light, even some too gingery, but there seems agreement in the breed that the standard colour is the one we all like and wish to see. In general the dogs that are shown display a uniform colour.

Quoting from *Your Vizsla* again:

Coat colour in America originally came in two predominant shades – a light sandy

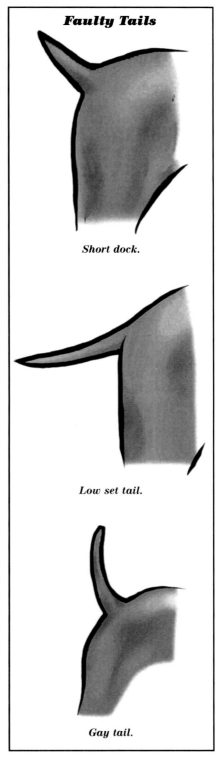

Faulty Tails

Short dock.

Low set tail.

Gay tail.

yellow-tan, and deep red, almost as dark as the coat of the Irish Setter. The lighter coloured coat generally was found on large, big-boned dogs, while the darker colour seemed to have seen more often on the smaller, more compact dogs. The darker reddish colour seems to be dominant, for the majority of the breed now carry this coat.

In general this cannot be said of the Vizsla here but could so easily happen. *Your Vizsla* continues, saying that: 'Some of the finest specimens in the breed carry the 'Esterhazy saddle' or stripe, as it is known in Hungary today'.

Our Vizslas certainly have it to some degree. It is a darker shading of the coat colour over the back; it slopes downwards over the shoulder and from there it narrows and goes back to the tip of the tail.

Too much white is rarely a problem. Maybe this is because most conscientious breeders would not breed from stock with too much white. One or two puppies in a litter may appear to have too much on the chest (5cm is allowed) or four white feet; but it can disappear after several days if the white is not pure and the skin is not bright pink beneath.

An ageing Vizsla usually starts to go white under the chin, then over his face; his feet will go white at the same time. As he reaches old age he may go completely white, giving a red roan effect.

Weight and size
Weight: 22–30kg (48.5 to 66lb)
Height at withers: Dog 57–63cm (22.5–25in), Bitch: 53–59.5cm (21–23.5in)

Faults
Undue lightness of bone, size too large or too small, bad colouring, too much white, spotted or black nose, entropic or ectropic eyelids, pendulant lips, mouth overshot or undershot, coarseness of head, thin coat or defective teeth.

If your Vizsla conforms to every word of the Standard but is too large or too small, it will make little difference if he is a pet or a working dog. It will make a difference, however, if you want to show or breed him. Any consistent winner may be used for breeding and the progeny used in other breeding programmes, so a stud or bitch who is too short, too lightweight, too tall or heavyweight could change the breed radically in no time at all if consistently bred from.

There is no point in mating a short animal to a tall one, hoping the puppies will be the correct size. Genes do not work that way. Even then the litter may not be even!

Finally, the Standard is the only blueprint we have to try and follow. It could be too easy to interpret it to fit our wishes rather than fit the dog to the standard. Lyons' *Dog in Action* puts forward as a positive start to a positive breeding programme the following advice:

If we like dogs for the sake of owning them or the pleasure of using them, we should want the individual to have the requisites of a functionally sound animal.

Breed Standard of the Hungarian Vizsla (British 1983)

Medium sized and elegantly built, he is an outstanding all-purpose gundog combining an excellent nose with stable pointing, good retrieving, and a positive enjoyment of working in water. He has great stamina and is happy to work in all weathers. He has an aristocratic air, with a lively but stable temperament. His short coarse, easy to care for coat is richly coloured in russet gold.

An intelligent dog with a good memory which makes him easy to train, he is responsive to intelligent handling. A popular pet in his native Hungary, where he adapts to living in house or apartment.

General appearance: Medium sized, of distinguished appearance, robust and medium boned.

Characteristics: Lively, intelligent, obedient, sensitive, very affectionate and easily trained. Bred for hunting fur and feather, pointing and retrieving from land and water.

Temperament: Lively, gentle mannered and demonstratively affectionate, fearless and with well developed protective instinct.

Head and skull: Head lean and noble. Skull moderately wide between ears with median line down forehead and a moderate stop. Skull a little longer than the muzzle. Muzzle, although tapering, well squared at the end. Nostrils well developed, broad and wide. Jaws strong and powerful. Lips covering jaws completely and neither loose nor pendulous. Nose brown.

Eyes: Neither deep nor prominent, of medium size, a shade darker in colour than the coat. Slightly oval in shape, eyelids fitting tightly. Yellow or black eye is undesirable.

Ears: Moderately low set, proportionately long with a thin skin and hang down close to the cheeks. Rounded 'V' shape, not fleshy.

Mouth: Sound and strong white teeth. Jaws strong with perfect, regular and complete scissor bite, ie, upper teeth closely overlapping lower teeth and set square to the jaws. Full dentition desirable.

Neck: Strong, smooth and muscular; moderately long, arched and devoid of dewlap.

Forequarters: Shoulders well laid and muscular, elbows close to the body and straight, forearm long, pasterns upright.

Body: Back level, short, well muscled, withers high. Chest moderately broad and deep with prominent breast bone. Distance from withers to lowest part of chest equal to distance from chest to ground. Ribs well sprung and belly with a slight tuck-up beneath loin. Croup well muscled.

Hindquarters: Straight when viewed from rear, thighs well developed with moderate angulation, hocks well let down.

Feet: Rounded with toes short, arched and tight. Cat-like foot is required, hare foot undesirable. Nails short, strong and a shade darker in colour than coat, dew claws should be removed.

Tail: Moderately thick, rather low set, customarily one third docked off. When moving carried horizontally.

Gait/movement: Graceful and elegant with a lively trot and ground covering gallop.

Coat: Short, straight, dense, smooth and shiny, feeling greasy to the touch.

Colour: Russet gold, small white marks on chest and feet, though acceptable, undesirable.

Size: Weight: Height at withers: Dogs: 57–64cm (22½–25in). Bitches: 53–60cm (21–23½in). Weight: 20–30kg (48½–66lb).

Faults: Any departure from the foregoing points should be considered a fault and the seriousness with which the fault should be regarded should be in exact proportion to its degree.

Note: Male animals should have two apparently normal testicles fully descended into the scrotum.

Breed Standard of the Hungarian Vizsla (American 1983)

General Appearance: That of a medium sized short coated hunting dog of distinguished appearance and bearing. Robust but rather lightly built; the coat is an attractive solid golden rust. This is a dog of power and drive in the field yet a tractable and affectionate companion in the home. It is strongly emphasized that field conditioned coats, as well as brawny or sinewy muscular condition and honourable scars indicating a working and hunting dog are never to be penalized in this dog. The qualities that make a 'dual dog' are always to be appreciated not deprecated.

Head: Lean and muscular. Skull moderately wide between the ears with a median line down the forehead. Stop between skull and foreface is moderate, not deep. Foreface or muzzle is of equal length or slightly shorter than skull when viewed in profile, should taper gradually from stop to tip of nose. Muzzle square and deep. It must not turn up as in a 'dish' face nor should it turn down. Whiskers serve a functional purpose; their removal is permitted but not preferred. Nostrils slightly open. Nose brown. Any other colour is faulty. **A totally black nose is a disqualification**. Ears, thin, silky and proportionately long, with rounded-leather ends, set fairly low and hanging close to cheeks. Jaws are strong with well developed white teeth meeting in a scissor bite. Eyes medium in size and depth of setting, their surrounding tissue covering the whites. Colour of the iris should blend with the colour of the coat. Yellow or any other colour is faulty. Prominent pop-eyes are faulty. Lower eyelids should neither turn in nor out since both conditions allow seeds and dust to irritate the eye. Lips cover the jaws completely but are neither loose nor pendulous.

Neck and Body: Neck strong, smooth and muscular, moderately long, arched and devoid of dewlap, broadening nicely into shoulders which are moderately laid back. This is mandatory to maintain balance with the moderately angulated hind quarters. Body is strong and well proportioned. Back short. Withers high and the topline slightly rounded over the loin to the set-on of the tail. Chest moderately broad and deep reaching down to the elbows. Ribs well sprung; underline exhibiting a slight tuck-up beneath the loin. Tail set just below the level of the group, thicker at the root and docked one-third off. Ideally, it should reach to the back of the stifle joint and be carried at or near the horizontal. An undocked tail is faulty.

Forequarters: Shoulder blades proportionately long and wide sloping moderately back and fairly close at the top. Forelegs straight and muscular with elbows close. Feet cat-like, round and compact with toes close. Nails brown and short. Pads thick and tough. Dewclaws, if any, to be removed on front and rear feet. Hare feet are faulty.

Hindquarters: Hind legs have well developed thighs with moderately angulated stifles and hocks in balance with the moderately laid back shoulders. They must be straight as viewed from behind. Too much angulation at the hocks is as faulty as too little. The hocks are let down and parallel to each.

Coat: Short, smooth, dense and close-lying, without woolly undercoat.

Colour: Solid golden rust in different shadings. Solid dark mahogany red and pale yellow are faulty. Small white spots on chest are not faulted but massive areas of white on chest or white anywhere else on the body is a disqualification. Occasional white hairs on toes are acceptable but solid white extending above the toes is a disqualification. White due to aging shall not be faulted. Any noticeable area of black in the coat is a serious fault.

Gait: Far reaching, light footed, graceful and smooth. When moving at a fast trot, a properly built dog single tracks.

Size: The ideal male is 22 to 24 inches at the highest point over the shoulder blades. The ideal female is 21 to 23 inches. Because the Vizsla is meant to be a medium-sized hunter, any dog measuring more than 1.5 inches over or under these limits must be disqualified.

Temperament: A natural hunter endowed with a good nose and above average ability to take training. Lively, gentle-mannered, demonstrably affectionate and sensitive, though fearless with a well developed protective instinct. Shyness, timidity or nervousness should be penalised.

Disqualifications: Completely black nose, massive areas of white on chest, white anywhere else on the body, solid white extending above the toes, any male over 25.5 inches or under 20.5 inches and any female over 25.5 inches or under 19.5 inches at the highest point over the shoulder blades.

Breed Standard of the Hungarian Vizsla (Hungarian 1981)

Characteristics: Medium-size, short-haired, yellow gundog of elegant appearance. It is rather lightly than heavily built, reflecting a harmony of beauty and strength. Balanced, intelligent, with vivid temperament. History writers consider the Pannion hound as one of the ancestors of the Vizsla. The yellow gundog of the Turks also played a significant role in the development of the breed. Some writers, however, date back its first appearance to several years earlier. Latest researches indicate that the 'Sloughi' was among the common ancestors. The first present-form specimens of the breed appeared in the early 18th century. In conformity with the modernization of hunting habits in the 19th century, other gundogs had been used in their improvement and finally there emerged a separate yellow national dog. The breed recovered after the war to develop into its present form, characterized by the following:

It is trained easily and quickly. Its character does not tolerate rough treatment. Inherited qualities, excellent memory and good reasoning power, make it the gundog of modern times. In spite of its great passion for hunting, it likes house keeping as well. Because of this, and also because of its distinguished manner, many people keep it as a companion dog. It is widely known for its excellent ability for acclimatization and is an untiring worker even in immense heat. Out of its inherited traits, the following are deemed necessary: excellent scenting powers; staunch, figurative pointing; distinct trailing and retrieving qualities, love of water work and excellent response to handling.

Head: Dry, noble, proportioned. The skull moderately wide, slightly domed. A slight median line, extending from the moderately developed occipital bone towards the forehead, divides the top of the head. The bridge of the nose is always straight. The foreface is well arched, neither pointed nor wide, ending in a well developed nose with nostrils well open.

Measuring the straight line linking the tip of the nose and the inner corners of the eyes, the foreface is always less than 50% of the total length of the head. The fang is proportionately long, the jaw is well developed, well muscled. The teeth are powerful, the incisors close like scissors. The expression is vivid, intelligent, the eyes are slightly oval. The eyelids are tight. The colour of the eyes harmonize with the colour of the coat: the darker the eyes, the more desirable. The ears are of medium length set slightly back at medium-height and are flat against the cheek, cover the ear-holes well and end in a V-shape rounding off towards the tip.

Neck: Medium length, well muscled, slightly arched, free from disturbing dewlaps. Set on the trunk at medium height.

Trunk: Powerful, proportioned, slightly longer than with the quadratic breeds. The withers, pronounced, well muscled. The back is short, straight; the line tight with the upper line slightly rounding off towards the base of the rump. The chest is moderately wide and deep, reaching down to the elbows. The ribs are moderately arched. The shoulders are well muscled, the shoulder blades slant, the movement is free.

Limbs: The forelegs are straight, strong boned, the elbows close to the body. The hind legs are well muscled, moderately angulated; hocks slightly low set. The toes are strong, well-rounded, compact. The paws are slightly oval, the nails are strong, the pads tough.

Tail: Slightly low set, medium thick, narrowing towards the tip. It forms aesthetic entity with the body when only three-quarters of the original length is left. Usually, one quarter is docked. If, however, the fine-lined tail is carried standardly, ie, close to the horizontal plane, docking is not mandatory.

Skin: The skin is tight, free from wrinkles or folds. The skin is pigmented, the nose is flesh-coloured, the lips, the eyelids and the nails are brown. The pads are slate-grey.

Coat: The hair is laying flat close to the body; it is short, with rough feeling. The belly is slightly haired. At the ears the hair is shorter and more silky. The tail is covered with longer hair.

Colour: Various shades of sandy or dark sandy. Smaller white spots on the chest and on the feet are not faulted.

Gait: Far-reaching, vigorous, smooth. While hunting, the gait is a balanced, steady canter.

Height: The ideal height for males: 56–61cm, 22–24 inches. For females: 52–57cm, 20.5–22.5 inches.
A 4cm deviation from the above is permitted in either way, if it does not disturb harmony. Static and dynamic balance as well as symmetry are considered much more important than proportions measured in centimetres.

Type Faults: All those structural faults or significant defects that disadvantageously influence the harmony of movement and continuous work. Major faults are: extremely light or rough structure, significant deviation from the standard, disproportioned build, within this short but high structure over-size individuals with hindquarters. Faults of the head are considered of major importance, such as: disproportioned, either too wide or too narrow skull and forehead; pointed hollow or coneshaped head, hound head, overly expressed stop, short pointed muzzle, ram's nose. Important faults are: pendulous lips, loose skin on the head, small disproportionate, close, deep-set or protruding light-coloured eyes; loose lids, expressionless, ill-intentioned look. Too low or too high set, narrow, twisted ears. Irregularly closing teeth, undershot, overshot over 2mm; wry mouth, buck-tooth, scale, yellow teeth, bigger dewlaps on the neck.

Trunk: Slack muscles, loose back and narrow pelvis; short, sway-back or steep hindquarters; sagging or sunken withers; chest either not properly deep or chest too wide; flat ribs. With females, sagging belly after whelping.

Limbs: Set of the legs deviating from the standard angulations; loose, not closed, long paws.

Tail: Tail set high, carried considerably higher than the horizontal.

Coat: Thin, silky, extremely short; fine or thin, like the mouse-hair; and any deviation from the short hair.
Colour: Dark brown, rusty and pale yellow shades are not desirable. The darker stripe on the back (the king stripe), which is usually due to nourishment conditions, is not considered a significant fault. White spots around the throat, or marks are faulted only if larger than 5cm in diameter.

Disqualifications: Considerable deviations from the breed characteristics. Deviation from the standard height of more than 4cm in either way. Parti colour spottiness, bigger sports on the chest white feet. Pointed foreface, narrow greyhound-like or rough, hound-like skull. Light-coloured eyes, grey or contrasting colour eyes. Ectrophy, entropy, strong ram's nose; pink, slate-grey, black or spotted nose and black pigmented lips, or eyelids. Undershot; overshot more than 2mm; wry mouth, pendulous lips, salivation, strong dewlaps. Colours lighter than wax-yellow or brown colour. Shy, weak-nerved, albino, cryptorchid or monorchid dogs. Seriously constrained faulty gait. Dysplasia of the hip-joint.

Conclusion

The British Breed Standard today is limited in its description, having to conform in specific wording, titles and headings. We may have our own individual preferences but the Standard has to be a fundamental reference; there are features that cannot depend on personal choice. The words 'musular' and 'moderate' are used throughout for good reason. The Standard aims for conformation that will help the Vizsla to perform his function with maximum efficiency, his general appearance being 'medium sized and medium boned'. Our goal surely has to be to breed good looking, working Vizslas, remembering that in his country of origin he was bred to hunt, point and retrieve.

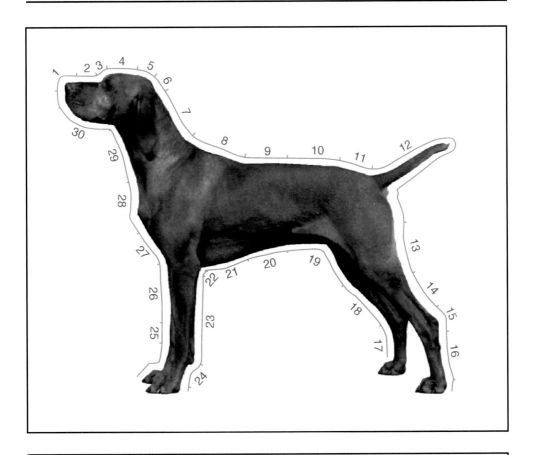

1.	Nose	16.	Pastern
2.	Muzzle	17.	Canon Bone
3.	Stop	18.	Stifle
4.	Forehead	19.	Tuck up
5.	Occiput	20.	Belly
6.	Pole joint, 2 vertebrae	21.	Brisket
7.	Neck, 7 vertebrae	22.	Elbow
8.	Withers, 8 vertebrae	23.	Forearm, radius & ulna
9.	Back, 5 vertebrae	24.	Pastern
10.	Loin, 7 vertebrae	25.	Knee
11.	Croup, 3 vertebrae	26.	Forearm
12.	Tail	27.	Upper arm, humerus
13.	Upper thigh, femur	28.	Chest
14.	Lower thigh, tibia & fibula	29.	Throat
15.	Hock	30.	Lip

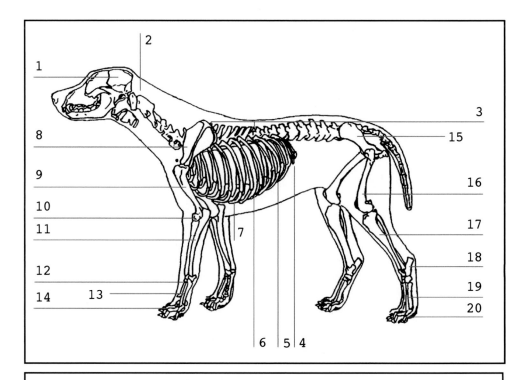

HEAD, NECK AND TOPLINE

1. Skull	Back - 7 vertebrae	Tail - 26 vertebrae
2. Neck - 7 vertebrae	Loin - 7 vertebrae	
3. Withers - 8 vertebrae	Croup - 3 vertebrae	

FOREQUARTERS

4. Floating Ribs - 1 pair
5. Joined ribs - 3 pair
6. Connected to sternum - 9 pairs
7. Breast Bone - sternum
8. Shoulder Blade - scapula
9. Upper Arm - humerus

10. Point of Elbow
11. Forearm - radius and ulna
12. Pastern Joint - 7 bones
13. Pastern - 5 bones
14. Toes - phalanges

HINDQUARTERS

15. Pelvis
16. Upper Thigh - femur
17. Lower Thigh - tibia and fibula

18. Hock Joint - tarsal bones - 5
19. Hock - metatarsal bones - 5
20. Phalanges

Introduction

The Wirehaired Vizsla is recognised as a pure breed in many countries today. On the Continent it is highly thought of, qualifying in the field and in the show ring at Championship level. The working Wirehaired Vizsla has many demands made on him, waterwork and wild fowling on the Great Lakes being especially popular and profitable. Many sportsmen travel to Hungary to shoot, and a dog who can work in these conditions is essential. The Wirehaired Vizsla, which can shed water easily from its thicker, warmer coat, has an advantage over the short-haired type.

When I judged Wirehaired Vizslas in Switzerland I found the coat type very varied, but the dog to which I gave the CAC and BOB was very handsome; his overall conformation was excellent and his coat, in my opinion, conformed to the Standard. He had a proud demeanour and great presence. I learned later that he was part of the 'Search and Rescue' team in the mountains – a truly multi-purpose dog.

Imports

Aranyos Tisza Dudas (David and Mic Layton)

In the late 1970s and early 1980s, two Wirehaired Vizslas were imported into Britain by Mr and Mrs D Appleton. The first to arrive was Aranyos Tisza Dudas, known as Zloty. She was later owned and handled by David and Mic Layton (Midlander), both judges in the ring and David an "A" Panel judge in the field. Zloty was shown with some success in Any Variety Not Separately Classified (AVNSC) classes. I remember first meeting her in the Layton's garden one warm summer afternoon. As we sat drinking tea and talking dogs, this appealing Wirehair strode about the lawn, coming up to each of us in turn, wagging her tail, gazing up with her soft brown eyes and her enchanting whiskery face. This was my first introduction to this breed. On going over her, it was clear that this breed is not a Shorthaired Vizsla with a wiry jacket.

Layton's Aranyos Tisza Dudas (right) and Appleton's Borostyanko Gulyas
of Carric Temple.

In 1983 a mate for Zloty was imported from Hungary, Borostyanko Gulyas of Carric Temple. Unfortunately Zloty never came into whelp.

Amor and Abafia Maya (Sheila Gray and Anna Coombes)

Mrs Sheila Gray, Hungarian Shorthaired breeder under her successful prefix Abbeystag, had taken a great interest in the Wirehair since the 1960s. She and her husband were advised that the breed had not yet been stabilised in their own country, the problem appearing to relate to the coat. There were also difficulties politically at that time, and approaching breeders of choice was prohibited. Hopes were rekindled when Sheila Gray saw the Appleton's Wirehaired Vizslas at the Game Fair.

By the 1990s, Hungary was free from the Communist régime and Sheila was informed that an excellent dog was available for export. At this point, Mrs Anna Coombes (Castlefield) joined Sheila in the venture of importing two Wirehaired puppies, a dog and a bitch. The male, Amor (Abafia Hires Humor ex Vadhozo Facano's Ada), was bred by Istvan Fa. The bitch, also bred by Istvan, was Abafia Maya (FA BX Hajduhegyi Aba ex Abafia Cifta). Both came out of quarantine proving to have excellent temperaments. Sheila writes: 'It was a great thrill to produce Britain's first Hungarian Wirehaired litter in 1992.' From nine puppies, five proved to have a good wire coat. Four of the bitches became good foundation bitches under Anna Coombes' and Sheila Gray's Shannamaya prefix. Oenone went to Mr and Mrs T Pearson. Mariska went to Mr P Hensey, Piroshka to Mr and Mrs R Thompson, and Margareta to Mr and Mrs B Robertson. Jean Robertson's greatest triumph was to win a magnificent first with Shannamaya Margareta at Greenwire at the Hungarian Vizsla Society's Novice Trial in November 1995. This was Jean's second trial ever and, of course, a 'first' in the breed. It was a great moment to witness, there were a few moist eyes as history was made. Sadly, Amor died prematurely, leaving a legacy of only one litter.

Abafia Hires Humor, Amor's sire, at a Hungarian show.

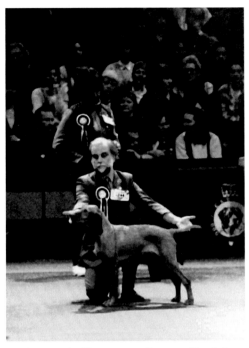

*Pearson's Shanamaya Oenone, Final 6
Crufts 1995. Photo: Dave Freeman*

*Coombes & Gray's Abafia Maya
(import).*

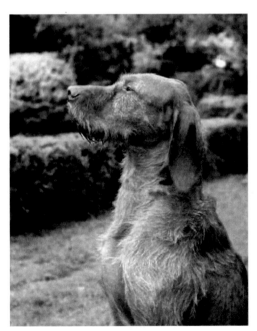

*Richard's Carpoff Du Domaine St Hubert.
BOB French National
May 1991.*

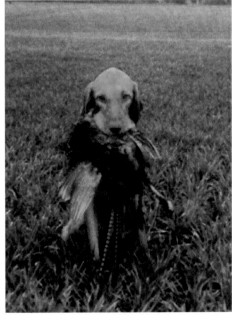

*Robertsons' Shannamaya Margaretta of
Greenwire, the first Wire to get an award at
a field trial.*

77

Hestia du Dumaine St Hubert (Sheila Gray and Anna Coombes)

The fifth import was brought in by Anna and Sheila from France in 1993. She was a bitch bred by Mad N Parent, Hestia Du Dumaine St Hubert (NL/Lux Ch Furjesi Alix ex NL/Lux Ch Volpi). She proved to be an excellent worker but did not enjoy the show ring. In the long-term interest of the breed, she was not bred from.

Abafia Vezer at Castlefield (Sheila Gray and Anna Coombes)

Again in 1993, Anna Coombes imported another dog, this time from Hungary. Abafia Vezer at Castlefield. Sheila and Anna travelled to Hungary to pick him up and were amazed at how well he took the return journey. Bred by Mr Istvan Fa, by Abafia Komisz ex Abafia Pletyka, he has proved to be a good sire. His first litter out of Abafia Maya produced Shannamaya Linz, one of the breed's top show bitches now in the hands of Mrs R and Miss Pinkerton.

Kecel Hatsagi Simi of Greenwire (Mrs J Robertson)

In 1994, Mrs Robertson imported a dog from Holland, although he had been bred in Hungary by Mr Gyozo Perjesi. Kecel Hatsagi Simi (Bren Z Prehyku CS ex Sabo Tomi) has proved an asset to the breed, siring Greenwire Wee Dram on his first mating to Margareta. Jean Robertson trained and handled this bitch to win a Novice Trial.

Arany Nezo Burny (Major K Bingham)

In 1995 Major Bingham imported Arany Nezo Burny (Brix Vom Rauhen-Busch ex Quodian's Lenke Kislany) from Holland where he had been bred by J Kors-Siegelaer. He has excellence conformation and temperament, and has proved a good sire of working and showing stock.

Further Imports

In the late 1990s, further imports have been brought in by Mrs P Wellstead from Holland, a brother and sister, Quodians Zanthos and Quodians Zelda (Sabo Tobi ex Quodians O'Mara, bred by Mrs V Lies Van-Essen).

Sheila Gray writes:

With all the imports thus far, the breed has been very fortunate with field trial and show successes within such a short space of time. We must strive to keep the quality of Wirehairs we have at the moment.

Interim Breed Standard issued by The Kennel Club in January 1994

General Appearance: Medium sized, of distinguished appearance, robust and well boned, without losing elegance.

Characteristics: Lively, intelligent, obedient, sensitive, very affectionate, fearless and with well developed protective instinct.

Head and skull: Head lean and noble. Skull moderately wide between ears with median line down forehead and a moderate stop. Skull a little longer than muzzle. Muzzle although tapering, well squared at the end. Nostrils well developed, broad and wide. Jaws strong and powerful. Lips covering jaw completely and neither loose nor pendulous. Nose brown.

Eyes: Neither deep nor prominent, of medium size, a shade darker in colour than coat. Slightly oval in shape, eyelids fitting tightly. Yellow or black eye undesirable.

Ears: Moderately low set, proportionally long with a think skin and hanging down close to cheeks. Rounded 'V' shape, not fleshy.

Mouth: Sound and strong white teeth, jaws strong with perfect, regular and complete scissor bite, ie, upper teeth closely overlapping lower teeth and set square to the jaws. Full dentition desirable.

Neck: Strong, smooth and muscular; moderately long, arched and devoid of dewlap.

Forequarters: Shoulders well laid and muscular, elbows close to body and straight, forearm long, pasterns upright.

Body: Back level, short, well muscled, withers high. Chest moderately broad and deep with prominent breast bone. Distance from withers to lowest part of chest equal to distance from chest to ground. Ribs well sprung and belly with a slight tuck-up beneath loin. Croup well muscled.

Hindquarters: Straight when viewed from rear, thighs well developed with moderate angulation, hocks well let down.

Feet: Rounded with toes short, arched and tight. Cat-like foot is required, hare foot undesirable. Nails short, strong and a shade darker in colour than coat, dewclaws should be removed.

Gait/movement: Graceful, elegant with a lively trot and ground covering gallop.

Tail: Moderately thick, rather low set, customarily one third docked. When moving carried horizontally.

Coat: Lustreless. Hair on head short and harsh, longer on muzzle, forming beard. Pronounced eyebrows. Longer and finer on ears. Longer over boxy, fitting closely to neck and trunk. Short harsh hair fitting closely and smoothly to forelimbs.

Colour: Russet gold. Small white marks on chest and feet should not be penalised.

Size: Height: dogs 57–64cm (22.5–25in), bitches 53–59cm (21–23.5in).

Faults: Any departure from the foregoing points should be considered a fault and the seriousness with which the fault should be regarded should be in exact proportion to its degree.

Note: Male animals should have two apparently normal testicles descended into the scrotum.

The Standard of the Wirehaired Hungarian Vizsla from the FCI Standard 239/6 1982 asks for a medium-sized, strongly built, yellow wire-haired gundog, with bones that are somewhat stronger than those of the short-coated variety. It is somewhat stronger and resistant to cold and water, and is thus preferred for working in water. In spite of being more robust, it resembles the short-coated dogs in elegance. It is intelligent, affectionate and well-balanced.

The Wirehaired Vizsla was developed in the 1930s, with the German Wirehaired Pointer figuring importantly in that development. The selective breeding work that went on for decades emphasised form as well as working ability, since the aim was to develop a multi-purpose, hard-working Vizsla breed. After this objective had been accomplished in the breeding process, breed lovers primarily sought to achieve further homogeneity in the texture of the coat and also strove to improve this characteristic in the form. It is similar to the short-coated Hungarian Vizsla in character, since it is

Volpi, European & International Show Champion.

easy to handle, a quick learner and is sensitive to rough treatment. It has good scenting powers, is especially fond of working in water, and retrieves at command. Its style, vigorousness and pointing places this breed on par with Continental short-coated pointers.

When the first imports arrived, many supposed innocently that this was a short-coated Vizsla with a wire jacket, but this has now been disproved and it seems that most judges and breeders recognise this.

Sheila Gray writes:

It is essential to note that, although the beard stands up and away, as do the eyebrows, the coat lies flat and close. Its jacket is similar to the Irish Terrier; it must not be wavy, nor wild or profuse. The coat usually fans out in the spring, but in general it needs little grooming and no trimming. It does not mat after getting wet.

She goes on to say: 'For myself, the greatest joy in living with the Wirehaired Vizsla is the cheeky expression on their whiskery faces.'

Madame N Parent is a successful and well-known breeder in France. She has bred shorthairs and wirehairs in France for many years and is 'passionate' about the wirehaired variety, finding them very intelligent, gentle, and happy to work and learn. She finds them calmer than the smooth-coated Vizsla and 'more of a clown, if that is possible'. Madame Parent has trained and worked her wire-hairs, the most successful being Volpi, a Show Champion in France, Holland, Luxembourg, a European and International Show Champion, with qualifications in the field in France, Belgium and Hungary. Volpi's sire is a World Show Champion.

Farkas' Du Domaine Saint Hubert, a Volpi daughter, aged 6 months.

Madame Parent states: "Puppies are born with smooth coats. Then, from about six weeks to four months, the difference can be seen between the different qualities of fur. Approximately ten to twenty percent of puppies will stay smooth (but they cannot be registered as smooth because the breeds are separate now, not a breed with two varieties) and approximately ten to twenty percent will have long, curly or woolly coats. Thus in a litter of ten puppies, one or two would be smooth and, of the wirehairs, one or two would have an incorrect coat".

The Wirehair Show Scene

On the show scene more breed classes are now put on, the Wires having had success in Rare Breeds and AVNSC, notably at Crufts 1995. Shannamaya Oenone, owned and handled by Mr T Pearson, came through to the final six in the Gundog Group under Valerie Foss. At Crufts 1997 there were 23 entries and four classes compared to Crufts 1996 with two classes and an entry of ten. Thus the breed is becoming more popular.

There was an inaugural meeting to form the Hungarian Wirehaired Vizsla Association, and the HWVA was recognised by The Kennel Club in December 1996.

The Longhaired Vizsla

It is reported that in Hungary, in 1937, an Irish Setter was mated to a Shorthaired Hungarian Vizsla, Kobra Z Povazio. Her name appears in most extended pedigrees of British Vizslas. It has been suggested that this mating is the true origin of todays Longhairs.

The Longhaired Vizsla is not recognised as a separate breed but accepted as purebred and registered as such. There seems to exist a gene for this feature; I have seen them in Switzerland and Holland. Longhairs have also appeared occasionally when Shorthair imports from Hungary, Holland and America have been mated. Nevertheless, they are rare. The difference first becomes apparent in the puppy as the fur grows wavy on the ears. The coat is Vizsla colour, soft and fine.

Until such time as a controlled programme is meticulously determined, these attractive Vizslas will remain an enigma. Their gentle aspect and working ability make them desirable and lovable companions.

Petrie-Hay's Berberis Bonney Boy.

chapter 5

Feeding and exercising are so closely connected in this breed that it is difficult to discuss one without the other. Good feeding and good exercise will produce excellent condition. Whether your Vizsla is a pet, a show dog or used as a gundog, he needs the very best.

A healthy Vizsla must be alert and lively, well muscled and lean. He must have no excess fat. Since his coat is so short, every ounce he takes off or puts on shows. This can certainly present a problem, for some Vizslas can be picky eaters and others never seem satisfied. When the dog is standing, neither the back bone nor the ribs should show, but if both show slightly when he is bending that gives an indication that he is looking right. If he is too fat, those bulging sides are a sign of too many titbits! A dip just before the root of the tail can also indicate overweight. A healthy Vizsla, of course, has a glossy coat, bright eyes and a willingness to work, exercise and play.

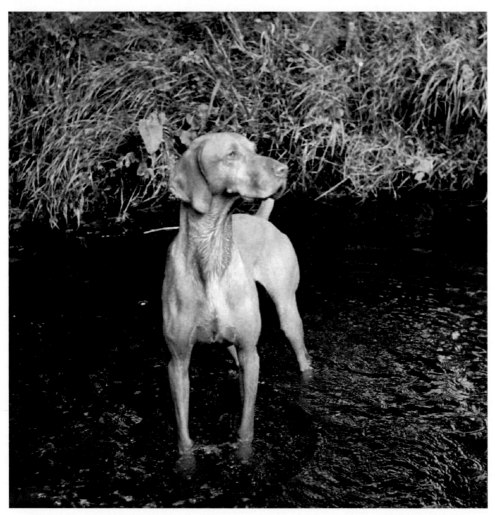

Buller's Duncarreg Sea Storm at Huntingate. A well muscled, alert and active dog.

Diet

No two people feed their dogs the same way. Each owner evolves his own formula and, having found the one that suits his dog and puts it into perfect condition, sticks to it. A Vizsla does go off condition for no apparent reason. This is bound to occur if he is working, because he will be using so much energy one day and the following day may have little exercise. However, it can still happen even though he is eating regular meals and taking regular exercise. It is no mean feat to keep a dog permanently in peak condition.

Some owners swear by dry dog foods, some by semi-moist foods and some by canned foods or meat by-products. Some will only feed raw meat, others would never dream of it. One thing is certain; a gundog must have food that will give him plenty of stamina. A Vizsla could not work all day if he were fed only on titbits from the table nor, for that matter, if he were fed on the most expensive fillet steak. He must have a correctly balanced diet and that means protein, carbohydrates, and fat, all of which are energy providers.

Protein is the essential constituent of muscle. The main foods that provide this are all meats, eggs, cheese, milk and fish.

Carbohydrates provide food that is most rapidly converted into energy, but excess carbohydrate is quickly converted into, and stored as, fat. The main foods that provide carbohydrates are cereal and biscuit.

Fat is burned much more slowly than carbohydrates and is thus a reserve fuel. It is a source of vitamins A and D, essential for sound bone and tissue structure.

Therefore, whether a complete diet is fed, and there are many on the market, or a diet of meat and biscuit with other additives, the Vizsla needs a high-quality, high-protein diet since he uses up so much energy and he needs to be a dog full of vitality.

Let us consider quantities, and here I am going to give the quantities and the type of food that I feed. I do not expect everyone to agree with it, but it is the method I have found that suits all my dogs, the old and the young and it also suits me! I feed a high-quality, complete dry food. I also add meat and good stock to that, which provides the extra protein that I feel this type of dog needs; so they get beef, chicken, lamb, turkey, fish or tripe, or whatever I can find that is cheapest at the time. This is partly because that extra protein is vital for those dogs that are showing, breeding and working to be in top condition. It also encourages them to eat the boring processed food, although I have one or two who would eat Charlie Chaplin's bootlaces anytime!

A fastidious eater prefers to have his palate tantalised by apple cores or lettuce leaves or even a little grated carrot, and Camembert cheese is never to be sniffed at! The quantities of feed given to an adult Vizsla are: 0.6kg (1.5lb) of complete food a day and 0.6kg (1.5 lb) of extra protein a day.

I qualify these amounts, monitoring the Vizslas at every meal. How do they look, how are they eating? Are they ravenous, are they being finicky? Do they look off colour, are their stools normal?

One Vizsla may need more to eat, another less, depending on the circumstances.

During the shooting season, the team may be out two or three days a week, flat out come rain or shine. Duck shooting especially takes it out of the dogs, as they are in and out of the water. On a frosty day it is tough going, and waiting for the next drive in pelting rain and cutting wind takes it out of handler and dog. Fast running Vizslas on the grouse moor have bulging muscles but the weight drops off. These dogs will be given as much as they can eat but, even so, by the end of the season they can look pretty lean. Therefore, be prepared to adapt and vary your Vizsla's diet, decrease or increase the amounts required, and be flexible.

If I were feeding a non-complete diet - that is, meat or some sort of protein and biscuit, plus the additives necessary, vitamins and minerals - the quantities would be the same as above.

Feeding your Puppy

If you intend your adult Vizsla to be a perfect specimen, it is essential that he is correctly fed from birth; first by the dam, then by the breeder who weans him onto his first solid food and finally by the owner who, on acquiring the new puppy, should follow the diet sheet provided to the letter. Even if the feeding programme does not seem to be the best, it is only fair to the puppy and his digestive system to follow the diet his tummy knows and accepts until he is totally established in his new surroundings. Then if his diet needs changing, do it gradually, step by step. Never change two foods at the same time, because if the puppy is upset and is sick or has diarrhoea, it is impossible to know which new food has caused it. So slowly, slowly. Do not be too eager. Better still, if you respect the breeder, perhaps his way may be the best. When you need to try something new, give it at just one meal. If the puppy is

There is no reason why a Vizsla cannot be exercised in any weather. Photo: Hauser

upset, do not give it again. Try after a week or two when he may be able to cope with it. Go back to the food you know agrees with him and try another food when there is no sign of upset. If you do need advice on feeding, ask someone you respect and whose own dogs look fit, and stick to their recommendations. If you seek help from several, you will not know where you are and your puppy certainly will not know where he is.

The puppy's diet has to have the correct amount of proteins, carbohydrates, fats, vitamins and minerals as does the adult's, but in his case these foods need to be palatable so that he eats the correct amount. They must be the right consistency so that his tender young stomach can digest them. The puppy's baby teeth cannot really deal with chewing and breaking up food and, later on, as the first teeth fall out and the second teeth begin to appear, the mouth can be very sore and the puppy may go right off his food. Therefore his food needs to be fairly soft until his adult teeth have come right through. The puppy will certainly need other bones or objects to gnaw on (preferably not the human hand or chair legs). As you prepare the food, be guided by him and you will see what consistency suits him best.

By the time the puppy is four or five months old, he will probably be on three meals a day. I say 'probably' because all puppies are different. Some drop the third meal quite early on, others continue until they are about six months old. If he seems to be bored by the cereal and milk meal, drop it, remembering to increase the quantities of the two remaining meals. As the puppy grows (and at this time of his life his growth rate is enormous) obviously his food must be increased, and it is helpful to decide on a particular day each week to add another ounce or two.

Sample diet for a puppy from 3–6 months
Meal 1 Cereal or biscuit meal, powdered goat milk.
Meal 2 Complete food or biscuit meal, plus meat.
Meal 3 Complete food or biscuit meal with meat.
The consistency of the food is such that the puppy can chew it. He can now have Bonios or a good hard biscuit last thing at night.

To this feeding programme I would add vitamins for the first six months, but it is always sensible to be advised by your vet.

It cannot be emphasised too strongly that regular meals are important. As a baby cries if his meal is late, so a puppy needs the same attention.

Problem Eaters

A Vizsla eating on his own can become an issue. He can be choosy, especially when a puppy or young adult. As he matures, the conflict seems to resolve itself. If a dog is eating in competition with others the problem rarely arises. Of course this does not include a sick dog. It is difficult to recognise whether the Vizsla with his sensitivity feels the tension and worry of the owner or whether at times he is genuinely not hungry. However, there is no doubt that a vicious circle can develop. The more the owner worries and fusses, the less likely the dog is to complete his feed.

I had a Vizsla who would not eat until all the other six feeding with her had licked their bowls clean. She waited until one of them could not resist the temptation of taking a quick nibble of hers then she leapt to the bowl and would finish it off as though she were starving.

chapter 5

If a Vizsla puts on too much weight, it is simple enough to cut the amount he is being fed. However, there is much more of a problem if he is too thin and will not eat the correct amount. I find it is unwise to leave food down. Old, fly-blown food does not stimulate the appetite. If the dog does not eat his meal, take it away and put fresh food down three or four hours later – if you can afford it!

I find it better a policy to feed my dogs twice a day. First, one enormous meal seems a lot to give all in one go. Second, having owned another breed that was prone to bloat, it was always recommended to feed two meals a day and, third, any finicky eaters seem to prefer a small amount at a time.

I have various ploys up my sleeve to encourage the appetite of a poor eater. Cheese sprinkled over the food or good tasty stock often does the trick. Some cannot resist pieces of delicious raw or cooked shoulder of lamb mixed in the food. This is expensive but ideal. There is a lot of fat on this cut which can put on those few ounces in no time. A teaspoon or two of Marmite well mixed in can be tempting. Sainsbury's Yeast Extract has saved many a Vizsla from looking like a toast rack. It contains vitamin B which also helps to stimulate the appetite, as do yeast tablets, obtainable from any chemist. Many a time have I sat handing out a variety of biscuits to a Vizsla who has gone off peak form. Many dogs find tripe irresistible and therefore this is worth trying. It could do the trick; there is something about the stink. It is best to prepare it out of the house. You may have a fit Vizsla, but find your partner has flown the nest!

Pilchards, chicken giblets, liver, kidneys and heart, even liver paté, all may entice the palate. However, what might suit one day may not suit the next. Variety is the only answer.

A stud dog may lose his appetite if he gets the whiff of a pheremone. There is little to be done until it is resolved, either by mating the bitch or the bitch finishing her season. A bitch in whelp may lose her appetite alarmingly, even two weeks before she is due. Entice her with tasty morsels if you can and give her three or four small meals a day. If she's 'knitting for the team', she won't have much room left.

I do not allow my dogs to have bones. I know they are supposed to be good for the teeth, but I find the problems are not worth the worry. They create endless arguments between the Vizslas who normally get on very well together. I have been so brainwashed by warnings from vets as to the possible dangers of small pieces of bone causing obstruction and resulting in life-saving operations. Having had a chicken bone wedged across the roof of a dog's mouth, piercing the skin, I believe them absolutely and do not want to take risks. If you feel that it is essential that you give your Vizsla a bone, never give cooked bones: the reason being that they break easily and a dog will swallow the splinters. A large uncooked shin bone is the least likely to splinter although a determined adult Vizsla can break one up.

A dog will slink off with a bone and bury it if he does not want to eat it straight away. If he is allowed to take it off and deal with it somewhere on his own, all well and good. But if you expect him to eat his bone in your house, in your human world, gnawing it by your fireside, then you are asking him to deal with a confusing issue. Bones seem to be part of his primitive animal world. They can stir up feelings of aggression in some dogs, whatever the breed. Many a time a dog will growl to protect his bone. On the one hand his animal instincts are being induced by you but on the other he has to deal with them in a way that is alien to him.

If you deal with him and his bone when he is a puppy he may be able to accept that he has to be civilised. Give him the bone and then firmly take it away. Dig some of the marrow out and give it to him, then return the bone, talking and praising him all the time. He may learn that this is a treat that only you can give. Since he cannot reach the marrow, he will appreciate the help. But if your dog remains 'chancy' over a bone, it is not sensible to give him one. Never allow your Vizsla to put you in a position when you are afraid of him.

Obviously it is important that your dog has something that he can gnaw on. There is nothing harmful in a large beef hide bone or similar items which are on the market. They do not seem to produce such strong reactions as the real thing.

Exercise

A working Vizsla is well on his way to attaining his full potential. Work satisfies his need to use his intelligence, his gundog instincts, his powerful body, his wish to serve his owner and to enjoy a close relationship with a human. If he does not work then it is obvious that he should be satisfied by other means.

He must have space to run, freedom to play, greenery to root about in, good scents, fresh air to sniff and plenty of room to stretch his long legs. He needs at least an hour of energetic exercise a day. He should be taken out for a walk. A dog does not exercise himself by pottering about in the garden on his own. A Vizsla's sparkling coat and good condition are all to do with feeding and exercise and very little to do with bathing or grooming aids you use. Without correct exercise you will have a poorly-muscled, miserable, fretting, shy Vizsla who has lost the use of his natural instincts.

One of the top field trainers in America, Paul Sabo, considers the Vizsla to be generally more highly strung than other pointing breeds. Whether or not this is so, an owner can treat the Vizsla in such a way that the dog can become totally hysterical and out of hand. Nowhere can this be demonstrated more clearly than during exercise. If the dog is encouraged to tear about, chasing sticks or leaping up and down for bouncing balls while the owner shrieks this name, telling him to do this and that and never expecting him to obey for one moment, in no time the dog will become as witless as his owner. All hope of that Vizsla working, or being a sensible companion for that matter, would be lost.

Fit, energetic Vizslas. Photo: O'Connel

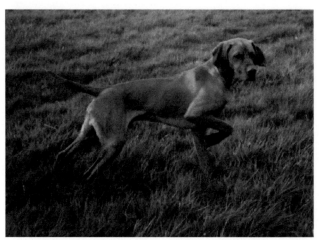

A youngster well on his way to attaining his full potential, pointing on sight not scent. Photo: Petrie-Hay

Exercising and Training your Puppy

A puppy needs gentle, playful exercise until he is about three months old, to grow strong, sturdy and sound. After that he should have restricted exercise, plenty of play and short walks, partly on the lead and partly off. This way he learns the discipline of walking to heel and has the freedom he needs when off the lead. At no time should he be allowed to tire or wear himself out. This will only take off weight and, since his bones are still quite soft at this age, his whole bone structure can alter if too much physical strain is put upon him. He will not be fully mature mentally or physically until he is over two years old.

If your puppy plays in the garden with your children, try to teach everyone to play

*Sh Ch Russetmantle Mace.
As a Vizsla matures you can expect more of him. Photo: Sara Hart*

gently and calmly as they would have to with a toddler. Children's wild games will only cause him to become over-excited, teaching him habits that are difficult to cure such as non-stop barking, nipping and holding onto clothes. All this may seem fun at the time but, as he grows to adulthood, he can become an anti-social nuisance and a problem. By that time, he will find it very difficult to control himself. Teaching mental discipline to your puppy does not mean repression but exactly the opposite. We must train him to use his natural resources, respecting him as an animal instead of using him as a plaything for humans.

By four months any self respecting puppy, if taught sensibly, should be able to walk to heel on the lead and, dare I say it, off the lead! He should sit on command, on and off the lead, should stay, not for any length of time perhaps but at least be absolutely steady with you by him and at a short distance. If you are gentle and firm he will enjoy his lessons. All this can be done as you exercise him. Thus he will learn to behave when he is out. You will find he is not difficult to teach to come to you when you call. The more you work with him, the more attached he will be. His responsiveness will improve every day, and your walks will bring great enjoyment to you both as he develops and matures into a sensible dog. One of the joys of a Vizsla is that he will rarely let you out of his sight. Many times I have tried to hide from mine but, however far they range, they always seem to have you in sight.

As the Vizsla Matures

As your Vizsla matures, basic exercise and training is very necessary whatever you intend to do with him – showing, working or as a companion – and well worthwhile. He can take more and more exercise as he grows on and develops.

You can expect him to obey your commands without having to make allowances, as you would when he was a young puppy. On the lead, never allow your dog to cock his leg at every corner, nor should he sniff at every person or dog that he passes. Teach him to walk quietly by your side.

When he is off the lead, let him range wide, giving him every opportunity to be independent and think for himself. It is especially important to allow him to do this if you wish to work your Vizsla. If he is over-trained in obedience, particularly in heelwork when he has to stay close, the Vizsla can become too dependent on his owner, waiting for orders anxiously, becoming tense and over excited, not wishing to leave his owner's side. If you are aware of this and recognise it happening you can usually solve the problem by letting the pressure off. Allow him to walk quite loosely on the lead. Forget the sit and stay

Riches' Gardenway Freebooter. One of the joys of a Vizsla is his versatility. Photo: Robertson

exercise close to you, try to do more distance work, but a little at a time. If that does not cure the problem forget any formal training for a week or two and encourage him to run freely. Do not call him if he begins to range far, it is rare that this one will go out of sight! A good tip I was given by a gundog trainer that seems to apply particularly to the Vizsla is, 'Any fool can get a gundog to walk to heel, it's getting him out on a 'send-away', teaching him to be steady when he's at distance, that's the difficult one'. It is easy to train a Vizsla in basic obedience as he learns so quickly, sometimes too quickly for his own peace of mind. This is when he can come unstuck. Too much pressure too early will make him either very bored by the whole thing and dig his toes in or, worse, he will become senseless and stupid.

When walking your puppy, as he roots about in a hedge or moves away showing interest in a scent on the air, encourage him to 'seek on". The moment of excitement

The Vizsla can become too dependent. Photo: Chisholm

is to watch your Vizsla lift his head to catch a sniff on the breeze, to move forward with purpose. These are the early beginnings of hunting. Let him be and just watch; you will have the privilege of being included in his maturing working instincts.

If you are lucky enough to have water nearby, encourage your Vizsla to swim. Most love the water and take to it naturally. Allow a puppy to paddle about on the edge. If you throw something in and make it a game at first, he will soon learn to swim. Better still, let him play on the edge whilst older

Most Vizslas love the water and take to it naturally.
Photo: Hauser

dogs go in for a swim. He may soon find himself following them! The water retrieve is a lovely sight to see and is one of the Vizsla's natural abilities. It is essential if you want to work him, for he has to retrieve in and out of the water. Vizslas love the sea, leaping into the waves, putting their heads beneath the water to search for seaweed. They will swim far out with any member of the family willing to swim with them. So, whether you exercise your dog in the country or in your local park, it is possible to train him up to the point where he can acquit himself as an intelligent, well behaved dog that is a pleasure to be with.

Exercising for Peak Condition

If you show your dog it may be necessary to change your exercise routine at times, especially as the all-important show looms ahead. I have discussed basic exercise and all it can entail. If you show, there is a specific type of exercise your Vizsla needs in order to have him in top condition.

Top condition means your dog's body has achieved the highest possible muscle tone throughout. This allows him efficient muscle co-ordination under any condition, at work or at rest. If he has too little muscle tone, is too fat or too thin, or has too much muscle, his ability to function correctly will be limited. So the type of exercise he needs will be based on developing every muscle he has and the best way this can be achieved is to give him gentle, rhythmical, steady trotting or walking day after day on hard ground. It does not have to be as boring as it sounds. Choose a walk that has hard and soft ground. Give him half a mile trotting or walking on the lead with his

Gottlieb's Russetmantle Aspic in top condition. Photo: Kent

head up. He cannot develop neck muscle if his head is down and, when his head is held correctly, the rest of the body will be properly balanced, allowing all the muscles to come into play. Trotting is the natural pace for the dog. If you jog at the same time you will both be as fit as a fiddle. If you have a bike handy, there is nothing like making your dog do all the work while you sit back. Give your Vizsla three or four weeks of this form of exercise, allowing him to run freely for the other half of the walk and there will be a marked difference. It may also tighten up his loose elbows, feet and pasterns as well as creating a second thigh you never knew he had.

The judge Percy Whittaker once said to me *'I like your dog, but for goodness sake get on a bike.'* I had no idea what he meant and asked him to explain. *'Look at this front. It needs to tighten up. His bones are good enough but he needs his muscles tightened.'* For three months I pedalled and my dog trotted. It did the trick. The dog became a show champion and gained 13 championship certificates. The trotting treatment cannot improve incorrect bone structure, it can only improve the muscle tone. Never try it too early – 18 months is soon enough otherwise the strain on under-developed limbs could cause problems and create deformities.

There is no reason why a Vizsla cannot be exercised in any weather; he will adapt if he is taken out in snow, rain or heat. Although his coat seems thin, it must be dense and greasy to the touch for good reason. A working Vizsla may be out in the wet all day with no ill effects at all. He may shiver at times but, as often as not, this is due to excitement. If the caring owner cossets him too much he will find the change from duvet or jacket to winter weather difficult to adjust to. However, treated sensibly, he is

The Vizsla is not a dog for those who do not like to brave the elements. Photo: Hauser

delighted to accompany you at all times, encouraging you to roll in the snow, swim, walk, trot, jog or amble, whichever you wish as long as you are out together. He is not a dog for those who do not like to brave the elements, nor is he suitable for those who do a quick turn round the block and back to bed. He is a dog who must have exercise and should not be denied that for one day of his life.

Equipment for your Vizsla

For the Puppy, the Adult, For Working, Showing, and General Care

All these items listed I have selected as being the most practical over the years. Of course it is a matter of individual preferences and each owner will know what suits him and his dog best.

Bowls: Two metal bowls; one for food, and one for water which should be available at all times. Plastic bowls are not advisable for this breed as the Vizsla has strong, sharp teeth and, although it is not generally a 'chewer', a plastic bowl is tempting.

Rug: Choose a blanket that is warm and easily machine washed, and is also almost indestructible.

Box: This type of bed, although not as aesthetic as a basket, will last much longer, is easily washed and indestructible. It comes in different sizes; the medium or large is ideal for the Vizsla.

Rubber glove: Rubber glove, with a thumb or without, recommended for removing hair and dirt as well as toning up the muscles.

Rasp: A rasp for scraping the teeth can be obtained from the vet, dentist or good pet shop.

Nail clippers: The Vizsla's nails are very strong and need sturdy, well-made clippers.
Leather puppy collar: Small, light collar with buckle. I do not recommend a slip lead and collar because the puppy can choke easily and become frightened. His movements are very erratic and it is difficult for the handler to anticipate which way the puppy is going from one moment to the next.
Choke chains: Some Vizslas never need a choke chain but others definitely benefit from a form of correction sterner than the word 'Heel'. A choke chain must only be used by the handler who knows how it functions. A puppy of three months old needs correction and discipline and it is often kinder to use a choke chain correctly rather than the alternative, which is to berate the dog incessantly, meanwhile allowing him to do just as he wishes.

The versatile Vizsla.

Benching collars: Several types of benching collar are available. The one made out of webbing is smart and light. The handmade, unstitched leather collar is of the highest quality soft leather and very strong.
Leather lead: A little light lead which does not need to be tough is all that is necessary for the first few months. Later, you will need a larger lead of good-quality soft leather.

The spring clip is very strong and allows for quick release. It is used in conjunction with the choke chain for obedience training.

Slip lead: A light cotton and nylon lead for the well-trained Vizsla, used when a dog has to be 'on a lead' but could manage perfectly well without one. Would not be practical for a dog who pulls!

Working slip lead: The ideal lead is expensive, made of nylon rope and fine leather. It is tough, weatherproof and washable and is ideal for the gundog out in all weather conditions. A leather lead is not advisable to use if it is likely to get wet as it becomes soggy and slippery to hold.

Light show slip lead: Many different types of show lead are on the market. Choose one that suits a gundog, is strong enough to check a dog, is easy on the hands and looks workmanlike.

Benching chain: Essential equipment to go with the benching collar. The chain is long enough to allow the dog freedom to lie down. The two clips are on swivels so that the dog is less likely to get tangled up. One clip is attached to the collar and the other to the bench ring.

Dummies: Dummies are all used for initial gundog training in early retrieving work, but all can be home made.

(a) The canvas dummy of medium weight.

(b) The canvas dummy with pheasant wing. This dummy familiarises the gundog with the feel of feather (but not the scent).

(c) The canvas dummy wrapped in rabbit skin. The skin can be sewn round or kept in place with rubber bands. The soft fur familiarises the dog with the feel of fur (not the scent).

(d) A pheasant wing. This little wing is for a puppy or adolescent. It accustoms him to the shape and strangeness of the feathers in his mouth.

Whistles for the gundog:

(a) A whistle and adjustable cord to hang round the handler's neck: any type of whistle can be attached to it. Whistles made of horn are the very best quality, a good shape to hold and the tone is neither too harsh nor too loud.

(b) A cheaper version of the horn whistle, made in plastic and not so heavy.

(c) Stop whistles: two types that I use are the referee-type whistle in plastic and the other a police-type whistle in metal, but this is hard on the mouth and inclined to rust. These two whistles can be used as 'stop' whistles. A good blast on one of these should halt and steady a dog if he is not heeding his handler.

chapter 6

Routine grooming, nail clipping, care of the teeth, ears and eyes should be started from puppyhood, so your Vizsla will learn that they are part of his life just as he has to accept his collar and lead.

Care of the Nails

Click, click, click, click, I hear as we walk down the road. I know what that means – the nails are too long. Click, click, click, the tiled floor in the kitchen tells the tale. I knew they were too long last week: why do I always put the job off? Because my Vizsla hates having his nails cut. Force, pleading, anger, even a stocking over the head (highly recommended) does not work. My own inexperience and an acquaintance's over-enthusiasm when helping gave him a poor start. The first time my dog's nails were cut every single nail bled, resulting in a Vizsla with an aversion to anyone touching his feet, let alone cutting the nails. To make matters worse, I persuaded a member of the family to hold him while I did the cutting but this was no answer. We struggled away while he panicked and we lost our tempers with him and each other. Another member of the family passing by this dreadful scene asked us innocently, 'Why does he need his nails cut anyway?'

Well, many years of experience later, the answer remains the same. Nails need to be cut. The nail grows in a curve and, if it grows too long, at worst it can curve back into the foot, but before it reaches that condition it touches the ground. As the foot is placed on the ground, the pressure forces the toes and pads apart because the nails touch the ground first. This causes discomfort and erratic movement so the dog tries to shift his weight off his forehand to his quarters. Thus he will not be balanced, creating a sort of strutting action in the front. If the nails are short, the pads will touch the ground first and, if the foot is correct, the muscles will keep the foot sufficiently tight to bear the weight.

It is generally believed that a dog with a good front will automatically wear his nails to the correct length if given enough road work. However, I have had dogs with poor fronts who did not need their nails cut and dogs with good fronts who did.

Guillotine nail clippers.
1 Blade open 2 Blade partially closed

A small puppy has sharp claws that can scratch his dam and his siblings so it is important that they are cut when he is very young. Of course this is a good opportunity to condition him to the practice of having his nails attended to regularly. When he is tiny, use a pair of the smallest nail scissors as his nails will be too soft to cope with the guillotine type of cutters which I find the best type for the older Vizsla. Never be tempted to cut the nail too far back, even if your Vizsla is behaving himself. Cutting little and often, and never to the point when he winces, avoids the trauma of giving the dog pain and a bleeding nail. Once he is hurt he will begin to fear the whole operation. It is, unfortunately, too easy to cut too much off, because it is very difficult to identify the blood supply in order to avoid it.

Arterial blood is brought from the heart with each heartbeat to the entire body. As the arteries get smaller and smaller they are known as arterioles. Finally they narrow down to allow the passage of only one blood cell at a time. These very fine tubes are the capillaries, a network which allows the oxygen in the blood to pass freely into the tissues and carbon dioxide from the tissues to enter the capillaries and back to the heart through the veins. The same process occurs in the nails, but the terminal arterioles are more exposed and are near the tip of the nail. Thus, when cutting the nail carefully, the pink you observe is the network of capillaries which will not bleed but, if you cut further back, the artery will be severed.

I have found a method of cutting nails which suits me and my Vizslas. I make the sitting arrangements as comfortable as possible. A large armchair, good light, and some biscuits are provided. I sit on the chair, my dog behind me or lounging on my knee. I have the biscuits to my right but these are only to be used as a reward. I gently pick up one paw, holding it loosely in my left hand. I cut one claw a little at a time and deftly reward him with a small piece of biscuit from my right hand and praise him. Part of the trick is to talk to him 'non-stop' which will reassure him to the point of boredom. Other dogs, I find, want to respond in kind by licking your face and generally nosing about. This character is best given a firm command or even a low growl from you. I have a Vizsla who defies all my ploys. She has found the solution herself; she lies under a low coffee table and as long as she cannot see what is going on, she is willing to stick out a paw. For yet another dog, a pile of cheese nibbles after each snip is reward enough for the torture she succumbs to! If you are desperate, a visit to the vet can be a solution. If you are determined enough in your own mind that you are going to remain gentle, calm and firm, the most difficult customers who have had years of non-co-operation, dare I say it, succumb in the end! It may take a few sessions, but each one will become shorter and the dog more confident that you are not going to hurt him.

If you do make a nail bleed and it causes discomfort, without fuss take the other paw and token cut at least one or two nails in order that your Vizsla keeps his confidence in you (as a rider is advised to re-mount after a fall). If he settles, finish cutting the nails on the paw that was bleeding.

This method excludes severe chastisement or force, so nail cutting days are no longer a dreaded task but are taken in everyone's stride. I have written at length on this subject because it is raised so often as a problem. Having tried so many methods myself, I understand why it should be so.

Care of the Ears

If there is dirt clinging to the outside of the ear, the Vizsla usually shakes it off when it dries. The inside of the Vizsla's ear is hairless so it should keep clean, but this is not necessarily the case. The Vizsla's coat is quite greasy as is his ear, so the inside of the ear should be inspected periodically because it may need cleaning. Usually, the dark deposit you see in the inner ear is a mixture of wax and dirt. It is never advisable to poke about with a cotton wool bud or a piece of material twisted round a matchstick. It is dangerous to force anything into the tender regions and narrow passages of the inner ear.

The outer ear can be cleansed with cotton wool dipped into a mild solution of witch hazel or a little olive oil. Witch hazel leaves the ear smelling sweeter. If the wax and dirt is difficult to remove from the inner ear, an infallible remedy is to apply a few drops of Otodex. It softens and frees the secreted wax which the dog can then shake out. It is simple to apply. My vet recommended this treatment and, on reading *The Dog's Medical Dictionary* (first edition published in 1906) the author, A J Sewell MRCVS suggested using Otodex. And I always thought it was the latest remedy on the market! It can be bought at some chemists and, of course, at any good pet shop.

The Vizsla's ear tip may dangle in his food bowl when he is eating. This can cause crusted, dry hard lumps to cling to the edge. Do not be tempted to pick them off as the skin is tender and the fur thin, and a patch may be left. Wash gently with disinfectant. I have found that during the shooting season when the ears can become muddy, wet and scratched, infected lesions can form around the edge. Usually the answer is to wash with disinfectant, but it may be necessary for the vet to have a look and he may prescribe an antibiotic.

If your Vizsla shakes his head, constantly flapping his ears, it is advisable to consult the vet. The dog may have ear mites or an ear infection that should be attended to professionally.

Care of the Eyes

The Vizsla's eyes need little attention if they are neither deep nor prominent and the eyelids fit closely as the Standard requires. Any slight accumulation of mucus in the corner of the eyes on waking can be removed by soaking a small piece of cotton wool in salt solution – enough salt to cover a sixpence in half a cup of warm water. (For those of you who are too young to remember what a sixpence looks like, use one teaspoon of salt and one pint of warm water). Bathe each eye with a separate piece of cotton wool, thus avoiding any possible infection being transmitted from one eye to the other. Always wipe the eye from the inner to the outer corner. If there is any persistent discharge of pus, take advice from your vet.

Care of the Teeth

The cleanliness and health of the gums are important. The teeth can be cleaned with a toothbrush and toothpaste. Dog toothpaste is on the market now. I know of a certain Vizsla who waits patiently each morning whilst his master cleans his teeth, and then this faithful companion opens his mouth to have his cleaned as well!

Until the age of two years, a good diet and plenty to chew is usually sufficient to keep them healthy. As the Vizsla ages, tartar often forms at the gum margin. This is the name given to the brown, yellow and black matter which hardens into a calculus, spreading under the gums. If it is not treated, it can cause deterioration of the gum, causing tenderness and bleeding, and become infected, leading to offensive breath. I find a weak solution of hydrogen peroxide most beneficial; the bubbling action cleaning between the teeth as well as the gums. If the tartar persists to a degree, a

Permanent teeth.

dentist's scaling instrument can be very effective, otherwise it may have to be removed by the vet under anaesthetic.

Care of the Coat

Having owned a long-coated breed, I appreciate the Vizsla's short coat. His smooth coat requires little routine grooming except when moulting and this he does moderately. I find a rubber glove the most effective tool. It can be bought at most shows from one of the many stands. This glove fits over the hand like a mitten. When you use it on a youngster, go gently, or he may find it too painful, but a thorough rub-down on an adult stimulates the circulation and the secretion of the natural oils as well as toning up the muscles. Any loose hair or dirt will come away. Polish the coat with a velvet duster or a piece of silk and the Vizsla coat will shine with added lustre.

It is not necessary to bath the Vizsla, even before a show. If his coat is really muddy give him a good swim. Shampooing his coat will remove its natural oiliness and tends to produce dandruff. If a Vizsla is pampered, he will behave as if he is. Keep him hardy; bathing him and allowing him to wear a coat will not help him if he has to stand in the rain for long which he may have to do if he works or shows. On the other hand, if he has had a pleasurable roll in some disgusting mess, you may be forced to bathe him!

In America, it is the custom to trim the facial whiskers. In England, so far, the whiskers endearingly remain.

Finally, ears that smell, a breath that smells or a coat that smells can indicate that the dog is not well. When a dog has a temperature, his coat often has a musty smell so the warning signal should not be ignored. It is best to call your vet.

Car Sickness

Many young puppies are sick in the car but, apart from the unpleasant task of clearing up, it does not need to be taken too seriously and generally the youngster grows out of it as he becomes used to the motion of the car. Rarely does it continue into adulthood. Most Vizslas love the car and are very good travellers, but there are exceptions which lead us to wonder what causes car and travel sickness.

The condition in animals is based in the main on some disfunction in the inner ear. In all mammals, the inner ear is fundamentally concerned with the maintenance of balance. It consists of the labyrinth, which is three semi-circular canals all structured at right angles to one another, each consisting of very fine cartilage and containing fluid called the endolymph. This fluid does not quite fill the canals. Any movement of the head, either slight or violent, will cause a shift in the levels of the endolymph in the semi-circular canals. This will immediately be transmitted to the higher centres in the brain, where the movement is at once appreciated at the level of consciousness and so the animal makes immediate adjustments to its position in order to retain its balance.

When travelling, the car makes all manner of deviations in terms of its horizontal angle, so the animal will experience frequent shifts of his head and body angle causing the fluid balance in the semi-circular canals to change. The dog's brain receives a message that imbalances are occurring and immediately the animal adjusts his head and body to rectify the movement. However, if there is any impairment in the inner ear such as injury, infection, or inflammation, the fluid levels may be affected. Therefore the nervous impulses to the brain will be impaired and the animal will not be able to adjust his head and body accordingly, and giddiness, nausea and vomiting will ensue.

A puppy of seven weeks will travel more comfortably than an older puppy whose sense of awareness and fear is more developed in every way.

To try to avoid travel sickness, never feed your puppy before he goes on a journey. He is less likely to be sick if he travels in the front rather than the back of the car. Try not to become apprehensive yourself; a dog will sense it and, if his discomfort continues, his own nervousness may be enhanced so that what began as a physical problem also becomes psychological. This may result in a dog developing fear of the car. He may be conditioned to fear travelling and this is the problem that eventually needs to be sorted out. Initially a visit to the vet is essential so that any infection, injury or inflammation can be dealt with. After that the dog must be re-conditioned – first by simply sitting in the car and then by short car rides taken calmly and without fuss. These can be lengthened as he becomes reassured and eventually he will gain confidence. With maturity the problem in most cases will be solved.

Occasionally the discomfort remains, perhaps because the conditioning has not been effective. I have an old bitch who still disappears if she anticipates a car ride. If I put her on the front seat where she is quite comfortable, she does not pant, she does not dribble, she just looks unhappy. She cannot forget.

Giving Medication to Your Vizsla

If your Vizsla's health depends on a form of medication, be it a pill or medicine, he is in a risky situation if his owners hope that he is not bright enough to notice that the goodies are wrapped in his favourite piece of meat or crushed in a teaspoon of raspberry jam placed in his tripe. If it is not eaten, disguised or otherwise, it is no wonder his owners become agitated; they are counting on luck.

As with every other aspect of Vizsla ownership, if he is treated sensibly and firmly he will behave accordingly. A foolproof way of administering medication is to give it personally. Sit your dog between you and a kitchen unit, talk to him calmly and firmly and, as you count out the pills, place them on the unit. If he has to take medicine, have someone close by with it ready poured out on a teaspoon, unless you are clever enough to do it yourself. Bend over your dog and, with the left arm over the back of his neck (so he cannot move backwards), slip the first and second fingers of your left hand into the corner of his mouth on the off-side, placing the thumb into the corner of his mouth on the near-side as soon as his jaw relaxes. While you do this, say 'open' and praise him. Keep the first, second and third fingers in his mouth, firmly and deftly put the pill into the back of his throat, pushing it as far as you can, quickly close his mouth, hold his mouth gently and he will swallow the pill. Praise him but do not let him move until he has taken the prescribed amount.

If he has to take liquid medicine, open his mouth as instructed, slip the teaspoon in from the side and tip the contents down his throat. It may be a messy job to begin with but, with practice, you will both become adept and the medicine will go down in seconds! Praise your dog and he will feel pleased to have earned it.

The Vizsla Bitch in Season

The first season can commence at nine months but could be as late as 15 months. If your Vizsla bitch has not shown any signs of coming into season by then, perhaps it would be advisable to ask your vet look at her. In general, Vizslas seem to vary their season. The cycle should be every six months but many come in every eight or nine months, or even once a year.

The duration of the season, or heat, is from the first day to the twenty-first. There are particular days in the cycle when a bitch ovulates. It is during this time that she will accept the male and, if mated, can conceive. It is generally understood that the 10–14th days are the most likely days of oestrus. It is rare that if she were mated on the 15th day that she would conceive. However, I have known a bitch who was not ready until the 29th day. She was mated on that day and duly whelped a large, healthy litter.

It is possible to have certain simple tests done by the vet to indicate the correct day of ovulation. If the bitch's owner is travelling from John O' Groats, it saves fruitless days on the motorway. Sometimes, however, it does not seem exact enough, contributing more confusing information.

The pre-oestrus cycle commences when the vagina thickens, and the vulva swells, the skin colour changing from pink to grey. The early signs are not difficult to see because the Vizsla coat is so short. The second sign is the commencement of her discharge. This should be deep red. As the heat continues, the discharge will usually lose colour, becoming pink and even paler up to the day when she reaches oestrus.

Oestrus

This is the period when the ova are shed and the bitch 'stands'. This is the term used when she stands stock still with her tail twisted to one side, indicating that the male may mount her. Her vulva should be enlarged and soft and, as she twists her tail, she should present herself with the vulva slightly upturned. Some bitches, although ready, may swell very little and, instead of upturning, slightly crouch. An experienced stud can cope with this, but a novice dog will be bemused and confused; searching to enter her but way off the mark! Her discharge will be straw-coloured and almost negligible after the days of oestrus, then the discharge will disappear and the vulva will return to normal unless she is in whelp when it may remain slightly enlarged.

These are some of the facts. It must be recognised that there are many variations at every stage. It can be very bewildering. No two bitches behave alike. A bitch can vary her timing from one season to another. Some bitches bleed profusely, others hardly at all. If there is little loss, it is difficult to follow the cycle but, fortunately, it seems to have nothing to do with the bitch's fertility. I had a bitch who bore 26 puppies in four litters in her time and she hardly bled at all. I also have a bitch who always has a pale pink discharge up until the 21st day whether she mates or not. It has been known for bitches to have a very dark discharge for four or five days after mating. Contrary to belief, these bitches have conceived and produced good sized litters.

I have always found that a Vizsla in season is very meticulous; she cleans herself endlessly, her fastidiousness reaching the point of obsession!

Care of the Vizsla in Season

Take no risks; keep your bitch away from any chance encounter! Confine her from day one. She may need to be kept away from dogs until the 21st day, whether she has been mated or not. Although it is very unlikely that she could conceive after the 15th, it could occur! Reconsider your wish to take her out to give her a good run, even though it may be before anyone stirs or late at night when the owls hoot. You may look around and, to your surprise, find two animals attached to your lead, one of them not a Vizsla! Better to confine her in an enclosed space and stay with her while she is outside – some dogs can climb over very high fences.

Various anti-mate powders are on the market. These can be useful towards the finish of the season, but such are nature's arrangements and so strong the pheromones, if two animals want to mate and the time is right, no anti-mate is going to get in the way! If the bitch is mis-mated, consult the vet immediately. She can be given an injection to deal with the situation.

Years ago, I had one of my bitches' season delayed for selfish reasons. I know that it is a widely-used practice, but it can be found to affect the bitch's cycle and fertility. My experience was that her season was delayed for a year, and whereas beforehand she had had two healthy litters of nine, the subsequent contained only one. Many breeders share similar experiences and vow never to attempt it again.

If you own a Vizsla bitch, inevitably the question will arise of whether to breed from her. Those who have been in the breed for any length of time will probably understand the market for Vizsla puppies, but those who are new to the breed and have not had the opportunity to appreciate what breeding could entail ought to consider the pros and cons. I must make it quite clear that there is little profit in breeding Vizsla puppies. If the puppies are well reared and cared for, costs may just be covered if they are sold at seven or eight weeks old, but since the Vizsla really is only for the specialist they are certainly not suitable for all homes. Anyone wishing to breed their bitch should consider where their responsibility lies.

Some vital questions need to be answered:

- Can you sell the puppies and, if you cannot, have you the facilities for keeping them as they grow?
- If you sell a puppy to a home that turns out to be unsuitable, are you prepared to take him back? Will you care enough to spend many hours helping to rehouse him? If the answers are not in the affirmative, perhaps the next question should be how much are you prepared to care for the puppies you have bred?
- Is it good for a bitch to have a litter? This is debatable. Some vets agree that it is, many state that it is unnecessary. I feel the question is irrelevant now with so many dogs roaming the streets. Whether or not it is better for the bitch, what is the quality of life to be for the progeny? And if she produces, say, five bitches are they also to be bred for their own good? In my experience, there has never been any significant change in a bitch's behaviour after producing a litter. A silly, excitable type of animal does not transform into an intelligent, sedate, sensible matron. She usually reverts back to all that she ever was, showing no sign of maternal fulfilment, satisfaction, or happiness after the puppies have gone. Her figure may be a little fuller, but not necessarily so since ageing can have the same effect.

The potential purchaser may want a puppy for showing, for working or as a pet. If he wants a Vizsla for showing he will, if he is sensible, go to a breeder who has had some success in this field and is knowledgeable about it. If he wants one for working, knowing that the best gundogs come from stock bred and trained to point, hunt and retrieve, he will go to a reputable breeder. There are breeders, of course, who work and show their dogs. Nowadays, there is a strong belief and aim in the breed to maintain the Hungarian Vizsla as the all-purpose dog he should be. The goal to keep the breed as one and the same dog means that a Vizsla puppy bought from a responsible breeder will have the potential to be an affectionate, loyal member of the family, as well as doing himself proud in the ring and capable of filling the game bag.

So where does this leave the pet owner with ten puppies? It must be made clear that a litter reared in the warmth of the kitchen with plenty of loving care from all the family and every desire satisfied has received the start in life it needs. But the only market may be other pet owners, and how are they found? All those friends who so wanted a Vizsla puppy tend to fade away when the puppy is a reality! The owner of the stud dog can sometimes provide help. Advertising in the dog papers, or magazines such as *The Field* or *Shooting Times* can produce many customers or none, depending on the time of year and whether there are other Vizsla litters born during the same

Gottlieb's Russetmantle Whitsun aged 7 weeks,
deep in thought. Photo: Dr S Gottlieb

period. For example, July or August is generally a difficult time of year for selling, as nobody wishes to take a young puppy on holiday. Neither does anyone want a puppy at their feet over the Christmas season (let us assume that no one would wish to sell a puppy for a child's Christmas stocking).

The delightful little Vizsla puppies are no longer sucking. After three weeks, their doe-eyed mother no longer cleans after, looks or gazes at her offspring as she did when they were warm and contented, unable to use their tiny legs with their perfect feet and nails, eyes shut, tails still long, tiger stripes not yet dry. Imagine what those few you cannot sell will be like at 12 weeks. Even advertising has not relieved you of all of them, and some of the replies you refused because they did not seem suitable homes. But by now you are feeling desperate, and any home would do! You cannot accommodate or contain these sharp-toothed, chewing, lively puppies who escape from anything into anywhere, and are capable of such destruction and mess, let alone smell.

The conclusion is that proper facilities for puppies are vital. If these are provided, unsold puppies can be accommodated easily, thus relieving the necessity of making a quick and possibly unsuitable sale.

Choosing a home for a puppy under pressure can frequently result in a decision you might later come to regret.

The Cost of Whelping (A Cautionary Tale)

This is an example of the sort of problems that a Vizsla breeder may have to face if things do not go according to plan and the bitch has a difficult time whelping. It is as well to know what you may be in for in terms of time and cost.

The bitch started to whelp in the middle of the night, had four puppies and then stopped. She had no more whelps for two hours, so we called the vet. She attended to the bitch and more puppies followed. She promised to return if there were further problems and, indeed, there were. Two more anxious hours followed, with no sign of a puppy. The bitch was by now in great distress. Out came the vet again and, to our great relief, more puppies arrived safe and sound. There are now ten beautiful puppies and the vet leaves.

The bitch and whelps were, no doubt, saved by the prompt attention and skill of the vet. However, in many areas, vets cannot be called out at any time of the day of night. They insist on the animal being taken to the surgery. This could cost you not only the vet's fees, but also the life of the bitch and her pups. A worrying scenario, of course, is the need for a Caesarean, with perhaps one puppy alive or two dead. At worst, if the dam dies, new-born whelps need all the attention the Vizsla would have given them. If we decide to breed, these eventualities need to be thought through. The fantasy can turn into a nightmare. My nightmare came true when 10 puppies had ringworm at two weeks. They were not cleared to go to their new homes until they were 4 months old!

After Puppies Leave the Whelping Box

It seems appropriate at this stage to discuss the provisions needed for the puppies once they can climb out of their whelping box. By this time, the bitch has decided that she is happy anywhere but with her demanding team of puppies. She will go to them to

105

'Don't disturb me, I'm relaxing'. Photo: Chisholm

relieve the discomfort of her breasts filling with milk, but prefers to leave them before she is mauled and scratched by them. This takes place around the fourth or fifth week after whelping, and at this stage the puppies will have commenced weaning. They need to be in a place where they can run and play in an enclosed area – not the kitchen! Before they are born, one fondly imagines a few sweet puppies tottering about one's feet, never needing to urinate or defecate. It is unbelievable how a litter of puppies can wreck a room in no time at all once they are running about. Ideally, the puppies need a place to sleep, a place to play in the warmth, free from draughts, and an outside area of concrete safely wired and puppy-proof where they can play when the weather is fine. When the weather is good they need a place outside so they can feel the warmth of the sun on their backs, enjoy the fresh air and feel a sense of freedom without coming to any harm.

Bedding

The indoor area needs some form of bedding, such as straw or shredded paper. I have never found that straw gives the puppies ticks or fleas, but they do sometimes smell of faeces and urine. Puppies kept on shredded newspaper are warmer, and they don't smell as the paper absorbs the mess immediately.

Space for Play

This room or kennel should have plenty of space where the puppies can run freely. The pups can still sleep in their whelping box or a cosy, boarded-in area free from draughts. It should be made totally puppy-proof, so that they cannot escape; free from furniture of any use or value, a place for puppies rather than humans, the only furniture provided being their playthings! Of course, it must be heated, with plenty of natural light, and a source of artificial lighting which is necessary for tending the puppies in the evening or at night.

Time for the Puppies

I hope these few facts help you to understand more clearly what breeding from your Vizsla bitch really entails. It is quite an undertaking. One item that has not yet been discussed at all is the amount of time it is necessary to spend on rearing a litter. This is infinite and I can only warn you that, if it is to be done well, it is a non-stop job. It is impossible to have a full-time job and a litter of puppies as well unless there is another helping hand. After weaning, they need to be fed four or five times a day so that by the time one meal is over and the dishes washed, it seems as if it is time for the next! Nevertheless, many would say the reason they like to breed is because of the unaccountable hours spent enjoying a litter, watching every move the pups make. It is true that this period is only for a short while if the puppies are sold at the right age. Everyone should be prepared for the certain disruption of the general household routine for an unknown length of time.

The Decision

Undaunted, you may feel you can manage a litter of puppies; you know you can find good homes, you are able to cover the costs, you have plenty of room for them, and you are satisfied that you have the time. Have you taken into account that enormous litter of 12, 13 or 14 puppies who will need a helping hand from the start because the dam has not enough milk to go round? Supplementary feeding every two or three hours will be essential. Without intervention, you will have poor puppies and a very tired and exhausted mother.

Any deformed puppies in the litter, for example, with a cleft palate or a damaged limb, need to be destroyed by a vet. A small, feeble whelp needs your constant attention, day and night, for he may be pushed out by the dam. Survival of the fittest is an instinct which is evident in a litter of pups. However we think of our Vizslas, they are still part of the animal world and, like all animals, will deliberately push away the weakest.

Some breeders choose to keep only six or seven puppies in a litter, destroying the rest in order to leave the dam with the ideal number of whelps. She can then feed herself and they will not leave her drained. Culling comes easy to some, while others cannot countenance such a policy.

You will also need to decide what to do if you have a puppy with four white legs and a snow-white chest. Although only a cosmetic fault, this is not allowed in the Standard and is absolutely wrong for a Vizsla. A British pet owner may think these faults unimportant, but may not understand that, if this pup were bred from, incorrect marking could easily be passed on. The condition of the sale must be 'not to be bred from' but, of course, if homes are hard to come by, the breeder may not feel he can call the tune.

Do not feel that, if you decide to keep a large litter and are going to supplement feed by hand, that this in any way gives the puppies a bad start in life. It does not – on the contrary, it gives them a very good start. To feed from the mother and have such close contact with a human so early on will help the puppy thrive emotionally and physically. In fact, the process of imprinting by a human cannot start too early. The runt of the litter is often the best adjusted puppy of the lot, because he has been given special attention by the breeder.

To conclude, the bitch you own may have the home that gives her all she requires. Her puppies may not be so fortunate.

Your Bitch as a Brood Bitch

It is now necessary to consider the suitability of the bitch you own as a brood bitch. However fond you are of your Vizsla, it is essential that you look at her from a breeder's point of view, so you have to be objective. Can she contribute to the breed? Can you appreciate her faults as well as her qualities? Read the Breed Standard so that you know it back to front, take a good look at as many other Vizslas as possible and, in this way, you will learn more about your Vizsla by comparison. Be advised by others in the breed whom you respect.

A good brood bitch is invaluable as foundation stock for any kennel. She may not be the showy winner of all the prizes, or have the extra something that always catches the eye first, but a second look may reveal some of the essentials – a sound temperament, imperturbable outlook, composure, lack of nervousness, and a steadiness of character that you can trust. A good 'doer', she could work, make a good family companion and show with the best. This is the bitch who is more likely to care for her puppies, provide milk and security for them and, hopefully, contribute to the breed. The bitch to breed from should be strong, well built and fit. It is no good expecting her to produce good pups if she is not strong enough for the task. If she is not well muscled she will find it difficult to carry the weight of her whelps. If she has a saggy top-line, it will sag even further. If she has poor feet and weak pasterns she will tire easily and if her elbows are out they will 'go out' even further. If her quarters are weak, her unborn puppies will become a burden and, what is more, she can pass all these unpleasant faults on to her offspring.

It is not advisable to breed from a Vizsla bitch before she is about two years old. She is not mature fully, either mentally or physically, before this age and the strain of carrying pups too early could stunt her growth.

How many litters should she have? My vet always advises that as long as a bitch is fit and well and still comes on heat, be guided by her. However, since we are responsible for her welfare and she is not living in the wild usually three litters are plenty, but there is no rule of thumb and one or two litters may be enough for a bitch to bear. There has to be good reason for breeding a bitch after five or six years of age. By that time she is more likely to have problems. You could be risking her life and her whelps by doing so. Do not go by what you wish, but be guided by the health, age and behaviour of your bitch.

It is not acceptable to mate her 'on the trot' (by which I mean mating her in successive seasons). It could take too much out of her. She should have at least one season between each litter. She will not know or understand this, and will mate at every season if she has a liking for it.

Having considered the suitability of your Vizsla as a potential brood bitch, and satisfied yourself that she is able to fulfil at least some, if not all, of the requirements, now is the time to consider which stud dog you wish to use. In order to make your task easier we should now consider the practical genetic management of breeding.

Breeding Objectives

When adding up the pros and cons of which stud dog to use for your bitch, it is important to remember that mediocre stock breeds mediocre stock, and no wishful thinking can possibly change that fact. Let us start by asking the question, what sort of stock do you want to breed and what are your priorities?

It is essential to have a clear objective. Is the idea to breed one or two litters, hoping to produce an outstanding puppy, or to establish a kennel, laying down the foundations for future generations? The Vizsla breeders in Britain over the years have managed to maintain the characteristics as the Standard states:

...lively and intelligent, obedient, but sensitive, very affectionate and easily trained.
It was bred for hunting for fur and feather, on open ground or in thick cover, pointing and retrieving from both land and water.

It will not be the Vizsla who is to blame if the characteristics are not maintained but the present and future breeders. We should be proud indeed that there is no division between working and showing types as there is in some gundog breeds. I believe this is so because working stock is well to the fore in many of our pedigrees. Looking at the pedigrees of today it would be fair to state that the breed is well stocked with working bloodlines. Many of our imports were brought over to work and certainly the early pioneers of the breed were dedicated to working their Vizslas. Few of the early imports have been brought in as pure show dogs.

A decision must be made when considering any kind of breeding programme that the aim is 'to breed a sound Vizsla of good temperament, capable of working and as good an appearance as possible'. By sound I mean free from disease, defects, and all structural faults. To quote from David Layton's excellent book *All Purpose Gundog* (although he was writing about the German Short-Haired Pointer, it is highly recommended to all Vizsla owners):

> It is perhaps even harder to breed good German Short-Haired Pointers than some other breeds. One is not only concerned with handsome dogs fitting the Standard and being a credit to their breed, but also with producing dogs with inherent characteristics and suitable temperaments potentially fitting them to the task of being good all round gundogs.

Lodge's Ponsonby Mr Bojangles. Photo: Buller

The only way to establish that the stud dog you choose has at least some of these qualities; that he is likely to be dominant in any of them and that he could complement your bitch is to study the pedigrees. Gather as much information as you can about the predecessors – the sire and dam, grandparents and great-grandparents. Better still, try to see some of them. Look at the progeny that the dog has produced, remembering that, however good he is, you cannot expect miracles if he is mated to a mediocre bitch. There is no easy way. I had thought, studied, talked about and looked at a particular dog over and over again, who on paper had all that I was looking for but somehow he and the dam did not click for me when I saw them together. When mated, the litter was not especial either. Pat Lanz, breeder of Rottweilers, Komondors and Pulis, whom I have admired for years and who has consistently bred top class stock (her kennel Borgvaale is known throughout the world), has patiently answered my questions on breeding since I was first in Vizslas. She told me once, 'Breeding comes down to instinct. If it feels right, it is right.' But that remark was based on years of good, sound acquired experience and basic knowledge of dogs, and years of selection of good breeding stock, of selecting puppies for future breeding thus building up a pool of desirable genes for typical stock. A breeding programme which is concerned with only one feature has much more chance of success. However the dog breeder is dealing with much more than this. Breeding presents a constant weighing up of good features and bad, based on knowledge of specific parts. Since the breeder cannot know for certain what characteristics are controlled by which gene combination – would that science and technology were so advanced as to enable the breeders to deal with separate genes – all he can do is observe and acquire a grasp of genetic principles.

A feature that appears in one parent but not in the other but is inherited by all the puppies is probably the result of a dominant pair of genes in the parent who had the feature. If half the puppies have this feature probably the parent had a single gene for this trait. Genetic make-up can only be surmised over a period of time and each feature has its own genetic code. Therefore in breeding risks are taken all the time. Like an iceberg there is much more beneath that you cannot see than there is above the surface. Even so, there are obvious pitfalls that even the novice can learn to avoid. A breeder must remember never to mate two animals with the same defect. Also, remember to breed two animals who look similar – breeding two extremes only produces extremes.

In aiming to breed a sound animal, that is, one which is free from disease, defects and all structural faults, in principle soundness should be sought for well before cosmetics. Do not misunderstand me – of course breeding for type is essential but, in establishing a breeding programme, a sound dog surely has to be the basis if you wish to continue to breed a dog who can work. It is incumbent on the breeder to strive to eliminate a disorder such as hip dysplasia before worrying about the tail set, which is a detail that rests entirely upon opinion and does not cripple the animal.

This practical genetic management may sound simple enough, but of course it is not. It consists of breeding from the best stock available, selecting those lines in which the defect appears infrequently, which means learning to disregard rare cases of defects which may result from environmental causes and, in the meantime, attempting to eliminate those lines which repeatedly produce the defect. For the practical breeder, the

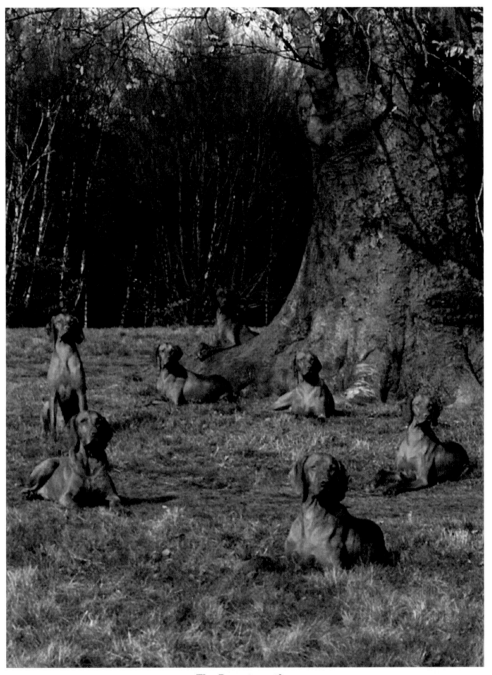

The Russetmantles.
Front: Sh Ch Russetmantle Paris. Front left: Ch R. Troy. Front right: Sh Ch R. Ochre. Far left (sitting): Sh Ch R.October. In front of tree: dog on left - Ch R. Gleam, dog on right - Sh Ch R. Poppy. Dog behind tree: Ch R. Quiver.

widespread occurrence of inherited physical faults means that any breeding programme must be based on multiple criteria. For instance, you may find that you finally produce a Vizsla with the correct front but little behind or elsewhere to commend it.

So let us discuss in more detail the practice of breeding, always keeping in mind the sire and the dam you wish to mate.

Each puppy inherits an equal number of genes from its parents. To illustrate this let us take the total value of the ancestors' influence as 100%. Each puppy inherits 50% from each parent. From its grandparents it gains 25% of its inheritance and 12.5% from its great- grandparents. So it is clear that a gene inherited further back is not likely to contribute very much. But if the gene for the same characteristic is received from both sides it will be double and therefore a stronger genetic characteristic. If closely-related animals are bred they are likely to possess more genes in common than are those that are unrelated. We will consider three basic breeding programmes that are used: in-breeding, line breeding and out-crossing.

In-breeding

This is the practice of breeding two very closely-related individuals, such as father to daughter, mother to son, or brother to sister. It is not advisable for the novice to attempt this form of breeding because he cannot have had enough experience or knowledge of the 'family tree'. (For example, if two animals with entropion were bred together it is not going to improve the condition in the breed, especially if the breeder discovers too late that the condition was known to be found in both lines.) In the right hands, if both the dam and sire are outstanding something really good could be produced, but new characteristics cannot be added. The puppies cannot be better genetically than either parent. Good qualities are fixed by in-breeding, but so are bad and they may be difficult to eliminate, so there is no chance of success if two inferior animals are used. The ever-optimistic breeder, having turned a blind eye, will find the changes of success ever diminishing. Even though he may decide to cull drastically, there are conditions such as hip dysplasia or epilepsy that often manifest themselves long after the puppies have gone to new homes.

Louise Petrie-Hay writes in one of her many articles in *The Shooting Times*:
In-breeding, as far as I am concerned, is out. Good clean incest is always tricky. Look at what it does in humans – father and daughter, mother and son, sister and brother – that's in-breeding. If we knew everything there was to know about the dog and bitch and everything we knew was good, then by in-breeding everything would be accentuated and 'tied' and we would have the perfect dog.

Line-breeding

This is a modification of in-breeding. It is the mating of related stock but not as close as that used for in-breeding: grandmother to grandson, grandfather to granddaughter, uncle to niece or aunt to nephew, son or daughter to the mother's half sister or half brother, and half-brother or half-sister if the common parent is outstanding. This method may not produce such spectacular results and demands no less high standards in the choice of breeding stock, but can produce high-quality progeny, taking longer to establish but much less risky than an ill-chosen in-breeding programme. In a well-chosen breeding programme, if only desirable progeny are used from each litter, future generations will become uniform and of the best quality, reproducing itself, displaying the same characteristics, and an even litter will be seen. More significantly, they will look alike as adults so a particular line will be recognisable.

Out-crossing

Out-crossing is not a specific breeding programme. It is a fundamental part of line-breeding and in-breeding programmes and is used to introduce 'new blood' or a new characteristic into a closely bred line. It is the breeding of two totally unrelated animals. It is recommended that the sire be in-bred, so that (probably) fewer faults will be introduced than a widely line-bred sire. In this way, it is hoped to introduce different qualities needed in that line, but it is then advisable to breed the progeny back to the original line. The reason for this is that having introduced the quality the out-cross provided, the stud dog may also have introduced new faults which could be difficult to eliminate. But if at least one of the resulting progeny still retains a strong resemblance to the original 'type' but has obviously inherited the new factor from the outcross, the constant characteristic of the line will continue. Be prepared to travel to use the stud dog who really suits, however easy it is to use the dog you have at home.

Breeding Vizslas

Breeding animals can be a heart-breaking business. Just as it seems that the slow process of improvement is coming right, all can be lost – a fine dog can prove impotent, a bitch barren, or some hereditary fault appears or a new characteristic never seen before rears its ugly head. As a kennel becomes established and does well, the type known to that kennel may become over exaggerated without the breeder realising. It is very, very difficult to be objective. 'Kennel blindness' is a fault that should be bred out, but it can be firmly established in breeders. It is very difficult to confirm failure when there are so many factors involved and even worse to have to abandon years of work. Trying to breed your dream Vizsla is like that game when you have to juggle five silver balls into five tiny holes. Sometimes, when it all comes right, it is a sheer fluke – but perhaps this analogy is not entirely apt because there are specific rules that need to be adhered to and, if they are followed, there is a much more positive chance of success sooner or later. It is imperative to have a good eye for a dog. If you have not got this, borrow someone else's!

I think it is true to say that there are few dogs who have repeatedly given the breed the same qualities of excellence. In all modesty, no breeder in Hungarian Vizslas could say there are many Vizslas of outstanding quality and excellence easily found in this breed. Serious breeders had an uphill task from the start because the first Hungarian Vizsla imports were brother and sister, Ernest and Agnes. They were the original stock that was bred from in England. Some of their progeny were also in-bred, so bad qualities as well as good were well and truly fixed. Although there is no longer any information available to prove otherwise, I doubt whether poor old Ernest and Agnes were 'the perfect Vizslas in every respect'.

It must be emphasised that for anyone wishing to breed seriously, a good strain must be established and this is rarely achieved unless the immediate forebears are of good quality. Each ancestor's genes become diluted in each generation. A particular animal cannot influence his descendants unless he carries dominant genes which pass on his virtues to his progeny down the line. One good dog amongst mediocrity is not likely to guarantee a desirable pool of genes. Therefore the relative values of the immediate forebears can be more rewarding if there appears to be consistency in sound typical stock.

Mating

Once you have selected the stud dog you wish to use, approached his owner and agreed on the arrangements, now is the time to learn 'the facts of life'.

The Act of Mating

When a bitch is in season she produces the chemical known as pheromone in her urine and it is this scent that the sexually arouses the male. When the bitch is ready to be mated, the two animals will go through a preliminary courting stage which can last from two minutes to half an hour or more. The dog will nuzzle her, lick her ears, her face and her vulva especially, both displaying great excitement. They may run together, he may clasp her over the withers with his front legs attempting to manoeuvre her body beneath him. When both are fully aroused, the bitch will present and display her enlarged vulva, her tail twisted to one side. She will stand motionless ready to receive him. He will mount her, clasping her with his front legs firmly round the flanks. He will search for the entrance of her vulva with his erect penis. If he is not successful, he may dismount and remount, making another attempt. When he does find the entrance, his hind legs will make fast jerking, frantic movements. He will get a good purchase on the floor in order to make complete penetration. When he has succeeded and ejaculation has taken place, the prepuce of the foreskin of his penis will have been pushed back and the swollen bulbous glandis will be held in the restricting band of the vagina. This is known as the 'tie'. Neither dog can now be separated. The dog's semen has entered the bitch's vagina and 'mating' has taken place.

The tie may last from five minutes to half an hour, or even to one hour. It is said that it is not essential for fertilization that the 'tie' takes place, but it is thought that it prevents the semen from leaking back. While the animals are 'tied' they may stand side by side, but usually the dog turns so that they stand tail to tail with their heads facing outward, away from each other. It is thought that this position is adopted because in the wild, dogs are vulnerable whilst mating takes place. If they are standing in this manner, they are better able to defend themselves.

As the bulbous glandis has reduced to normal, the mating pair is released and a small amount of fluid will come away. Now the mating is over, the animals will take very little notice of each other. Sadly there seems little ecstasy, passion, or love in the act. Even the Hungarian Vizsla whom we cherish so much is no different from any other breed. He, with all his need to give and receive love and affection from his humans, is totally promiscuous and fickle when it comes to loyalty either to his bitches or to his progeny. No nest-building or feeding the dam for him while she cares for his puppies, nor does he recognise his progeny when he sees them.

The Vizsla at Stud

The Hungarian Vizsla presents few problems as a stud dog if he is handled correctly as a youngster. He needs no particular preparation before mating as long as he is free from any infection, is fit and healthy and his diet is correct. Some owners will add extra protein to his diet but there is little need for this unless he has a lot of stud work. In this breed no stud dog is likely to have bitches coming to him every day! The Vizsla should not be large or heavily built compared to big breeds, so he should have no trouble mounting a bitch as long as they are well suited in height and weight. His short coat presents no problems. There are no curtains of hair to keep out of the way.

The gentleness and sweetness of the Vizsla character is often demonstrated while courting is in the preliminary stages. He seems to prefer to flirt and wrestle, enjoying the bitch's playfulness. He is not usually the aggressive type of stud dog who dismisses the preliminaries, mounting the bitch before she knows it. Some seem to need encouragement and reassurance from the bitch that she will accept him. I think most owners would agree that the Vizsla is considerate at stud, rarely wishing to force himself on a bitch if she rejects him. I have observed a Vizsla losing interest in the whole affair when the bitch appeared to have no liking for him or if she lacked interest in the proceedings even though she was ready to 'stand' and even though he was keen to start with.

The Vizsla temperament is such that he can be over-conscious of the human element in the exercise, seeming almost shy at times. He sometimes mounts the bitch and then dismounts again quickly, regarding his owner. This is not unusual and is entirely understandable if we realise that we are dealing with animals. We have arranged the mating, not they. In the wild there would be no human contact. Little wonder that the dog may be confused if the observer is a dominant party in this primitive act. In order to mate successfully, the male needs to be dominant. This influences his behaviour when approaching the bitch sexually – an overbearing bitch may not allow a subordinate male to mate her. Thus the role the human plays should be as retiring and as quiet as possible. Handled with sympathy and understanding, the Vizsla will gain confidence at stud and become an expert on the job.

As in all aspects of owning a Vizsla, be there when he needs you but do not over-handle him or he becomes dependent and finds it difficult to assert himself except in a totally subordinate fashion.

The Owner Handler

The owner of a dog will soon learn that he cannot request the use of a bitch, a mistake many new owners make until they realise that the apple of their eye may not be anyone else's. The owner of the breeding bitch makes the choice, choosing the male best suited to produce the best puppies by the bitch. The owner of the bitch has all the work of whelping and caring for the offspring and selling them, therefore it is he who will request the 'use' of the dog. Once this has been arranged then the owner of the dog dictates the terms, such as stud fees and where and how the mating takes place. If the mating does not 'take', it is necessary for the owners of the dogs to decide whether to allow a free mating when the bitch has her next season. It is generally accepted that this is the procedure.

In order to ascertain the correct date of ovulation, the bitch can have a smear test done by the vet. The vet uses a microscope to look at the red blood cells that line the epithelium of the vagina. The test shows the changing conditions of the cells in ovulation. When the bitch is ready to be mated, the normally large, round cells are flat. Now the picture can be confusing, because the bitch may present herself as ready to be mated, tail to one side, discharge pale, but some of the cells may not have completed their change so she is not in full oestrus.

The stud dog can also confuse the picture. There can be some variance in the length of time the sperm can last in the uterus. Some dogs may produce sperm that last for one day, others may produce sperm that last for five days after mating. Invaluable is the stud dog who mates the bitch who is not in full oestrus but is willing and his fertile sperm hangs around a bit. Conversely, if we learn that the stud dog's sperm does not endure, obviously a second mating is necessary if the bitch is to become in whelp.

It is important to decide whether one or two matings are necessary when the bitch comes to the dog. Every breeder will have his own opinions and methods based on his experience. Basically it is sensible to mate a maiden bitch two or three times. This will give her experience and it is not quite so easy to know when a maiden bitch is absolutely ready because she may be so confused by the new circumstances she will not know whether to stand up or sit down! It is kinder to give her a chance to settle.

One mating is all that is necessary as long as it is certain that the bitch is in full oestrus, if both Vizslas are mature and both have proved themselves as a sire and dam.

Personally, I always prefer to mate Vizslas twice, the reason being that I am not very good at ascertaining the exact moment the bitch is ready. I also find that if the Vizslas are from my kennel, they know and like each other. The bitches will accept the dog so easily they may be a couple of hours out! It is very rare but it has been known that a bitch accepts the dog kennelled with her at any time of the year!

The timing of the second mating varies, depending on the dog's owner. Some will mate them four hours later, some 12, some 48 hours. After mating I count that as day one, leave them the following day and mate them on day three. Others may disagree but I have always found it successful. Obviously, it is difficult to do this if the bitch has travelled from a distance, but the stud dog owner should give those visiting an opportunity to choose. Whether it is convenient to either is another matter.

It is usually understood that, if the dog has not been mated before, his first attempt at mating is free, the reason being that the dog needs to have a chance to 'prove' himself. Can he sire puppies? The first mating is a trial and just as important to the owner if he wishes to use his dog at stud as it is for the owner of the bitch. Therefore it is courtesy not to ask for a fee. If this mating is successful and, as time goes on your dog proves himself a potent and worthy sire, depending on his merit and the demand for him you can decide what you wish to charge. You may charge for any subsequent matings, or you can ask for 'pick of the litter'.

The stud dog owner has every right to refuse a request to use his dog if it does not seem to be a suitable match. He has as much responsibility as the bitch's owner in spoiling or improving the breed.

A dog who proves to breed untypical Vizslas can do great harm and actually changes the breed if used repeatedly. The dog's owner may feel that the puppies are not his responsibility, but they are if he really cares about the breed, so when your dog is in demand it is helpful to acquaint yourself with a few facts. Does the bitch's owner have customers for the offspring? If not, what will happen to them?

As the dog's owner gains experience he will learn that each mating is different: some easy, some difficult, some complicated. He will discover whether his dog prefers to manage on his own or whether he needs his owner to help him 'turn'. He may like his owner to hold and comfort him during the 'tie' or, alternatively, he may hate being fussed over, preferring to be left entirely on his own. Whatever the procedure, the owner should 'be in charge'. He will need to assess the bitch and her owner. If the owner is experienced in these matters, he could stay and handle the bitch for you. If not, perhaps it would be simpler if you suggested that the bitch is left with you and her owner collect her later. It is a very uncomfortable experience to mate two animals in the presence of someone who is shy, embarrassed or squeamish. A noisy, impatient or talkative human will disturb the calm atmosphere necessary if the dogs are not to be 'put off' or disturbed.

Where to Mate

The stud dog always 'stands' on his own home ground. The bitch should always be brought to him. It is essential that the dog is settled and relaxed in surroundings that he knows well. He may be fearful and tense in a strange place and, however good his temperament, he may fail to consummate. Therefore, always use the same place that is familiar to him. He will soon learn that it is where he mates. Choose a room that is warm, light, and airy, a place away from other dogs and normal household activities. Make sure that the family knows that you cannot be disturbed. You are not available socially for at least an hour, or more!

The room should not be too large; there should be enough space for the dogs to run, but the area should be small enough for the handlers to reach their Vizslas quickly once the dog starts to mount the bitch after the pre-mating courtship. The floor must not be slippery because the dog has to get a good grip with his back legs. This rules out vinyl, lino and wood – even straw can be very slippery. The ideal is the best Wilton carpet! Failing that, a rough cement floor or grass will do. So, if you have a long, narrow, well-lit, warm room, well away from civilisation, carpeted with fresh spring grass, cement, or an unwanted Indian rug, with facilities for making tea, coffee or something stronger with one hand, you have the ideal conditions!

Some owners may prefer to have their dogs mate outside, and some dogs prefer it. In this case, the bitch should be on a lead so that the handlers are close enough when the time comes to assist them. Weather conditions have to be taken into consideration.

The First and Last Mating

After the first mating and puppies have been produced the male can be said to be a 'stud dog'. This first mating is obviously very important. Ideally it should take place at about 10 to 12 months, so that he learns the procedure when he is young. If he is fortunate enough to have his first mating with an experienced bitch who has a good, sensible temperament, she will help him over his naivety without upsetting him. She should be a bitch who is keen to mate and who likes it, and preferably knows the dog well. He will be bemused and shy at first and it is she who will chivvy and flirt with him endearingly, gentling the young dog into his first mating.

At what age is a stud dog too old to use? There seems to be no hard and fast rule. The owner will recognize the signs of old age creeping on and perhaps feel the dog cannot manage it any longer. This could be from nine years onward. In my experience, Vizslas of 11 and 12 can still be very potent sires, capable of siring good healthy puppies. The worry is that they could collapse on the job!

Handling

If the owner of the dog is a novice it is advisable to seek expert advice and help for the first few meetings. It is not just a matter of putting two Vizslas together in the garden or field and leaving them to get on with it. The maiden bitch could be badly frightened by a male. He could be bitten by her or he could be torn very painfully if he mated her and she pulled away or laid down. Both could decide that they would not like to go through that experience again! So it is sensible not to have to learn by your mistakes in this case! Ask for assistance, do not be proud.

There are many different methods of handling a breed when mating. Each individual will work out his own method of helping the dog to succeed. Meanwhile, let us consider the handler's role in an uncomplicated mating, with one person handling the bitch and the other the dog. Both Vizslas should be wearing their collars. They should be allowed to relieve themselves before being introduced, giving the bitch plenty of time to familiarize herself with the surroundings. Once they have met in the area where they are to mate, leave them as much time as they wish to prance and play, the handlers remaining quiet and removed but alert to assist when the time is right. When the courting stage is over and the dog mounts the bitch, her handler should be close enough to hold her collar gently, placing the other hand beneath her belly, firmly supporting her weight. This will prevent her from turning on the dog if she is so inclined and stops her from sitting down or twisting around. Some bitches will stand rigid to receive the dog but there are many exceptions and it is as well to be prepared. With this method, the dog is well protected.

The tie may last for 10, 20 or 30 minutes. The longest I have experienced is one hour. I was on my own and, as the minute ticked by, my mind was beginning to fantasise. I was becoming anxious: 'Suppose they don't part, what do I do? Put them in my car, arrive at the vet's surgery with two dogs doing 'you know what'! I have since learned that, eventually, the bitch releases the dog – yes, it is she whose muscles relax to release the penis.

It is questionable whether the tie is necessary at all. I know we feel reassured that a good mating has taken place if there is a tie. However, I have witnessed matings where there has been no tie, and the bitch has come into whelp. The myth of the longer the tie, the more puppies, has been disproved time and again.

When they are tied, the dog usually turns in order to stand back to back. A novice dog may find it difficult to effect this manoeuvre. His handler can gently raise the front leg and then the hind leg over the bitch's back and so ensure little or no discomfort for either. At this stage both Vizslas may be happier with their handlers by them. The bitch may attempt to pull away from the dog so both need coaxing to relax. Both handlers can feel content the dogs have mated. Now they need to wait until the 'tie' is over. Two low stools and a cup of tea will be welcome at this point. The dog will need little attention by now but the bitch will still need her handler to hold her head if she is restless. Both will have calmed down after the excitement and will appear passive. They may not seem particularly comfortable, their ears back, eyes red, panting and drooling. Little can be done for them at this stage When the dog's penis is finally released, the handlers have little more to do than feed and water them and leave them to rest separately.

Handling a mating is an art; some people never manage to achieve the right attitude. Their tension and unease for the welfare of the dog or bitch is quickly transmitted to the animals, causing confusion. It has to be accepted that, if it hurts, the bitch will cry and whine. If the dog does not manage to mate he will be uncomfortable, but not for long. Those who are expert at supervising matings are those who calmly accept the course of events, giving the animals a sense of security.

Complications for the Stud Dog
It would seem ridiculous to discuss mating difficulties with the owner of the curly-tailed Don Juan of the neighbourhood – a strong force to be reckoned with for any unfortunate owner of a pedigree bitch. And I am sure those Vizsla owners who have always found the exercise runs smoothly will wonder that such a heading as 'Complications' is necessary, but there are those, and I am one, who have needed advice at times when, usually through lack of experience, things have not gone according to the book.

1   Frequently the courting stage becomes protracted until both dogs are exhausted and bored, neither appearing excited enough to copulate. The most common reason for this is that the bitch is not in full oestrus, perhaps it is too late or too early. If she repeatedly sits and snaps at the dog, especially if she has been mated before, then be guided by her and try some hours later or the following day. If it is after day 14, it could be too late. If the dog does not show much interest it could be for the same reason.

2   If the bitch is not ready to 'stand' she will often sit down if a dog shows interest. She will also behave in this way after she has finished ovulating. If the dog does not get the message that she no longer accepts him, she may also snap, a sure sign that she may have come out of purdah.

Many young, inexperienced dogs will take time to comprehend which end is 'the place for him' and in doing so will become exhausted and over excited, frantically trying to mount the bitch from every angle. A short turn around the garden may calm him. If patiently handled, he will sort it out. In this case, it is necessary to take into account the Vizsla temperament. He can become over-anxious. He needs reassurance from his owner in case he feels he is causing displeasure, which will increase his bewilderment.

4   Occasionally, the dog may not be able to penetrate the bitch, leaving him in a very uncomfortable predicament with his penis exposed and drying and the bulb partially enlarged. He may also have ejaculated outside the bitch. This can be due to his over-enthusiasm or difficulty in penetrating the bitch. She may have moved at the crucial moment or he could have misfired or he could have penetrated her but not completely. The wisest thing to do is to separate the two for 10 minutes or

so, allowing the dog to remain quietly by himself. I have found that usually he will be quite comfortable by then and ready to return and mate the bitch. If he is still disinterested, separate them for a few hours, in order that he may forget the unpleasant experience. Some advise applying cold water to the exposed membranes but I have never felt it necessary, feeling the cure may be more painful than the temporary condition.

5   It has to be accepted that some dogs have their preferences and do take a dislike to a bitch and vice versa. In some cases, it is best to recognise this and call it a day.

Types of Stud Dog

Specific problems can arise due to the type of dog that is being used. For instance, an over-enthusiastic Vizsla could terrify a young maiden bitch. This one will not wait for any introductions or preliminaries but completely and accurately hurl himself onto her. He needs to be restrained for the bitch's sake, until she has had the chance to accept him. I would suggest that it is rare behaviour for a Vizsla.

The dog who shows little enthusiasm is difficult to deal with. He may not show any interest in the bitch, however keen she is. If she is a maiden it may not be a productive proposition at all. Have patience, do not despair, and use some ingenuity. First try him on a mature bitch. She may behave in such a way that he finds her irresistible. You can help him to feel more confident by encouraging him to play, by jollying the two up, even throwing a tennis ball can get them into a playful mood. Sometimes this mood then changes to courting. Another trick that sometimes works is to remove the bitch for a few minutes and then return her with a flourish, hoping to change the atmosphere of boredom to ecstatic excitement.

If this Vizsla's problems are deep seated, however, then we should look further and try to find out why he is behaving in this manner. Perhaps he has spent his entire life with humans, protected, petted and shielded from other nasty dogs? In that case, if he is young, this could be rearranged in some way. If he has lived with a dominating dog or bitch or played a very subordinate part in the pecking order in his kennel he may not have had the opportunity to mature sexually. In both these cases, the dog will manifest his lack of interest towards a bitch. The answer is that he should be placed for some time in an environment where he can establish his own identity. Probably an old dog would not respond, but I have known a case where a young dog living with his sire could not mate any bitch. The owner was advised to remove him and allow him to run with the other young stock. This was done and, after a couple of months, the problem was solved. He no longer behaved as if he were suppressed. In fact, with a bit of practice and a lot of encouragement, he became a very competent stud dog.

I have been flummoxed by a young, untried dog. On presenting him with a mature bitch who 'stood' for him (proving the day was right) he sniffed her and that was that – showing no further interest. A few minutes later he climbed on and mated her! He lived with his top dog father and six bitches, one of whom was his dam, who dominated the whole kennel. He displays the same pattern every time he mates a bitch, even in his father's presence, disproving many theories.

The hesitant Vizsla may appear to be interested and excited by the bitch but, as he mounts her, he feebly gives up and slides off. Often the behaviour can be attributed to his lack of experience. If this is the reason he will learn soon enough. He could be shy.

He may find the proximity of his owner too embarrassing, especially if he has been chastised for his interest in bitches when it has been inconvenient. If the owner is over-dominating and interfering it may put him off. If the owner is sensible and allows someone not emotionally involved but who the dog knows to handle the dog, all may go well. If not, then it may be one of the rare occasions when the humans have to remove themselves entirely; not advisable, but perhaps the only answer. I know a stud dog who has mated many times but will have nothing to do with the Vizsla bitch unless he is left alone with her and another who will only mate under a certain rose bush in the garden.

The dog may also hesitate to mate if he has been injured or hurt in any way during the previous matings. Given time and patience and much encouragement from a fond and flirty bitch, he may forget all about it unless he is a shy, nervy type. But in this case, perhaps it is unwise to consider putting him to stud in the first place.

I have seen two cases when the bitch has had a vaginal cyst which caused an obstruction in the organ. This, of course, can cause great discomfort to the dog, complete penetration being impossible. His behaviour would seem unreasonable, dismounting the bitch at the very last minute, attempting to mate her time and time again, becoming more and more distressed until, totally dejected, he stands pathetically, his passion spent.

The Stud Dog Who Knows His Business

This is the Vizsla with the solid temperament, the one that works, or could if given half the chance, the one that presents no problems when mating or, if he does, can overcome them pretty well on his own with a little help from his owner. His gentle, responsive nature is ideally suited to adapting to the temperament of the bitch if she is well disposed toward him. Expect him to take time. Expect him to have likes and dislikes. Do not expect him to be aggressive or forward or demanding in any way. Expect him to be as you have found the Vizsla to be, if he is well adjusted – romantic, affectionate, passionate, excitable, whimsical and persistent in getting the job done. He is totally reliable once he has confidence in himself and he knows what he is up to, learning by his own mistakes, but always needing his owner's approval.

I give two examples when the experience of the dog allowed him to be in charge of the mating. A mature bitch showing all the signs of her 'readiness' came to be mated. Both animals behaved as if they had no idea why they were there, neither seemed to concentrate on each other for any length of time, preferring to trot about wagging their tails as though they were going for a walk. The bitch's handler decided to hold her steady, but this only encouraged her to sit by her handler. If all concerned were novices, this may have been a 'non event', but the bitch's owner knew his bitch was 'ready' and the dog was totally reliable. Both dogs were encouraged to play, the handlers standing well away. Then the dog decided now was the time, pulled the bitch towards him, wrapped one leg round her thigh, held her firmly by the other, and mated her.

The second incident involved a maiden pet bitch. This mating proved to me the worth of a truly reliable, confident dog, with a good sound temperament. The bitch also had a good temperament, for I am sure we could have been bitten if she had not. The dog was strange, the place was strange and she had no experience. She clung to her owner, who handled her well; he encouraged her to run with the dog and sensibly remained as kind but aloof as he could. She stood and was mounted by the dog and in a flash she turned on her back screaming, taking all by surprise. The dog was not deterred nor disturbed. He mounted her again, and this time the handlers were prepared and both held her firmly while the dog turned calmly on his own. Meanwhile the bitch screamed and screamed, no amount of comforting pacified her. The dog remained quiet and the noise reduced to a whine. She was mated a second time and behaved very differently, flirting and presenting herself as soon as he appeared, apparently unaffected by her traumatic experience. It could well have been painful to begin with, as a bitch can have a spasm of the vaginal musculature (vaginismus) during mating. Now a young dog could well have been put off, from mating this bitch, nor is it the sort of mating a novice dog should be faced with for the first time.

Code of Ethics

Finally, I quote from the relevant sections of the Code of Ethics drawn up by both the Hungarian Vizsla Club and Society, giving guidelines to responsible breeders.

Hungarian Vizsla Club Mandatory Breeders Code of Conduct

- Members will only breed from Vizslas which are temperamentally and physically sound and will always strive to produce Vizslas which show natural ability and conform to the Breed Standards as published by The Kennel Club.
  Members will not allow their stud dog to serve any bitch of:
  (a) less than two years of age, or
  (b) more than seven years of age.
- Members will not allow their bitches to whelp:
  (a) more than once in any calendar year, or
  (b) if younger than two years of age.
- A bitch in her lifetime shall not have more than four litters.
- Members will ensure that any stock from which they breed is Kennel Club registered.

The Voluntary Code of Ethics of the Hungarian Vizsla Society

- Members will only breed from Hungarian Vizslas of sound temperament, which show natural ability and will always strive to produce Hungarian Vizslas conforming to the Standard as published by The Kennel Club.
- Members will not knowingly allow their stud dogs to serve bitches of less than two years of age, or over the

age of seven years. Neither dogs nor bitches in poor health, of unsound temperament, or with any serious hereditary disease, will be used for breeding.

- Stud dog owners will use their discretion as to the number and suitability of bitches covered each year.
- Members will not allow their bitches to whelp more than once in every 12 months or before two years of age, or over the age of seven. A bitch will not have more than three litters during her lifetime, or be mated before two years of age.
- Members shall ensure that any stock from which they breed shall be registered with The Kennel Club in accordance with the rules in force at that time.

This dog is nothing like me!

chapter | 8 |

The Expectant Mother

One of the most fascinating and exciting aspects of Vizsla owning and breeding must be watching a bitch whelping. They are such natural mothers, they need little assistance while giving birth. They don't fuss or panic, they seem by instinct to understand what is required of them.

The construction of the Vizsla bitch is such that there is nothing to inhibit a normal birth. There is no reason why any bitch should not give birth quite naturally without complications and with minimum help from the owner. A visit from the veterinary surgeon afterwards to check that all is well is all that is needed.

Pre-Whelping

The first 3–4 weeks

The first three to four weeks after mating, the Vizsla bitch should be treated exactly the same as usual, with the same feeding routine and the same exercise. Do not give her extra titbits in your zeal and anticipation.

Week 5

The first outward signs of pregnancy are the swelling and reddening of the nipples; those at the back will be the first to swell. This may not occur before the fifth week and is the first positive evidence of pregnancy that the owner will have. If the bitch becomes fatter and broader across the back but there is no physical change either in her nipples or the fullness of her belly, then it is more probable that she has been overfed and has a slight hormone change. This is very easily done and is a trap many of us fall into. Changes are imagined, and the bitch is overfed and cosseted as our maternal and paternal instincts come to the fore.

Some bitches have an unnerving habit of producing similar signs of pregnancy after their season. This is due to hormonal changes and seems more frequent in maiden bitches. Although the nipples redden and the bosoms at the back swell, the belly does not enlarge. Usually phantom pregnancy, as it is called, does not go to full term. It is rare that a bitch produces milk. Even if the bitch reaches the stage of nest building she will return to normal afterwards, usually with no ill effect, but it can be confusing and very worrying, especially if the bitch goes to an extreme stage when she is nest building and digging up frantically. Although it is said to be normal, it seems anything but; it appears to be wildly obsessional and manic. It is said that wild bitches living in a pack would feed other puppies when in this state. A bitch may also present some or all these symptoms if puppies have been re-absorbed.

Weeks 6–9

After the fifth week the bitch should have her meals divided and the protein content increased. Her diet should be of the very highest quality. It is always sensible to be advised by your vet as to which vitamins he would recommend, if any.

Exercise as usual until she is obviously in whelp and is carrying quite a burden, but care should be taken that she is not knocked or pushed if she is exercised with other dogs. She may behave as if she has no idea that she is in whelp. I feel this should be encouraged – if she is spoiled and petted – 'poor little dog, be careful, don't do anything silly now, stay by me' – your Vizsla will look at you and catch on very quickly. Your mood becomes her mood, your worrying becomes her worrying. She thinks there is something wrong. She does not know that she should be knitting for nine. She knows only that you are in a state of anxiety and she had better be in one too. So give good food and sensible exercise (swimming is not advisable – one of mine, when I was not looking, had a quick dip two days before her puppies were due. There was no harm done but this was taking my nonchalance a bit too far).

Continue to increase the bitch's food as the weeks go by. It is not so much the amount she eats but the quality. She must have the very best. She deserves it since she is producing puppies and you will want them to be a credit to the breed. As her pregnancy continues, the extra demands of the whelps upon the mother increase and it is the protein content in her diet that is the most important for her welfare as well as the whelps!

On no account increase the fat or carbohydrate content such as biscuit or starchy food. She should not be overfed; a fat pregnant bitch is an unhealthy one. As time goes on, when the bitch lies on her side, the puppies can be seen moving, providing the final proof that she is definitely in whelp. Early on in their pregnancy some bitches will heave and sigh and look enormous, seeming thoroughly uncomfortable. Others will not be affected at all almost to the day of whelping, the size of the litter making no difference in either case.

About three weeks before the birth, it is sensible to introduce the future mother to her whelping box. If she will sleep in it happily, she will be more comfortable there than anywhere else but, unless it is in your bedroom, she will be happier near you and you can keep an eye on her. In the wild, a bitch hides herself and her puppies to obliterate any trace that they have been born. This is the only defence she has against an enemy. Her chosen place to whelp would have a small entrance opening into a chamber, just large enough for her. The roof would be low and the light subdued, the atmosphere humid. We need to re-create an environment for her that will give her a similar sense of security. Even the most civilised and gregarious bitch becomes primitive to some extent at the time of whelping. She may not know what she wants – either to be with people or to seek solitude.

From the date of mating to the date of the birth is 63 days (the gestation period).

The Whelping Box

It is as well to have all the necessary items for the bitch prepared in advance. A whelping box is the major item.

Place the box somewhere secluded in a quiet, dimly-lit room, preferably beneath a table or low shelf and well away from open doors or draughts. I enclose the front with a blanket flung over a clothes horse. You need a room where the bitch can be left in peace without fear of being molested by other animals or children. The whelping box needs to be a solid, long-lasting, serviceable piece of equipment. It is possible for an amateur to make a sturdy box at quite a reasonable cost, taking from three to four hours. The method may shock the true carpenter but as long as the local wood merchant is there to give advice, and as long as he cuts the wood to exact specifications, the box can be put together by anyone who is practical and handy with a hammer and a screwdriver. The box must be large enough for the bitch to lie comfortably, and the sides must be the correct height so that the bitch and whelps can be tended easily and she can get in and out without effort, as well as affording enough protection to contain the puppies for the first few weeks. Some breeders do not use a 'pig rail' or 'shelf' fitted inside the box but, from experience, I have found an 'escape route' essential to ensure the puppy's safety should his dam lean on him. I prefer narrow shelving set at the correct height all the way round the inside of the box, because it prevents an errant puppy nearly strangling himself by poking his head between the pole and the box.

To make a whelping box 105 x 105cm (42 x 42in)
- 4 pieces of deal 105 x 22cm (42 x 9in)
- wood for base of box – plywood or block board
- oval nails 3.5cm (1.5in)
- glue, pencil, hammer, screwdriver, gimlet

For the shelf:
- 2 pieces of wood 102 x 7.5cm (40 x 3in)
- 2 pieces of wood 89 x 7.5cm (2.11ft x 3in)
- 12 shelving brackets 6cm (2.5in)
- screws to fit brackets

Method
1. Glue and nail the three pieces of wood to the base, one by one. Spread the glue liberally along the edges before nailing. Remember to place the nail with the grain of the wood or the wood may split. Use about six nails for each side.
2. With the pencil, trace a line 7.5–10cm (3–4in) from the base of the box all the way round. This will give the height at which the shelves must be fixed.
3. Screw three shelves into place along the pencilled line, the brackets uppermost.
4. The 4in panel and the 4in pig shelf are for the front of the box. They must be removable so that you can have easy access and the puppies can toddle out eventually. Make two slots, front right and left, for the 4in panel to slot into.
5. Nail and stick on the outer right and left edges a small piece of wood approximately 16 x 2.5cm (6.5 x 1in). About 2.5cm (1in) apart, nail and stick another piece 10 x 2.5cm (4 x 1in). This will also accommodate the loose 10cm (4in) rail. The 4in panel can now slip in and out. Thus the front of the box can be entirely removed when necessary.

Adding height to the box
If the puppies are to remain in the box after they are agile enough to walk and climb, it is simple to add another panel to give it more height so that they cannot climb out. You will need:
- Two pieces of light wood, measuring the length of one side – approximately 22cm (9in)or more.
- Eight pieces of wood approximately 30 x 5cm (12 x 2in).
- Two pieces of carpet measuring the length of each side and long enough to fold and nail over the top of the added panel.

You may not need four panels. If your box is in a corner, two will do. I have since

The lamp can hang from a hook screwed beneath the table or shelf.

Nail or screw the legs exactly opposite to one another, with carpet long enough to fold over the top of the panel.

The Whelping Box with drop front, added panel and shelving fixed to the inside of the box.

Drawings by author.

modified the luxury model! Now I put a spare piece of vet bed or soft heavy material placed over the panel instead of nailed carpet.
1. Nail or screw the 'legs' of wood exactly opposite one another about 10cm (4in) from each end.
2. Fix the carpet or material in place.
The whole panel should fit over the side of the whelping box. The soft carpet/material allows the bitch to jump in and out without hurting herself. At this stage she may be more comfortable lying outside the box and, if she has a comfortable bed nearby, she will stay near her puppies and tend to them when necessary.

Floor covering
Whilst the bitch is whelping, layers of newspaper are the most practical lining on the base of the box, as they can be replaced as soon as they are soiled. After whelping, a softer warmer covering of thick material can be fixed. There are products on the market now that can be bought in quantity, and cut to the size of the box. You can have one in use and one in the wash. A square of this can be fixed to the floor of the box by screwing a metal door sill on either side. This can easily be taken up and replaced by a clean piece. I have now modified this method in that I fix the cover round the edge with a heavy duty stapler; however determined a bitch may be to scrape up the box, she cannot unpin the flooring. Some bitches do insist on digging

up after whelping. It is a worry that a whelp may be smothered, so it is not worth the risk by leaving loose covers about.

The infra-red lamp

An infra-red heat lamp is an essential. It is no use thinking the puppies will be fine in the kitchen where it is warm. It is cold at night or when a door is opened. Unless there is constant heat, the puppies will become cold and, if they have to struggle to keep warm, inevitably it will give them less chance to 'do well'. At worse, they may not survive. The temperature required is about 25°C (75°F). The puppies need this heat for about two to three weeks. If the lamp is suspended slightly to one side of the box it enables the puppies and the mother to move beneath it or away from it as they wish.

Items Necessary for the Birth

- whelping box
- infra-red lamp
- a low table – here you can put all the items necessary for the whelping
- newspaper
- waste paper basket
- towel, bowl and soap for washing hands
- sharp-ended scissors for cutting cord or bag
- cotton wool for wiping whelps' eyes, nose and mouth
- towel for drying whelps
- clock for noting the time between delivery of each whelp
- scales, pen and paper for weighing and recording birth weight
- drink prepared for the hard working mother while giving birth
- some sort of matting – this is to prevent housemaid's knee while attending the birth – you may be kneeling for hours. It would also be good to have a comfortable chair for you when there is a lull in the proceedings!
- cardboard box with hot water bottle covered with a blanket – this is for the whelps. The whelping box becomes crowded if the mother has a large number of pups.

The Pre-Birth Signs

There are two signs that the puppies' birth is imminent: one is a sharp drop in the bitch's temperature and the other is loss of appetite. Take her temperature twice a day, a few days before the expected date of birth. This is easily done by inserting the thermometer gently about half an inch into the anal passage and leaving it in for three minutes. When it is obvious that the bitch's temperature is several degrees below the normal temperature of 37–38°C or 100–101°F, depending on the time of day and the individual dog, then this coupled with loss of appetite – although not all bitches lose their appetite – is a good indication that the long-awaited puppies are due to arrive.

Some bitches make a great fuss nest building, attempting to scrape and dig up their bed. They will move about restlessly, unable to settle anywhere. Other bitches will seem unaware of the life moving within them until the last moment.

There are times when the oldest of hands can be caught out. One evening, my pregnant bitch, due to whelp five days later, lay by me on the settee. I could feel the puppies having a fine game stretching their legs inside her. She had not been eating well and this evening she felt quite cold to the touch, especially her ears. I took little notice of these indications but, oh dear me, I should have done so. The following night she had six of her nine puppies all by herself! They came on Wednesday night and were not due until the Saturday. I was completely taken by surprise. Granted, she had shown no sign of scraping up or digging, but I had ignored very significant signs. It is probably more usual for puppies to arrive late than early; however it is better to be prepared for either eventuality.

A small amount of sticky opaque fluid (the plug) is lost, indicating that the cervix is opening. The first puppy will not be long in coming. It will start to move down the birth canal. The bitch will lick her quarters, she may attempt to squat, she may frantically dig up, pant fiercely as contractions begin or may gaze into the distance. Something is about to happen. The whelp is descending – a last push and it has arrived. There is nothing to do but remain calm at this point. A quiet voice and a gentle presence will help her over this stage, which can be bewildering for her, especially if she is a maiden. She may cry in her discomfort but, after she has given birth to one or two puppies, this stage seems far less painful to her. Let the birth be as natural as possible with the least obtrusive help.

The Birth

As the puppy is born head first it may shoot out at an alarming rate, bag broken, umbilical cord trailing along, no sign of a placenta. Another may arrive still in its bag, encased in the finest membrane looking like a burglar with a stocking over its face. A maiden Vizsla bitch may not necessarily be able to cope, but one who has whelped before may break the bag, bite the umbilical cord and mop up the mess herself.

If the maiden bitch is bewildered by the whole procedure do not be alarmed if she is frightened by her first whelp. It will not take her long to learn but, meanwhile the bag will need to be carefully nicked with the scissors or pulled away carefully and the umbilical cord cut or tenderly torn about 1.2cm (0.5in) from the puppy's abdomen. The remaining piece will dry up and eventually fall off. The afterbirth to which the umbilical cord has been attached within the mother will usually appear as a dark mass. Sometimes there is so little of it you hardly realise it has come away. Most dams will eat the afterbirth but it is not advisable to let her eat too many as she may vomit and it could also cause diarrhoea.

Draining the Fluid

The next job, and it's a crucial one, is to drain the fluid. Turn the puppy upside down – he may not have shown any sign of life at this point – and literally drain the fluid that has collected in his mouth and lungs. Holding the puppy in your left hand let the body hang down head first, place your right hand under the throat running your hand up to the corners of the mouth. At this point the mouth will open – if it is not open already – and usually a small quantity of fluid will flow out. The whelp will cry and, to the relief of the dam, you can return her newborn.

After the birth of the whelp, it is surprising to see that he is like a tiger. It can be quite a shock if you are not expecting it, but it is normal. The stripes disappear after a couple of days, looking very pretty while they last. The bitch will lick the newborn from top to toe, pushing him about quite roughly with her muzzle. Thus he is

129

The whelp enclosed in the finest membrane.
Photo: Osinga

Breaking the membrane.
Photo: Osinga

Mopping up the mess.
Photo: Osinga

Severing the umbilical cord.
Photo: Osinga

Fifteen minutes old. Note the stripes. Photo: Millson

stimulated by her in the most natural way to urinate and defecate. Her instinct to do this is a wonder to observe. She will continue this stimulation and swallow the results until the pups are old enough to 'perform' on their own, but she continues to keep the box clean until the puppies are weaned. Her competence is remarkable to observe.

While the bitch is whelping she should be allowed as much to drink as she pleases, warm milk as well as water. If she is unused to cow's milk, powdered products are less likely to upset her. She could also have an egg or two added to the mixture. The general opinion is that this régime is continued for about 24 hours after the birth of the whelps, thus allowing her digestion to settle after eating the afterbirths and her general cleaning up. It is also recommended that for the following few days she is only allowed white meat such as chicken, fish or rabbit.

I have a Vizsla bitch who is now a great-grandmother. She loves everybody's puppies, but puppies and people need cleaning. To sit next to her is fatal. She insists on washing you. Her poor puppies were always violently cleaned by her. Her last family – she gave birth to 12 – had such a hard time as they were born we had to restrain her, as her licking became furious. She soon tired, and with her excitement and enthusiasm waning by the end, her obsessive cleaning became a brief wash and brush up before the next arrival.

It is amazing to watch the maternal feelings of the bitch manifests itself, her protective instinct already showing her anxiety as she sees her young picked up.

Putting the Puppy on the Breast

The whelp may need a bit of help in feeding for the first time. Some puppies feed easily from the start, others find it difficult to hold on to the nipple until they get the feel of it in their mouth.

To help the puppy, the easiest method is to hold the mother's nipple in the right hand. Place your left forefinger and thumb on either side of the puppy's mouth, squeeze slightly and the mouth will open, put the nipple inside and away you go! It may be necessary to repeat this several times as the puppy does not always get the message and seems determined to starve. But when he does latch on and the dam is licking and nuzzling him, there is a sense of relief all round. The tiny whelp, finding it unnecessary to suck now, holds on while the milk flows down his throat.

The Length of the Birth Period

The next whelp may arrive soon after but, if there is no sign of another whelp after two hours, then you should seek the advice of your vet. If all goes according to plan, however, further contractions will announce the next whelp. There will be a sort of rhythm – a whelp arrives, he will learn to feed, then he can be placed under the lamp to dry off and be out of the way. As further whelps are born and the numbers increase to a stage where it is difficult to manage and the box becomes overcrowded, place some of them in the cardboard box which you have already prepared with a warm hot water bottle under the blanket. They will be safe until the mother has finished whelping, then they can join the others.

The ideal number for a Vizsla mother to cope with is six or seven whelps. A larger litter does tire and bring the mother down. If you have seven puppies, preferably more bitches than dogs, then you should be well pleased.

It is not always clear when the last whelp is born. If you can no longer feel a lump or see any contractions, if the abdomen looks and feels empty, if there has been a long lapse since the last whelp, then usually these signs indicate no more puppies. But beware! Sometimes there is another tucked away so when you take the bitch outside to give her a change of scenery and to relieve herself, keep a good eye on her just in case another drops out – it has been known! Of course, if the bitch seems in distress and is clearly exhausted, call the vet.

You may also leave her sleeping peacefully with 10 puppies and come down in the morning to find 11 or 12.

All the whelps have finally arrived. They are asleep, the dam sleeps also, content and exhausted. Her milk has come in and the puppies have fed. She left her puppies reluctantly to relieve herself and, on her return, she assured herself that each puppy was still in the nest – touching each with her nose. She had a good drink and lay down beside her newborn.

You yourself are exhausted, need a drink, a feed and a good sleep. But just for the moment relax and recall an experience you will never forget, watching and listening to the newly born litter of Vizsla puppies. The bitch's cleanliness and neatness, her fastidiousness and caring, the lack of fuss and the ease with which motherhood is accepted is impressive. There is nothing more delightful than listening to the murmuring and mewings of the contented litter.

The Vizsla needs you to be close at this time. She will reward you by giving utter devotion to you and the puppies. The little help that she requires from you is nothing to the pleasure she and her puppies will give in return.

Whelping Problems

When to Call the Vet

Uterine inertia
When the dam does not produce contractions.

Eclampsia
The symptoms are shuddering, great agitation and panting. This can be due partly to insufficient absorption of calcium. This condition must be treated immediately. It may occur before or during whelping, but it is most likely three weeks after the puppies are born.

The whelps' position
A whelp may be positioned in the birth canal in such a way that contractions are not sufficient to expel it. It is advisable to call in a professional.

Deformed puppies and large litters
If there are any deformed puppies in the litter, obviously it is advisable to put them down.

Although a large litter may present difficulties, as long as the pups are healthy and vigorous, I feel they should be given the right to live. It will be more work for the owner and the dam, but a bitch can handle a litter of 11 or 12 if she is fit and well.

Weaning and Feeding

The Vizsla puppies will establish their routine of feeding and sleeping, provided that the dam has adequate milk and the puppies have plenty of warmth. The litter will sleep closely together in a huddle a little away from their dam if they are contented. As one wakes, the others will too when it is time to feed. The dam will keep her puppies and whelping box spotlessly clean for the first few weeks. Although she may tolerate the humans she knows and who are close to her, do not expect her to accept strangers anywhere near her puppies. Her instinct is to protect her young against any predator as she would in the wild.

Early Feeding

You will notice as the puppy moves towards his mother to feed, he searches for the nipple. When he has obtained a good suction, he kneads the mammary gland with his tiny feet, thus stimulating lactation. The puppy wraps his tongue around the base of the nipple and, once the milk is flowing, he will relax while he fills his tummy. If a puppy continues to fuss, sucking and slurping noisily, pushing the breast with his nose, it is a sign that the milk is not coming. Either someone else has been there first or the breast is so engorged with milk that he cannot get the whole nipple in his mouth. When all the whelps are settled and feeding side by side like sardines there is no more contented sound than their grunts while the bitch lies relaxed but ever watchful.

My first experience of a large litter makes me chuckle in hindsight, at the tine I was extremely anxious. The bitch had whelped 11 puppies, she was well and so were they. I was appalled - how were they all to feed? She only had 7 nipples. I rushed around making up milk feeds and sterilising bottles. When they had had a good sleep I attempted to feed one, then a second and a third. To my distress they would not suck the rubber nipple. In exasperation and exhaustion I sat back. The dam lay there watchful and alert, relaxed in her maternal duties. Some whelps were noisily slurping and sucking, others were sleepily moving about and a third group were sound asleep. I realised that she could cope perfectly. It was I who tried to mess the routine up by interfering. I learned to respect the Vizsla, to trust that in most situations this breed is resourceful and instinctive. To my admiration she fed her litter without mishap until they were weaned. It was a lesson I never forgot.

If all is well, the puppies will grow rapidly and gain weight. By the third or fourth week, depending on the size of the litter, it will be time to think about weaning the puppies. This is the process of introducing solid food so that by the time the puppy has reached six weeks he will not require his mother or her milk although, if he is still with his dam at eight or nine weeks, depending on her maternal instinct he may still feed from her as well as taking solid feeds. Contrary to many theories, the dam is usually happy to stay away from her puppies as they grow. They become demanding and tend to maul her. It is a pathetic sight to see a bitch stand to feed her puppies while they hang from her nipples. They try to cling on with their claws and can scratch her belly. The puppies' nails must be snipped with nail scissors as soon as they begin to grow or they become as sharp as pins.

Weaning

While the puppies are being weaned, they will not take so much milk from the dam. Thus a natural process takes place: as they require less so she will produce less, until her milk dries up completely. A bitch feeding puppies may need to take in four times her normal ration during the time the puppies are making the heaviest demands on her. A high protein diet is essential, so plenty of fresh meat should be added to her normal diet. Most bitches look in good health during their pregnancy but they can look pretty poor after whelping. For the first few days, the bitch may pant and fuss, sometimes giving every indication that another whelp is tucked under her belt, but then she will settle into a rhythm of sleeping, feeding and caring. It is not necessary

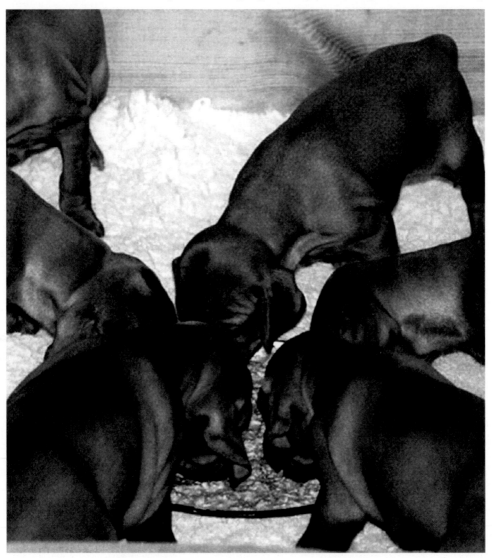

Puppies no longer dependent on their dam. Photo: White

to give her milk in order that she produces milk – this is an old wives' tale. So also is that the poor mum must be starved so that her milk reduces and dries up when the time comes for the puppies to be weaned. Gradually remove her; to begin with a couple of hours before the puppies eat. Once they are on four meals, aim to have her away from them with a quick top-up after the last meal to relieve her.

Sometimes milk may drip from her nipples but do not be tempted to express it to relieve the engorged breasts, otherwise the cycle will be perpetuated. Give her plenty of exercise, restrict her fluids and, if the weather is warm and she likes swimming, this will help to relieve much of her discomfort. The vet can provide pills to aid drying up the milk but the condition will right itself after two or three days. The bitch usually gets her figure back after 10–12 weeks. I had a bitch who won a CC three months after whelping! Obviously some bitches do take longer than others. Also much depends on how many litters she has had, and how soon she comes off her pups.

Weaning is a crucial time in the puppy's life. A set back at this stage of development can severely affect his growth. Some breeders wean their puppies onto a semi-solid milk feed to start with. Others prefer to commence weaning by giving good quality cooked or raw minced meat, such as beef, lamb or chicken. The bitch will often indicate when she feels the puppies are ready to wean by regurgitating her food for them.

When the time comes to start weaning, it will be necessary to organise the procedure in such a way that all goes calmly without confusion. If there is no routine, puppies will be crying and whining in the most distressing way. For instance, if puppies are being hand fed to start with, those who have fed should be separated from those who have not, otherwise there is no way of knowing which has eaten and which has not.

As the puppies grow on and feed from dishes, it is much easier to feed the litter divided into two, for instance four bitches in a penned-off area and four dogs outside it. Thus the control over what seems like an army is greater and each puppy can be observed as he eats. When dividing the puppies, always put the large ones together to feed. In this way the smaller ones are not pushed out.

If a supplementary milk feed is necessary after a week or two, one of the simplest methods is to feed the pups three hourly and then four hourly. For the first feed, for example, feed four bitches by hand leaving the four dogs to have a good feed from the dam. For the second feed, hand feed the dogs allowing the four bitches to have a good feed from the dam. After each feed those that have been hand fed should go back on the dam so that they can feed from whatever is left. Puppies normally lap towards the end of the second week. If supplementary feeding is necessary before that, they will need to be bottle fed.

Weaning - the method

To give the puppy the idea of chewing and eating instead of sucking, roll a small amount of raw, finely-chopped beef into a ball in the palm of your hand. Sit the pup on your knee, and hold the morsel of meat in your right hand. At first, the puppy will take time to get the idea. This is his first venture on his own, and how he reacts to the experience will give the breeder quite a bit of information concerning his character. Does he seem timid? Does he gather confidence? Is he a good eater? Does he

135

concentrate? Observing these early patterns will give clues to the pup's needs, even at this age. After the puppy has had its first taste of meat, put him back to feed from the dam. This will help him to settle.

Give the puppies the same routine the following day and, if all is well, try cooked finely-chopped beef and a complete food the following day, ensuring that it is mushed to resemble the dam's regurgitated food. Feed it in a shallow bowl on the floor – use two or three bowls if necessary – and observe closely. If one or two puppies are not interested, encourage them a little by putting some food on your finger and letting them lick it off. Allow the dam to go back in with the puppies to feed them afterwards. Increase these two feeds as the weeks go by and, as long as there are no tummy upsets, you can feed chicken, tripe and fish, as well as beef. When these meals are well established, introduce a milk and cereal meal in the morning, following the same principles, until the litter is well established on one milk, one meat, one milk and one meat feed. Feed the litter four times a day, four hourly. Meanwhile, gradually keep the dam away from the puppies after their feeds. By this time she will probably be heartily sick of them! As they grow on, the dam can find them very demanding, and it is quite distressing to see her mauled by her young ones. Sometimes a bitch will refuse to go into her puppies once they start being weaned, feeling her maternal duties are over. Somehow she realises that they are no longer dependent on her. She will happily see them off to their new homes without a backward glance. Now she can return to gentle exercise, and if she has a swim each day, all the better. It will help her to muscle up again and her undercarriage will soon disappear.

At seven weeks the puppies should be on four meals a day, two cereal meals a day and two meat meals. For example:

8.00am
milk and cereal meal
2 tablespoon powdered milk
2 tablespoon cereal
approximately 7oz of water

12.00pm
meat and biscuit or complete food meal
2–3oz of minced meat
2–3oz of meal or biscuit
The food must be soaked to a palatable consistency.

4.00pm as morning feed

8.00pm as lunchtime feed

Meat can be chicken, beef, tripe, ox hearts or rabbit; whatever suits the puppies and, of course, whatever is available and suits the purse.

The puppies must have the correct vitamins so they may also have eggs, fish or even Heinz baby foods. At this stage the bitch will need approximately 1kg (2lb) of meat a day and 0.8kg (1.5lb) of biscuit or complete food, split into three or four meals as well as plenty of fluids – water and milk drinks.

By the time a puppy is three months old, his feeding routine and his capacity for accepting any new food should be fairly well established. However, one of my puppies had an eating problem that defied my feeling that no puppy is stupid enough to starve himself. This once-lovely russet bundle of puppy fat shrank visibly to a bag of bones and limp skin. Obviously, an ill puppy will not eat, nor will a wormy one. I'm talking about the puppy who drives you to distraction, who takes a couple of mouthfuls and then races about full of energy. Obviously the gastric juices are not functioning the way they were. Somehow the routine and conditioning have changed. This can coincide with a change of environment, pecking order, missing litter mates or routine. In this case, I had kept the puppy from the recent litter and he was now eight weeks old. I tried all the usual ploys to no avail: delectable, tasty, warm dishes of anything I thought he'd take to, small amounts four-hourly, no titbits in between to dull the appetite. His mate was an older bitch whom I thought might encourage him to eat in competition, no headway there. One day in despair I was trying to handfeed him. I dropped some food on the floor; like a demon he scoffed it up, just as puppies do when the dam regurgitates. Tail wagging, he asked for more and, step by step, we progressed from floor, to hand, to bowl, with me sitting with the older bitch who had already eaten hers. After a week there was a marked improvement. If he relapsed, we went through the whole procedure again. The trick is to stay calm, still and quiet in order not to break his concentration. It is fatal, of course, to have the general hubbub of the family around you. Pavlov proved how repetition induced behaviour patterns with his dogs. This is what we are trying to do with our tricky eaters.

While the puppies are on a milk diet, they drink very little water, but it is as well to offer them a drink after a meal. It is not advisable to leave the bowl down all day as they will only paddle in it – all right in the summer but a bit cold in the winter.

Worming Puppies

Even though the dam's worming programme is up to date, and even though there is no sign of worms in the puppies' faeces, it is absolutely essential that the puppies have a strict worming routine recommended by the vet. All dogs have worms and all puppies have them also or, rather, the larvae of the worm is in their system.

The most common worms in the dog are the roundworm and the tapeworm. It is the roundworm that can infest the puppy. If the infestation is severe, he will lose condition and his growth will be stunted, because the worms feed off his tissues. The symptoms may be loss of appetite or a ravenous appetite, diarrhoea, potbelly, and lack of sparkle. If the condition has not been treated, worms like fine grey threads may be seen in the faeces and, of course, the older they get the larger they grow.

Generally, the puppy receives his first worming dose at four or five weeks old. This is usually a syrup. After that he may be given a pill recommended by your vet at seven weeks, nine weeks and so on until he is six months old. The pills are best given after a meal and popped down the puppy's throat. The method of putting any pill in food, hoping the dog may eat it without knowing, is hit or miss. Much better to educate him from the start to accept that you will open his mouth and place the pill on the back of his tongue. One day he may need life-saving pills such as antibiotics. If he is trained to accept pills from you, you will have no trouble.

Approximate Pattern of Development
From Birth to Twelve Weeks

7–10 days:	eyes open.
14 days:	ears open.
18 days:	barking begins.
18–20 days:	early play movements.
3 weeks:	stand upright.
4 weeks:	walk and run.
21 days:	baby teeth.
3 weeks onwards:	eat from dish.
3–3$^{1}/_{2}$ weeks:	balance on their own for urine and bowel movement.
3$^{1}/_{2}$–4 weeks:	vigorous play among pups.
4 weeks:	body twitching during sleep disappears.
4–5 weeks:	pecking order established within litter, personalities begin to emerge.
5 weeks:	hearing acute.
5 weeks:	play with toys, play constructively with litter mates, hiding, chasing.
5–6 weeks:	learn mouth and paw skills, body control.
10 weeks:	able to sleep continuously through night (11pm–7am).
12 weeks:	gradually through to five or six months: voluntary control of urination and defecation.

The Litter Develops

Healthy whelps are quiet, sleep, warm, round, firm and plump. The skin and mucous membranes are pink, and a fold of skin collapses as soon as you let it go, as it does in all healthy dogs. Poorly puppies are limp when they are picked up. They have wrinkled, cold skin which feels damp. They squirm and cry constantly, or lie cold and inert. It is hard to believe that the obsessively caring dam will leave a sick whelp alone, out in the cold, but in fact, she leaves it to die.

For the first three weeks, the puppies feed and sleep. They are born with certain patterns, but they can neither see, hear, nor walk, and they are not able to urinate or defecate without the dam's stimulation. The dam will keep both the puppies and the whelping box spotlessly clean, until the litter is ready to be weaned. By the end of the third week, the whelps make enormous strides. The brain, which is inactive at birth, develops rapidly, and from the 21st day the puppy's environment starts to shape its entire life, its intelligence and its emotions. This little being will start to relate to all that is going on around it. This is a time when a pup can become extremely upset, and it cannot adjust to great change, as it will do in two weeks time. I have often observed that contented puppies in the whelping box become extremely disturbed if it is opened up; clearly they are not ready for the outside world. But when they start trying to climb out, and then the whelping box is opened up, they welcome the extension of their freedom.

A puppy is born with certain functional patterns, such as sucking and sleeping, that enable him to survive. As he grows from day to day, his behaviour is influenced by his earliest experiences. Therefore the way in which he is imprinted is vital to his welfare if he is to reach his full potential. Emotional sensitivity is a necessary part of the socialisation process and this (automatically) makes the puppy susceptible to psychological damage if he is not treated well. I am suggesting that those of us who have known a shy Vizsla, an aggressive Vizsla, an excitable Vizsla, a fussy one, the clinging type or the one that could not work, should not always put the blame on the poor gene and the well-worn pedigree. I am proposing that some of this behaviour could be a result of ignoring a critical need in our puppy's rearing.

Extension to the puppies freedom. Photo: I Smith

What is Imprinting?

Imprinting is an irreversible process by which a puppy is exposed to repeated stimuli appropriate to his stage of development. He is programmed as a computer so that an impression is established in the central nervous system. This 'impression' is physical and is termed a 'nervous pathway'.

It has been established by intensive research programmes on dog behaviour, one of which was run at the Jackson Laboratory in America for nearly 20 years, that there are particular periods in the very early life of the puppy when this process is at its most effective. John Paul Scott and John L Fuller have written the most authoritative volume, *Genetics and the Social Behaviour of the Dog*, based on their research at the Jackson Laboratory. Particularly important was the discovery of 'critical periods' which exert a lasting influence upon adult behaviour and a dog's relationship with humans. I will discuss these 'critical periods' in detail later but first let us establish how 'imprinting' takes place. Unlike the learning process which requires some active participation from the subject, imprinting is an entirely passive process; the puppy has no choice in the end result.

chapter 9

With the advances in scientific understanding of the structure and function of the nervous system we could talk of any dog's attributes in terms of the underlying 'neuronal structure'. A neurone is the elementary cell of the nervous system. Billions of neurones make up the brain, spinal cord and all the nerves emanating from them to the entire body, also from all the body's structures, organs and specific senses back to the brain and spinal cord.

A neuronal pathway consists of a series of connected neurones along which an impulse must pass. Thus a puppy exposed to artificial feeding from a human instead of its dam will have this repeated experience impressed or imprinted on a selected pathway. In his original work with goslings, Conrad Lorenz found that in the absence of the true geese parents, the young birds adopted him as a parent substitute. The gosling's infant nervous system was exposed exclusively to the reception of stimuli from a human and so humans were imprinted instead of geese on the susceptible neurones. What can be observed at a very early age in a developing puppy is the interaction between the environment and the definitive qualities of the animal. It will be found that a litter of Vizsla puppies, all raised under the same conditions, with identical dam and sire and identical feeding routine, will still react differently to their environment because their innate qualities will not be the same. Thus the puppy's personality is affected by its inborn temperamental characteristics and shaped by the stimuli he receives from his environment.

An example of this is given by an incident affecting two 12-week old puppies, a brother and sister reared together. We were standing at a zebra crossing and a lorry came hurtling past. Too late, I realised that both puppies were badly frightened. They were shaking and panting, their ears pinned back and their tails clamped between their legs. I reassured them both as best I could. The bitch responded immediately. From birth she had been adventurous, taking each unknown step without a backward glance, very bright and quick to learn, always full of confidence. She had had a fright and showed fear but handled it quite differently from her brother. He had always been a gentler puppy altogether, slower to accept changes, hesitating at each unknown step but, once taken, he would be full of confidence. His reaction lasted much longer. He shivered and shook all way home, wishing only to slink into the house. He stayed there pathetically, his eyes darting round fearfully. It took days to reassure him, repeatedly taking him back to the same spot when there was little traffic about, until one day he was able to walk across glancing neither to the left nor to the right, nor behind him. As we stood on the same spot where the lorry had gone by, his tail would be up and no sign of worry. They had both received the same imprinting and socialisation from birth, both had received the same stimuli in experiencing the 'fright' but had dealt with it differently.

It is not profitable to attempt to estimate what is the proportionate contribution of 'nature and nurture' but it is profitable to stress the need for domestic dogs to be allowed to grow up in an environment in which correct imprinting by human beings comes about. It must be stated that the brain of any species, be it dog or human during infancy, does not distinguish between a good or useful trait or a bad or harmful trait. It is up to the breeder and owner to assure themselves that they are doing all they can to socialise their puppies in the best possible manner. Any puppy which has not been handled by humans will never attach himself to humans in later life; he will appear shy and display a great lack of trust in people.

Goran Bergman states in his book *Why Does Your Dog Do That* that the results of imprinting are in some respects different in different breeds. Some appear to be easily imprinted, others less so. Some become, through imprinting, extremely strongly tied to one person while other breeds are always just as friendly towards all friendly people they meet. He also states that Setters, Springers, Spaniels and other related game dogs have a reputation for being friendly and unaggressive. The Vizsla is part of this group. I think most breeders would agree that he is not difficult to imprint. His capacity for loving and desiring human affection and his need to serve – as with all gundogs – allows him to enjoy his working relationship with humans. His attachment to the human race is a delight. A Vizsla which has not had the advantages of good socialisation is a poor, shy, cringing creature, longing to be friendly but terrified to put his trust in

Russetmantle Marsh (Hogan); a well adjusted puppy.

anyone or any other Vizsla – or breed for that matter. The Vizsla is not necessarily a one-man dog although obviously he will be more attached to the person who cares for, feeds and exercises him. I have known instances where he has been expected to be a 'one man dog' and this type of relationship has not succeeded. In one case, a newly-acquired puppy had been expected to show total loyalty to one member of the family and it resulted in confusion, the puppy becoming fearful of the member who insisted on forcing his affection and firm discipline in order to make the Vizsla puppy 'his' dog. The puppy finally refused to walk or accept food from his 'owner' but would from any other member of the family. Thus not only was the puppy psychologically disturbed but the family was upset too!

The Critical Periods

Let us now consider these critical periods in a puppy's life when he is most susceptible to imprinting. It is important to say that some experienced breeders feel that it is too dogmatic and rigid to insist that unless puppies are introduced to particular stimuli by a certain date they will miss out. There are exceptions to every rule and I am sure in this case there are many exceptions. We are dealing with living beings, not inanimate objects but it is as well to know and understand the well-researched data first and then to apply this to the experience.

Michael Fox's book *Understanding Your Dog* provides us with well-researched information about how the puppy's brain develops and how its maturing relates to what behaviour the puppy is capable of at different stages of growth.

Clarence Pfaffenberger, who wrote the fascinating book *The New Knowledge of Dog Behaviour,* and also Scott and Fuller after extensive study all agreed the premise that **if a puppy experiences proper socialisation from 3–16 weeks he will reach a satisfactory level of behaviour.** They submit that if this is not observed and the puppy has not been allowed the dignity of being an individual, it will have no ties with people.

Beginning to stand. Photo: Dr S Gottlieb

Scott writes:

...the evidence is that puppies have a short period early in life when positive social relationships are established with members of their kind, after which it becomes increasingly difficult or impossible to establish them. The same applies to their relationship with human companions.

Clarence Pfaffenberger writes:

a puppy who has no socialising before it is sixteen weeks has little chance of becoming the sort of dog that anyone of us would want. The time is so short, once it has gone it can never be retrieved. The implications of this in the development of the dog are so great that it behoves a puppy raiser to employ this time wisely. It can never be made up at an older age.

So when are the clearly recognisable critical stages that are characterised by certain behaviour patterns and emotional reactions? The first three weeks of a puppy's life are spent surviving. It needs food, warmth, maternal care, plenty of sleep and its litter mates. It makes enormous physical strides by the end of the third week. It can urinate and defecate without being massaged by its dam. Its teeth begin to appear, it can hear, its eyes may have opened by the tenth day or thereabouts. It has learned to crawl backwards and forwards and it may be able to totter.

Its brain, inactive at birth, starts to develop a number of neuronal pathways but it is not until the puppy is three weeks of age that these are fully functioning and this is when the puppy reaches social awareness. His environment starts to shape his life, his intelligence and emotions begin to function, socialisation, as the Americans call it, or imprinting can begin. Thus, from 3–7 weeks is the first critical stage.

It is said that the brain and nervous system develops to the capacity of an adult at this time, but without the experience. This is the period when ideally the puppy should be imprinted by its own dog world, that is, its dam and litter mates, and by a human being or human beings in order to form stabile relationships with humans and dogs. In nature, most animals and birds are imprinted by their own species but, since the dog needs to form attachments to the human world at this time, the more the humans have to do with the puppy, the stronger the imprint will be. This little being will start to feel sociable, he is aware of his Vizsla litter-mates, his mother, or any other dogs or humans who come into his field of vision. He will wag his tail and totter towards his owners. If he is taken from the nest at this time and socialised alone with humans he can become over attached and will find it difficult to relate to other dogs. He will become 'dog-shy'. If he does not get sufficient human contact, he will grow up to be 'people-shy'. If he has too much human female contact, he will be shy of men and vice-versa. Thus at this stage without close attention to these specific needs, the puppy will not reach a satisfactory level of behaviour.

Pfaffenberger states in his book:

the period of twenty-one to twenty-eight days is so strange to the puppy that at no other time in a puppy's life can he become so emotionally upset, nor could such an upset have such a lasting effect upon his social attitudes. I believe, if there is a time when a puppy needs its dam more than any other time, it is probably the fourth week, from the twenty-first day to the twenty-eighth day. This is the time of very rapid development emotionally, he should not be moved from his mother for any length of time during this week. To wean at this time may upset him so that he may never be able to compensate from the abrupt break. A week after at twenty-eight days he has already become so well adjusted that weaning will have much less effect.

At this point I have to say that I always wean puppies at three weeks. A large litter brings a bitch down, and at 21 days baby teeth can soon become pinpoint sharp. Sensitive and cautious weaning takes time and patience and, although I certainly agree that at this stage puppies can become extremely upset, as long as the process is not rushed and the dam is there to comfort, by five weeks the puppies can be completely independent of the dam.

So we can see that at this time the puppy's life in the nest becomes suddenly very active and interesting. He needs as much affection and fondling from humans as possible. He needs to have children visit him and play gently with him. He can be removed for much longer periods and, by the sixth week, the dam can be removed from her pups without any harm done. After the fourth week, if he spends some time each day with humans on his own, he will form his attachments as a companion. It allows him to develop as an individual, shaping his character and gaining self confidence. If his life until now has been filled with loving care from his own kind and from humans he will be well on his way. The second critical period is from 7–12 weeks.

This is the time to form the man-dog relationship. The puppy has been weaned by now. His dam is no longer interested in spending much time with her young. He can make the transition from his litter mates to his new home (if he is to be sold) without trauma as long as he has all that he requires – plenty of care and attention. He needs this change. It is not necessarily as desirable for him to stay with his dam or his siblings as could be supposed. If he is left with his siblings in an enclosed area without the chance of experiencing new people, new places, new territory, new noises, he will suffer from institutionalisation. An outgoing puppy may adjust later, having had the necessary treatment at the 3–7 week period, but an innately more timid individual may find each new experience in his life becoming a dreadful trauma. If Vizsla puppies

Russetmantle puppies ready for the next stage. Photo: White

are not sold at this time, the breeder will need to spend a lot of his day socialising the puppies – no easy task. The Vizsla is a lively, vital, intelligent dog and, when a puppy, cannot be left to his own devices for long. He requires his very active brain to be put to full use. The sort of treatment he receives from humans during this period will affect his attitude to them. Because every dog inherits the 'pack instinct' this is when he will be ready to accept human dominance. Never again will he be so prepared to yield, or the human leaders so able to bind him to them in order to shape the character traits, as during the first and second critical stages. Training can only be in the form of games but, with affection, gentleness and firmness, the puppy learns who he must respect.

The third critical period is from 12–16 weeks. This is also the start of the juvenile period which continues until the puppy reaches full sexual maturity. Serious training can and should be effected. I am not necessarily including training for work. Many trainers differ in their views as to when a Vizsla puppy should be trained for the gun. I mean elementary obedience and manners.

At this time, although a puppy may have accepted his human pack leader, and had all the advantages of maturing as an individual, he will be feeling his feet, asserting himself and trying out everyone and every dog in his world. It can be a disturbing time for any other Vizslas he may be living with, for he will challenge each one playfully and, if he is not 'put in his place' in the hierarchy, he can be very disruptive as he can be in the human world. At this stage, a Vizsla puppy's boisterousness and energy seems to be at its height. He is no longer a cuddly little puppy, but lithe and strong. At this age he is too big to carry and will find every chance he can to wilfully flout authority. This sense of fun and need for activity seems boundless. It is a difficult time for his owner, but it can also be a very enjoyable time, for a Vizsla can enchant you if you have a sense of humour, because he has learned to clown.

One of my puppies amused us for hours at this stage. She would sit on a chair with a tennis ball, gently pushing it to the edge. She would hesitate and look up, regard her audience and deliberately push it over the edge with her nose, wait until one of us picked it up for her and repeat the performance all over again. She had us all retrieving her ball beautifully and dutifully, but trying to teach her to retrieve anything to us was quite a different matter.

It is absolutely crucial that by now the Vizsla puppy respects his owner and the human world. If there is any sign of an aggressive challenge, then he must be reprimanded. If it is not corrected at this stage, then it could become a serious problem as he grows older. A sense of territorial rights will be developing as well, so it behoves the owner to prepare himself. If the reason for this probable behaviour is understood and it is dealt with firmly and explicitly, the puppy will learn that there are certain modes of behaviour that are totally unacceptable and he will obey.

For example, if a puppy is sitting on a chair and the owner requires him to move and the puppy growls, the owner has the opportunity to confront the situation and settle it once and for all. If it is shelved, the puppy will learn in no time that growling, and biting too, is very effective if the end result is that he gets his own way every time. So we go back to the repeated stimuli of what we want in order that he behaves in a particular way. But here we have an example of conditioning wherein the puppy by now is playing an assertive role. The puppy growls, he is removed forcibly off the chair with appropriate verbal remonstrance such as 'No!'. The puppy may respect this and learn his lesson, but if he jumps back and growls again then he is deliberately challenging authority, so he needs to be taught that:

- he can only sit on the chair when allowed
- he must never growl at you

It must be demonstrated clearly by the owner that this behaviour is not acceptable and the remonstration must be repeated over and over again until his challenging ceases. He has to respond now, not tomorrow or next week, but now. I believe that Vizslas rarely show challenging aggression if they are sensibly handled when they are puppies.

A puppy from three to four months can develop phobias, demonstrating a sudden fear of strangers, unfamiliar places and loud sounds. This can be very worrying if he has been or appeared to be perfectly well adjusted before this. Provided that he has had all the necessary rearing up to this time and is well adjusted, he will grow out of this anxiety period. He needs reassurance and repeated stimuli of the same experience that caused the anxiety, understanding of course that there are some unpleasant experiences such as fire or the dog next door who would fight to the death, that no dog would ever be expected to accept without fear and if he did he would be foolish. But the puppy will be reassured if he is given the opportunity to meet many strangers, taken to unfamiliar places, has car rides, train rides, even boat rides. Widen his horizons; do not cosset him, but help him to learn that his fears are unfounded. Sheltering him in the kitchen or kennel will only aggravate his anxiety. What he needs is experience. If this stage is taken too seriously by the owner, the Vizsla's tension can increase. I find that he can be laughed out of this mood and that jollying him along by playing with him can help him to forget.

Russetmantle puppies. One major quality to look for in gundog puppies is confidence.
Photo: White

Beginning to adjust to the outside world.

In Conclusion

Donna Brander, behaviour consultant and Honorary Fellow of the Small Animal Behaviour Unit at the Royal (Dick) School of Veterinary Studies at the University of Edinburgh, has had over 25 years' experience of diagnosis and treatment of behaviour problems in companion animals. She also owns a Vizsla. In a 1996 article written for *'Gundogs' magazine*, she discusses the difficulty of assessing a puppy's temperament since he is evolving as he develops and, in the first few months of life, spends much of his time role-playing. She writes:

One major quality to look for in a gundog is confidence. Look for the puppy who has a quick recovery time. New experiences can be met by an initial startled reaction but should fairly quickly be followed by recovery and curiosity. Be wary of the one who repeatedly hides from new experiences with a slow recovery because even intense socialisation will not necessarily help in such a case.

The single most important issue in successful puppy ownership is socialisation and habituation at the critical age of 3–14 weeks. This period was determined as long ago as 1963 by behaviourists Scott and Fuller, who found that if puppies were not handled and accustomed to a range of stimuli and environments by 14 weeks of age, there was a lasting detrimental effect on their character and ability to cope in the big wide world.

At three weeks, she notes:

The puppies become truly mobile, there is a surge of electrical activity in the brain. They begin to interact increasingly with their environment and companions. From this age onwards we should 'drip feed' as many good experiences as possible so that puppies grow up to be sociable and confident. It is generally considered that the ideal average age for a puppy to leave the litter is 7–8 weeks of age.

Observations on the puppies in the box are crucial from the breeder's point of view:

The first one out of the box may be a puppy showing confidence or may be a puppy pushed out by the more determined members dominating the territory. This puppy may find it more amenable to join the human group peering into the box. While this puppy may bond with humans, it may not react so well with its own. Whilst the obviously shy, fearful puppy should never be a sensible choice, the quiet, aloof puppy may not be shy but may have attained a certain status in the litter which allows it to have a special place and does not require the submissive fawning behaviour of its mates. This puppy may be seen to have attained a particular sleeping area for itself, already demonstrating confidence and independence, allowing it to pull away from its litter mates and establish a place of its own.

Even though it is very difficult to believe that the difference of a week or two could have such long-term effects, having the knowledge that there are such important stages in the life of a puppy must inevitably increase the breeder's awareness of his needs. In my opinion, the Hungarian Vizsla, with his particularly high sense of awareness and intelligence, his gentle temperament and the need for giving and receiving much physical affection, his contrariness and strength of will, is such a complex, emotional creature that incorrect socialisation makes him a very insecure, fearful, unstable dog who goes to pieces with little provocation. Such a dog would be absolutely useless for work, and does not makes a trustworthy pet.

But given all the rearing he needs, no one could deny that he can be the most constant companion anyone could wish for.

A well adjusted adult. Photo: Buller

chapter 10

A Puppy's Characteristics

The litter is ready to leave the nest and each puppy ready to make his own way. From a breeder's point of view this is a crucial time. All the previous planning and arranging has come to fruition. Is there the Vizsla of all time in this litter? A future dual champion? Such are the questions and the excitement, intensity and anticipation engendered by these little scraps of russet gold.

Wilks' Sh Ch Russetmantle October aged 10 weeks.
Photo: Dr S Gottlieb

'How can you bear to let them go?' puppy purchasers ask. I can bear to let them go, if I feel the quality of life provided is just what they need. I love the hours spent deciding which puppy would best suit which home. After pairing them up, I am thrilled when I hear that the new owners are pleased and enchanted by the little Vizsla who will share the next 10–14 years of their lives. Any breeder has a great responsibility in this respect. After all, if you sell someone a coat and it does not suit, it probably ends up in jumble sale. What happens to a puppy if it does not suit?

The breeder needs to assess which puppy will best fulfil the customer's requirements. The more time spent watching, handling, petting and understanding the puppy, the more familiar each puppy's characteristics become. One puppy tries to scramble up, another pushes him aside, already asserting himself. Another sits and gazes, patiently watching, while the others vie for every attention. Meanwhile, who is that sniffing and snorting around on his own with an independent air? He's using his nose and seems to be onto something, his tail wagging furiously. The quiet one who gazes at you so persistently and loves to be petted may suit the loving family who have owned dogs all their lives, perhaps he may be too gentle and doesn't have enough 'oomph' to work. Now there is one who really takes your eye. Trotting about bossing all the others, getting into mischief. Good topline already, chest well down, plenty of skin to grow into. As he sits you laugh as his skin falls in folds over his rump. He looks at you and wags his tail. His front is already acceptable at seven weeks so perhaps he has good show and work potential?

And so the gazing and choosing continues. Meanwhile their relationship with you and with each other flourishes. You will soon learn who accepts your authority more readily than others. You have noticed one more reluctant and less outgoing. If you put your hand out he does not approach you. He is the one who is always last, he does not seem to heed you. This is the puppy who needs special care and attention. As likely as not, individual loving and socialising by gentle children can help a puppy of this type learn to communicate. Once he has gained confidence away from his litter mates, after a few days of this 'treatment', although he may never be a bouncing extrovert, he will be a perfectly happy, well-adjusted puppy.

Beware of any very shy, nervous, overly-sensitive puppy who flinches at any noise. Also watch out for the overly-aggressive one, the one who at a few weeks old growls or snarls if you pick him up. You cannot blame your breeding programme, for even puppies from the same litter cannot have the same genetic construction and every now and again extremes can occur. Even so, it is the breeder's responsibility. Puppies like this should not be sold to unsuspecting customers. It could cause heartbreak.

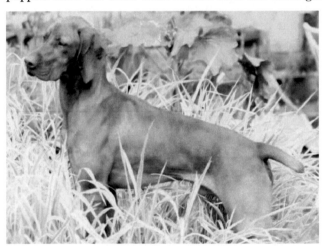

Gottlieb's Sh Ch Russetmantle Crisp; a muscled adult dog.
Photo: Dr S Gottlieb

Although the breeder may take great care counselling future owners, it is always advisable to encourage them to see as many adult Vizslas as possible if they do not know the breed well. A photograph can be very deceptive. The reality could be quite a shock! This muscled, lively dog may not be what they require after all. So three visits may be necessary:

(a) to see the adult Vizsla, the dam and sire if possible, before booking a puppy
(b) to visit the puppies in the nest at 5 or 6 weeks old
(c) to pick the puppy up to take home at 7 or 8 weeks

By this time it will be much easier to match the puppy's temperament to the needs and lifestyle of the future owners. The couple who like an active life with their pet, the person interested in shooting, the retired couple or a family with noisy children, the show home or the gamekeeper who kennels his dogs, all provide different environments that suit some Vizslas better than others. It is vital that the breeder is prepared to refuse a customer if he feels the home would not be suitable.

On the sale of the puppy, the new owner will require:
- a diet sheet
- details of worming and injections
- Kennel Club registration papers (if available) signed by the breeder for transfer
- the pedigree
- any information available on the breed

Unfortunately, some new puppy owners do not follow feeding instructions in spite of painstaking advice from the breeder. It can be very disappointing for the breeder and, of course, disturbing for the puppy because as likely as not he will have a bad tummy ache.

In spite of the hazards of selling puppies, there is nothing so satisfying or so pleasing as when doting owners return proudly, presenting their adolescent Vizsla, strong and healthy and obviously adoring his family.

Buying a Vizsla Puppy

Whatever your purpose in selecting the Hungarian Vizsla as your breed, you may find you have to wait some time if you wish to buy your puppy from a reputable breeder. It is clearly sensible to do as much research as you can into every aspect of the breed before embarking on buying a puppy. Seek out a breeder who will willingly answer your questions, understands and indeed encourages your wish to have as much information as possible and your request to visit the kennels. There are various types of Vizsla and it is only when the purchaser has seen a good many that he can discover which he prefers. Never allow yourself to be pushed into a sale. Any caring breeder will be pleased to spend time with a customer who is offering a good home. It is never wise to buy a puppy if partners do not agree. It can cause grounds for separation! Meanwhile the puppy suffers unbearably in the ensuing arguments, however good his temperament. No Vizsla of seven or eight weeks old can tolerate stress and tension. He is extremely susceptible to physical and psychological trauma at this age. He is entirely dependent on the humans in his life to supply his needs and does not have the comforting support of his dam or litter mates any longer. If he is the centre of arguments and shouting matches, it will not take long before he displays signs of deprivation. He will become disturbed himself, may be restless and clinging, whining incessantly. He may show signs of aggression or fear or destructiveness. His sensitive hearing can be affected by the constant rumpus. To escape from it all he may creep away and hide. All these signs indicate his desperate loneliness, isolation and unhappiness.

I do not feel a puppy should be left alone all day. If all members of the family are out, he could tolerate two or three hours alone, but the kitchen could be demolished by the family's return! Neither do I feel a puppy is happy kennelled by itself all day. In both cases it would be strongly recommended that he has a companion. This should be discussed with the breeder before acquiring a puppy.

If you are offered a puppy much older than eight weeks, you will need to make certain that he is a happy, outgoing little Vizsla. For instance, if he is as old as three or four months, it would be very risky to buy him unless you knew the circumstances in which he had been reared. You would need to be quite satisfied that he had been socialised adequately. If he is still in a pen with other unsold litter mates, he is not likely to have had the chance of leading any sort of independent life. Although he may appear a forward, friendly puppy when with his brothers and sisters, on his own he could show signs of shyness, hesitation and stress, having lost all the support and security of his pack that he has known and lived with from birth. I would suggest that you have him on trial for a week so that you are able to see how he behaves away from his environment. A breeder should be satisfied with this arrangement and may suggest it himself if he cares for the welfare of the puppy.

Be very suspicious of a breeder who guarantees a perfect pet, show or gundog. Few dog people, even with years of experience behind them, would ever commit themselves. It would be misleading a customer. At best, he could say 'In my opinion, this puppy has the essentials at the moment.'

The most successful show or working dogs do not necessarily produce the best puppies so do not be blinded by all the winning rosettes and cups on the sideboard. It does not always follow that all the progeny will be excellent, although the *likelihood* of getting a good dog from good stock with working and showing lines in the pedigree increases the chances – but many a bad workman blames his tools.

Author with puppies. Photo: Smith

What to Look for in a Vizsla Puppy

Temperament

A bold, lively, exuberant, playful puppy is how he should appear. An aloof, reserved manner is not the true Vizsla temperament. The pup should be interested in everything and everyone, his nose seeking out every interesting smell. As he walks towards you with his tail wagging, showing pleasure and confidence, you can be assured that he is a puppy who wants your affection and will give you as much. When you pick him up he may freeze for a moment but relaxes as he licks or gnaws you, whatever the case may be. He should feel settled in the warmth and comfort of your arms, enjoying his contact with you even for a brief moment. It is important that you feel his confidence and sureness of you. He may struggle to get down but you have felt that moment of contact and contentment. That puppy will be the one who has the true Vizsla temperament, regardless of his potential.

The puppy who wriggles incessantly, neither allowing you to cuddle nor stroke him can turn out to be a livewire, a fidgety, restless Vizsla, one you will find difficult to relax with in your sitting room. Clearly, the hesitant, shy puppy will need much reassurance, love and support. The bold puppy who shakes when you pick him up may develop into the aggressive, fearful Vizsla who may bite. Although many Vizsla puppies are hesitant and shake at strange new experiences, they regain their confidence in a matter of seconds. Thus the purchaser needs to spend time with the puppy he is offered and, if he does not like what he sees, he has every right to change his mind, just as the breeder can change his mind if he feels the customer is not right for the puppy.

Some Physical Points

A Vizsla puppy should be sturdy and strong. Although at seven or eight weeks he does not have the elegance and grace of the adult, at this stage he should look in proportion, his conformation having a balance that is not exaggerated. Look at him after 10 or 11 weeks and the length of his body or length of leg would not form the compactness that it should and can have at eight weeks. By that time his legs will have grown too long and, as likely as not, every part of him will be out of proportion (because frequently the bone structure develops at a different rate) but, as he matures, his good outline will reappear. His chest should look broad and deep. Never expect a puppy to develop a deep chest if it is not so to start with. His chest must be well down to his elbow as he stands sideways. A straight back is essential at this age and, again, for a while this may be lost before the muscles develop. He needs to have rather strong, thick legs with good feet. A puppy with enormous flat, flabby feet with toes splayed apart standing easterly and westerly is not going to have good feet when he reaches adulthood. The foot should not be out of proportion, although soft and un-used. When the puppy stands alert his foot should look compact and the leg straight. A fiddle front at this stage does not grow into a good front. Do not worry about the knobbly knees as the knee is one of the growing points, rather beware a smooth, flat one, because the puppy may remain small. At this stage the quarters should have strength and a good, almost exaggerated turn of stifle. The second thigh should also be well developed. A straight back leg is required for the dog that needs strength for pulling, the Vizsla needs to move his body forward, powering his body into action as he moves.

If a puppy constantly holds his tail 'gay' (perpendicular instead of horizontal) or if he has a sickle tail (a 'gay' tail with a bend towards the forehand) he will probably continue to do so into adulthood. As likely as not, he will pass the condition on to his progeny and it has probably been passed down from his ancestors. Thus, it is important to look for a puppy who holds a horizontal tail.

The head should be in proportion to the body, appearing neither too large and heavy nor too small and narrow. In profile, the muzzle should not look tapered nor the lip too tight. The eye should be fairly tight, covering the whites. Beware of a loose lower rim, because even at this stage the shape of the eye should be correct. The colour of the eye will be difficult to assess at eight weeks because it will still be in the transitional stage. If the sire, dam and the grandparents have the correct eye colour, it is practical to suppose that the eye will eventually become a shade darker in colour than the coat. The coat will probably be paler than in adulthood but, as the puppy matures, the coat starts to darken down the centre of the back and the ears and the legs. The last to darken are the shoulders so at this stage the Vizsla can have a rather mottled appearance. Again when attempting to assess a puppy's future coat colour it is better to rely on the knowledge of the breeder and the pedigree. For example, if the line is known to have light coats or ginger coats or very dark coats, it is likely that the progeny will inherit the same colour.

Unless the purchaser has no preference for the type of Vizsla he owns and does not plan to breed, it is well to know that the small, light-boned little specimen will not develop good strong bones, nor will an enormous one reduce to the correct size when he reaches adulthood. A Vizsla puppy is surprisingly heavy, and his legs are certainly not on the spindly side if he is a 'good un'. If he looks like a model of an adult he will have little to grow into. The coat should be loose and the head should have wrinkled skin, not as exaggerated as the Bloodhound or the Shar Pei, but at this stage it must not be tight. If there are any signs of physical abnormalities such as lameness, skin problems or diarrhoea, it is risky to take the puppy home unless you are perfectly satisfied that the condition has been dealt with by the breeder or the vet.

Preparing for Your Puppy's Homecoming

Be prepared to have your time consumed by the newcomer. Hours will be spent enjoying him if he is right for you. The naughtiness of the Vizsla puppy is incalculable. He will drive you to distraction with his rowdiness and sharp teeth, but his intelligence, charm, and familiarity will captivate you and his trainability will amaze you. From the start, he will make you respect him. That little golden dog has a quality of knowingness that can only be understood once you have acquired a Vizsla puppy.

A puppy is bound to feel strange and uncertain in his new surroundings, but he soon learns his way about, where he eats, where he sleeps, and who to relate to. The puppy needs warmth and affection, and will be desperately unhappy if he is left alone at first. Once he feels safe and secure, he will not mind nearly so much. A Vizsla cannot tolerate being on his own for long. He is strictly a companion dog who loves to be part of the family; he is not at all a solitary type. Vizslas are gregarious and love nothing better than to share their zeal and zest for living with the people in their lives.

Ask the breeder what food the puppy will require about a week before you fetch him. This will give you plenty of time to obtain all that is necessary in advance. Do follow the feeding routine as closely as possible to start with, whatever ideas you have on feeding. For the first few weeks it is important to follow exactly the routine as the breeder recommends. Your puppy will need his own basket or base, his own blanket and a bowl for water and one for food, a small leather collar and lead or a slip lead – I recommend the leather collar. Unless you really know what you are doing, the slip lead can tighten and choke him if he is the type of puppy who is stubborn at first. Do allow your puppy to have his box somewhere where he knows he will be left alone in peace when he feels like it. He needs a place of safety. It follows that if he is constantly disturbed when he is tired, he will become bad-tempered, so the household should understand and respect his need for privacy. If a puppy starts to snap at children who constantly tease or pick him up when he is trying to sleep, it is not the temperament of the puppy that is at fault, it is the character of the parents and children.

It is advisable to decide who is going to do all the 'dirty work' before the puppy arrives. His life should follow a set routine at first: meals on time, toilet training consistent, times for sleeping and times for playing. He will soon settle into the pattern of the household. If he has one person responsible for organising him he will feel more secure, learning in a matter of hours who he can refer to if there are any complaints!

One of the vital issues that occurs again and again is 'where does the puppy sleep?' It seems against many owners' principles to allow the puppy to sleep for the first few nights in the obvious place, which is the bedroom where there is human company and security. If the puppy is put in the kitchen, in the dark and alone for the first time, away from the siblings he has been used to sleeping with in a heap from the moment he was born, naturally he is going to cry, naturally he will relieve himself out of fear and cold. Then he will have to deal with irate humans in dressing gowns, desperate for a bit of 'shut eye', angry on two counts: first, because the household will be awake and, second, because the puppy's house training has not got off to a very good start. In contrast, the little puppy sleeping warm and secure in his box by your bed may stir once to go out. After a few nights, you can take the box downstairs. If the puppy makes a fuss, he can be corrected and reassured firmly from the human he has grown to trust, know and love, who would do him no harm.

Injections

Your new puppy is at risk until he has had all the necessary injections. Whatever treatment he has had while with the breeder it is well to consult your vet on this matter. He is the professional and it is he who has all the up-to-date literature on the research programmes that have been initiated recently, especially on the disease Parvo Virus, which has caused such anxiety over the last few years. This fatal disease mainly affects very young puppies and the older dog. When it first manifested itself, there was no antidote except that which was given to cats for this disease and of course, little or no research had been done on dogs. At last, we have a vaccine well tested and researched specifically for the dog. The early symptoms are vomiting and diarrhoea which will be blood-stained due to internal bleeding. In a very short space of time the dog is listless and dehydrated and complications result in a weak heart. The vet should be called without delay since it is better to be safe than sorry in this case. So the basic essential injections necessary are the vaccines for protection against Parvo Virus, Distemper, Hepatitis, Hardpad and Leptospirosis.

Distemper: This is a contagious disease. The symptoms are: loss of appetite, loss of condition, rise in temperature, a cough, eyes weak and running, offensive breath and furred tongue. Possible vomiting and diarrhoea. The worst complication is the effect on the nervous system. The membranes which envelop the brain are invaded by the infection and this may lead to epileptiform convulsions.

Hardpad: Clinically, this disease may not be easily distinguishable from distemper until the characteristic hardening of the pad occurs. The symptoms may have an insidious onset and the disease may be well advanced before advice is sought. Early symptoms may be lethargy, loss of appetite, high temperature, a discharge from the nose which could be blood-stained ,and the nose may harden and crack.

Hepatitis: This is the term given to inflammation of the liver, the symptoms being loss of appetite, listlessness, vomiting and diarrhoea. When pressure is applied over the region of the liver, the dog may feel pain. He may be jaundiced; this can be seen in the white of the eye which becomes yellow.

Leptospirosis: This disease is an infection by a micro-organism known as spirochaete. It is a serious and sometimes fatal disease. No time should be lost in calling the vet. The symptoms can include listlessness, loss of appetite, loss of condition, high temperature, dehydration, external haemorrhaging and uraemia due to kidney infection. Uraemia is a failure of the kidney to excrete waste products into the urine and these therefore increase in their concentration in the blood causing severe nausea and vomiting and retention of fluid. This disease can be caught from rats' urine so it is vital that a puppy is protected from any place where rats may inhabit. A rat will urinate in a drinking bowl so it is advisable to always renew the water each day, especially if the Vizsla puppies or adults are kennelled.

It can be seen that there is little to distinguish one disease from another as many of the initial symptoms are similar. Nonetheless, the owner will know that his dog is ill enough to ask for the services of his vet.

Even though it may be very disappointing that your new Vizsla puppy cannot be aired for all to see, don't allow him anywhere he may be able to catch these diseases until he is fully inoculated. He should not meet strange dogs nor go any place where he may pick up an infection which means, in practical terms, that he should be kept within the confines of his own home unless he is carried or taken by car.

By the time your puppy has had his last injection, which could be up to 14 or 16 weeks, you will have grown accustomed to his face. The chaotic early days, disrupting the family, will have settled into some sort of pattern. Who could imagine this little golden puppy could cause such concern? Or jealousies for that matter between humans or other canines, imposing a re-arrangement of the pecking order? But ruffled feathers usually settle so that all can enjoy the new addition. So quickly will the new puppy settle into his 'niche' that it would be difficult to imagine life without him!

House Training

The Hungarian Vizsla puppy should not be difficult to house train. I am always delighted to hear from new puppy owners that they have trained their puppy in a matter of days. It means that the new owner had a plan of action and it worked, meanwhile establishing a good relationship with the puppy. A seven or eight-week-old puppy cannot be house trained if there is a hint of punishment in the air.

The bladder is controlled by the sphincter muscle. As the bladder fills with urine it reaches a certain point when the nerve supply to the muscles enables it to relax and the bladder will empty. A different set of muscles in the sphincter enables it to close. The nerve tracts in the frontal lobes of the brain which control the functions of elimination are poorly developed until the puppy is 5–6 weeks old. He can then learn how to consciously control by conditioned reflex the opening and closing of his bladder and how to eliminate in a particular place.

The owner must decide where and when he is to 'go' and who is to train him to 'go' there. If it is made clear to him, he will not be confused. He can be trained to use the newspaper method indoors or he can be trained to 'go' outside straight away. Obviously, if it is winter there is not much choice. The advantage of the newspaper method is that neither owner nor puppy has to brave the weather! The disadvantage is that sooner or later the puppy has to learn to go outside and he may become confused. If he does not get the message, he will continue going to the same spot in the house while the owner stands outside with the paper. I am not very good at the paper method. I traipse from one room to another with the puppy stopping to 'pee' on the way. I know I should stay in one room with the puppy and his heap of newspaper so that he will know exactly where it is but I find it difficult to confine my life to one room. The puppy should not be allowed the run of the house or he may find his own particular spot that suits him. I have a bitch aged nine and she still remembers a very comfortable bedroom carpet that she selected for her exclusive use when she was eight weeks old.

Training the puppy to go outside from the start seems a much simpler exercise although perhaps needs more concentration on the trainer's part. It means picking him up when he needs to 'go' and putting him down on the spot that has been chosen for him. A large patch of soil, grass or sand would suit him well and, once he has urinated or defecated there two or three times, he will know that that is where he eliminates when he is put outside. The trick for success in this method is timing. A pup cannot ask to go out, but the owner can observe his pattern of behaviour. For instance, he will need to eliminate after every meal so this is a good opportunity to condition him. He will learn to associate the door with going outside and soon enough he will start to go towards the door when he feels the need to go. A puppy generally needs to urinate every two hours – often it seems like every five minutes! There will be accidents at first but if the owner learns to anticipate, a Vizsla puppy gets the message sooner than most. The golden rules are:

- Decide to have your puppy with you every minute of the day for the first few days and concentrate on housetraining him.
- Always take him to one spot to 'go'.
- Praise him when he succeeds every time.
- Never punish him, but be firm. If he makes a mistake, it has happened because he has not 'got the message'. Since it is you that is 'giving the message', maybe it is the teacher and not the pupil who is to blame.

I overheard a puppy owner relating the terrible misdemeanours his puppy had perpetrated. 'I'll get the better of the little bugger. He's not going to get the better of me. I shut him outside in the rain for ten minutes. I said to myself "That'll teach him"'. Asked by the listener what had transpired, he droned on "So you know, the bugger wouldn't go. He stood there shivering in the rain, defying me!" The puppy was all of eight weeks old! The result was that at a year old the 'much loved puppy' would do all he needed to do outside for anyone else in the large family but not for the owner.

If a puppy passes water frequently, he may have cystitis. This is inflammation of the bladder which can be caused by an infection or a chill. A puppy can easily catch a cold by sitting on cold concrete or wet grass, especially if he is kennelled. He should be kept very warm and given plenty to drink but if the condition persists it is wise to call a vet. Usually it can be dealt with easily.

If your puppy has a loose stool probably it can be cleared by a slight change in feeding and, of course, a change in his diet may have upset him. If he has frequent diarrhoea but seems fit enough, it could be due to an infestation of worms. If he suddenly appears to be ill and has diarrhoea, keep him warm and keep calm for a couple of hours. You may find he is himself again in no time. I have never found the real cause for this but I suspect that the puppy has chewed some object such as a pebble, and it is passing through. If at any time there is any sign of a high temperature, or blood in the urine or faeces call a vet immediately.

Hereditary Diseases and Conditions

The Vizsla is still small in numbers compared to some other gundog breeds, but every breed has its peculiar susceptibilities to hereditary diseases and faults. However, a responsible watchfulness has been adopted to ensure the essential qualities of the breed are retained. Thus the likelihood of hereditary faults and diseases becoming a major problem is reduced.

A number of conditions have been observed and continue to be monitored in the breed.

Hip Dysplasia

Improper bone formation in the hip joints. Many more Vizsla owners now take advantage of the hip scoring scheme, and the hip score average shows that the breed is in a healthy state. Your vet will explain the procedure, which involves x-raying the dog's hips. The x-ray plates are then sent to be scored by the British Veterinary Association. The lower the score, the lower the degree of dysplasia. Scores range from 0 (the best possible score) to 106 (the worst possible score).

Entropion

The lower eyelid does not fit tightly and curls inward. The eyelashes thus rub against the corneal surface, resulting in constant watering of the eye and could cause a slightly bloodshot eye. It may be noticed in a pup and in extreme cases the puppy may find it difficult to keep his eyes open. The condition is thought to be hereditary. Entropion can be treated by a cosmetic operation.

Tail Deformities

Either crooked, bent or stubbed. Little is understood concerning this condition. It is thought that the tail could have been bent in utero. Usually it affects the end of the tail, but because the breed is customarily docked, it is not a problem. Tail deformities never right themselves. It is thought that tail deformities may be hereditary but this has not been proven to date.

Epilepsy

Spontaneous release of nervous impulses from within the brain leading to fits, varying in intensity from a fleeting disturbance of consciousness to a fully-fledged convulsion. Petit Mal is of small consequence but Grand Mal is a fully fledged convulsion. It can usually be treated effectively by closely monitored medication under veterinary supervision. There is a wealth of research dealing with this condition. It is thought to be hereditary but may also be caused by trauma (for example colliding with a stationary object) or lead poisoning. Another cause may be infection leading to high temperatures in puppies. It has been alleged that booster injections in some cases have led to fits.

Whilst the dog is having a Grand Mal it is usual veterinary advice to leave him alone in a darkened room. Some dogs come out of it quietly, others appear disorientated for a while

Skin Rash

One or two whelps or the whole litter at 3–4 days old can develop spots, varying from one or two tiny ones to large, scabby areas. It is believed that the whelp's immune system cannot deal with mites that are normally in the hair follicles. Once the system has adjusted, the problem should disappear. However, if the spots become infected, the condition must be treated.

Finally, it must be taken into account that defects and diseases are not always hereditary, and it is essential to eliminate other causes such as injury, infection, poisoning and stress. In order to go forward in organising an effective breeding programme, facts and statistics are vital. Hearsay is not scientific and therefore it is worthless.

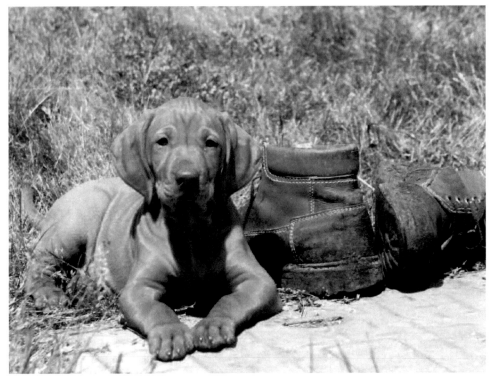

Smith's Russetmantle Caillie (Dollar). Photo: Smith

chapter 11

Wilks' Sh Ch Nicael Rully handled by Maureen
Wilks. A top show dog in unison with his handler.
Photo: Buller

Watching a top show dog can be an exciting experience, perhaps never to be forgotten by the handler and the spectator. It is exhilarating and moving to see an animal in absolute peak condition displaying all the qualities for which he has been bred. No dog is perfect, but he must be as near to perfection as can be as he goes round the ring in unison with his handler – standing and gaiting together, moving as one. His character and temperament should make him ooze with confidence and happiness – he could not and would not be in this company, however good his conformation, if he did not enjoy the job in hand.

The Ideal Vizsla

Who can use the term 'just a beauty contest' when the dog before him in the group is so superbly constructed? Beauty is in the eye of the beholder; here the beholder may find beauty but he must not and cannot deny the facts. The more experienced will like the pretty head, the attractive coat, the lovely colour, but he will know that this is not all by any means. The framework beneath the flowing coat or the short thick fur has to be correct and that has nothing to do with beauty but the parts of the dog put together correctly and functioning without fault.

Each breed has its own Standard which lays down guidelines to which it must conform. This is to preserve the particular type and function of that breed. Whether or not the dog in the ring actually performs the task for which he was developed originally, he must be bred so that he has the conformation and temperament to make him capable of pulling a sledge, baiting a bull, rounding up cattle or sheep, going down a hole or retrieving a pheasant, running across the desert or racing.

Few people come into a breed expecting to go right to the top. The hard core of show folk are those who go from show to show meeting their friends and enjoying the fancy with others. They are thrilled to win when they do and, in the main, appreciate those dogs who beat theirs if they are better. It is they who give the atmosphere to the showing days, who are cheerful and still keen after hours of travelling, who will talk dogs all day and part of the night and help any newcomer who needs a hand, giving away willingly whatever dog know-how they have.

Everyone showing dogs, top breeders, top handlers, top judges came into the fancy as amateurs at some time or other. There is no GCSE or 'A' level, no degree, no university. If someone wants to learn, if he takes part, he will. Knowledge of dogs has little to do with money or class. An enthusiast need only watch, ask and listen and a wealth of knowledge is at his feet.

If a newcomer finds he does not like showing, then he should give it up and leave it for others who do. Some people love to show, some love to work a dog, some love a dog as a companion and pet and some may have the pleasure of all three, but to discriminate and condemn those who may not have the fortune or wish to combine all these is presumptuous and foolish.

Turtle's Sh Ch Russetmantle Swallow (handled by Lynette Turtle). Photo: Dalton

So where does the Hungarian Vizsla stand in the winning stakes in the company of other breeds? Not too high. It is still a relatively new breed. The first recorded registration at The Kennel Club was in 1953, but other breeds have been imported since then which have become established more rapidly than the Vizsla in every way. In 1997 however, our records prove the Hungarian Vizsla competed successfully in the gundog group.

It is an invaluable lesson to sit by the ringside of the gundog group at a show. Compare the Best of Breed Vizsla's structure with the Best of Breed Labrador or Pointer, for instance – the top winners of the established breeds are so sound and well made, the Vizsla cannot yet compare. Sh Ch Swanside Miklos, now dead, bred by Roger Simkin (by Bingo vom Wurmbrandpark ex Sh Ch Swanside Czarina, owned by Minecke Mills de Hoog) was placed RBIS at the National Gundog Championship Show in 1975. An elegant dog and always beautifully handled, he never put a foot wrong in the show ring. Others have been pulled out in the last six or four of the gundog group and some have done well at smaller shows.

Ten years ago, those people trying to establish the breed on a footing with other gundog breeds in the show ring and in the field were having an uphill struggle. Much of the imported stock made a worthwhile contribution but, although there was been a gradual improvement in temperament and some physical aspects, the main fault in the breed – 'a bad front' – was still a problem. The result of this was that there were Vizslas who did not appear to have that particular fault but may have carried it genetically so it recurred again and again in the progeny. If the progeny were bred from, the merry-go-round started again.

It is interesting to compare the breed now, in the 1990s, with what was happening a decade ago. The uphill struggle has had its rewards. The Vizsla is establishing a positive footing in the field, he can and does compete successfully with other HPR breeds.

His conformation and the 'bad fronts' have improved. It is quite rare now to see a front 'you could drive a bus through'! Although we cannot be complacent, the general construction is sounder. It is possible to judge a class on the finer points of the breed rather than comparing 'a poor animal with one not so poor'.

However, the downside is that the beautiful, noble, distinguished Hungarian Vizsla head has suffered, and the truly aristocratic gundog aspect of 10 years ago is difficult to find. Heads can be broad and heavy with the muzzle too short. Judges have commented on the subtle changes over the years but now, alas, this head seems to be here to stay.

The only way to learn about good dogs is to watch good dogs. Question why one dog wins and another doesn't, why the judge looks at certain points of a dog, why he ranks the exhibits in a particular order, and so on. The more you study and question other participants, the more you learn about your breed.

If your intention is to show the breed seriously, while learning and enjoying showing you will be gaining more and more knowledge. You will find that you have a good idea of your ideal Vizsla, your dream Vizsla. One day, it may be you and your Vizsla in the big ring winning Best in Show or one of your breed standing on the red carpet. The late Arthur Westlake said to me *'One of the most rewarding experiences is to be at the ringside watching a dog that I had bred taking top honours!'* Most breeders would agree with this sentiment.

The Ideal Show Career

Let us suppose that you are a complete novice. You own your first Vizsla and you are really pleased with him. You have no idea whether he is good enough to show except that the breeder said he 'could be'. If the breeder said that the pup you bought at seven or eight weeks old will make a top winner, that breeder must have knowledge that no other has, because at that age it is impossible to be positive since a Vizsla goes through many stages. At seven or eight weeks old you think you have a world beater, but at 10 weeks he can look as if he has every fault in the book.

It is sensible to visit a couple of local shows, just to observe and glean information. Find out what is expected of you and your dog, talk to the show goers. There are a wealth of facts you need to know so here are a few to start with.

A puppy cannot be shown before he is six months old. For his first entry, choose a small show, an Exemption or local Open show. You will find it easier and more relaxing, and the competition is not nearly as formidable as at a Championship show. Novices frequently enter their puppy in every class available. This is not sensible. It is tempting but a young puppy can tire quickly and become bored, so only enter him in one or two classes if you want him to enjoy his day. Aim to arrive early, giving yourself plenty of time to familiarise yourself and your puppy with the atmosphere and the venue. For your Vizsla's debut, you will need to equip yourself with:
- Your admittance card and schedule.
- Safety pin or metal tag for pinning on your chest to hold class number.

Winter's Stregaya Celebrity of Glendun. Excellent example of free standing/topping & tailing. Handled by Paddy Winter.

- Money for buying the show catalogue. (This is vital because it gives your bench number, ring number and all essential information.)
- Bag for carrying the following: show lead, rubber glove, velvet duster, benching collar and lead, blanket (for dog), water and water bowl, food for dog (and something for you too), clothing for snowstorms, pelting rain or a tropical heatwave.

So you have been to your first show, and you enjoyed it. Whether or not you won a prize it seems you have acquired a taste for this side of the dog game. You then try to gain as much experience as you can, entering your puppy in small shows with a Championship show in mind in a couple of months time. Remember that some Championship show entry applications must be received two months before the show date.

Depending on classification for Vizslas, there may be a Puppy and a Junior class. If not, you will enter your dog in the first one or two classes that are offered. If you have found that your Vizsla is a natural, loves every minute of showing and is an extrovert you could enter the Puppy Stakes, but do not risk it if he is likely to tire and become bored.

When you have reached Championship Show stage your puppy will have had some good wins in the smaller shows that you have been to so, although nervous, you will probably have gained confidence and a certain aplomb. You know that your Vizsla is not shy, he may stand and trot if in the right mood. Even so, neither of you could have been prepared for the noise and tension or the magnitude of the place, nor the thousands of dogs and people – you will see more Vizslas than ever before. You will have the opportunity to compare different types and lines that you have heard and read about. You will meet the breeders and enthusiasts and some of your puppy's relatives too, perhaps.

We will suppose that your puppy wins both his classes. Now you can feel that you may have something good! You will then have to compete with all the Vizslas who have won their classes. That means you are up against the winner of the Open dog class who, as likely as not, is a Show Champion or a full Champion so you would not expect to beat him at this stage. But as you come out of the ring, you should be feeling very pleased. Stay and watch the other Vizslas being judged. Find out who does win the Open bitch class. The best bitch, having won her Challenge Certificate, competes with the best dog who won his Challenge Certificate.

At this stage the tension mounts round the ringside – everyone is playing at judging and trying to guess which one will be put up. The two Vizslas are standing perfectly in the middle of the ring, the strain telling as you see the hands of the handlers shaking, their faces serious, not a muscle moving. The judge asks them to move their dogs again – he is finding it a difficult decision. They both stand again, the judge goes over to the table, collects the Best of Breed card and rosette and gives it to the winning animal's handler. Everyone relaxes, both the dogs and their owners, and the crowd claps. The winner is kissed by the loser, a kind gesture and nice to see. The judge has a brief chat with the owner then the winners do a lap of honour and come out of the ring amid congratulations. When that happens to you for the first time, you will never forget it.

Suppose that it happens to you a year or two from now and it is you holding the precious prize, your dog's first Championship Certificate. You have gained your Junior Warrant and qualified for Crufts. You have worked your way up from Puppy classes to Junior, Maiden, Novice, to Post Graduate and Limit and, finally, if your Vizsla gains his 3rd Challenge Certificate his title will be Show Champion. He can only enter the Open dog class after this. Usually, the competition in this group is really hot because he will be competing against the other champions and show champions in the breed. By this time you have done a lot of winning, and losing too, so you know what it feels like to go cardless. Even so, you have managed to smile and be gracious to those who beat you even if you felt their win was not justified. But, more important, you have asked questions, been modest and sensible enough to take good advice and recognised virtues and faults in your dog. Your handling has improved and you feel that it is a good partnership between you and your maturing Vizsla. Perhaps he has been through a stage of listlessness and boredom when you had to lay him off showing for a time. Good walks and a bit of fun tend to cure this problem and the dog should come back as if he had been on holiday and start to show again with liveliness and energy for the job.

Some of your friends and competitors will have experienced similar difficulties with their bitches. Invariably, they go 'off the boil' when they have been in season and, during what would be the gestation period of nine weeks if they were in whelp, their minds are on nests rather than show rings.

You need to gain two more Challenge Certificates before you can call your dog a Show Champion. You will find it difficult not to take everything too seriously; your showing days are not the naive win or lose days that you felt in the beginning. Now they are tinged with not a little cynicism and wariness as well as a deeper understanding of people and dogs. It is important to recognise that you are ambitious and need to win, as long as this ambition goes hand-in-hand with the wish to gain more knowledge of the Vizsla and see him find a place with the best in the ring and in the field – not just your dog but the Vizsla as a breed. Then, it will not be such a blow if you go home cardless. You may have discovered a new dimension in yourself where your pleasure in seeing a really good Vizsla win transcends your losses.

When you do gain your three Challenge Certificates, you may have had it easy. For some exhibitors it takes a long time. Sh Ch Chantilly Jester of Oroshaza, owned and bred by Heather McCabe, waited until he was over two years old. From then on he never stopped winning, taking on every newcomer until he was retired. He died in 1984.

Many Vizslas in the breed never achieve the final Championship Certificate. They may win well in early classes as youngsters and seem to have a promising future but, eventually, never quite make the grade. It is difficult to cut your losses, but you may have to. It is difficult to retire a top-winning Vizsla too, since the best in breed needs to be seen. There is no point retiring a good Vizsla to make way for mediocre stock. One thing to remember is that our breed can mature late. So, with your third Championship Certificate in your hand and Best of Breed rosette pinned to your chest for all to see, the rest of the day will be spent in a pleasant haze. If you have really worked hard for it you can spare a moment congratulating yourself. If you have won easily, then you have been very lucky.

Now you have to go into the big ring. If you go into that ring expecting it to be a piece of cake, you will not have learnt a thing on your way up! If you know that it is unlikely that you will even be pulled out in the last six or eight then you have learnt a lot. If you understand what your chances are, you have come a long way from the day when you first showed your puppy. You have assessed your Vizsla as a judge should, not as a novice.

What the Judge Wants to See

The judge assesses the conformation of the dog to the specification of the Standard. He can best achieve his final decision by examining the dog standing in a show stance and gaiting so that he can see how the structure of the dog functions in action. Therefore, to allow the judge to see your Vizsla at his best advantage, you need to understand how to place him and move him correctly. Firstly we will discuss the different ways of handling and then how to set up your dog.

Setting the Dog Up

With your dog standing on your left, hold his muzzle with your left hand. Place his right foot, then change over, placing his left foot parallel to the other. Check that the feet are in line with the tip of the elbow and the top point of the shoulders; this will demonstrate the angulation of the shoulder and forequarters immediately. Holding his head either by the muzzle or with his lead up behind his ears, run your left hand over his back in order to place his back legs so that they too are parallel to one another. Bend down and reach for one leg and then the other. They should be so positioned that, when viewed from behind, they are straight and, when viewed from the side, the dog presents a balanced picture, covering the ground adequately, demonstrating the correct

Handling faults: tail not horizontal. Neck should be stretched to produce flowing topline.
Handler: M Williams. Photo: Pearce

angulation, the hocks being perpendicular to the floor. Check the balance again by stretching his head and neck slightly, so that he has to adjust his weight so that it is distributed correctly. Finally position yourself so that you have control of his head and forequarters with your right hand and hold his tail horizontally with your left hand. This is best done by placing the palm of the hand under the centre of the tail allowing it to lie there – never hang on to your dog's tail to control him. Your Vizsla should feel relaxed and comfortable because his whole body is being correctly supported. Smooth his back every now and then, and talk to him so that he knows that he is pleasing you.

Practise opening your dog's mouth. This is necessary because the judge should always look at his teeth. Once the dog becomes accustomed to you handling him he should not mind a judge going over him.

How to Gait Your Vizsla

Your Vizsla has to learn to trot by your side. This is the pace that demonstrates whether the dog's structure is functioning at its most effective. The judge will instruct the handler to trot the dog in a triangle and in a straight line so that he can assess the dog's movement from different angles, his stride, topline and ground-covering ability. When practising, place the lead up the dog's neck. The head must stay at the same level throughout, the lead should be neither too tight nor too slack so that the dog remains 'collected'. The pace should be a 'moderate but lively trot' and the handler can best do this by synchronizing his pace and the dog's in order to move as one. Keep him 'going forward' at all times when he is gaiting; do not allow him to pull away from you otherwise he will not be balanced and he will start to crab, creating problems in his movement that he would not have naturally. Always keep the dog between you and the judge. Be attentive to the judge's wishes. If he requires a triangle, use as much of the ring as possible and trot your dog into the corners. When going straight, make sure it is not a diagonal! Never allow your dog to 'run into the judge'. Stop a few feet away from him, keeping your dog standing as alertly as you can on a loose lead – this is when all the faults show up because you do not have a chance to pose him. If your dog can do all this with his tail wagging, it will indicate his happy temperament and he will be a pleasure to watch.

How to Spoil Your Dog's Chances

1. If you string him up too tight on the lead, he will compensate by standing on tiptoe which will cause him to knuckle over and his elbows to come out. Some handlers prefer to place the forequarters by standing in front of the dog, lifting the feet off the ground together and lowering them into place. This can cause the hindquarters to be overstretched if the forelegs are too far forward, and it can also create a gap between the elbow and the brisket when the dog is viewed from the side.

2. Placing the back legs too far beneath the dog or too far back will distort his frame. He will hunch his back to try to compensate for the discomfort. If his legs are placed too far back it will appear as though he has little turn of stifle.

3. Holding the tail too high spoils the topline, too low has the same effect, giving the dog a lifeless look.

Timing

Timing is an important factor if the dog is to be seen at this best. Never have your dog at a disadvantage whilst in the ring. Don't relax yourself, nor allow him to forget that he is in the show ring, and that you expect a lot of him. When you first come into the ring, set him up so that he knows why he is there, and this steadies him as well as you. If you have to wait too long for the judge to walk down the line, let your dog relax by walking him round you and set him up again.

While you are waiting your turn to be gone over, make sure your dog is ready to go when the judge calls you up. Take your time setting your Vizsla up correctly and do not fuss him. A good judge will give you time to set your dog up so that his best points may be seen. The golden rule of showing is never take your eye off the judge.

Handling

Your ideal show career depends on how good a specimen your puppy develops into but, whatever happens, you need to learn how to show and handle him to the best advantage. There are very few dogs who cannot be taught to behave as they should. Anyone who does obedience training learns very quickly that it is always the handler who has not learnt to teach the dog correctly rather than the dog's inability to learn. With this in mind, and however good or bad a dog's conformation, a well-handled dog is always a treat to see.

Back legs overstretched. Photos: Dr S Gottlieb

Roach back, frame distorted.

Tail too high, spoiling the topline.

*Tail and head too low, giving the dog a
lifeless look.*

Faults in Handling

A Vizsla should not be difficult to train. He is a gundog so it should be his nature to want to please and work for you. He is usually very easy to train in basic obedience. As a youngster of three months you would not expect him to stand for long or tolerate much formal teaching but, as he matures, with patience and firmness you can expect a high degree of showing ability if you teach him correctly. He should be perfectly capable of standing and moving in the show ring to a very high standard. The handler's personality, feelings and skills will directly affect the way the dog behaves at a show. If you feel your dog cannot learn to stand still or move correctly he is certainly not going to learn by himself. Give yourself confidence and some knowledge by watching good handlers, then try it. It is important to be patient with yourself and your dog. Of course you will make mistakes but, as long as you admit to them instead of blaming your dog, no harm is done. When you show him, have the attitude that he is your pride and ever-hopeful joy. It is difficult when he does not show as well as you know he can but, as you both become more and more accustomed to the performance, you and he can enjoy the experience together. If you are able to keep your sense of humour at the same time, everyone will enjoy watching you. Never believe that you are the only one who has difficulties or that you are the only one who is nervous and tense as you stand in the ring – some people are cleverer than others at covering up feelings. Of course your dog will feel the tension but this can be put to good use as, combined with the excitement and sense of occasion, he can rise to it. Many, if not all brilliant performers in other fields, can only give their best when they are really keyed up. You can liken the day of the show to a performance in the theatre – months of hard grind with rehearsing until the day arrives. The tension mounts, tempers quicken, come the moment it can either be a complete flop or a resounding success. Whatever the outcome, if there is talent there, it will come out sooner or later.

Head facing forward. Back legs overstretched resulting in straight stifle.

Teaching a puppy how to stand and move correctly and learn ring manners is quite a task. You will need to be guided by his temperament and stage of maturity as to how much you can expect of him. From very early on, give him a few minutes of some sort of training each day. You can do this in your kitchen, hallway, or in the middle of the garden, park or field – in fact, anywhere with a bit of space. Kneel down and stand him in front of you. It does not matter how he stands at first, just get him used to covering the ground so that his legs are taking his weight equally. You can help him by holding his muzzle from underneath with your right hand or, if he does not like that, steady him by holding his neck. Try running your left hand over and over his back to relax him. Talk to him and praise him so that he enjoys it. Then place the back legs, either separately or by putting your hand between his back legs and lifting his quarters off the ground. Replace them gently again so that he is standing squarely on his four legs, then place your left hand under his tail and lift it so that it is horizontal. Of course it will not work at first – one end will go up, the other down, but it will come in time. You may get a surprise. He may do it perfectly well if you are firm. The golden rule is, always finish any lesson on a note of success and praise, no matter how old the dog. If a lesson does not go well, take him back to an exercise you know he can do in order to end on a good note. If lessons always end in failure and tension and your displeasure is obvious, your Vizsla is not going to want to repeat that lesson, so you will have a stubborn dog on your hands. If you feel you are losing your cool, leave your Vizsla in peace; do something with him that you can both enjoy and leave the lesson for another day.

The dog needs to get used to being touched all over, so get into the habit of looking at his teeth regularly, inspecting his ears, picking up his feet, running your hands underneath and over his back, inside his back legs, and in the case of a male, his scrotum. The judge has to check that he is entire. Get him used to every move you know the judge will need to make. Once your puppy is used to his collar and lead you can introduce him to his show lead. There are many different makes and types on the market. Personally, I like a narrow leather slip lead that is not too long, the reason being that leather is easy on the hands and is strong enough to check a Vizsla if necessary. I also like the colour of leather against the Vizsla coat, but it is important that you find something that suits you and that you find comfortable. Keep the show lead just for show training him and for shows, because a dog soon picks up the idea

Try standing in front of a mirror. It can be quite a shock! Photo: Dr S Gottlieb

Above and below: Perkins' Gardenway Chekov learning how. Photos by Pearce

that his every day lead means walks and the other means using his brain as well as fun with you.

You need to teach your puppy to trot correctly as you would in the show ring. At first he will be all over the place but, if you trot gently, encouraging him, talking to him, keeping his attention and teaching him to keep his head up (which he will do if you keep up an incessant chatter), he will be keen to hear what you are saying. When he does it right, take the lead off, let him leap and play, knowing he has pleased you. Then stop, put the lead back on and trot, saying 'trot' so that he learns the word. Soon he learns that when the lead goes on, you mean business. As soon as you take it off, he knows it means fun and games. This way, he really does enjoy the job in hand. The Vizsla loves working and pleasing and he loves to play. This will stand you in good stead throughout his life. In every aspect of owning a Vizsla, this is how you will get the very best of him. You must never forget to praise him.

There are many different methods of showing the various breeds and there is an art to handling dogs well. The professional handler is there to display the dog to its full advantage. He will do this with such skill that it looks simple, but anyone who handles well knows it is not easy at all and takes much practice, time, patience and insight. It is said that a good handler can make a poor dog look good, and a bad handler make a good one look poor. Maybe that is so, but if a dog is handled badly no judge can see enough to make his own mind up.

The time will come when your

Vizsla is old enough for you to decide what method you will use, which manner of handling suits him best, taking into consideration that the freer and less cluttered up any dog looks, the more the judge likes it. Also, the Vizsla does not like being overhandled. He is best left alone and independent. He is also a natural fawner and will do so if encouraged in any way, so the less you touch him the better.

In the Vizsla breed it can be said there are three main methods of handling. We will not talk about idiosyncratic methods, but accepted forms of showing in the gundog world! Whichever method you choose, and I suspect we all use a bit of each, it is essential that we are decisive so that the Vizsla can understand what we are asking of him. Some dogs have more grey matter than others, but they cannot learn to show by themselves.

When practising with your Vizsla, try standing him before a full-length mirror sideways and frontways (this is what the judge sees). It can be quite a shock. You think your Vizsla is set up just right, but you look in the mirror and everything is wrong! A friend is just as useful as a mirror if not more so, because you can discuss, criticise, take it in turns to look at each other's dogs. The work and anticipation is almost more fun than the day itself.

Even though your Vizsla is your beloved pet and gundog, the purpose of showing is to perpetuate the breed, as it should be. A Hungarian Vizsla is a gundog which hunts, points and retrieves. He should look like a Vizsla and be able to fulfil his function as one. All who show should be protective of his unique qualities.

The Free Standing Method

This must be the ideal style. It can be seen in the Labrador ring to perfection. The dog stands alone with the handler in front of him holding the lead loosely, with a titbit at the ready. The dog stands stock still with his tail slowly swinging from side to side. This is a lovely sight, accentuating the dogs excellent temperament and conformation. If your Vizsla has a calm, placid temperament, is extrovert and enjoys standing freely, it is well worth giving it a try. There is no doubt that it is very effective when it works.

To train your Vizsla to show this way takes time. Titbits, firmness and praise must be used as always. To start with, try standing in front of him with the lead loose, and titbits in your hand. Concentrate on his eyes and say 'stand' (it does not matter how at this stage). If he sits, put the titbits away, go back to him, stand him, using the word, run your hand along his back so that he begins to associate the hand movement with the word. When he feels steady enough, stand in front of him again and repeat the performance. If he stays for two seconds praise him and give him the food, but do not over-excite him. Stay calm, then try again and again and again. You can stand him correctly if you find he is getting the message and he seems really steady. Then the fun begins. Each day practise and you will find that he will stand longer and longer enjoying his sense of balance, until eventually you may find that you can count up to 100 (under your breath) without his moving. By that time I am sure you will have found that this method suits you both. The drawbacks to this way of showing are numerous. First, it is difficult to achieve with a Vizsla. His lively, vivacious temperament does not lend itself too well to having the handler stand so far away. Secondly, there is nothing like it for showing up faults such as bad feet and elbows, and you cannot keep nipping back to put them right. Nor are there many Vizslas who

Gottlieb's Sh Ch Russetmantle Paris with handler M Williams demonstrating the free standing method. Tail incorrect.
Photo: Pearce

will hold their tails horizontal on their own, so the correct outline cannot be achieved. If your Vizsla is the fussy type, he will keep smiling and wagging his tail at you for food. On the other hand, some Vizslas are not tempted by any titbit, or even curious once they are in the show ring. I have used this method and I found that if I put the titbits in my pockets, it seemed to be more effective. My Vizsla did not get quite so excited but he knew they were there, and his eyes would be rivetted at just the right level. All I needed to do was to keep my hands waist high.

Topping and Tailing

This way of showing a dog has exactly the opposite effect to the free standing method. The advantages are that the Vizsla is close to his owner which he likes. If he moves his feet or head they can be quickly corrected without the handler moving. The tail is held horizontal and it does not take so long to set him up.

To train your Vizsla to show this way takes less time and patience than the free standing method but you need all your skill to prevent him from turning his head towards you, since you are practically eye to eye. Stand your Vizsla as you have taught him. Holding his muzzle, you kneel on one knee or two, whichever you prefer. Support his tail in the usual manner, allowing the lead to drop loosely round his neck.

The disadvantages are that first, the outline can be marred by the handler looking over the dog. If your Vizsla does not like being held by the muzzle, he will lean away from your hand which will shorten his neck or he will lift his muzzle too high in the air, causing his back to hunch in protest. Thus he will not be correctly balanced. If you are over a certain age, struggling to get up and down on your knees will not do your lumbago any good! I do not think this method is for a gundog breed, at least not the larger ones because they should have an independant aspect and be allowed to stand as naturally as possible.

Free Standing/Topping and Tailing

This is a compromise between the free-standing and topping and tailing methods. The handler stands, holding or supporting the muzzle or neck, or he can hold the lead up behind the ears, leaving the head entirely free. Meanwhile the tail is held in the correct position. The advantage to this method is that you are not restricted in any way, either by standing in front of the dog, or kneeling down. You are free to shift your weight either toward the dog's head or to his rear. You can stand close to or at arm's length. If your dog is showing really well that day, full of confidence and as steady as a rock with the minimum of handling from you, you can stand back. On the other hand, if he has the fidgets you are close enough to put him right.

Many handlers like to use titbits – a bit of biscuit, meat or whatever the dog fancies best. The Vizsla does not usually respond all that well. It can over-excite

This dog obviously does not like being held by the muzzle. Photo: Dr S Gottlieb

him and, in many cases, instead of relaxing him, makes him fuss. If titbits are used, better to have them in your pocket out of the way so that he can smell them. If you hold them out, the dog either leaps for them or manages to be chewing a piece just as the judge approaches to look at his teeth! I have to add, from the judge's point of view, that it is very difficult to look at the teeth whilst the dog is chewing and licking his chops! Thus timing is of the essence and needs skill.

As far as I am concerned, I cannot handle the titbit. Either it gets stuck in my pocket and I cannot reach it or I drop it so that both my dog and I end up searching in the grass for it. It is better not to confuse the issue with food unless you are very skillful.

Some handlers are aided by a relative or friend, the plan being that the dog's attention is attracted by waving, calling, coughing or whatever from outside the ring. This can work very well if they always place themselves somewhere in front of the dog. This exercise is not allowed by The Kennel Club regulations. No-one other than the actual handler is allowed to assist the dog, either inside or outside the ring.

Types of Dog Shows

Exemption Shows

Most people's introduction to showing comes from attending the small dog shows which are often held in conjunction with local fetes and agricultural shows. These shows are held under the jurisdiction of The Kennel Club and are known as Exemption Shows. A dog need not be registered with The Kennel Club in order to compete at Exemption shows. Only four pedigree classes are allowed which usually come under class headings such as sporting, non-sporting, working and utility. There are also novelty classes such as best short-haired dog, dog with the 'waggiest tail', dog with the prettiest face and so on. After all the novelty classes have been judged, the class winners compete for the Best in Show title. Wins at Exemption Shows do not count towards any titles.

The Vizsla does not like being overhandled. Photo: Dr S Gotlieb

The Vizsla is best left alone and independent. Photo: Dr S Gottlieb

Matches

Matches are often held by 'Ringcraft' clubs. They involve pedigree dogs only. Once again they are held under Kennel Club rules, although they do not need to obtain permission to hold the show. An outsider is often called in to judge. Matches are really just social affairs which give good grounding in ring behaviour.

Limit Shows

Often regarded as the next step up from competing in matches, a Limit show must have a minimum of 21 classes if more than one breed is scheduled or a minimum of 13 classes for just one breed.

Any dog which has won a Challenge Certificate is not eligible to be shown at Exemption shows, matches or Limit shows.

Open Shows

These can have any number of classes and are open to all breeds of pedigree dogs that are registered with The Kennel Club.

Championship Shows

These are the shows at which the much sought-after Challenge Certificates are awarded. These shows cater for nearly every type of pedigree dog found in Britain. They are held all over the country and winning a class at a Championship Show means that one can enter for Crufts.

Crufts

In order to enter Crufts – this world-famous show – a dog must first qualify at a Championship Show. A show champion or champion dog can be shown at Crufts without having to qualify as it has already proved its quality.

Definition of Classes

Minor Puppy: For dogs of six and not exceeding nine calendar months of age on the day of the show.

Puppy: For dogs of six and not exceeding twelve calendar months of age on the day of the show.

Junior: For dogs of six and not exceeding eighteen calendar months of age of the day of the show.

Special Yearling: For dogs of six months and not exceeding two years of age on the day of the show.

Maiden: For dogs which have not won a Challenge Certificate or a first prize at an Open or Championship show (puppy, special puppy, minor and special minor puppy classes excepted).

Novice: For dogs which have not won a Challenge Certificate or three or more first prize at Open or Championship Shows (puppy, special puppy, minor and special minor puppy classes excepted).

Undergraduate: For dogs which have not won a Challenge Certificate or three or more first prizes at Championship Shows (puppy, special puppy, minor and special minor puppy classes excepted).
Graduate: For dogs which have not won a Challenge Certificate or four or more first prizes at Championship Shows in graduate, post graduate, minor limited, mid limit and open classes whether restricted or not.

Post Graduate: For dogs which have not won a Challenge Certificate or five or more first prizes at Championship Shows in post graduate, minor limit, mid limit, limit and open classes whether restricted or not.

Bicknell's Sh Ch Pitswarren Isaac of Szentendre. Photo: Dalton

Limit: For dogs which have not won three Challenge Certificates under three different judges or seven or more first prizes in all at Championship Shows in limit and open classes, confined to breed, whether restricted or not, at shows where Challenge Certificates were offered in the breed.

Special Open: For open classes except that it is restricted as to weight, height, colour or to members of an association.

Field Trial: For dogs which have won prizes, awards of honour, diplomas of merit or certificates of merit in actual competition at a field trial held under Kennel Club or Irish Kennel Club field trial rules and regulations.

Special Beginners: For dogs and bitches shown by an exhibitor whose dogs have never won a Challenge Certificate in the breed. (Note: it is the exhibitor who has to qualify, **not** the dog.)

Brace: For two exhibits (either sex or mixed) of one breed belonging to the same exhibitor, each exhibit having been entered in some class other than brace or team.

Team: For three exhibits (either sex or mixed) of one breed belonging to the same exhibitor, each exhibit having been entered in some class other than brace or team.

Veteran: For dogs of seven years of age and over on the day of the show.

Special Regulations

When a dog is not fully registered at The Kennel Club, certain letters must be placed after his name on the entry form to indicate that permission has been applied for but that the owner has not yet received confirmation from The Kennel Club. These are as follows:

NAF: Name Applied For
TAF: Transfer Applied For
ARAF: Active Register Applied For

chapter 12

Introduction to the Working Vizsla in Britain by Louise Petrie-Hay

Gay Gottlieb writes:

This text was contributed to the First Edition of this book by Louise Petrie-Hay (Waidman). It is as relevant today as it was then. I wish to pay a special, warm tribute to her continuing contribution as judge and mentor in all working and field trial activities. Her unchallengeable deep knowledge of her beloved breed will always be cherished.

The years 1973 to 1984 were important ones for the Vizsla being trained for the field. Included here are the year by year accounts of the field events held between 1973 and 1984 as many Vizsla owners, both old and new, find them a fascinating insight into how a breed develops. Also, many of the people who first introduced the Vizsla were ardent field triallers and handlers, and their history is also the history of the breed. There is a résumé of those achieving success to date, both old-timers and newcomers to the Vizsla world, to bring the story of the Vizsla in the field right up to date.

Versatile Shooting Dog

Originally the Vizsla was bred as a hunting dog, to find food for his master. Then he had to find game for hunters working with falcons or nets. Finally, with the advent of the gun, the Vizsla became a gundog. He must not be thought of purely as a bird dog (as in America) since, if properly trained, he must hunt fur or feather on command. In Hungary, the word 'madar' tells him to run high headed in search of birds and 'nyul' warns him that he must hunt rabbits and other ground game. As an all-purpose gundog, the Vizsla is rapidly gaining popularity in this country and many are being exported to the continent, America, Australia, Africa and New Zealand to people who wish to use them as gundogs.

Two pups were sent to Greece and their owner tells me that the bitch pup has grown into a splendid animal who performs particularly well when pointing birds. Sometimes she even seizes the quail from the air! The dog, he says, is with him day and night, is very obedient, and his performance as a hunter and pointer is excellent. He is also a good watch dog. He does not interfere with the domestic animals, rabbits, pigeons, hens, etc, and if one wanders away he will shepherd it back. He is such a master of his trade that one forgets to shoot, one is so lost in admiration at his performance! Surely the Vizsla is the aristocrat of dogs, writes this owner.

Similar letters of praise have come from many countries from people who have bought Vizslas as shooting companions. From Denmark I am told that the pup that was sent over is very aggressive in the way he dares to go into any bush to see if there should be some game. From Scotland I received a letter saying that their dog was not used for shooting but had adapted so well to the conditions of the hill farm he made a wonderful sheepdog and it would not be possible to work the hill without him, particularly during the tupping season. Another tells me that he has

Wilson's Ch Cuzco Laski, a dog who is both shown and trialled.

Hunter's Vadasz Velvet, a successful Field Trial Vizsla.

yet to find a breed of dog that can match the Vizsla for hunting and dogwork. He tells me that he has owned many different breeds but the Vizsla, as far as he was concerned, outshines all others.

Mr Gillan, who was the headkeeper at Balmoral, had considerable experience of training these dogs and considers them superior to German Shorthaired Pointers and Weimaraners. Lord Londonderry's keeper was so impressed with one that he saw running in a trial that he bought a couple of pups the following season.

One report I had about a bitch said that she had never been known to be sulky or do anything underhand, that although she was very feminine she was as tough as any dog when it came to facing cover whilst hunting, quite fearless, with an outstanding doggedness and determination of character. She had a first class nose and was a tireless worker. Another bitch, who died two days before her 17th birthday, had worked all her life not only as a gundog but also with falcons. All this is a testament to their adaptability and proficiency as gundogs, but they are also used by many falconers and also for deer stalking.

In a copy of *Shooting Times and Country Life Magazine* in 1966 there is a report of the Welsh Hawking Club and a photo of Mr Jackson and Mr Lorant de Bastyai with their Vizslas. Lorant says of his Pacal that there was great harmony between Pacal and Durak, his goshawk. The bird would watch and follow the dog, both were quite free, and he felt completely unnecessary in their company. John Gassman, well known as an experienced shooting and stalking man, wrote *"One thing I am sure, having been with Pointer/Retrievers all my life, that the Vizsla will compare favourably with any of these breeds."*

Reports taken from *The Hungarian Vizsla Society's Newsletters*

Until 1973 the activities of the Hungarian Vizsla Society were confined to newsletters and information about the breed but, in this year, the first field trial was organised. From then on, a number of other events were introduced to encourage the non-shooting Vizsla owner to learn more about the working ability of his dog and how to train and control this ability.

The First Field Trial Held by the Hungarian Vizsla Society

Report and results of that first Novice Stake by Eric Greig

The 3rd November 1973 was quite literally a field day for those members who visited Margaret and Bill Sanderson's delightful home at Thorphill, Morpeth. On that day, the Society ran its first field trial, and if this first attempt may be used as a guide, the future of subsequent meets looks to be bright.

Eight dogs were entered and that number ran, although Louise Petrie-Hay's Bella was sportingly substituted with Sipa, as the former was in season. The dogs came from as far apart as Worcestershire and Perthshire, and the distance travelled did not seem to have any adverse affect on their fitness. Some handlers travelled to Morpeth the previous day staying overnight locally in a pub or, as one enthusiast did, slept out under the stars with his dog ensconced on her bed in the vehicle; whilst others had an early start from their homes, trusting that fog and ice would not be too severe.

The day was without rain, mild and humid with a very light variable breeze which changed its direction often. This made for difficult scenting, and game seemed to realise it, as they either sat tight or, as we suspect, moved low leaving the dogs with a problem. Only one entrant, the winner, had a warm retrieve; in fact he had two in very quick succession on pheasant; the others had to be content with cold retrieves at the water test on pigeon. The judges, Margaret Sanderson and Roger Phillips, were most patient, giving the dogs and handlers every chance to come onto game, but it was, with a couple of exceptions, not to be; and they were confined to judging mainly the quartering, facing cover and handling, before the break in proceedings for lunch.

Whilst in the morning the work had been on the north side of the farm, the afternoon's work took the southerly direction which had more cover, and eventually ended at the river where the water test took place, just before dusk. After the test, the whole party were taken by tractor and trailer back to Thorphill Farm, where the judges and steward did their sums to place the dogs in their order of ability on the day.

The judge's notes and comments give the technicalities of the meet, and they are shown below; but it should be noted and remarked upon that the handlers of the first, second and third prize winners had never previously taken part in a field trial. On the strength of this the Society hopes that all those members who thought they would like to run a dog but did not have sufficient experience will take heart and enter the next event. One cannot thank Margaret and Bill Sanderson too much for allowing us the privilege of using their ground, which in itself is a major concession; but also to shoot for us, judge and feed us as well, places their hospitality in the highest possible bracket.

181

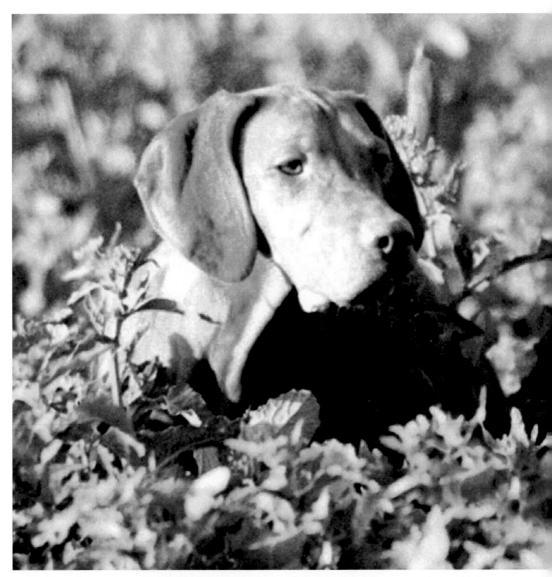

Petrie-Hay & Cox's Archenfield Crusty of Waidman. Crusty became the second Field Trial Champion in the breed during the 1997-1998 season.

Judge's notes by M Sanderson

The Hungarian Vizsla Society held their first field trial at Thorphill on November 3rd by kind permission of Mr W Sanderson. This was not an easy trial to judge as scent was very poor, with little or no wind; apart from this I personally enjoyed judging the Vizsla's work, placing as follows:

1st Mr E W Berry's Windover Ripp who worked well on open ground and in hedgerow; had a very good point, was very steady to flush and shot. He did a quick retrieve and a very good water test. He was well handled by his owner.

2nd Mr G E S Grieg's Saline Caroline. This bitch worked well on open ground; had a good point; was steady to shot; did a very neat water test and retrieve. Well handled by Sorley Grieg.

3rd Major G Maitland-Smith's Starleypoint Ulles. This dog worked his open ground well; was very steady to shot. He did a good water test and retrieve. Well handled by Mrs Maitland-Smith.

Two Certificates of Merit were awarded to Mrs Auchterlonie's Saline Achilles, handled by Mr A MacRae, and Mr R Anthony's Capeland Cascade, handled by her owner. Both these dogs worked well and did good water tests; they just did not have the luck of the first three dogs.

Field Trial in Suffolk (1974)

The Society's second field trial was held in Suffolk. The following is the report:

Report and results

A Novice Stake for Vizslas only was held on Saturday October 26th at the Marshland Estate, Sudbourne, Suffolk by kind permission of Mr A Heyman, QC. Fourteen entries were received, four withdrew owing to the ill-health of the owners, and one failed to attend – so in fact nine dogs competed. The weather was unbelievably good considering the storms on the previous day and the rain on the following. Scenting conditions varied considerably as the sun warmed and dried out the wet cold ground. Stubble, cut seed kale and sugar beet was worked, also a small area of potatoes. Game was plentiful, consisting of a plethora of hares, some partridges and a quantity of pheasants. The two guns performed their task admirably and the dogs had ample opportunities of retrieves on feather – no fur was shot over novices. The water retrieve was held on the Iken Estate and the dogs were tested with a swim of about thirty yards, which all were allowed to partake in as there was a special award for the best water retrieve, kindly presented by the secretary, Mrs K Auchterlonie, who very sadly was one of those unable to attend.

The outstanding winner was Mr Heyman's bitch, Matai Vica, who put up an excellent performance showing style, speed, nose and exceptional retrieving ability both on seen and blind retrieves. She was steady both to flush, shot and fall of game and had a staunch point on a myxy rabbit right under her nose which she made no attempt to move in on. She also won the water award by a very bold entry and a quick return but only by one mark above Mrs Phillip's dog, Waidman Buda. Mr Greig's Saline Caroline came 2nd. This bitch worked well and sensibly, showing her experience over the younger dogs. She found game and pointed staunchly – was steady and made a good retrieve. 3rd prize went to Mintalla owned by Mr Van Helvoort and handled by Mrs Petrie-Hay – this 20 month old dog did all that was asked of him, he was steady to a number of hares, pointed in the roots and retrieved to hand. He completed the water retrieve but his inexperience was obvious. Two dogs were eliminated for falling into the temptation of numerous hares, one for hardmouth, one of them failed on a retrieve, another who had completed the card finally refused the water, and another inexperienced bitch failed to find and point the game owing to poor ground treatment.

In the judges' final assessment at the end of the day they agreed that, apart from the winner, the obvious potential working ability of all the dogs was hampered by the lack of competent handling. More experience by the handlers will go far to improve the performance of the dogs. The judges expressed their enjoyment and interest and thanked all those who competed under them.

The prizes, which were kindly given by Major W Petrie-Hay, went to:
1st Prize: Mr Heyman's Matai Vica, Kinford Trophy, (Prize for best Water Retrieve)
2nd Prize: Mr Grieg's Saline Caroline, Provanston Cailleach Challenge Trophy
3rd Prize: Mr Van Helvoort's Mintalla

GSP Association Field Trial (1975)

On 11 January 1975, the German Shorthaired Pointer Association held a field trial in Hampshire.

It was a Novice Stake – 12 dogs ran – 8 German Shorthaired Pointers, 3 Weimaraners and one Vizsla (Waidman Brok). The dog with the highest marks was Brok – so a little bit of Vizsla history was made in that this was the first time that a Vizsla had competed in this country against German Shorthaired Pointers and Weimaraners and beaten them. BUT, and here is the rub – no 1st or 2nd prizes were awarded, Brok got 3rd prize and one Certificate of Merit was issued to a German Pointer.

According to the judges, after the first round the standard of work was exceptionally high. After the second round only 6 dogs qualified for the water retrieve. Two refused to enter the water and out of the four remaining dogs (1 Weimar, 2 German Pointers and Brok), Brok was awarded 3rd prize as his total marks were not high enough to warrant better. He made two mistakes and both of them were avoidable by better training on my part.

His ground treatment, game finding and pointing marks were above average. The retrieve he had in the second round was a pricked hen pheasant dropped about 100 yards in high marshland grass. He marked it well, went straight to the fall, found the bird, picked it up and started to come in. He stopped once, put it down to get a better hold (this is not penalised by the judges) and came on – when about 15 yards from me he fell into a cross dyke, he recovered, came out still with the bird but then he put it down, shook and said 'that's enough' – this was only about five yards in front of me so I went forward and collected the bird – but he should have brought it to hand and, as a result, got a low mark. At the water the bird was thrown into a fairly fast running narrow river, it drifted almost to the far bank, so that when Brok retrieved he went up onto the far bank – having climbed up with the bird he was reluctant to return, but after considerable persuasion on my part he did bring it back. But of course this again lost valuable marks. In both these instances more attention in training would have made the difference between a 1st and 3rd prize. That is why I say although I am delighted with the success it is not good enough. A Vizsla must get a 1st prize next season when competing against the other pointer/retriever breeds – I shall do my damndest to see that it is Brok, but this surely should give an incentive to other Vizsla owners to take just that extra bit more time and trouble in training during the summer months so that we can prove the true working ability of our dogs.

Three Field Trials held by The Vizsla Society

Later in the year the Society organised three field trials:
Mr J Brockbank and Mr E Young very kindly invited us to their moors at Dufftown and Tintohill and once again Mr A Heyman offered us the Marshland Estate in Suffolk. These trials were a 'qualified' success, not owing to any lack of game, entries or enthusiasm but entirely to the element which is out of our control – the weather. All three were novice stakes.

Report by Lord Joicey

Dufftown, Banffshire. Saturday August 16th 1975. There were 12 entries and one reserve – 10 runners consisting of 5 Vizslas, 4 German Pointers and one Weimaraner. Conditions were made difficult by continuous rain and, although the whole morning was spent advancing into a steady breeze, the dogs found conditions too difficult for them and only one point on grouse and two points on hares were recorded during the whole of the first round. In these conditions, the judges had inadequate information to express their views on individual dogs. Coveys took wing several hundred yards ahead of the line but a few single birds sat tight, enough for nine points to have been registered had the dogs covered their beat more thoroughly and had they worked closer in front of the guns. There is room for much improvement in quartering and ensuring that the dog's nose covers the whole of the beat with the minimum waste of time. After lunch the handlers asked that the stake should be abandoned and the judges agreed to do so and go straight to the water retrieve where all the dogs entered and retrieved their pigeon.

On September 6th we foregathered again, this time on Tintohill, and Evan Young was our host. Tony Jackson and Sandy Levanton from *The Shooting Times* were with us to shoot and take photographs. The report and pictures were published on September 18th and 25th. Our Judges this time were Mr Rankin Waddell and Mr Eric

Greig. George Richmond very kindly acted as a gun and Mr G Sterne, the president of the German Shorthaired Pointer Club, was with us on the hill for much of the day. There were 12 entries and 4 reserves – 13 dogs ran – 6 Vizslas and 7 German Pointers. Yet again the weather was unkind – intermittent light rain and no wind at all. There appeared to be no scent whatsoever. Grouse were seen in plenty and within shot, but the dogs ran into them, indicating lack of scent. The points obtained were all on a few hares who decided to sit it out instead of tempting the dogs with a mad dash. After lunch the judges decided that all game must be shot regardless of whether it had been pointed or not, and in this way retrieves were available and a result obtainable. This time the water test was carried out in a reservoir.

The results were:
1st: Mr I Sladden's Inchmarlo Jasmine
2nd: Mrs Layton's Midlander Oriental Ranee
3rd: Mr I Sladden's Sh Ch Inchmarlo Raphoe
(All German Shorthaired Pointers)
Reserve and Certificate of Merit: Mr A Heyman's Vizsla Matai Vica
Certificate of Merit: Mrs K Auchterlonie's Vizsla Saline Achilles who was awarded the Provanston Caileach Challenge Trophy.
The Shooting Times kindly gave a box of cartridges to the Guns' Choice. This was Mr Elliott's German Pointer Inchmarlo Solas. Again it was a very enjoyable day, marred only by the lack of scent.

On October 11th we all met at the Marshland Estate by kind permission of Alan Heyman. Last year we hd an excellent day on this ideal ground and this time we were lucky again. 12 entries and one reserve. 11 dogs ran, Vizslas only this time. Lord Joicey and Mr G Sherring judged.

Judge's Report
1st: Mr J Parke's Matai Pirok, 79%
2nd: Mr A Heyman's Matai Vica, 68%
3rd: Mr T West's Galfrid Gelert, 64%
A few heavy showers later in the day did nothing to spoil this excellent novice trial, run on the lovely wide stubble fields and sugar beet of the Marsh Estate. Most of the eleven runners obviously lacked much experience of the shooting field, but nevertheless displayed great keenness and potential ability. Quartering of the ground was for the most part free and unrestricted and, on a rather difficult scenting day, nearly all the dogs reacted to the scent left by the plentiful head of pheasants, partridges and hares seen. The majority of dogs did not have the experience to interpret the meaning of the scents they were picking up and, in some cases, the handlers did not understand the messages which the dogs in turn were trying to convey to them.

The three eventual prize winners, however, showed themselves to be no strangers to the shooting field. Mr Parke's bitch, Matai Pirok, was beautifully handled; she ranged freely, but under complete control, and all the time was working to find game. She indicated clearly the near presence of game in the roots, tracked with caution a pheasant running on ahead, and then held it in a steady point. When this was flushed and shot, she made a good job of the retrieve. Mr Heyman's bitch, Matai Vica, also quartered beautifully, having a stylish point on some partridges in the open, which rose wild. She too gave an excellent performance in the roots, but overshot her mark for the retrieve, and for a brief moment became over excited. The third dog, Mr West's Galfrid Gelert, did not quarter with quite the same fluency as the other two, but showed himself a reliable game finder both in the open and the roots. This was an excellent performance for a first appearance in field trials. The ground placed at our disposal was superb for pointers to work on, and also for the spectators to see what was happening at all times. Mr Heyman and his keeper gave the judges every help in advising how best to work it to show game to the best advantage of the dogs. The water test caused 2 eliminations, but otherwise was well performed. An excellent lunch at the Orford Oysterage completed a thoroughly enjoyable day for which much gratitude is due to our hosts, Mr and Mrs Alan Heyman.

John Parke is to be doubly congratulated as the day before he won the Weimaraner Club novice stake, running against German Shorthaired Pointers, Weimars and a Munsterlander. This is the first time a Vizsla has been placed first in a stake for all breeds which hunt, point and retrieve. Well done, John!

Field Trial (1976)

In 1976 a field trial was arranged at Biggar in Lanarkshire but this had to be cancelled owing to lack of sufficient entries.

The First Open Stake Field Trial (1976)

The first open stake field trial was held this year and the judges were Sir Michael Leighton and Mr Howard Fisher.

Judges' report

The Hungarian Vizsla Society held an open stake field trial on 30 October 1976 at Marshland Estate, Woodbridge, Suffolk, by kind permission of Mr A Heyman.

The day was warm and misty with occasional outbreaks of drizzle. Wind conditions varied from nil wind to a strong wind and scenting conditions were generally not too good. The ground worked was open stubble and roots taking in hedges and rough pit. Game was pheasant, partridge and hare, rabbits were also seen.

The standard of work was not very high and we were unable to award a first prize. One or two dogs were going well and showing a good standard of work but committed cardinal sins, so putting themselves out of the stake. In this category fell Mr K Stammer's German Pointer Maylock Maree, who impressed in the first run very greatly. Also, Louise Petrie-Hay's Waidman Zimba who worked nicely in the roots but spoiled himself after finding game well. No first prize was awarded. Second was Mrs M Layton's German Pointer bitch Midlander Oriental Ranee, handled by Dr D Layton. This bitch was disappointing on her first run by being unwilling to get out and quarter freely. She was steady to a shot hare but rather spoilt her retrieve by not delivering to hand. On her second run she went much better, finding game in the roots and being steady. Again, a sloppy delivery spoiled an otherwise very good retrieve.

No other placings were possible but Certificate of Merit went to the Vizsla of Mr

The first get together in 1997 at the Petrie-Hays. Photo Dr S Gottlieb

T West, Galfrid Gelert. This dog ran nicely on the stubble, scenting well and indicating good game finding ability. He also went well in the roots finding birds, being steady to flush and shot and retrieving well. His water test was very poor which removed him from contention or a placing. His handler should, however, take encouragement from the dog's general working.

Meeting at Inkberrow (1977)

August 1977 saw the first Vizsla get together at Inkberrow.

The author in charge of stays at an HVS training day in Shillingford. Photo: Ryan

Programme

11.00am Welcome by the President and chat-about.

11.30am Basic obedience in two groups for dogs under and over one year old:

- Walk to heel on and off the lead.
- Sit on command. Sit and stay, return to dog.
- Sit and stay and recall. Sit, stay, recall and drop half way.
- Walk to heel, shot fired, dog to sit.
- Walk to heel, shot fired, dummy launched, dog to sit.

A 'stay' at the get together in 1977.

Retrieving:

- Simple seen retrieve.
- Blind retrieve.
- Memory retrieve.
- Double retrieve.
- Retrieve over jump.
- Running rabbit on elastic for steadiness test.

12.30am Instruction by Sheila Gray and practice in dog show technique and requirements.

12.45am Pointing caged rabbit and pigeon either on scent or on sight. No flushing or retrieving. Initial quartering up wind.

1.00pm Dog Race (The Vizsla Derby)

1.15pm Demonstration on dizzying pigeons and the advantage of training in their use in pointing and flushing.

Simulated field trial demonstration given by Sheila Gray and Virginia Phillips.

Quartering allotted beat, point on pigeon, steady to flush and shot, and fall retrieve on command.

2.00pm Break for lunch.

3.00pm Convoy to water.

An enthusiastic retrieve over wire.

General swim about for all dogs, competitive retrieving to encourage the less bold to swim.

Retrieving:

- Simple, thrown dummy, dog allowed to run in.
- Launched dummy, dog to retrieve on command.
- Unseen retrieve from water with no shot fired.
- Unseen retrieve across water with no shot fired.

4.30pm Dogs dried off and carriages called.

It was with great pleasure that the President, Mrs Virginia Phillips, opened the day with a speech of welcome to exactly 50 people and their dogs. They had come from as far afield as Kent, Dorset, Essex, Wales and Derby.

The enthusiasm and appreciation of so many Vizsla owners was most satisfying for the organisers. The class was split into two groups, with the dogs going through the exercises according to their ability. The object was not to train the dogs on the day but to demonstrate to the handlers what to aim for and how to achieve it. The programme attempted to go through the whole schedule of basic training up to field trial standard.

The training session was divided into three periods – basic obedience and retrieving, pointing and flushing, and water work; it was stressed that the training of a pointer/retriever should follow this pattern until all facets were perfected for steadiness and ability. Only then should hunting, pointing, flushing and retrieving be combined. Basic obedience and retrieving of all sorts were tackled first with a wide variety of standards and results. Generally speaking basic obedience was good and the speed and delivery of seen retrieves was good. Steadiness seemed to cause no problems but much work will have to be done by those present on handling their dogs onto a blind retrieve. This can be made easier if, for every seen retrieve, two blind retrieves are also given. There were no failures when the dogs were asked to retrieve over a jump.

The class was then instructed by Sheila Gray on the art of dog showing and I think this was probably the largest single class that any judge has yet seen in this country! It was a glorious sight to see so many Vizslas parading round, with not as much variation in conformation as one might have expected.

We then moved into the small field where the dogs were encouraged to point the caged game. No easy task as many dogs will not point as the game seldom gives off a fear scent. However, with perseverance and the example of the dogs who did point, most of the dogs were seen to be pointing and were encouraged to hold their point. Finally the dogs were lined up at the top of the track with their 'slippers' while their owners went to the lower gate. On 'go' a cloud of russet gold was seen blowing at gale force across the hay field in two directions – one towards the calling owners and the other in the direction of the caged game! There had to be two winners of that race!

Dogs and owners reunited, we moved across the lane to the big field where the general requirements for, and behaviour at, a field trial were explained. Virginia and Sheila then put their dogs through simulated conditions to demonstrate the importance and purpose of the exercises previously done.

By this time food and drink was much needed and enjoyed, and sincere thanks and appreciation go to Virginia Phillips and Jeannie Smith who brought the chicken, hard boiled eggs and salads, and Nigel Smith who supplied us with the excellent red and white wine.

When everyone appeared satisfied, a long convoy assembled and set off for Mr Platt's trout reservoir. 'All in' was the order of the day, and all it was. Even though one or two did not quite go out of their depths, nevertheless confidence was built up by seeing so many of the dogs swimming and retrieving successfully. The highlight was one chap who did his utmost to catch the rising trout, a very sensible idea for a working dog, and it was quite a time before he could be persuaded to give up the hunt. By 4.30pm we had all had enough and, as the dogs were being dried off, the rain, which had miraculously kept away all day, came down in buckets. But I am sure, despite the long, wet drive home that many had to suffer, everyone enjoyed and benefited from this get together and it was agreed that it should be repeated, if possible at the end of the summer.

A Novice Stake at Loton Park (1977)

Report
A novice stake was held at Loton Park on October 8th 1977. The ground work consisted of stubble, hedges, grass and potato fields, game produced was pheasant and partridge. The weather conditions were good with a fresh wind all day. Scenting conditions were good.

1st: Mr Parke's Matai Pirok. She worked her ground well all day. She had two very good points – a useful, steady gun dog
2nd: Mr Farmer's Waidman Bogar. Very little to choose between this dog and the winner. He had good game finding ability, style and drive, also several good points. He lost marks on an untidy retrieve
3rd: Mr West's Galfrid Gelert. He worked well, good treatment of his ground but rather unsure of himself
Conclusions: The standard of the first two placed dogs was well up to novice stake. The general handling has improved a lot. The average age was high for novice dogs. We would have liked to have seen them working with more drive, confidence and speed.

Award Winning Dogs of 1977

The Vizsla Club held two novice stakes in the season, officially for Vizslas only, but on both occasions had to invite other breeds in order to fill the cards. Over this year's trialling season, the following dogs were in the awards:

Mrs Auchterlonie's Saline Cabal: 3rd open stake all breeds
Major Wilkinson's Galfrid Otis: 3rd novice stake all breeds
Mr Farmer's Waidman Bogar: 2nd novice stake Vizslas only; Reserve novice stake all breeds; 1st novice stake all breeds
Mr West's Galfrid Gelert: 3rd novice stake Vizslas only; 1st novice stake all breeds
Mr Parke's Matai Pirok: 1st novice stake Vizslas only

Vizsla Gathering at Inkberrow (1978)

On Sunday 4 June 1978 the Society held their second annual get together and training session at Lower Bouts Farm, Inkberrow, by kind permission of the Petrie-Hays. Much work was done by the organisers and this was well rewarded not only by an excellent turnout of 53 members, friends and visitors with their dogs but also by the improvement both of the dogwork and handling since last year. The president, Mrs Phillips, welcomed everyone and a short session of basic obedience followed ending with a simple test for dogs under 20 months – thirteen competed and Sylvia Cox with her ten-month-old puppy won by a whisker with a good performance.

Everyone then moved over the lane into the big field and there was a five-minute playtime with Vizslas romping in all directions. Then came walking in line with gunfire and the dogs dropping to shot at heel and away from their handlers. On the return there was shot and also falling dummies to contend with and finally a stay – recall – and drop halfway. After this all the dogs had a variety of retrieves – marked, memory, blind, double and over a jump. This ended with another test of a double retrieve, one thrown over the jump and the other launched across the field into thick hay. Nigel Cox pulled off a family double by winning this convincingly with his three-year-old dog. The line-up for the annual race was next; there were a couple of over-keen early starters but Sheila Gray's Emilio just got his muzzle over the line first. Back in the yard, Sheila Gray and Commander Val Hawes organised a beauty competition divided into dogs and bitches. Everyone sportingly entered and the judges made Mr Berry's dog puppy Best in Show with Mrs Young's bitch taking Reserve.

At last lunch and much-needed refreshment. At 2.30pm Martin Jones gave a most interesting talk on falconry and the use of dogs. Question-time followed which proved the interest he had elicited. A short walk up the little field where pigeon in release traps awaited to be pointed, flushed and shot at. This gave everyone the opportunity of seeing some excellent, staunch points and also some nice steadiness to flush and shot. Finally the grand exodus to the water; the convoy drove about five miles to Mr Richard Hocknells' trout lake where two Canada geese and their five goslings were waiting to watch the fun. The party walked down to the far end and the dogs had a short free-for-all, swimming and splashing happily. Then one at one time they completed a retrieve of a dummy, first thrown from the near bank and then from the far bank. The Canadas were totally unperturbed, in fact swam in line abreast to referee the proceedings and a common tern also joined in and gave a demonstration of a diving retrieve. With only two non-swimmers all the dogs completed both retrieves with ease. Styles of entry and swimming varied but the dogs' enjoyment and natural ability was very evident.

The First Grouse Trial (1978)

In September the first grouse trial was held.

Field trial report

Everything augured well for the field trial this year. A good report from the moor, a satisfactory entry and fine weather during the preceding week. Saturday 16 September dawned – grey clouds covered the sky; the wind, which had blown away the night's rain, decided to increase its force and, although by 9.30am conditions were not perfect, the trial started cheerfully. We were honoured by the presence of Mr G Sterne, president of the German Shorthaired Pointer Club who came to spectate, as did Hilbre Smith, our ex-chairman of committee. Carol Auchterlonie reported for duty as chief steward. Out of the mist, and berry-brown from the deserts of Dubai, came Eric Grieg, bringing his friend who now has charge of Saline Caroline. Mrs Lewis came from Montrose and a German Shorthaired Pointer owner with his wife from Glasgow. Nine out of the ten entries were present, Mrs Eppie Buist and myself were judging and our host Evan Young with two friends were shooting.

The first dog to run, Mr Farmer's Waidman Bogar, showed his inexperience of grouse at the beginning. Birds got up ahead of him and he made no effort to work round and draw on to where they had pitched. But as the day progressed this dog's work improved considerably and, had the conditions been more favourable, he would have undoubtedly shown us good sport. His quartering down wind was very professional and his handler knew better than to interfere with him. He dropped flat to flush and was 100% steady to hares. He retrieved a hare to hand but lost marks in an untidy pick up.

The second dog, Mrs Nixon's German Pointer bitch Quintana Tyr, had the misfortune to have a hare shot in front of her. The temptation was too great and she was eliminated for running in.

Mrs Auchterlonie and Saline Cabal came next. This strong, sensible dog settled down to his work immediately, covering a lot of ground. He could be faulted by his use of the cheek wind but, working into the wind, no ground was left unsearched. He had a good point on a hare and was steady to shot. He was asked to retrieve an unmarked snipe in conditions where no scent was obtained. The bird had fallen in the lee of a stone wall, with the wind coming over the wall towards him. It was entirely a question of handling the dog onto the bird. After a good try, Mr Elliott was called into the line and achieved this with his German Pointer bitch. Mrs Auchterlonie got high marks for her handling which was quiet and effective.

Dog No 5 was Mr Elliott's German Pointer bitch Inchmarlo Solas. Her quartering was fast and efficient and she looked very pretty indeed as she covered the ground. She also showed a good sense of game and acquired top marks for steadiness. There was obviously a close bond between her and her handler and perhaps the only criticism might be that she was a little too reliant on him, but no doubt time and more experience will overcome this. She retrieved the wounded snipe to hand nicely.

chapter 12

Sheila Gray's Abbeystag Bruna started off well and her handler left her to get on with the job. After not many minutes she had a beautiful point which she held really well. She then worked this point out in copybook fashion, flushing a very young pheasant; a shot was fired at the bird and alas Bruna decided to chase, not far, but far enough to be eliminated – a great shame when she had found and flushed game so well.

The next dog down was Major Wilkinson's Wirehaired Pointer Alphonse. He started off with some indifferent quartering and some unsteadiness to a flushed hen pheasant. But as the day wore on, his groundwork improved and he seemed to be settling. Unfortunately just as he came into the line a second time, a hare got up behind him and he was fired at. Alphonse was nothing but a hairy monster disappearing over the hill – a great pity but I am sure further training is all that is needed.

Mrs Auchterlonie then ran her bitch Ella Elia of Saline; a beautiful mover and efficient worker, very thorough in her ground treatment. In her first round she was steady to fur and had a retrieve of a hare but, alas, fell into temptation later when another hare was shot and she ran in; what a shame as she was in the lead in my book till then.

Mrs Nixon's other German Pointer bitch Kirklade Tanzen then started off well, showing us how an experienced grouse dog should tackle a difficult wind, but a bird was shot and she overkeenly anticipated her retrieve and had to be eliminated.

Lastly came Major Wilkinson's Galfrid Otis. This little bitch worked well, covering her ground carefully although not always as thoroughly as she should and her handler made no effort to correct this. A hare was shot on one flank and supposedly wounded. The gun pointed this out and he was asked to shoot again before Otis was sent to retrieve. A shot was fired and, as there was no movement, Otis stopped and returned to her handler; an extremely creditable performance in steadiness. She worked on well, despite her size and the fact that the heather was making a right mess of her undercarriage, which was red and sore. Later on after a snipe had been shot and Otis was coming over to retrieve it, an obviously wounded hare got up and went off across the heather and down along a narrow ditch out of sight. Major Wilkinson was told to send his bitch for this hare as it obviously had priority over what was supposed to be a dead snipe. He was a little bothered as he did not think Otis could carry a hare – 'Try her,' was all the sympathy he got. She was put on the line and followed it well. The last we saw of her was way down the hill going towards a bit of woodland. A long pause – Major Wilkinson sensibly refrained from calling her as the wind was far too strong. In the distance the little Vizsla could be seen carrying the hare, head high and trying not to trip up over its legs. A very proud handler went to meet her and relieve her of her burden. It was an excellent piece of tracking and showed courage and determination.

That is an overall picture of the dogwork; the weather was far less pleasing. By lunchtime a gale force wind was blowing with intermittent rain. Plenty of birds were seen but none would hold long enough for the dogs to have the opportunity of a productive point. Evan invited us into a barn for lunch and this was a most welcome break from the roughening weather. Having sustained ourselves with liquids and some solids it was agreed to brave the elements again on the chance that it might clear –

what a forlorn hope. Mrs Buist requested to be relieved as the pace and conditions had taken a heavy toll of her resources and, as she was due for an operation in the near future, it would have been foolish to undergo further stress. Eric Grieg, an experienced judge, agreed to replace her, with the agreement of the competitors. He strode into the teeth of the gale with that rear profile which fills us Sassenachs with envy! Our luck was right out and, as we advanced, the weather worsened. Nevertheless the dogs continued to work with style and pace. Eventually as we neared the reservoir it was agreed to call the competitors and report that owing to the conditions it was not possible to get a result. If they were game we proposed to give them the water retrieve and then assess the marks and award the cups on an unofficial basis; the trophies would not be awarded. It was felt that the dogs and handlers had acquitted themselves well enough to warrant a token of appreciation from the Society for their efforts.

Four dogs were in contention and their final placings were:

1st Galfrid Otis; 2nd Inchmarlo Solas; 3rd Saline Cabal; 4th Waidman Bogar.

A vote of appreciation and thanks to our host, the guns, the judges and the steward ended the day and, despite the disappointment, it would seem that those present really enjoyed themselves which, after all, must be one of the main objects of any trial. I would like to mention that our vice-president, Mr Alec MacRae, was unable to attend but very kindly sent a donation, as did Mrs Lewis who withdrew her entry. Mr Hilbre Smith brought some very useful towelling materials which were sold at the end of the trial, for which a lot of very wet dogs were most grateful, the proceeds being donated to the Society.

The Hungarian Vizsla Society have held trials since 1973 under the rules and regulations of The Kennel Club, novice stakes at first and then non-qualifying open and all-aged stakes. The time has now come to apply to The Kennel Club for permission to run qualifying stakes. The winner of two such stakes becomes a field trial champion.

Get Together (10 June 1979)

Once again we were lucky with the weather and the Petrie-Hays much enjoyed welcoming so many Vizslas and their owners to Lower Bouts Farm. Among the new members were Mr and Mrs Armstrong, Mr and Mrs Hargreaves and Mr and Mrs Chaffe. The petrol shortage was responsible for a slight decrease on last year's numbers but the enthusiasm was great. We sadly missed the presence of Mr and Mrs Hilbre Smith and extend the greatest sympathy to them for the loss of Katy who was killed on the road two days before. The tests were kept as simple as possible in order to encourage everyone to have a go and nearly everyone sportingly did.

Puppy test: for dogs of 12 months and under
1. Walk to heel on lead from A to B. Stop and sit. Continue to heel to C. Stop and sit. Leave dog at C and walk back to B. Stand and count ten. Return to dog. Walk to heel off lead to A.
2. 25 yards marked simple retrieve with shot fired. Dog to be steady on or off lead.
3. 50 yards memory retrieve.

Novice test: for dogs between the ages of one year plus or four years minus
1. Walk to heel from A to B, sit. Leave dog and walk to C. Recall dog and sit. Leave dog and walk to C. Walk to A, recall dog and drop at B.
2. 100 yards memory retrieve.
3. Blind retrieve placed in the same position as memory.
4. Two dummies launched left and right. Handler to select order of the retrieve of both dummies.

Open test: for dogs over two years old
1. Dog to quarter field up wind. Shot fired (no dummy) and dog to drop to shot then redirected. Continue quartering dummy launched ahead and dummy dropped behind. Dog to retrieve both dummies, back one first (blind).
2. 200 yards L-shaped memory retrieve with diversion of running rabbit on return.
3. Seen retrieve over jump and blind retrieve to the side. Retrieves to be made in jump/blind order.

Dogs may enter one or more of the tests if eligible. The Marion Trophy will be awarded to the member with the highest placed dog in the Novice Tests. We can have a water test at the lake, but this will not be included in the marks.

The puppy test was won by Mrs Phillip's Ibi
The novice test was won by Mrs Cox's Barley Broth with 88%
The open test was won by Mr Cox's Hal with 82%
Mrs Cox won the Marion Trophy, many congratulations to her
Mr Chaffe with Anya came a very close second both in the novice and open with 86% and 78%
The Grand Derby was won by 'Pasha' Hambi
Sheila Cox very kindly agreed to judge the dog show. Mr Berry came first with his dog and Mr Hargreaves owned the best bitch. Overall winner was Mr Berry

Field Day at Donhead St Mary (1979)

The field day was held on 13 October and was kindly organized by Sheila and Jim Gray on ground that was generously provided by Mr Hall. Sheila had prepared a wonderful lunch and tea for everyone who attended this Vizsla gathering.

Roger Phillips acted as judge and reported as follows:

The intention of holding this field day was to give dogs and their handlers an opportunity to run their dogs on the lines of a field trial, without actually competing and those who attended certainly thought that it was well worthwhile and should be repeated if suitable ground could be found. It was unfortunate, and nobody's fault, that the game was absent on the day. Six dogs with their owners were present, and most had driven a very long way, so it shows how much enthusiasm there is.

The day was fine and damp after rain, ideal for scenting conditions but, alas, no game could be found in the morning so, apart from observing the dogs working and quartering, and the owners' handling ability, nothing much could be learnt about the dogs.

After lunch, a water test was laid on with pigeons thrown into the lake and a shot fired. All the dogs entered the water and retrieved, though one only did so at the second attempt and with some persuasion! We then went to a very tall kale field; a difficult test at the best of times for experienced dogs, and more so with inexperienced dogs especially if rabbits and game are moving about. It was here that the only two pheasants were seen departing unscathed at the end of the beat, by which time everyone was more interest in getting out of wet trousers and into dry ones.

Extract from a letter from one of the competitors at the above field day:

As a 'competitor' may I say how interesting and rewarding my dog and I found the day and how helpful the comments from our very patient judge. I am not a great public performer and, although enthusiastic, must admit approached the occasion with some apprehension. But the atmosphere of work without the pressure of competition was such that with each run I gained more confidence and so therefore did the dog. I feel the day gave my dog a very interesting experience which we very much hope can be repeated at some time.

Two Field Trials held by The Vizsla Society (1979)

The Society organised and ran two field trials this year. On 6 October a novice stake was held at Loton Park by kind permission of Sir Michael Leighton Bt and on 27 October our first open stake carrying championship status was held at the Marshland Estate, by kind permission of Mr Alan Heyman, QC.

The novice stake at Loton was judged by Sir Michael and Mr Peter Moxon. A very unfavourable report of this trial was published in *The Shooting Times* on 25 October. On the other side of the coin I think the Society should feel pleased that this was the first trial to be held for Vizslas only with a full card of 12 runners and that all competitors should be thanked for supporting the trial. I do not agree that the ground, which the dogs were expected to work during most of the day, was ideal. This consisted of sprayed potatoes, neither suitable nor conducive to any breed of dog in any stake. This was very noticeable when, late in the afternoon, we eventually came to grassland and roots, and the dogs called up to work this were awarded the certificates of merit. No dog was put out for hardmouth, no dog failed on the water retrieve. I think it was unfortunate that Mr Moxon did not even do us the minimum courtesy of spelling the name of the breed correctly.

Certificates of Merit were awarded to:
Mr Berry's Galfrid Dali
Miss Boy's Galfrid Odo
Mr West's Galfrid Gelert
Mrs L Petrie-Hay's Waidman Crumpet
We must thank Mrs Gay Gottlieb for acting as chief steward and also Mr Ron Martin for coming as picker-up.

The open stake in Suffolk was a much happier affair. This stake was open to all breeds which hunt, point and retrieve and the winning dog achieved a qualification towards the necessary two required to be a field trial champion. Fourteen entries were received, eight Vizslas and six German Pointers. On the day seven Vizslas and five Pointers ran. It is interesting to note that four of the Vizslas had run in the trial at Loton.

Judging this stake were Mr J Wylie (Kennel Club Panel 'A' judge for Pointers and Setters, Retrievers and Spaniels) and myself. It was a beautiful day with good scenting conditions and, as usual, really suitable ground, consisting of large areas of lucerne, stubble and roots. Partridges, pheasants, hares and rabbits were seen. The best report I can give of the Trial is to repeat what Mr Wylie had to say. He enjoyed judging the trial very much and thought the standard of work was very high. This is what he wrote to Mr Moxon:

> After reading your write-up of the Vizsla novice trial, I had my eyes open when I judged the open stake. The hunting and quartering would put plenty of our pointers and setters to shame. The steadiness and retrieving were as good as plenty of Labs. Several runners were collected first class. It was a very tough water test over a quite wide piece of water on a planted pigeon. It was a blind retrieve with no shot fired and the majority of dogs went over with very little trouble. It was a very commanding performance all over. The trial was worth a lot of praise, I enjoyed every minute of judging.

One can assess from that and I confirm that the dogs went well, with plenty of drive. The final results were:

1st: Mr Hale's Trakevlyn Commanchero (GSP)
2nd: Mr Musselwhite's Ft Ch Fruili Asta (GSP)
3rd: Mr West's Galfrid Gelert (Vizsla) handled by Mr Williams
Reserve: Mrs Nixon's Quintana Tyr (GSP)
Cert. of Merit: Mrs Stammer's Moylock Maree (GSP)

Working Tests (1980)

The Vizslas' get together was held in June, and in September the Society's working tests took place.

Puppies: not under 6 months but born after 1 January 1979

1. Walk to heel on lead – sit on command – sit and stay – handler to return to dog. Sit and stay – handler to recall dog. Walk to heel -- off lead – sit and stay – handler to walk on – recall – heel.
2. (a) Seen retrieve in long grass with shot; (b) Memory retrieve; (c) Blind retrieve.
3. Seen retrieve from water with shot.

Novices: any dog under 5 years old

1. Walk to heel – sit and stay – handler to walk on – recall – heel – sit and stay – recall and drop half way – recall and sit.
2. Quartering – dropping the dog twice and redirecting. Drop – launch dummy retrieve – continue quartering – shot fired and blind retrieve.
3. Double launched retrieve in order directed by judge.
4. Seen retrieve from water – shot fired – dog and handler 10 yards back from a bank.

Open: all dogs other than puppies

1. Quartering to point caged pigeons. Shot fired – seen retrieve. Continue quartering to second point – 2 shots fired at (1) seen dummy (2) blind dummy. Blind retrieve first then the seen.

2. Retrieve over fence from cover – seen with shot.
3. Retrieve across water – no shot fired.

Report

On Sunday 7 September the Society's first working test took place at Wotton Underwood near Bicester by kind permission of Mr and Mrs Mike Farquhar. It was a beautiful and ideal setting for the tests and the weather was perfect. The entries had come in well and we were lucky to have John Gassman, Rosemary Jones and Sir Denis Smallwood to judge for us. John Gassman had presented a cup to the winner of the open tests and the Cox's had presented the rosettes. There were 3 leather slip-leads as specials.

The puppy and novice tests took place in the morning and were judged by Mrs Rosemary Jones and Sir Denis Smallwood. There were seven entries in the puppy test:

Winner: Juno, owned and handled by Mrs Sweetman
Second: Mr Greig's Maggie handled by Mrs Petrie-Hay
Third: Messrs Jones and Williams' Alex (Maggie's brother)
Fourth: Mr Coller's Jaffa handled by Mr Coller
The special prize for the most promising puppy was awarded to Freddie, owned and handled by Mrs Farquhar

There were nine entries in the novice test and the results were:

Winner: Mrs Cox's Barley owned and handled by Sylvia
Second: Mr Chaffe's Anya
Third: Mr Berry's Bruce
Fourth: Mr Bennett's Miscka
The special prize for the best handler was awarded to Mr Chaffe

After a break for lunch Mr John Gassman started judging the open test. There were six entries and the results were:

Winner: Mr Bennett and Miscka
Second: Mrs Cox with Barley
Third: Mr Cox with Hal
Fourth: Mr Farquhar with Vikki
The special prize for the best water test was awarded to Mr Bennett and Miscka.

After the prize-giving our host, the judges, the stewards and everyone who had helped organise this event were gratefully thanked.

Field Trial – Invitation Novice Stake for Eight Dogs (1980)

Report

Mr and Mrs Farquhar very kindly offered us part of their shoot for a field trial. Because we had not held a trial here before it was decided to limit the stake to eight dogs. Myself and Mr Gerry Webb were invited to judge and Sir Denis Smallwood took a book. The weather was not good. There had been driving rain on the previous night and in the morning there was drizzle and a cold wind which did nothing to encourage the birds out of the coverts.

There were eight entries but only seven ran as number 8 failed to arrive. These dogs all had three or four runs each and were well tested for ground treatment and game finding, but conditions were severe for novices and, at the end of the day despite all efforts, it was agreed that no awards could be given as not enough game had been shot to ensure that all the dogs had been tested fairly. Nevertheless, the competitors benefited greatly from the experience of running in a trial and the general standard of work and handling was good. No dog was eliminated for hardmouth and all the dogs completed the water test. The dogs which were submitted to temptation proved steady. The judges agreed that in many cases the dogs were over-handled owing to lack of confidence in them by the handlers, but this will obviously improve with experience. It was good to see how all the dogs faced thick cover without hesitation.

Because of the number of field trials open to all breeds which hunt, point and retrieve organised by the other societies this year it was decided that The Vizsla Society would hold only this one.

Our congratulations to Mr Bill and Mrs Auchterlonie who came 1st and 2nd in a novice stake at Pitlochry for all breeds which hunt, point and retrieve run by the German Shorthaired Pointer Association.

1980 field trial awards
Three Vizslas featured in the 1980 field trial awards. Mr Bill's Saline Gambler won a German Shorthaired Pointers Association's Novice Stake. Mrs Auchterlonie's Saline Fulmarx Blue came second in the same trial and won a certificate of merit in a German Pointer Club's novice stake. Mrs Cox's Calversam Barleybroth came second in two novice stakes, one run by the Hungarian Vizsla Club and the other by the German Shorthaired Pointer Association. It would be nice to see a lot more dogs in the awards.

Hungarian Vizsla Working Test (1981)
(27 September, Piddington, Oxon)
Report
It is very encouraging to find more Vizslas and their owners having a go at working tests, and this year's Society working test saw an increase in the entries to puppy, novice and open. We were very fortunate in having a lovely field loaned to us by Mr J Johns and arranged by Mr and Mrs Farquhar. We were also very lucky in the weather; it was cold but stayed dry and the whole day was enjoyed by all. The judges were very patient and gave each dog every opportunity to do its best. The puppies were judged by Sir Denis Smallwood, novices by Mr Martin Gibbins and Sir Denis and the open tests were judged by Mr Martin Gibbins. I donated some leather slip leads for specials and Mr Peter Faulk presented the Society with a super trophy for the winner of the puppy tests in memory of his Vizsla puppy Saddleglade Moni. A plaque for the open winner was also donated by Mr Coller to be won outright. Many thanks for their generosity. Results were as follows:

Puppy
1st: Viszony of Vallota, Mr N Cox

2nd: Laser Duite, Mr J Churchill
3rd: Abbeystag Josie Mrs S Gray

Novice
1st: Czassa Camboge, Mr N Coller
2nd: Viszony of Vallota, Mr N Cox
3rd: Perdita's Puzzle of Szajani, Mrs S Harris

Open
1st: Calversham Barleybroth of Valotta, Mrs S Cox
2nd: Waidman Brok, Lady Smallwood
3rd: Galfrid Dali, Mr E Berry

A Working Day at Piddington (November 1981)

Report by Jeanne Smallwood

There was an excellent turnout, with all the usual 'suspects' plus several new faces, both canine and human. Was it my imagination or were one or two of the dogs larger than the norm?

The tests for Purdey's class were interesting, as the first one (split retrieve) was done in a paddock full of sheep. It was very satisfactory to note that not a single dog blinked an eyelash at the sight of them all day.

The pointing was done on a caged pheasant – very nice for the dogs but somewhat disastrous for the poor victim, who departed this world before the day was over! I did not have a chance to watch the puppies but gather that there was quite a lot of potential about. The dog show was judged by Mr Elliott in a very professional style, and again, as far as I can remember, it was won by a very handsome large newcomer to the scene. The water test went well. A few reluctant candidates but, on the whole, most dogs entered with enthusiasm and enjoyed themselves.

Field Trials (1981)

On Saturday 17 October the open qualifying stake was held on the Marshland Estate, Woodbridge by kind permission yet again of Alan Heyman. Chris Church and Eddie Hales were the judges and we had a full card of twelve runners. Sir Denis Smallwood was in the line taking a book. At the end of the day Mrs Marina Dumas, Alan's daughter, kindly agreed to give out the prizes. The winner was Mr Wagstaff's Clara of Abberton, a large Munsterlander, the first open win for this breed. Second prize went to Mr Street's German Pointer bitch My Lady Belladonna, third to Mr McErlean's German Pointer dog Friuli Cougar. Mrs Kathleen Auchterlonie's Vizsla dog, Saline Fulmarx Blue, was awarded a certificate of merit. Two other Vizslas ran – Mr Bennett's Waidman Chico and Mr West's Galfrid Gelert. They both worked well and with enthusiasm but blotted their copy books, alas! There was also a German Wirehaired Pointer running. With his usual generosity, Alan gave the officials an excellent lunch at the Oyster Bar in Orford.

On Thursday 22 October we held a non qualifying All-aged Stake at Sansaw, Shropshire by kind permission of Major Thompson. Lord Joicey and Mr Graham

Nixon judged and Maureen Nixon acted as Chief Steward. Twelve dogs were entered with one reserve, but on the day there were only nine runners. Four of these were Vizslas. The winner was Mr Musselwhite's German Pointer bitch, Friuli Duchess, she also won the Waidman Bock Trophy for the highest placed member. No other awards were given.

On Saturday 24 October a novice trial was held at Apley Park, Bridgnorth by kind permission of Brigadier Goulburn and the Hon. James Hamilton. Here was an entry of twelve dogs and five reserves but on the day, due to withdrawals, there were nine runners. The judges were myself and Geoff Sherring. Amongst our competitors was Mr Jim Pryke, aged 76, which has got to be a record age for a competitor. On top of this he managed to gain a certificate of merit. He was congratulated by all.

The winner was Mrs Harris' Vizsla Perdita's Puzzle of Szajani. Second Mr Hargreave's Foxbrae Flora, third Mr Martin's German Pointer bitch, Zhexe of Waidman. The reserve and winner of the puppy cup was Mrs Cox's Vizsla, Viszony of Vallota. Certificates of merit went to Mr Pryke's Waidman Foxi and Mrs Phillip's Llewellyn Ibi.

Other results this year: Mr Bennett's Waidman Chico won 1st prize in an All-aged Stake and a certificate of merit in an Open stake. Mrs Cox's Calversham Barley Broth won 2nd prize in a novice stake.

The 1982 Annual Get together

Report

On 13 June this annual event was once again held at Inkberrow by kind invitation of the Petrie-Hays. Despite the date the weather was very pleasant and the turn out was even better than ever. Apart from all our old friends it was very nice to welcome Mr and Mrs John Gassman and also Gay and Sydney Gottlieb who had not attended before. Sidney clicked away with his camera and produced some really superb pictures, capturing not only people and dogs but also the carefree atmosphere which pervaded.

The fun work this year consisted of a sponsored walk. Members, their dogs and families followed a trail round the fields, taking part in various exercises at intervals. There were no judges, but any dog who failed an exercise requested his owner to report this to the steward who then penalised him 10p. Twenty dogs played this game and, by the end of the day, the Society was £10.00 better off. This included one or two kind donations or perhaps it was conscience money! There were three winners who amassed no penalty points at all; these were Jean Smallwood with Purdey, Sheila Gray with Katy and Sylvia Cox with Solly. At lunch time Sheila Gray very kindly gave us a talk and demonstration on the art of showing your dog. As usual there was the annual Vizsla derby, won again by Sue Farquhar's Freddie, the fastest Vizsla in the south.

In the afternoon, after some retrieving tests, the pigeons were put to good use again and some very nice pointing was achieved and good steadiness to flush. At five o'clock we returned to the house and everyone agreed that it was time to go home, so this year the water party had to be skipped. But, despite this, everyone seemed to have really enjoyed themselves which makes the effort of laying it all on worthwhile. Very many thanks to the dummy launchers, dummy throwers and to John Dickinson who worked very hard as Chief Steward, also to Denis Smallwood our dead-eye-dick shot.

HVS Working Test (1982)

Report by Sylvia Cox

The Society held its first working test open to all hunt, point and retrieve breeds on Sunday 12 September at Little Ponton, near Grantham in Lincolnshire.

The weather was rather blustery but otherwise conditions were good. The ground was stubble and rough grass and was kindly given by Mr A McCorquodale who unfortunately was unable to present the awards at the end of the day. However he did come along to watch in the afternoon with his son and daughter-in-law, Lady Sarah, who is very fond of the 'ginger ones' – probably because she is ginger headed herself!

The entry of dogs was very encouraging with 13 Vizslas, 12 German Pointers, 1 Large Munsterlander and 1 Weimaraner. Even more encouraging was the amount of people who said they had enjoyed the day – for myself and Nigel it made all the work well worthwhile.

The judge for puppy and open was Louise Petrie-Hay and the judge for novice and open was Mr Gibbins. The results are below:

Puppy

1st and winner of the Saddleglade Trophy: Mr M Gibbins GSP dog, Isara Kurzhaar Voyager
2nd: Mr J Gatcliffe's GSP dog Geramers Shannon
3rd: Mr A Stammer's GSP dog Lockpointer Mr Chips
4th: Mr and Mrs Gray's Vizsla bitch Abbeystag Katy

Novice

1st: and winner of the Ch Abbeystag Bruna Trophy: Mr J. Churchill's Vizsla dog, Laser Duite
2nd: Mr D Bennett's Saddleglade Zoli Vizsla dog
3rd: Mr and Mrs Horsefield's Fineshade Quail Run Weimaraner bitch
There was no fourth award

Open

1st and winner of the Braeville Award: Mrs M Simon's GSP dog Ch & Ft Ch Swifthouse Tufty
2nd: Mrs M Cox's GSP dog Trolanda Black Tern
3rd: Mr J Churchill's Vizsla dog Laser Duite
Certificate of Merit went to Weimaraner bitch Fineshade Quail Run
There was no fourth place awarded
The best Vizsla puppy winner was Abbeystag Katy and the Best Vizsla overall and winner of the Marion Trophy was Laser Duite.

Other Working Test Results (1982)

Large Munsterlander Club, Sandpeck Park, 25 March 1982
Open: 4th Vizsony of Vallota, owned by S Cox. Judge: Mr I W Sladden
Novice: 4th Laser Duite, owned by J Churchill. Judge: J W Malesa

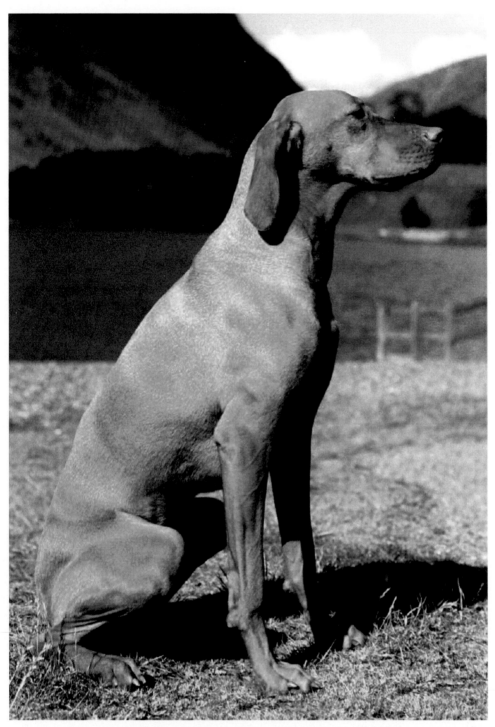

Newbury's Gleam of Dalgarth successfully trialled in the 1980s.

Large Munsterlander Club, Hall Barn, Beaconsfield, 16 April 1982
Open: 2nd Calversham Barleybroth of Vallota owned by S Cox. Judge: Mr C Church
Graduate: 4th Laser Duite, owned by J Churchill. Judge: Mrs S Kuban

GSP Association, Lowdham Mill, Notts, 23 April 1982
Open: 4th Viszony of Vallota, owned by S Cox. Judge: Mr G Roberts

GSP Club, High Wycombe, Bucks, 30 April 1982
Open: 2nd Waidman Chico, owned by D Bennett. Judge: Mr E Hales
Novice: 4th Laser Duite, owned by J Churchill. Judge: C Snelling

GSP Club (Eastern Counties Group)
Puppy: 3rd Dalegarth Gleam, owned by Mr Newbury

Field Trials (1982)

The Society ran two field trials this year. Both were well supported.

The Open Stakes

The open stake was held once again on Alan Heyman's ground in Suffolk and, as usual, supplied everything any field trial secretary could dream of to ensure success. Unfortunately our senior judge, Lord Joicey, was unable to come as he was still shooting in Denmark, so I replaced him and had great pleasure in judging with Roger Phillips. Sheila Gray came and acted very efficiently as chief steward.

Report by Roger Phillips

Hungarian Vizsla Society open field trial held on Saturday 16 October at the Marshland Estate by kind permission of Alan Heyman, QC.

There was a full card for this trial, consisting of 4 Vizslas, 6 German Shorthaired Pointers, 1 Weimaraner and 1 Munsterlander. The weather forecast for the day was not promising, with rain spreading from the west; however it luckily remained dry all day – it was still in the morning, with increasing wind through the afternoon.

The land worked consisted of large tracts of stubble, kale and sugar beet. The first stubble field produced a surfeit of hares, which was indeed a severe test to all the dogs that were given a run at this stage. However, all but one survived and most proved to be rock steady. Several retrieves of hares were accomplished. All except one were large and heavy, and only Mathams Goshawk (German Pointer) achieved a clean and efficient retrieve. The second large stubble field produced fewer hares, but sadly Waidman Chico (Vizsla) after some promising quartering succumbed to the hare problem that most handlers have at some time experienced.

A field of kale showed a few pheasants, but Fossana Blue John (Weimaraner) developed a lack of interest in his handler, and so was withdrawn. Here, Vizsony of Vallota (Vizsla) completed her run with some good work; a nice point, steady to flush – fall of bird followed by a faultless retrieve. Earlier an inexperienced hare retrieve by this young dog cost her a few points.

There were nine dogs left at lunch and a picture began to emerge in the judge's mind as to what the final result might be. How wrong can one be! The promising dogs of the morning failed to improve on their position in the afternoon and good work was put in by other dogs to nudge them ahead.

All the remaining dogs achieved the water retrieve in an efficient manner and we then entered a large sugar beet field where there were plenty of pheasants. Mathams Goshawk did a useful blind retrieve from a wood, but failed after two runs to get a point and so had to be discarded. Swifthouse Tufty (German Pointer), a really strong-looking dog who looked like he would work for days without tiring and who moved and quartered really well, failed to retrieve a wounded bird which unfortunately had fallen in or near a patch of wild mint. The same bird produced a negative retrieve by Clara of Abberton (Munsterlander) who subsequently retrieved an unseen bird efficiently. Trolanda Common Tern (German Pointer), a nice bitch not yet three years old, improved on her morning run doing a good point and was rock steady ending with a nice retrieve. More experience and she will be really good. Also in the same ownership, Feltimores Redpoll (German Pointer) improved on the morning run but tended to be erratic when quartering, ranging too far ahead and returning on the same line. Birds could have been missed, but she was really too steady to shot and fall and finished with a good retrieve.

At the end of the day the judges felt unable to award a first prize, the second prize going to Mrs Winser's Trolanda Common Tern, and the third to Sylvia Cox's Vizsony of Vallota, handled by Nigel Cox. Both these dogs have great promise and with more experience will soon be in the winning positions.

If there is a general criticism to be made of most of the dogs, it is that the quartering was erratic; often the dogs were not going to the extremities of the line, and too frequently going directly away from the line and back again. Also when turning, even in a strong head wind, they would turn away from it rather than into it. It was a most enjoyable day, and we were sincerely thankful to our host, Alan Heyman, for his hospitality.

The Novice Stake

The novice stake was held for the second time at Bridgnorth by kind permission of Brigadier Goulburn and again we were lucky to be supplied with ideal ground for the dogs to work on and to be seen working. This time Eric Grieg had hoped to come down from Scotland to co-judge with Wing Commander Pat Godby but alas, Eila his wife, was not well enough for him to be away from home overnight. This occurred at the last minute which made it difficult for me to try and replace him with an outside judge, so I withdrew my dog and judged with Pat. At the end of the day we compared our assessments of the dogs in order to place them in order of merit and found that our placings were identical. Pat sent me his critique after the trial and which is below and in his covering letter he says 'Mary and I thoroughly enjoyed the trial. What a happy lot of people you have in your Society.'

Judge's report by Pat Godby
I was very happy when asked to judge the Hungarian Vizsla Society's novice stake on

Saturday November 6th as it was many years since I had seen them in action. And I must say I was very impressed with the general standard of work, particularly for novices.

The main weaknesses were failing to retrieve to hand, especially with pigeons at the water. Handlers must learn not to push forward as this will lose them marks as they move up to open stakes. The other failure was in not covering the ground allotted, a fault not always corrected by handlers.

The winner, Saddleglade Zoli, was steady when a cock pheasant ran from a point in heavy cover. Later the handler accepted a retrieve on a hare though it was the first time the dog had been asked to do this. Though this was not a very clean one, a later retrieve from rough cover was very sound. The dog entered water and made a quick retrieve. The runner up, Calversham Barleybroth, was slow to warm up, but picked up marks with a good point, and very two good retrieves. His water retrieve was sound.

Throphill Boss (German Pointer) earned his third place with a very good point although his quartering needs some attention. His retrieves were also not up to those of the dogs placed above him. The reserve, Zhexe of Waidman (German Pointer) covered her ground particularly well but missed a bird and was not too steady. Her retrieves were good.

I was very sorry that Eric Grieg could not judge with me, but it was a pleasure to be joined by Louise Petrie-Hay with whom I had enjoyed judging at previous trials.

There was plenty of game to test the dogs and the field work was ably handled by the keeper, Mr Fred Cooke. Competitors and spectators were quickly and efficiently organised by the steward, Mrs Sue Farquhar.

Major George Wilkinson makes this comment concerning a novice field trial held in Kent by the Large Munsterlander Club:

> *Two Vizslas completely outshone the other competitors. They impressed everybody with their tremendous drive and style. They were Saddleglade Zoli 1st, and Viszony of Vallota 2nd.*

At the very end of the season the GWP Club ran a novice stake and Mrs Cox's Viszony of Vallota came 2nd. The senior judge's comments on her work ran as follows:

> *What a super little bitch this is, she finished her run with a fantastic retrieve of a wing-tipped cock pheasant that ran a long way into the wood before being caught up with. She was under very good control and, besides being 2nd, was awarded a prize for the best retrieve of the day and also a brace of pheasants by the guns as being the dog they would soonest take home.*

The Vizsla Get Together (1983)

Report by Sue Harris

Major and Mrs Petrie-Hay kindly invited us to foregather at Inkberrow on Sunday 5 June, and made us most welcome on our arrival with a glass of wine – a lovely way to break the ice for new members. Personally I can still remember how nervous I was the first time I attended with my K9 accomplice who was shaking like a jelly!

About 40 handlers set off with high hopes to the paddock. First to show their paces were the youngsters – walking to heel, sitting, staying and the recall. They had obviously been working hard at home, and the standard was very promising. They are certainly going to give the older dogs something to think about in a year or two if they continue to progress at this rate. The old hands were then put through their paces in the obedience, finishing up with the 'Great Temptation' – a fur dummy on elastic which enticed only one victim. A great improvement on the last time it was used at a get together!

We then progressed on up the track to try our hands – or should I say dogs – at some retrieves. The intention was to have a split retrieve, however, the dogs, being much more knowledgeable, had other ideas and thought the hedgerows needed closer investigation. It is terrible the way a dog can bring you down to earth – especially in public! The junior dogs did some very creditable retrieves. It was fun to see the senior class all going for their unseen retrieves at the same time – needless to say, not everyone came back with their own dummy! Next it was the turn of the pigeons. The young entry showed great interest with their noses glued to the crate. After one or two came on point, the rest soon copied. What a lovely sight to see 4 Vizslas all on point together.

After a picnic we went to the lake for some water work. Sad to say there are still some non-swimmers in the Society, but they were given every encouragement and opportunity to take the plunge and certainly enjoyed splashing around and getting muddy. Meanwhile at the other end of the reservoir some very competent water retrieves were demonstrated.

The Working Test (1983)

Report by Sylvia Cox

The working test this year was held in the grounds of Little Ponton Hall, by kind invitation of Mr and Mrs A McCorquodale. We were very fortunate with the weather in that we had a short cool break in the morning, and then, unfortunately, cooked again in the afternoon in the heatwave we were having. Due to the large novice entry, Brian Backhouse kindly agreed to myself judging the water test, and nearly all the dogs made light work of it. Over half the entries got 8 marks and over out of a possible 10 which made the novice competition very close all day. It was very rewarding to have so many Vizslas running; Mr Berry having 9 entered in the puppy out of an entry of 13, Mr Backhouse having 11 out of an entry of 24 and Mrs Layton having 6 in the open out of an entry of 14.

Puppy

1st: and also best Vizsla puppy, Mrs S Harris' Szajani Csipke
2nd: Diela (Vizsla) handled by Mrs Petrie-Hay
3rd: Mr Bennett's Saddleglade Kasa (Vizsla)

Novice

1st: Mr Gibbins' Isara Kurzhaar Voyager (German Shorthaired Pointer)
2nd: Mrs Cowburn's Peckers Penny (Vizsla)
3rd: Mr Bucki's Andesheim Clemmy (German Pointer)

Certificate of merit went to Mr Gatcliffe's Geramers Shannon (German Pointer) and Mrs Harris' Szajani Csipke (Vizsla)

Open
1st and highest placed Vizsla overall: Mr D Bennett's Waidman Chico
2nd: Mrs C Snelling's Shaleward Esprit (German Pointer)
3rd: Mr H Girling's Monttaber Sparkel (German Pointer)

Working Day at Clearfields Farm (1983)

Report by Sue Farquhar
By kind permission of Mr and Mrs Johnie Johns, Sue Harris and I were able to hold a working day in ideal surroundings, luckily on one of the cooler days at the end of August. Many people travelled a long way to work their dogs. They were divided into two groups; one for beginners, the other for the more experienced dogs. The first group was involved in basic obedience, walking to heel on and off the lead, walking to heel bending in and out of other dogs, sitting, staying, recall and dropping to command, retrieving dummies seen and memory, also retrieving seen dummies over a fence.

After lunch we had an extremely interesting talk from Mrs Perkins on training puppies, outlining the basic do's and don'ts when first starting to train a new puppy. For the more experienced dogs there followed a working test kindly judged by Mrs Perkins. For the novice dogs a simple test involving the lessons learnt in the morning, also pointing at caged pheasants and a water test, ably judged by Air Chief Marshall Sir Denis Smallwood. Sir Denis said the standard of work was high considering that for many of the owners and their dogs it was a totally new experience.

Air Chief Marshall Sir Dennis Smallwood & John Gassman deep in discussion at a get together in the 1980s. Photo: Dr S Gottlieb

Field Trial News (1983)

The Society held three field trials this year – novice, all-aged and open qualifying stakes. We are greatly indebted to our kind hosts, Brigadier G Goulburn, Major Thompson and Mr Alan Heyman for once again inviting us to hold trials on their land. We would like to welcome our new honorary members, Mr Fred Musselwhite and Mr D Layton, who kindly judged for us and we would like to thank Mr G Nixon, Mr R Phillips, Mrs L Petrie-Hay and Mr E Hales for judging also – particularly those who so generously waived their expenses.

The Society's three annual trophies which include work in the field were all won last year by Mrs Cox's Viszony of Vallota, it will be interesting to see if she clears the board again this year.

Judges' reports and observations

In the all-aged stake at Hall Barn run by the Large Munsterlander Club, Viszony was awarded 2nd prize, the only award in the stake. In another all-aged stake in Kent, run by this club, Mr Bennett's Saddleglade Zoli came in second. In an all-aged stake in Yorkshire run by the German Shorthaired Pointers Club, Mr Churchill's Laser Duite came third. In the novice stake at Clapham run by the German Shorthaired Pointer Association, Mrs Cowburn's Peckers Penny was awarded a certificate of merit.

Novice Stake

Brigadier Goulburn has been host to the Society for many years and it is his kindness and hospitality which attracts the entries. The ground is also inviting. The judges were David Layton and Graham Nixon who proved understanding and helpful to the 11 Vizsla and 1 German Pointer handlers. Conditions at the start were not conducive to good scent as there had been a sharp frost which lingered till mid-morning; later the sun shone and the dogs had every opportunity of showing their paces. I was not in the line so cannot comment on the standards but, regardless of results, everyone had a happy and educative day and the spectators were well placed to watch all of the trial.

The winner for the second time on the ground was Mrs Sue Harris' Vizsla bitch Perdita's Puzzle, a great favourite with the Brigadier! Second was Mrs Cox's Vizsla dog Calversam Barleybroth and third was John Churchill's Vizsla dog Laser Duite. Two certificates of merit went to Mrs Harris' Vizsla puppy Szajani Csipke, who also won the Touchie Quaish for best puppy. The Quaish was suitably christened with the correct lubrication which will delight the kind donor from Scotland, Mr Eric Greig. Roger Phillips handling his wife's Vizsla bitch, Llewelyn Ibi, won the other certificate of merit.

All-aged Stake

Roger Phillips co-judged with me – he was a successful Vizsla pioneer trialler in the early 1960s. Of the 10 dogs on the card, 6 were Vizslas, 2 German Pointers, 1 Weimaraner and 1 Munsterlander. Seven of these were experienced dogs capable of competing in an all-aged stake and three were genuine novices. Despite this those three ended up in the awards, the more experienced ones proving to be unsteady. In the morning one dog could have been put out for not hunting, he was keen enough but just did not seem to know what he was meant to be doing. Because there was the time and the game we gave him a second round in the afternoon. It was hard to believe it was the same dog. He got out well, hunted systematically, pointed, retrieved and completed the water retrieve. Roger muttered to me 'must have had a double gin at lunch time!' Four dogs ran into shot, one of these John Churchill's Vizsla Duke proved himself to be a useful gundog if not a successful trialler on the day. He pointed and flushed a hen which was lightly hit and seen high-tailing down the far side of the hedge towards the covert. Duke went immediately down the near side to the bottom, cutting off the bird's escape into the wood, then went through the hedge and worked his way back up, found the bird and had it back to hand, alive and undamaged. Had he not done this, that hen would have been in the cover amongst live birds and virtually irretrievable.

Mrs Cowburn's Vizsla bitch Peckers Penny won 1st prize. This novice bitch worked with style and pace but lacked experience in handling the wind and was not helped by her handler. However no game was missed and she had an excellent point at the end of her run on a cluster of young birds. Despite the temptation she remained quite steady until they had all be flushed. A bird was shot and fell over the road, apparently a dead bird, but not so when the dog got to the fall. She eventually worked out the line and picked the bird bringing it to hand. In the afternoon her quartering improved, a bird was shot and she completed another good retrieve. Her waterwork was good.

Second prize was awarded to Geoff Hargreaves' Munsterlander bitch Foxbrae Flora of Ghyllbeck. Only one mark separated this dog from the winner in my book. Her ground treatment was good, she pointed but failed to produce a bird and worked on, a cock then flushed back and was shot. She was steady and retrieved well. She had productive points on a rabbit, another cock and a waterfowl and did an excellent retrieve on a pigeon which dropped well ahead in the roots.

Third prize went to Mrs Cox's Vizsla dog Calversam Barleybroth. This dog must always be in contention. What he lacks in style and pace is amply compensated by the game he produces. His handler is unflappable. He deals with the wind as it comes, he points steadily and his retrieving is reliable. He gives the impression of a very experienced hunter who knows what he wants and where to find it.

Certificate of merit went to Mrs Gottlieb's Vizsla dog Ch Russetmantle Troy. This is the dog who benefited from his lunchtime tipple and impressed enough in the afternoon to gain a certificate. Another certificate to Mr and Mrs Gray's Vizsla bitch, Abbeystag Josie, handled by Mrs Gray. This was Josie's first trial and she went with speed and style, very quietly handled. She made intelligent use of the wind on the stubble and in the roots. She had a good point and was steady but needed a lot of encouragement to retrieve. Experience will soon sort this out, she swam well and had no difficulty in finding and retrieving her pigeon. The third certificate was awarded to Brian Backhouses's Throphill Boss (German Pointer). His ground treatment was good but his handling of game running ahead was inexperienced. In roots, with a tail wind, he eventually got a good point on a pheasant and was steady. He had one good retrieve, but failed on two runners, only one of which was picked. His water retrieve was excellent.

Open Stake (1983)

At 4.30am on 29 October, 1983 I set off with my husband to steward the Vizsla Society's open qualifying stake on Mr Alan Heyman's Marshland Estate near Woodbridge. Alan has provided the society with this superb ground for nearly 10 years and, as ever, the judges Fred Musselwhite and Eddie Hales had the opportunity of testing the dogs as pointers. There were 7 German Pointers, 3 Vizslas and 1 Munsterlander running. They started in lucerne and then acres of stubble, giving all the dogs an opportunity of free hunting in varying wind conditions before going into kale and beet. Before the end of the day we had seen not only partridge, pheasant, snipe, woodcock, hares and rabbits but also a marsh harrier, geese, duck and fallow deer. Any dog unsteady to hares is wasting his time on this ground. By mid-morning 20 had been flushed, very few of which had been pointed although all the shot gave off sufficient scent for good retrieves. Not one dog was eliminated for chasing. Unlike pointers, hunt, point and retrieve breeds are expected to point and retrieve ground game. It is not the game they point, it is the scent, and it is accepted that if a hare has been laid up in its form for any length of time, no scent is given off. On one occasion in the roots a dog went on point, a hare flushed forward and was shot and a second hare flushed back from the identical spot. In the past on this ground I remember a dog pointing in stubble, a hare flushing and being shot and, as the dog sat to shot, another hare escaped from under him!

No 1st prize was awarded. Second went to Mike Street's German Pointer bitch Cocklebrook Tamarisk, third to Mrs Finan's German Pointer dog Ch Geramers Sea Venom handled by Mr Finan, reserve to Mrs Cox's Vizsla bitch Viszony of Vallota, handed by Nigel Cox and a certificate of merit to Dave Bennett's Vizsla dog, Saddleglade Zoli. Interesting to note that these four dogs were all born in 1980.

The fact that hosts at hunt, point and retrieve trials comment on the good sportsmanship is something to be proud of but some of the competitors would benefit by reading not only The Kennel Club rules for field trials but also the guide to judges which gives an insight into how and why the judges come to their decisions.

Thus over the last ten years there has been a considerable increase in the encouragement given to Vizsla owners by the Society, to enable them to train their dogs for work whether they have shooting facilities or not. The annual get togethers aim to give them an outlet to assess their success as handlers and trainers. The working days give courage to potential triallers and the trials give an opportunity to prove that the Vizsla can compete and win against the other hunt, point and retrieve breeds.

Vizslas at the Game Fair

The Game Fair is an annual event where sportsmen meet from all over the country. It is organised by the Country Landowners' Association and held at a different venue each year in order to give the maximum opportunity for people to attend. Once in five years it goes to Scotland.

Every year since 1973 Vizslas have been represented in the Parade of Gundogs and in the Gundog exhibition tent. Photographs and details of the breed are displayed and questions from the general public are answered by the Vizsla owners who are invited to attend with their dogs. This is an excellent shop window for the breed as a working gundog. It is only recently that it has been possible to demonstrate their working ability. In 1976 I was approached by the Game Fair Committee and asked to stage some sort of exhibition or competition which would help the general public to understand the work of the hunt, point and retrieve breeds. I gathered a committee and we decided that, as it was the first time such an exploit had been undertaken, we would have a working competition between

Petrie-Hay's Waidman Brok pointing a caged pigeon at Woburn Game Fair.

three German Shorthaired Pointers as these were the most numerous and best known of the hunt, point and retrieve breeds. Despite panics and set-backs during rehearsals, on the day the dogs put up a brilliant performance and convinced a lot of people as to the value of these versatile gundogs.

Proof of this was that I was invited again the following year to stage a similar show at Woburn. This time it was to be a match between a German Pointer, a Vizsla and a Weimaraner in order to demonstrate that, although the work of the breeds was similar, their styles differed considerably. The dogs had to hunt, point caged pigeons, retrieve a dummy over a fence and then another from the lake. The fair was on Friday and Saturday and there was a match on both days. Waidman Brok represented the Vizslas. On the first day the German Pointer won with Brok and the Weimar tying for 2nd place. On the Saturday Brok won so there was a run off between the German Pointer and Brok. The German Pointer was declared the winner, gaining 72 points out of 80 against Brok's 69.

In 1980 at Welbeck we were again invited to demonstrate the work of these dogs and it was agreed that this should take the form purely of a demonstration. A German Pointer, Vizsla, Weimaraner and a Large Munsterlander were represented and the fair lasted for three days.

The object of our demonstration was to cover the role of a pointer/retriever in the shooting field. The dogs would have to be seen to quarter the ground and hunt for game, to point steadily, to flush and to retrieve from land and lake. To do this in a controlled environment, on unnatural game, in public with an audience is quite a tall order for the most experienced of competitors – and it must be repeated for three days.

The hunting must be seen to be systematic and therefore the wind direction could not necessarily be used. The dogs would have to quarter as directed. The pointing would have to be on a caged pigeon, a scentless bird, probably partly visible. So the

213

Waidman Brok at Woburn Game Fair.

point had to be contrived as naturally as possible. The flush was definitely the most difficult obstacle. To persuade a pigeon to rise rapidly upwards can be achieved by a sprung trap, but sprung traps can fail to spring! The alternative is to tip the trap off the pigeon by pulling a piece of string. However, one can never guarantee the pigeon will feel like flying away. Some do, some do not, and those which do not are in considerable danger from an impatient, pointing dog whose next job is to retrieve. All credit to our dogs who remained statuesquely on point before a strutting dithering bird. Only one pigeon lost a few loose tail feathers!!

The retrieving was the least of our worries, apart from the fact when a bird is flushed and shot fired, the dog's instinctive reaction is to mark that bird until out of sight, rather than to watch for a thrown dummy.

To make it more realistic we decided to use a dead pigeon instead of a dummy, and to incorporate a jump in the retrieve to make it more attractive to the spectators. The retrieve from water had to be a dummy launched into the lake. We now had to find suitable dogs to fulfil these requirements, dogs and handlers capable of coping not only with the work but also the artificial conditions. Speed, style and steadiness was essential.

I approached the breed clubs asking for volunteers and we held an audition in June on the ground. This proved difficult as the 'ground' was covered in sheep but, nevertheless, we ran through the aspiring candidates and gave our commentator a vague impression of what we were attempting to achieve. This practice also gave us an idea of timings and the back-up team we would require – two guns, two pigeon replacers, one pigeon thrower, one water launcher and we were promised a military walkie-talkie gentleman. The plan was taking shape but we agreed a further meeting was necessary early in July to finalise the production.

Sylvia Cox was selected to represent the Vizslas with her dog Calversam Barleybroth.

We met on July 13th and, despite the date, were greatly heartened. The ground looked ideal, the grass had grown, it had been fenced off, the jump had been constructed and some offending reeds and rushes by the lakeside had been cleared, making it possible for the dogs to enter the water more spectacularly. We ran through the programme with the selected dogs and they went well. Jack Petit, the head keeper, brought us a couple of partridges to try in the traps to see whether this would produce a more effective point. It did, but the partridge flushed and flew very low, landing in the lake where it had to be retrieved by one of the dogs and revived by one of the handlers inside his shirt! We decided to stick to uncooperative pigeons. Nothing more could now be done other than to pray for good weather. Our preparations were complete.

And what of the show? The weather was kind, the spectators were numerous and appreciative. Our arrangements and timing caused us no concern and every member of the team played their part without fault. If you had seen some anglers taking up their stations on the bank exactly where we had planned our water retrieve they had disappeared when you looked again. From the comments heard or overheard we got the impression that those who had seen our efforts to increase the knowledge and understanding of pointers/retrievers had been interested and entertained, and more than that we could not have asked.

In 1981 the fair was at Stowe School and again a demonstration was staged with the addition of the Wirehaired German Pointer. Sylvia was elected to show up the Vizsla in its true colours and put up yet another superb performance.

In 1982 the fair was at Totton Park and the same pattern was repeated. This time Sylvia and Barley did the first and second days and Nigel Cox demonstrated with Viszony of Vallota on the third day. This young bitch worked brilliantly. This is the sort of publicity which is invaluable to the breed.

In 1983 the fair was in Scotland and there was no demonstration.

Gay Gottlieb brings us up to date and comments : *"Many of us have represented the breed with our Vizslas in the parade of gundogs over recent years, but there is no longer a demonstration of gundog work."*

Gay continues with 'Vizslas in the Field – mid 1980s to late 1990s'

I have been dipping into the *Dog World* breed notes to recall one or two instances to get the 'flavour' in the field. Roger Philips (Kinford) was instructing on a training day. Having done the serious work, we went to the water.

We spent a hilarious time by the delightful river as dummies or pigeons were or were not retrieved. Of course the Vizslas with their brand of humour joined in the fun, some plunging in with great gusto, others stealthily creeping in. We were firmly sabotaged by some stately swans who floated arrogantly by, refusing to move. So we had to retire, not too gracefully. A useful tip we learned: if your Vizsla is not too keen on picking a bird, try a retrieve from the water.

Judi Neill (Auchiner) gives an account of her first field trial in 1985, before she made Sh Ch Saline Judi into a full champion.

Sula worked well. She was congratulated on her excellent run, but later in the afternoon at the water, disaster struck. She looked at me when I gave the command to 'get in', paddled along the edge, another look which clearly said, 'There is no way I'm going into that freezing water to bring back a pigeon.' I knew right away that no amount of persuading would make her change her mind. I am sure other Vizsla owners will know the scene!

Ch Saline Judi and Ch Russetmantle Troy that year both won their field trial classes at Crufts. Both trialled and worked through the season.

Master & Pupil: Ernie Wheeler tutors Ryder's Stregaya Newsprint, 1997. Photo: Ryan

Saline Judi was bred by Kathleen Auchterlonie, who sadly died in 1989. There is hardly a pedigree without her Saline prefix. She was determined to do her best for the breed and, over the years, she demonstrated that the Vizsla can work and look good.

After Kathleen died, Judi had many calls from keepers who knew Kathleen and her dogs well. She worked her Vizslas on grouse right through. Keepers were keen to have her work her Vizslas on their shoot.

In 1989 I recalled an HVS field trial in *Dog World* breed notes:

It is no hardship to walk in the most beautiful countryside, chatting with friends and acquaintances whilst watching the HPRs work. Our hosts were Nigel and Sylvia Cox. They made everyone most welcome. What could be more fun than sitting in their warm kitchen at the end of a trial? Quite fittingly, the Cox's famous Soli (Vizsony of Vallota) has photos of herself hanging on the kitchen walls. From every angle these magnificent coloured portraits of great size looked down upon us. So far, no other Vizsla has come anywhere near her equal in Britain.

It was not to be until the 1997–98 season was nearly at an end that history repeated itself. The second field trial champion was made up, and by whom? The Coxs, with Soli's grand-daughter, Archenfield Crusty of Waidman.

I wrote in *Dog World*:

She was bred by John Gardener (Vallota Varazs ex Clare of Archenfield), and is grand-daughter of FT Ch Viszony of V. She was born in 1991 and has had one litter. She gained her title at the GSPA trial judged by Maureen Nixon and Keith Scattergood, handled by Nigel

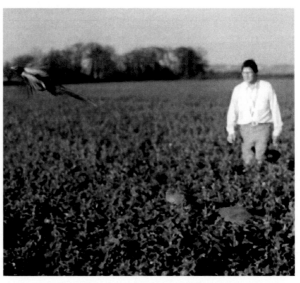

Petrie-Hay & Cox's Crusty, handled by Nigel Cox, demonstrating 'steady to flush'.

Cox. I am told by all who were at this trial and her first open winning trial a couple of weeks ago that she hardly put a foot wrong and that she went like a bird.

Crusty was sold as a puppy but her owner had found that she could not cope. Louise Petrie-Hay took her in for training. She had so much promise and potential that Louise decided she should have the best. Sylvia Cox and Louise shared her in partnership. Crusty went to live with the Coxs and so was set on the path to success.Her training paid off and, as she has matured, all the hard work has given us a Vizsla to be proud of. I know the champagne has been flowing – congratulations; what a great way to end the season.

Crusty on point.

She won her title by winning two Open Stakes in January 1998. The first was the WCGB and the second the GSPA.

The Weimaraner Club of Great Britain, January 1988
Judges - B. Botterman, C Simons.

Judge's field trial report by Brian Botterman
First: Petrie-Hay & Cox's Archenfield Crusty (H Vizsla).
On this bitch's first round, she covered the ground well, took scent, pointed, held until guns were in position, and produced a cock bird and retrieved efficiently. She then acknowledged a hare going away, was steady and made a smart retrieve. She continued working, took scent in the white grass alongside a small plantation, drew forward taking the guns with a high head carriage, kept contact before pointing and flushing a cock pheasant on command, but the bird was missed. In her second run, she ran open white grassland for some twenty minutes, sticking well to her task, covering lots of ground before taking scent, drawing forward some 40 yards before pointing, waited until the guns arrived, then followed with high head carriage, taking the guns on rapidly for some 200 yards before momentarily losing contact with the bird. She cut back right hand and nailed the cock pheasant which was attempting to double back. She produced the bird which was shot and made a smart retrieve tenderly to hand. Made an efficient water retrieve and was quietly handled throughout the day. A very polished performance.

Cox's Vizsony of Vallota; the first Vizsla Field Trial Champion in this country.

The German Shorthaired Pointer Association

Judges - M Nixon, K Scattergood.

Judges Field Trial Report, January 1988

First: Archenfield Crusty – Petrie Hay/Cox

Running no. 9 started her run on two blind retrieves, shot by the gun on the outside of the wood, one 30 metres, the other 80–90 metres, made two retrieves, very little handling. Working her on had a good point which produced two pheasant, both carried off flying.

Second run: had nice find in a bramble bush, a nice staunch point producing a hen pheasant, staying on point, then flushed a rabbit to order, ground game not being shot, the pheasant flew on, working on to the end of the wood had a point standing well off, as the guns were taking their positions, lifted a pheasant which was shot dropping two metres from the side of the dog, she stayed on point, then producing the bird when told, the pheasant flew on.

Third run: her run was on the side of a bank 25 metres wide, produced a cock pheasant which flew on.

Fourth run: working at the side of ride came on point producing a cock pheasant retrieve gently to hand. Completed a good water retrieve.

By the by

Louise Petrie-Hay successfully trialled through the 1980s with Diela of Waidman. I recalled in the breed notes:

> *...a happening that I hope will touch your hearts and remind us of our oldies who are past and present. The time to leave our old dogs behind is a decision that can be changed again and again by just a look. How heart-rending it is to retire and rend a partnership that has been so close and given so much fun and pleasure.*

> *Louise Petrie-Hay and I have been working our Vizslas on the same shoot for the last 15 seasons. Waidman Brok and W Che – long since gone – my Ch Russetmantle Troy and Ch R Quiver, also long since gone. We all worked on this shoot over the years and we have all a few more wrinkles and even more grey hairs.*

> *Louise and I have introduced young dogs but there are still one or two oldies, Waidman Jaques, all of 12, who still insists on coming out and does a good day's work. W Lulu is the oldest. A bit deaf and does not see too well, so it is a bit of a worry when she goes out of sight.*

Last week after the last drive, we were searching deep in a wood for a hard-running cock pheasant that had been pricked. Six Vizslas all hunted out, it was darkening as dusk fell, we decided to give up, called our dogs in – no Lulu. We whistled, called, no sign. We know of old that she will always come back, and always with the bird. But these days the worry is that she may lose her way.

We comforted each other with 'always trust your dog', but we were concerned. We stood in the ride quietly, not a sound, not a twig cracked, silence. In the gloom we saw the old girl slip out of the wood stealthily into the bottom of the ride, trotting toward us with the bird in her mouth, her old grey head held high. Our hearts and emotions overwhelmed us and we surely felt very relieved.

She must have wondered why on earth we made such a fuss when, after all, she had been doing this all her life.

Vizslas – My Problem

(First published in the *Shooting Times and Country Magazine*)

When God created the Vizsla he did so with his tongue in his check. He made a noble, beautiful, agile, lithe, affectionate and intelligent dog. He gave him the eyes of a hawk, the nose of a Bloodhound, the speed of the wind and mouth of velvet. He instilled an immense and urgent ability to work. And then for fun he threw in a pinch of willfulness as if to challenge man with the perfect shooting companion providing he had the patience and character to be master. He gave the Vizsla three commandments:

1. Thou shalt love thy master better than thyself.
2. Thou shalt work hard and joyfully.
3. Thou shalt bite neither man nor dog without just cause.

But on the Vizsla's family coat of arms the devil added the motto: 'My will not thine be done.'

It is said that if you have a Hungarian for a friend you have no need of any enemy. I can quote this in good conscience as it was told me by a Hungarian friend and perhaps it is the answer to this anomaly – the Vizsla. How can black be white? And is it not strange that with the years black and white fade into varying shades of grey?

This may seem an odd introduction to a breed which, once owned and understood, can be replaced by none other. To many, these enigmatic qualities would be distasteful and unattractive but, to the Vizsla lover, they are a glorious challenge which, if treated with kindness, patience, firmness and understanding, can bring rewards not often enjoyed by other dog owners.

Behind this eulogy there is a note of seriousness and a message which was sparked off by a letter from a worried Vizsla owner. By quoting (overleaf) and answering it maybe I can help to give a deeper understanding of this versatile and loving breed. If you read and heed what follows, bear in mind that I never blame the dog – the chances are that I bred it!

He writes: *He is well grown, fit and basically obedient. He quarters well in the open, faces any cover, and points steadily. But as soon as the quarry flushes the chase begins. If I use a check cord I have no trouble, and he is perfectly steady in a rabbit pen, but as soon as he is free in the field I lose control.*

How's that for contradiction? Not from the dog, but from his owner/trainer/handler. What does he mean 'basically obedient'? Of course it is obvious, but what he should have said was that the dog has been basically trained, that is, the training a youngster gets when it is explained to him the manner in which he must behave.

This should always be done without distraction or temptation. Once perfection is achieved by willing obedience to certain commands then distraction and temptation are introduced gradually, but this should never be done before the result of the basic training has become automatic.

There are two training rules for Vizslas:

1. No chasing of anything at any time
2. Willing and complete obedience at all times

These rules must be implanted and, as laws, implemented from the age at which the puppy leaves the nest for all time. No relaxation of either should ever be permitted. With other dogs, very often if given an inch they will take a mile – with a Vizsla if given a millimetre he will take two miles.

Once basic training is achieved successfully there are three more rules to observe when live game is introduced:

1. During his first season he should never be allowed to flush the game he is pointing. This should always be done by the trainer with the dog dropping on command as the game flushes.
2. If that game is shot the dog must remain dropped and not sent to retrieve. The dead game may be used as a retrieve but only after association of the point has been forgotten.
3. No retrieving of wounded game should be permitted during his first season. Only in this way can steadiness in pointing and retrieving be achieved.

It would be true to say that this training could apply to the other pointer/retriever breeds or, for that matter, to other gundogs. It is the application that differs. Remember that you are dealing with a loving, gentle, bloody-minded character, and that being firm is not as simple as it should be. An illustration of this can be shown by Vlada, a bitch who was given to me when 18 months old – thrown out by the trainer and unwanted by her owner (naturally enough, as he needed a gundog).

The history that came with her was that she had gone to a professional trainer at eight months. After the first month a good report was given, after the second difficulties were reported, six months later the trainer asked her owner to collect her as she was useless. She refused to retrieve. I found this hard to believe as, although in this case I did not breed her, I knew her breeding well. It was admirable. She joined my family and fitted in well and happily. During the summer I put her through her paces gradually. She hunted and pointed well, was steady to flush and shot and was obedient. We did no retrieving.

When the season started I took her out with an older dog and let her work but the retrieves were only asked of the other dog. At the end of the day I sent her for a bird dropped in sight but in long grass. She galloped out eagerly for it, found it and then looked straight at me and returned without it. No amount of persuasion or jealousy would make her pick it up. I repeated this three or four times during the following weeks with varying game but always with the same result. It was puzzling because she went so gaily for the bird. I had of course tried turning my back to her but to no avail. The answer came unexpectedly.

Yet again I had sent her for a bird; this time it fell on the far side of the hedge and for the first time I was unable to observe her. Luckily, unknown to her, there was a gun standing in the gateway. He told me that she went to the bird, picked it up and carried it through the hedge. She then stopped, looked in my direction, put the bird down and galloped in. Somewhere along the line she had been overpunished, either for running in or possibly for pegging a bird, but that punishment had never been forgotten nor was I able to overcome the effect.

So, returning to our problem trainer – his problems would never have existed if he had followed the rules. That is why perhaps, although in this case we are shutting the stable door after the horse has gone, this advice may be useful to those who have puppies now. It is also given as a serious warning to those who covet a Vizsla, having enjoyed seeing a well trained one working. Don't rush into buying one lightheartedly but only if you have a gentle, patient character that can return the love and loyalty which will be thrust upon you and are prepared to give the time necessary to achieve control of the boundless energy and enthusiasm which a Vizsla possesses for the work he was bred to perform.

In due course the Shooting Times received the following letter:

Sir, I am bemused by the article by Louise Petrie-Hay. I am Dutch and have shot over this breed on the Continent. Mrs Petrie-Hay writes that the Vizsla was given 'the eyes of a hawk, the nose of a bloodhound...' This is an unfortunate choice of words. One of the FCI disqualifications is hawk/windover eyes and it is accepted that the bloodhound was introduced to the breed in the late 19th century, so developing the heavy forehead that our breeders now strive to obliterate. Why must the English make lap-dogs from a tough and proven dog like the 'Magyar Vizsla'? J A Bosch van Drakenstyn. Holland.

The editor's comment ran as follows:

In defence of Louise Petrie-Hay we must make it clear that in referring to 'eyes of a hawk, nose of a bloodhound' she was extolling the keen sightedness and power of scent owned by the Vizsla and not commenting on its physical appearance. As for lap-dogs! We suggest that Mr Bosch van Drakenstyn pays a visit to the Waidman Kennels. He will be hard put to find any lap-dogs amongst the working retriever-pointers owned by Mrs Petrie-Hay. Ed.

The Vizsla as a Multi-Purpose Dog

(a letter from a friend in Scotland)

When my two Labradors met untimely ends within a short time of each other a few years ago, I decided not to replace them with the same breed, about which I was concerned with the results of breeding for show and inbreeding. I decided to pick a breed which I considered to offer both a high percentage of working dogs and a greater degree of 'dual purpose'. My Labradors were both excellent 'bird dogs' (as our friends over the

Atlantic might say) and first class for roe stalking. Since I consider it to be imperative that any woodland deer stalker has a dog available, I felt absolutely naked without a dog for a short period, during which my roe stalking was very restricted. Having been to Hungary a short time before and seen Vizslas for the first time, my wife and I decided that, despite their light coloured eyes, this was the breed for us. That this choice was, in our opinion, correct, we have confirmed by acquiring a puppy to understudy our 4 1/2 year old dog. I find it invidious singling out dogs that I have had in the past, all of which have been great pals and good workers, but I do feel that our older Vizsla has fulfilled my requirements better than most and, happy as I was to be told by a friend that my dog has the best nose of the dogs on our shoot, an even higher compliment was to overhear on a friend's shoot my host saying to another gun, "That's a bloody good gundog of Ian's". I hasten to point out that I really never trained the Vizsla – it wasn't necessary. Indeed he never had to be house-trained and really neither did the puppy (now 8 months old), because the situation never arose.

Although my dog's principal role now is grouse, partridge and pheasant shooting, originally it was primarily roe stalking. This entailed, and entails, either being on hand in vehicle or house whilst I am sitting in a 'high seat', or, more often accompanying me on a stalk. His first buck, when he was perhaps 8 months old, I remember well. My wife and I sat up a yew tree high seat and when the buck emerged I shot him, the bullet passing about one inch in front of his heart as it subsequently transpired. He turned and ran off, as one would expect with a heart shot, but a subsequent search failed to find him lying a few yards into the wood as expected. I went and fetched the Vizsla pup, and he immediately took me down the side of the little valley and started up the other side. I called him off as he had gone too far and was clearly on the wrong track.

To cut a long story short, my wife and I spent a restless night and were up at dawn next day and searched for two hours in vain. As we gave up I decided to follow the line taken by the Vizsla pup, and there, of course, 20 yards further on from where I had called him back lay the roe buck – or what was left of it, for clearly vixen and cubs had welcomed such a windfall in the night.

Since that time my Vizsla must have been involved in stalking well over 100 deer, and has been invaluable to myself and friends. I rely heavily on his judgement, senses and reactions both with regard to warning me of the presence of deer that he has seen or smelled and of which I was unaware, or with finding dead deer. He has been a regular companion on red deer stalks on the hill too, and whilst he is generally left behind for the final approach, he has accompanied me on a crawl, stealthily creeping low to the ground by my side. On frequent occasions he has warned me of the presence of deer ahead, and he indicates this by pointing red deer with his tail down (as a result of being whacked for starting to chase them when young.) He points roe with a slightly higher tail. Similarly one can tell from his reactions whether he is pointing a pheasant, partridge or grouse, or whether he is pointing a rabbit or just a warm, recently-vacated spot.

I have not taught him to 'bay dead', ie, give tongue over a dead deer, as expected in Hungary, because I don't know how to do so. However, he is able to convey the message to me in his own way without noise. Similarly, he is useful in my everyday work in finding calves on the hill, or sheep in thick bracken, etc. I am always amazed at how he seems to know when we are after deer, rabbits, pheasants or whatever, concentrating on the species being sought and largely ignoring the others. He accompanies me when I go to work in the fields on the tractor, staying close by the tractor, within 200–300 yards anyway, whilst I am ploughing or whatever. Occasionally he picks a vantage point where *he can watch me, and lies down, and rarely he gets fed up or cold or wet and goes home, but mostly he goes up and down the field parallel to me. Another useful feature of our Vizsla is his message carrying, varying from taking notes from my wife or myself to the other from the bedroom to elsewhere in the house, to bearing a note telling me that tea is ready from my wife in the house to where I am working at the far end of the farm yard, as he did yesterday.*

I have never subscribed to the view that working dogs cannot be pets. Our sheepdog prefers to sleep out in the byre at night, but otherwise shares the house in daytime, but the Vizslas live in all the time and appreciate warmth and comfort. The older dog always comes up to the bedroom when the alarm goes off, or when it should have gone off, and judging my wakefulness and receptiveness, either lies beside the bed or says good morning. He is then invited to lie beside me for a while before I get up, with his head buried under my arm. The puppy has, in the last few days, started to be allowed on the bed in the morning, though is as yet rather a fidget! He shares my wife's side of the bed, until she rises to milk the cow, leaving me to enjoy a few idle moments with a Vizsla on either side! In my opinion this 'softness' in no way spoils the Vizsla's working ability and indeed I feel that it enhances our relationship with each other. The Vizslas are good house dogs too, and whilst always friendly to authorized visitors, I feel that unauthorized ones might well have a less friendly reception.

Whilst always delighted at the prospect of a walk or a trip in the car, it is the sight, smell or even sound of the getting out of a gun or rifle which really makes the dog happy. To my mind the Vizsla is the ideal all-round rough shooter's dog. Though he will sit quietly at heel during a driven shoot, he prefers to work, hunt and point as well as retrieve.

I believe that in Hungary the field trial for Vizslas includes blood trailing a deer and retrieving a fox. My Vizsla would doubtless score badly in a strict Hungarian trial, since he probably lacks the style required in such things, largely because I am not interested in such perfection from him, but he can trail a deer and retrieve a fox and has done both. I should be sorry if British Vizslas were to lose their ability to perform as a really all-round sporting/hunting dog as a result of field trials concentrating on the 'bird' or small game hunting side of their ability.

Falconry – the Case for using a Vizsla

(An article by Martin Jones, the falconer published in *HVS Newsletter*)

The falconer's choice of dog tends to be a little confused at the best of times, and depends a great deal on the terrain and type of bird he flies. This I shall endeavour to explain.

Basically, the types of bird flown may be split into two main categories – falcons and hawks (with eagles and buzzards generally flown in the manner of a hawk).

Falcons are birds of open country, possessing long pointed wings and a short tail; they generally kill by stooping at their quarry. Hawks are more direct in their approach, possessing a far longer tail and a more rounded wing, enabling them to manoeuvre after their quarry in enclosed country.

Hawks may be flown with a modicum of success without the aid of a dog, but a good dog will increase the number of flights and help bring more game to book. A great many dogs can be pressed into service for the purpose of working out hedgerows and rough ground. I have seen Spaniels, Labradors, Terriers and an assortment of mongrels used with varying degrees of success, but my own preference has been the pointer/retriever breeds (though no retrieving is required) – I exclude pointers and setters for use in enclosed ground with a true hawk.

In all branches of falconry where a dog is used, there is an estimable value in the time a pointer gives one to move into a suitable position prior to the flight; a tremendous advantage when flying a hawk and a sine qua non when flying falcons at game. As the whole object of flying a falcon is to witness the stoop at quarry, there is no point in walking-up game and slipping a falcon as they flush. Indeed, the falcon is normally hooded to prevent her being tempted should this occur accidentally.

Very few falconers are able to afford the luxury of a separate dog handler, therefore, steadiness and complete 'handleability' is essential as the falconer will tend to concentrate on his bird.

The ground for flying falcons must be as open as possible with a minimum amount of cover for the quarry to seek refuge in and thwart the relatively unmanoeuvrable falcon. Density of game need not be very high – a good point every 20 minutes is considered ample.

On obtaining a point the falconer unhoods and casts his bird off; whereupon the experienced falcon, seeing the dog on point and appraising the situation, will start to mount. In level flight, falcons have little edge in speed over grouse or partridge, so an experienced falcon will mount as high as she thinks fit to ensure a good stoop. Game will often spring wide of a low-mounting badly positioned falcon, without any attempt being made to flush, as they know instinctively that in this way they are unlikely to be caught.

Whilst the falcon is mounting, the falconer walks round in a semi circle, to head the point from an upwind direction.

John Powell with Galfrid Milo and Goshawk.

When the falcon reaches her pitch (as high as she is likely to go) then the falconer and dog combine to flush the game. Frequently, the falcon will drift out of position and it is essential to be able to arrest the dog immediately and continue when the falcon is back in position. Eventually, one hopes, the game is flushed, the falcon stoops, there is a puff of feathers, and a grouse or partridge is dramatically brought to book.

The use of a dog for flying with the true hawks is generally simpler and is rather like using a dog for pot-hunting with a shotgun – get reasonably close and you're in with a chance.

So far no reference has been made to the Vizsla, as I thought it better to give a résumé of the sport and the involvement of dogs in it.

My preference for the pointer/retriever breeds as all rounders in the hawking field has already been stated, and a great deal of my hawking has been done with the aid of German Shorthaired Pointers. However, the last dog (or rather bitch) I obtained for falconry was a Vizsla, and I shall attempt to give my thoroughly biased reasons for this choice.

The need was for a dog that was gentle, co-operative, willing to please, not headstrong and yet not too much of a 'potterer'. I considered German Pointers but had been rather disheartened in recent years by the number of headstrong ones I had seen, that had ruined rather than enhanced several days hawking (was it dog or handler?). Wirehaired Pointers I knew nothing about at all which, together with their relative rarity, precluded them from my reckoning.

Weimaraners I had little experience of, but had seen one with foot problems (inherent?) and had heard reports of their unsociability towards other dogs. Also Munsterlanders were rather an unknown quantity, though I knew a couple of falconers who used them primarily with goshawks; besides which I have always been rather anti long-haired dogs (idleness on my part as I dislike the attendant grooming and dog hairs all over the place).

Although I had not seen many Vizslas, the breed had impressed me. They did not appear too headstrong, did not seem to have been affected by general popularity and consequent attendant evils, and appeared to fit my requirement for a general hawking/shooting dog.

That decision was taken two and a half years ago, somewhat hastened by the fact that Jock Shelley had a smart litter of pups close by, one of which (the smallest bitch) had really taken my fancy. Since when the bitch has performed well up to expectations both in the hawking and shooting field, including two seasons when I have been flying at grouse professionally, with frequent compliments.

If there is a complaint to be made, it is that she does tend to be puppyish if worked with another dog for a while, suddenly deciding it is playtime – to exasperated shouts of 'for heaven's sake grow up'!

A Critique of the Vizsla

Kathleen Auchterlonie, HVS Handbook, 1989

To some owners the Vizsla will not have great enough range; again, some others might expect him to work in water as well as a labrador. That the Vizsla is sensitive I would not consider a disadvantage; frustrated or unintelligent men should not spend their ire on an innocent dog.

As in any other dog, so the Vizsla – I would not consider more than 5% of the dogs as superior. The rest will be average though, in the case of the Vizsla, this average will be rather high due to the careful selective breeding, intelligence and disposition which places the Vizsla slightly ahead of the other breeds. Probably the handicap in proving the breed will be the lack of professional trainers who know the Vizsla sufficiently well, and can adapt themselves to the personality of the individual Vizsla. Besides the somewhat different climatic conditions, the heterogeneous class of owners and their treatment of the Vizsla might influence the behaviour of individual dogs so far that they will not come up to expectations. Many Vizslas have been and are the victims of commercial breeding, with the emphasis upon quantity and not quality. The lack of sufficient authoritative information made the situation even more serious. Several self-styled 'experts' backed by heavy advertising impress the people that they know everything about the breed; however, when it comes to answering certain questions, their replies are often confused, obscure, contradictory and widely different.

The true sportsman will find it a breed which is best adapted for all round hunting, a combination of a pointing and retrieving dog, the best combination so far achieved, but it requires an intelligent, personified handling and treatment for the best results.

Some of the Field Triallers, 1984–1998

Sue Harris

Sue Harris trialled her Szajani Csipke (Holly) successfully. When mated by Henry the Hun of Hookside, she produced Sue Farquar's Szajani Aniko, top field trial Vizsla in 1988–89. All through the 1980s and 1990s Holly won 13 field trial awards. She had two litters, one by Istvan Gyorn, the second by Ch Cuzco Laski. Sue Harris is field trial secretary for the HVS; she shows and works her dogs consistently. In 1997 her youngster Szajani Palinka, out for the first time, won COM at the HVS novice trial at 18 months old. She is by Hookside Solt (who was born in quarantine) ex Szajani Brokat.

Ted Huckle

Ted Huckle is not known in the ring but is a familiar figure in the trialling world. He trained and handled his first Vizsla, Abbeystag Mariner, to be placed first, second or third many times. His second Vizsla, homebred Caldicote Kestrel (Mariner ex Istvan Gyorn), did well for him in the 1990s, winning the GSPA novice trial in 1993.

Penny Easy

Penny Easy is a keen and successful trialler. Living in Scotland means that she travels many miles to compete. She trained her first Vizsla, Swallow Skylark, and handled her to win the GSPC novice trial in 1987. Swallow's daughter, Loguart Capercaillie (by Ch Russetmantle Quiver), did well for her too, winning the GSPA novice trial in 1993 and numerous placings in all-age and open stakes.

Nigel and Sylvia Cox

In the 1980s, the Coxes trialled successfully with Viszony Virtuoso and Visibility. Their breeding dominated the Vizslas placed in trials in the 1990s. Volatile Velocity, as well as Crusty, figured in the top placings. Sylvia also shows her dogs and is frequently in the cards.

Barry Wilson

Ch Cuzco Laski was another in the cards in both disciplines in the 1990s. Bred by M.

Harris' Istvan Szarka of Szajani on point. Photo: de la Rosa

Pia (Oroshaza Alicante ex Glenbek Gerda), Barry handled him to win the GSPC Novice Trial, as well as other placings in trials. Cuzco was always handled by Mrs Pat Wilson in the ring. His highest achievement was his exciting win – CC and BOB - at Crufts 1991. From his mating with Gryffe Rittia, Lambert's Mystical Megan of Gesztenye became a show champion.

Penny Patullo

Penny Patullo, another Scottish competitor, had many successes with Auchinner Cabral. Her most exciting win must have been the GSPC All-age Stake when he was placed first. Another triumph must have been his second place at the All-age Stake at GSPA in 1994.

Penny wrote after a trial:

> *Incidentally this trial was on grouse and hare! Every dog had at least 3 or 4 hares on each run! Judges were delighted with the standard of work. Vizslas always look at their best running across vast moors producing 'the goods' when there are hare about. The operative word may, of course, change to 'chasing' the goods.*

Norma Hunter

Norma Hunter enjoys showing and trialling. Her Galfrid Nymph of Vadasz had successes in the field, being placed second in a novice trial in 1996 whilst her youngster Vadasz Velvet gave her great excitement when she was placed third in the first HVC trial held in 1996. This was after several years when the club had no trials. (John Digby is the Club's Field Trials Secretary. With much dedicated work there are more trials held for the breed than ever before.) Norma also gained a 3rd place with Vadasz in a W A Novice Trial in 1987.

Keith Scattergood

Another competitor new to the breed but not to HPR work and trialling, is Keith Scattergood, GSP breeder, judge and handler. His first Viszla, Conigree Zelda, took the field trial circuit by storm. She won the Weimaraner Association novice trial first time out and gained 2nd & 3rd placings in 1996/1997. Conigree Amber, Zelda's sister, owned trained and handled by Philp Cox, has had success in the field, winning the HVS novice trial in 1996.

The first grouse. Phil Cox's Conigree Amber.

Sara Barnard

By the end of the 1990s season, other novices were trialling for the first time with success. Fresh from winning RCC at LKA, Sara Barnard (Daypack) was placed second in the HVC novice trial, working her dogs, picking up; this was her first trial. Her clever Vizsla is called Daxpack Seeking Cash.

Sue Millson

Sue Millson ended her picking up season by gaining third place in the Hampshire novice trial. Her youngster is Szolnoki Konyak at Lutra, and he is a consistent winner in the ring.

John and Ann Digby

The season ended with the Digbys making up Nicael Russe to a full champion by gaining a C.O.M. as well as a 4th at the H.V.C. Novice Trial.

Jennifer Hurley

In 1997 Jennifer Hurley trialled her Kenvee Habitat for the first time, gaining 2 C.O.M. and a 3rd in the H.V.S. Novice Trial. 'Higgins' is her first Vizsla.

In Conclusion

Of course, there are many others who trial and have had some success, but as we see, most who go to the top also continue on with Vizslas that they have bred themsleves, becoming hardened campaigners.

Thus we come to the end of the season and the late 1990s. Another stalwart of the working Vizsla, Sophie Mildwinsky, who trialled, trained and handled her first Vizsla with some success, expressed exactly a moment of triumph and delight plus pride in her Vizsla, Russetmantle Mist. Perhaps this is the reason for our ambition in any area of owning a Vizsla. On returning from her first run at a field trial, she joined us, the waiting competitors, gasping: *'I feel so happy, yes, at this moment precisely, I am happy!'*

A perfect dummy retrieve by Mildwidsky's Russetmantle Mist. Photo: Gliddon

A good water retrieve by Hurley's Kenvee Habitat.

Field Trial Results 1964–1998

Featuring Vizslas in the awards according to Kennel Club Stud Book Records.
The Stud Book did not include Certificate of Merit Awards 1992–1997.

Abbreviations

BCGB	Brittany Club Great Britain	HVC	Hungarian Vizsla Club
GSPC	German Shorthaired Pointer Club	HVS	Hungarian Vizsla Society
GSPA	German Shorthaired Pointer Association	LBDGA	Lothian Borders Gundog Association
GWPC	German Wirehaired Pointer Club	WCGB	Weimaraner Club of Great Britain
HGS	Hampshire Gundog Society	WA	Weimaraner Association
HPRCDS	Hunt, Point, Retrieve Club of Scotland	HGS	Hampshire Gundog Society
		NQ	Non Qualifier

Date	Club	Stake	Dog	Handler	Award
1964 Aug	GSPC	Novice	Sibriktelepi Tigri	MacRae	2nd
1964 Oct	GSPC	Novice	Creagan Anya	Phillips	2nd
1965 Sept	GSPC	Novice	Creagan Anya	Phillips	3rd
1966 Oct	GSPC	Novice	Creagan Anya	Phillips	2nd
1966 Oct	GSPC	All-aged	Kinford Ficko	Phillips	Res
1970 Oct	LBGA	Novice	Saline Achilles	Auchterlonie	3rd
1971 Nov	GSPC	Novice	Saline Achilles	Auchterlonie	Res
			Saline Czeppataki Csaba	Auchterlonie	C of M
1972 Oct	LBGA	Novice	Saline Caroline	Greig	C of M

Date	Club	Class	Dog	Handler	Place
1973 Nov	HVS (Vizslas only)	Novice	Windhover Ripp	Berry	1st
			Saline Caroline	Greig	2nd
			Starleypoint Ulles	Maitland-Smith	3rd
			Capeland Cascade	Anthony	C of M
			Saline Achilles	Auchterlonie	C of M
1974 Oct	GSPC	Novice	Waidman Brok	Petrie-Hay	3rd
	HVS (Vizslas only)	Novice	Matai Vica	Heyman	1st
			Saline Caroline	Greig	2nd
			Mintaka	Van Helfoort	3rd
	HVC	Novice	Galfrid Gerda	Gottlieb	C of M
			Matai Sari	Boys	C of M
1974 Dec	HVC	Novice	Waidman Brok	Petrie-Hay	C of M
1975 Jan	GSPA	Novice	Waidman Brok	Petrie-Hay	3rd
1975 Sept	HVS	Novice	Matai Vica	Heyman	Res
			Saline Achilles	Auchterlonie	C of M
1975 Oct	HVS (Vizslas only)	Novice	Matai Pirok	Parke	1st
			Matai Vica	Heyman	2nd
			Galfrid Gelert	West	3rd
	WCGB	Novice	Matai Pirok	Parke	1st
1976 Sept	GSPA	Novice	Saline Achilles	Auchterlonie	Res
1976 Oct	HVC (Vizslas only)	Novice	Galfrid Gelert	West	1st
			Galfrid Gerda	Gottlieb	2nd
			Galfrid Odo	Boys	3rd
			Ch Abbeystag Bruna	Gray	C of M

Date	Club	Class	Dog	Judge	Placing
	LBGA	Open	*Saline Achilles*	Auchterlonie	C of M
	GSPC	Novice	*Galfrid Otis*	Wilkinson	3rd
	HVS	Open	*Galfrid Gelert*	West	C of M
	NQ				
1976 Nov	GSPC	Novice	*Saline Cabal*	Auchterlonie	3rd
1977 Aug	GSPC	Open	*Saline Cabal*	Auchterlonie	3rd
1977 Oct	HVC	Novice	*Galfrid Otis*	Wilkinson	3rd
	HVS	Novice	*Matai Pirok*	Parke	1st
	(Vizslas only)		*Waidman Bogar*	Farmer	2nd
			Galfrid Gelert	West	3rd
1977 Nov	GSPC	Novice	*Waidman Bogar*	Farmer	Res
1978 Jan	GSPC	Novice	*Waidman Bogar*	Farmer	1st
	HVC	Novice	*Galfrid Gelert*	West	1st
1978 Oct	HVC	All-aged	*Galfrid Gelert*	West	Res
1979 Oct	HVS	Novice	*Waidman Crumpet*	Petrie-Hay	C of M
	(Vizslas only)		*Galfrid Odo*	Boys	C of M
			Galfrid Gelert	West	C of M
			Galfrid Dali	Berry	C of M
	HVC	All-aged	*Galfrid Gelert*	West	3rd
	HVS	Open	*Galfrid Gelert*	West	3rd
1979 Dec	HVC	Novice	*Calversam Barleybroth*	Cox	C of M
1980 Jan	HVC	Novice	*Galfrid Csaba*	Powell	1st
			Waidman Crumpet	Petrie-Hay	3rd

Date	Club	Class	Dog	Judge	Placing
1980 Aug	GSPA	Novice	Saline Gambler	Bil	1st
			Saline Fulmarx Blue	Auchterlonie	2nd
1980 Nov	GSPC	Novice	Saline Fulmarx Blue	Auchterlonie	C of M
1980 Dec	HVC	Novice	Calversam Barleybroth	Cox	2nd
1981 Jan	GSPA	Novice	Calversam Barleybroth	Cox	2nd
1981 Oct	WCGB	Novice	Calversam Barleybroth	Cox	2nd
	LMC	All-aged	Waidman Chico	Bennett	1st
	HVS	Open	Saline Fulmarx Blue	Auchterlonie	C of M
	HVS	Novice	Perdita's Puzzle	Harris	1st
			Viszony of Vallota	Cox	Res
			Waidman Foxi	Pryke	C of M
			Llewelyn Ibi	Phillips	C of M
1981 Nov	GSPC	All-aged	Waidman Chico	Bennett	C of M
1982 Jan	GSPA	All-aged	Viszony of Vallota	Cox	3rd
1982 Sept	GSPA	Novice	Viszony of Vallota	Cox	2nd
			Laser Duite	Churchill	Res
1982 Sept	GSPC	Novice	Calversam Barleybroth	Cox	C of M
1982 Oct			Viszony of Vallota	Cox	2nd
			Calversam Barleybroth	Cox	3rd
	LMC	Novice	Saddleglade Zoli	Bennett	1st
			Viszony of Vallota	Cox	2nd
	LMC	Novice	Calversam Barleybroth	Cox	C of M
	WCGB	Novice	Viszony of Vallota	Cox	3rd

Date	Club	Class	Dog	Judge	Placement
1982 Nov	HVS	Open	Viszony of Vallota	Cox	3rd
	HVS	Novice	Viszony of Vallota	Cox	C of M
			Laser Duke	Churchill	C of M
			Llewelyn Ibi	Phillips	C of M
			Calversam Barleybroth	Cox	2nd
			Saddleglade Zoli	Bennett	1st
1982 Dec	WCGB	All-aged	Viszony of Vallota	Cox	C of M
	GSPC	Novice	Saddleglade Zoli	Bennett	Res
	LMC	All-aged	Calversam Barleybroth	Cox	C of M
1983 Jan	GWPC	Novice	Viszony of Vallota	Cox	2nd
	GSPA	All-aged	Viszony of Vallota	Cox	Res
1983 Oct	LMC	All-aged	Saddleglade Zoli	Bennett	2nd
	CSPC	All-aged	Laser Duite	Churchill	3rd
	LMC	All-aged	Viszony of Vallota	Cox	2nd
	HVS	Open	Saddleglade Zoli	Bennett	C of M
			Viszony of Vallota	Cox	Res
	HVS	Novice	Perdita's Puzzle	Harris	1st
			Calversam Barleybroth	Cox	2nd
			Laser Duke	Churchill	3rd
			Szajani Csipke	Harris	C of M
			Llewelyn Ibi	Phillips	C of M
	GSPA	Novice	Peckers Penny	Cowburn	C of M
	HVS	All-aged	Abbeystag Josie	Gray	C of M
			Ch Russetmantle Troy	Gottlieb	C of M
			Pecker's Penny	Cowburn	1st

1983 Nov	LMC	Novice	*Pecker's Perchance*	Houghton	C of M
			Ch Russetmantle Troy	Gottlieb	C of M
	GSPA	All-aged	*Saddleglade Zoli*	Bennett	Res
			Viszony of Vallota	Cox	1st
	GSPA	Open NQ	*Viszony of Vallota*	Cox	C of M
1984 Jan	GSPC	All-aged	*Saddleglade Zoli*	Bennett	C of M
	WCGB	Open NQ	*Saddleglade Zoli*	Bennett	3rd
			Viszony of Vallota	Cox	Res
1984 Oct	GSPA	Open Q	*Viszony of Vallota*	Cox	CoM
1984 Oct	GSPA	Open Q	*Viszony of Vallota*	Cox	1st
	HVS	Novice	*Diela of Waidman*	Petrie-Hay	3rd
			Szajani Csipke	Harris	C of M
	WCGB	Novice	*Szajani Csipke*	Harris	2nd
1984 Nov	WCGB	Novice	*Hookside Harmony*	Smith	C of M
1984 Nov	GSPA	Novice	*Hookside Harmony*	Smith	C of M
			Szajani Csipke	Harris	C of M
	LMC	Open Q	*Viszony of Vallota*	Cox	2nd
1985	HVS	Novice	*Gleam of Dalegarth*	Newbury	C of M
	GSPC	Open Q	*Laser Duite*	Churchill	2nd
1985 Oct	HVS	Novice	*Diela of Waidman*	Petrie-Hay	1st
			Hookside Harmony	Smith	3rd
	GSPA	Open Q	*Viszony of Vallota*	Cox	2nd
			Viszony of Vallota	Cox	3rd
			Viszony of Vallota	Cox	1st
	GSPC	Novice	*Vallota Vizibility*	Cox	1st
	GWPC	Novice	*Vallota Virtuoso*	Green	C of M

Date		Class		Judge	Place
1985 Nov	WCGB	Open Q	*Saddleglade Zoli*	Bennett	C of M
	GSPC	Novice	*Saline Judi*	Neil	C of M
1986 Jan	GSPA	Open NQ	*Viszony of Vallota*	Cox	2nd
			Vallota Virtuoso	Green	1st
	GWPC	Novice	*Vallota Vizibility*	Cox	1st
	HVS	Open Q	*Vallota Virtuoso*	Green	Res
	GSPC	Novice	*Saddleglade Zoli*	Bennett	C of M
		Novice	*Gleam of Dalegarth*	Newbury	2nd
1986 Oct	HVS	Novice	*Diela of Waidman*	Petrie-Hay	C of M
	HVS		*Abbeystag Marina*	Huckle	3rd
		Novice	*Fandango in the Sun*	Elliott	C of M
		Open Q	*Viszony of Vallota*	Cox	2nd
		Novice	*Diela of Waidman*	Petrie-Hay	2nd
	GSPC	Open Q	*Vallota Vizibility*	Cox	C of M
	GSPA	Novice	*Abbeystag Marina*	Huckle	2nd
		Novice	*Kinford Miska*	Phillips	3rd
1986 Nov	HVS	All-aged	*Abbeystag Marina*	Huckle	2nd
	GSPC	Novice	*Abbeystag Marina*	Huckle	1st
	HVS	All-aged	*Abbeystag Marina*	Huckle	2nd
1987 Jan	GSPA	Open NQ	*FT Ch Viszony of Vallota*	Cox	2nd
	WCGB	All-aged	*FT Ch Viszony of Vallota*	Cox	2nd
1987 Sep	GSPA	Open Q	*Vallota Vizibility*	Cox	3rd
1987 Oct	GSPC	Novice	*Swallow Skylark*	Easy	1st

	KC	Championship	FT Ch Viszony of Vallota	Cox	Dip
	HVS	Novice	Szajani Csipke	Harris	2nd
			Gleam of Dalegarth	Newbury	C of M
			Russetmantle Quiver	Gottlieb	C of M
			Kinford Miska	Phillips	C of M
1987 Dec	GSPA	Novice	Kinford Miska	Phillips	2nd
	GWPC	Novice	Swallow Skylark	Easy	3rd
1988 Jan	GSPA	All-aged	Vallota Vizibility	Cox	R+ C of M
	WCGB	Novice	Szajani Aniko	Farquhar	C of M
	WCGB	Novice	Swallow Skylark	Easy	1st
			Szajani Aniko	Farquhar	3rd
	GWPC	Novice	Swallow Skylark	Easy	2nd
	WCGB	Novice	Szajani Csipke	Harris	3rd
	GSPC	Novice	Kinford Miska	Phillips	C of M
	WCGB	Open Q	Vallota Vizibility	Cox	3rd
1988 Oct	HVS	Novice	Szajani Aniko	Farquhar	1st
			Pitswarren Zephyr	Ryan	2nd
1988 Oct			Striders Time	Smith	3rd
	HVS	All-aged	Gleam of Dalegarth	Newbury	C of M
	WCGB	All-aged	Gleam of Dalegarth	Newbury	3rd
			Szajani Aniko	Farquhar	1st
1988 Nov	GSPA	Open Q	Vallota Vizibility	Cox	2nd
1988 Dec	LM	Novice	Ch Russetmantle Quiver	Gottlieb	3rd
	HVS	Novice	Castlefield Midnight Blue	Dimond	1st

chapter 12

Date	Club	Class	Dog	Judge	Award
1989 Jan	GSPC	All-aged	Szajani Aniko	Farquhar	C of M
			Szajani Csipke	Harris	C of M
1989 Sept	GWPC	All-aged	Szajani Aniko	Farquhar	3rd
1989 Oct	GSPA	Open	Vallota Vizibility	Cox	C of M
	GSPA	Open	Vallota Vizibility	Cox	2nd
1989 Nov	HVS	Open	Vallota Vizibility	Cox	2nd
	GSP	Open	Vallota Vizibility	Cox	C of M
1989 Nov	WCGB	All-aged	Castlefield Midnight Blue	Dimon	2nd
	GSPC	Open	Vallota Vizibility	Cox	C of M
1990 Jan	GSPC	Novice	Swanton Agatha	De Giles	C of M
1990 Aug	GSPC	Novice	Cuzco Laski	Wilson	C of M
	GSPA	Novice	Auchinner Cabral	Petullo	C of M
1990 Sept	GSPA	Open	Vallota Vizibility	Cox	C of M
1990 Oct	LMC	All-aged	Pitswarren Zephyr	Ryan	3rd
	HVS	Novice	Galfrid Bisque	De Giles	C of M
1990 Nov	GSPC	Open	Szajani Aniko	Farquhar	3rd
	GSPC	All-aged	Auchinner Cabral	Farquhar	3rd
	GSPC	Open	Vallota Vizibility	Petullo	4th
1990 Dec	WCGB	Novice	Russetmantle Quiver	Cox	3rd
	GWPC	Novice	Russetmantle Fennel	Gottlieb	C of M
1991 Jan	GSPA	All-aged	Vallota Vizibility	Wilks	C of M
	GWPC	All-aged	Vallota Vizibility	Cox	3rd
	WCGB	All-aged	Castlefield Midnight Blue	Cox	C of M
				Dimon	C of M

Date	Club	Class	Dog	Handler	Place
1991 Sept	GSPC	All-aged	Vallota Vizibility	Cox	1st
	GSPC	All-aged	Vallota Vizibility	Cox	2nd
	GSPC	All-aged	Castlefield Midnight Blue	Dimon	3rd
	HVS	Open	Cuzco Laski	Wilson	4th
1991 Oct	GSPC	All-aged	Auchinner Cabral	Petullo	1st
	GWPC	Novice	Vallota Volatile	Cox	3rd
	GWPC	Novice	Vallota Velocity	Cox	4th
1991 Nov	Dukeries	Novice	Caldicote Kestrel	Huckle	4th
	HVS	Novice	Vallota Volatile	Cox	3rd
		Novice	Stregaya Echo	Coote	C of M
	HVS	All-aged	Szajani Aniko	Farquhar	C of M
	HVS	Novice	Vallota Volatile	Cox	3rd
	HVS	Novice	Russetmantle Mist	Milwidksy	C of M
1991 Dec	WCGB	All-aged	Castlefield Midnight Blue	Dimon	C of M
1992 Jan	GWPC	All-aged	Szajani Aniko	Farquhar	C of M
	GSPC	All-aged	Szajani Aniko	Farquhar	2nd
1992 Jan	GSPA	All-aged	Szajani Aniko	Farquhar	2nd
	GSPC	All-aged	Castlefield Midnight Blue	Dimon	2nd
1992 Aug	GSPC	Novice	Cuzco Laski	Wilson	1st
1992 Aug	GSPC	Novice	Loguart Capercaillie	Easy	2nd
1992 Oct	GSPA	Novice	Valleyhunter Special Envoy	Kleinman	3rd
	GSPC	Novice	Cauldicot Kestrel	Huckle	3rd
	Dukeries	All-aged	Loguart Capercaillie	Easy	3rd
1992 Nov	HVS	Novice	Vallota Volatile	Cox	1st
	HVS	Novice	Caldicote Kestrel	Huckle	2nd

Date	Club	Class	Dog	Judge	Place
	GSPL	Novice	Valleyhunter Special Envoy	Kleinman	1st
	WA	Novice	Stregaya Echo	Coote	4th
	HVS	All-aged	Castlefield Midnight Blue	Dimon	2nd
1992 Dec	SPA	Novice	Vallota Velocity	Cox	4th
	BGGB	Novice	Vallota Velocity	Cox	3rd
1993 Jan	WCGB	All-aged	Vallota Volatile	Cox	3rd
1993 Aug	GSPA	Novice	Loguart Capercaillie	Easy	1st
1993 Oct	GWPC	Novice	Caldicote Kestrel	Huckle	4th
	HVS	All-age	Caldicote Kestrel	Huckle	2nd
	HVS	Novice	Archenfield Crusty	Petrie-Hay/Cox	3rd
	GSPA	Novice	Cauldicot Kestrel	Huckle	1st
1993 Nov	HVS	All-aged	Loguart Capercaillie	Easy	3rd
	Dukeries	All-aged	Caldicote Kestrel	Huckle	2nd
	HVS	Novice	Osprey Moon	Dimon	1st
	HVS	Novice	Archenfield Crusty	Petrie-Hay/Cox	4th
	BCGB	All-aged	Szajani Aniko	Farquhar	1st
	GSPA	Novice	Archenfield Crusty	Petrie-Hay/Cox	1st
1993 Dec	GSPC	Open	Cuzco Laski	Wilson	3rd
1994 Sept	GSPA	All-aged	Auchinner Cabral	Petullo	2nd
	GSPA	All-aged	Loguart Capercaillie	Easy	4th
	GSPA	All-aged	Loguart Capercaillie	Easy	2nd
1994 Oct	HVS	Open	Loguart Capercaillie	Easy	3rd
	GWPC	All-aged	Vallota Volatile	Cox	1st
	HVS	Novice	Alsziv Pasque	Digby	2nd

Date	Club	Class	Dog	Handler	Place
1994 Nov	GSPC	Novice	*Valleyhunter Vallhalla*	Kleinman	1st
	WCGB	Novice	*Galfrid Bisque*	De Giles	4th
	GSPC	All-aged	*Vallota Volatile*	Cox	3rd
1994 Dec	GSPC	All-aged	*Valleyhunter Vallhalla*	Kleinman	4th
	BCGB	All-aged	*Vallota Volatile*	Cox	1st
	BCGB	All-aged	*Szajani Aniko*	Farquhar	3rd
1995 Jan	GSPA	Open	*Loguart Capercaillie*	Easy	4th
1995 Oct	WA	Novice	*Conigree Zelda*	Scattergood	1st
	GWPC	All-aged	*Archenfield Crusty*	Petrie-Hay/Cox	2nd
	HVS	Open	*Archenfield Crusty*	Petrie-Hay/Cox	2nd
1995 Nov	WA	Novice	*Nicael Shining Star of Alsziv*	Digby	3rd
	GWPC	Open	*Archenfield Crusty*	Petrie-Hay/Cox	3rd
	HV	Novice	*Russetmantle Aspic*	Gottlieb	3rd
1996 Jan	WA	Novice	*Galfrid Nymph of Vadasz*	Hunter	2nd
	GSPA	All-aged	*Conigree Zelda*	Scattergood	3rd
	HVS	Novice	*Conigree Amber*	P Cox	1st
	BGGB	All-aged	*Osprey Moon*	Dimon	4th
1996 Oct	GSPA	Open	*Vallota Volatile*	Cox	3rd
	WA	Novice	*Stregaya Highlander*	Coote	1st
1996 Nov	HVS	All-aged	*Stregaya Highlander*	Coote	4th
	HVC	Novice	*Vadasz Velvet*	Hunter	3rd
1997 Oct	GSPA	All-aged	*Conigree Amber*	P Cox	3rd
	WA	Novice	*Vadasz Velvet*	Hunter	3rd

Date	Club	Class	Dog	Judge	Placing
1997 Nov	HVS	Novice	Valleyhunter Edrador	Reed	2nd
	HVS	Novice	Kenvee Habitat	Hurley	C of M
	HVS	Novice	Kenvee Habitat	Hurley	C of M
	HVS	Novice	Szajani Palinka	Harris	C of M
	HVS	All-aged	Conigree Amber	P Cox	C of M
	HPRCS	All-aged	Castlefield Arizona	Wittaker	C of M
	HVS	Novice	Kenvee Habitat	Hurley	3rd
	NSGA	Novice	Castlefield Arizona	Wittaker	C of M
	GSPA	Novice	Vermilion Villarsia	Cox	C of M
1997 Dec	GSPA	All-aged	Conigree Zelda	Scattergood	2nd
	GWPC	Open	Archenfield Crusty of Waidman	Petrie-Hay/Cox	4th
	WCGB	Novice	Vermilion Villarsia	Cox	1st
1998 Jan	WCGB	Open	Archenfield Crusty of Waidman	Petrie-Hay/Cox	1st
	GWPA	Novice	Nicael Russe	Digby	C of M
	HVC	Novice	Nicael Russe	Digby	4th
	HVC	Novice	Daxpak Seein Cash	Barnard	2nd
	HGS	Novice	Russetmantle Auriole of Gardenway	Perkins	C of M
	HGS	Novice	Szolnoki Konyak of Lutra	Millson	3rd
	GSPA	Open	Archenfield Crusty of Waidman	Petrie-Hay/Cox	1st

The Trainer's Objectives and the Dog's Capacity

Before going into the details of training a young dog for the gun it is essential to acknowledge your own objectives and the capability of your pupil. There are two very important basic rules involved in training Vizslas:

1. Mean what you say and say what you mean
2. Trust your dog

Vizslas take many roles in the field – a rough-shooter's dog who accompanies his master on forays up hedges, in woods, over stubble and across water. Here he is expected to be a genuine jack of all trades. He must work as a Pointer over stubble and open ground and as a Spaniel when hedging and ditching and in cover. He must be prepared to retrieve rabbit, hare, partridge, pheasant and water fowl. His points on stubble must be precise and staunch. To find and not miss game, his ground treatment (his quartering) must be methodical and expansive. In cover, although his ground treatment must be thorough, the pattern will vary with the density of the cover. When on point, he must be prepared to get in and flush the bird bravely from the hedge, ditch or brambles in order that the bird springs into flight, thus giving his master a sporting shot. Where you have a dog that creeps into flush, the chances are that the bird will do likewise and creep away rather than fly. This sort of shooting requires a dog that will adapt all the facets of his work to the conditions and be prepared to get after a wounded bird quickly, not only to save time in searching for it, but also to ensure that it is in the bag and not lying up in the next county with pellets in its body.

As a non-slip retriever his role is very different and is not really ideal for a pointer/retriever but it is work and, if that is all that is available, it is certainly better than no work. But here the dog is used purely as a retriever and in many ways it is better not to encourage free hunting for live game but to confine his training to retrieving exercises only. On the other hand, a dog can be used solely as a pointer, as by a falconer, and his retrieving ability actively discouraged as it is the hawk, not the dog, who picks up the game. Many Vizslas are also used on deer, either as their main employment or as an adjunct to the general shooting scene. Here the training of the dog must include some advanced training exercises and teaching the correct behaviour when stalking. It never ceases to amaze me how many dogs take to deer hunting who never had any specific training and how they will quickly differentiate between a rifle and a shotgun. Get out of a Land Rover with a shotgun and the dog is all ready to start searching for game, the sooner the better; take a rifle and he is at your heels, ears pricked and alert to the slightest smell or sound of the quarry ahead.

Some Vizslas never get any nearer to the shooting field than working tests, where a canvas dummy must take the place of the real thing, and dummy launchers simulate the gun. But here his innate instincts are given expression and being controlled and, provided this gives the dog and his owner pleasure, a lot of enjoyment and sensible training can be acquired. The other extreme is the person who revels in the competition of field trials and keeps a dog solely for that purpose. This is a necessity if he or she is going to be a successful contender as very, very few winning field trials dogs will go on winning if they are used as regular shooting dogs. Why? Because in a trial the dog must be 100% attentive to his handler at all times. Admittedly he must

A strong swimmer in training.

find game, point it and then retrieve it when he is ordered to do so, but he must never use his own initiative whereas your shooting companion is the dog who will not bother to cover ground where he knows full well he is not going to find game, he is not going to hang around on point while the judges and guns all position themselves and the bird is already starting to creep away; and he is not going to wait one or even two minutes when he can see a wounded bird hot footing it for the nearest cover. Then there is the picking-up dog and the dog who is destined to be purely a family pet but who is taken out for long walks or with the horses.

Every one of these dogs must have not only a basic education in manners but also advanced training, if only in controlled obedience, in order to prove themselves to be intelligent and co-operative companions.

If you decide that your pup is destined for the shooting field then, before the intensive training which this involves, you must be sure that he is neither gun-shy nor has a hard mouth.

Gun-shy

Many people think that if a dog is nervous of gunfire he is 'gun-shy'. This need not be the case. With careful handling, many a pup that has shown disquiet on hearing a shot has turned into an excellent gun dog. There are two kinds of gun-shyness, inherited and man-made. A truly gun-shy dog will turn tail and go, and I mean **go**, very far away from the band when a gun is fired. If either of this dog's parents were also gun-shy then it is sensible to presume that the condition is inherited. I would say that this was comparatively rare in the breed.

It is extremely easy to make a dog gun-shy by insensitive handling, particularly if the pup is gun-nervous. Gun-nervousness is not unusual; the noise of a gun, rifle or blanks from a launcher can be frightening, particularly if the pup has lived a quiet life with not many sudden noises to put up with. Many a young dog dislikes the sound of blanks whereas a cartridge will have no effect. The reason for this is the difference in the tone of the explosion, the blank being very much higher and sharper. A gun fired over the head of a young dog can damage its ear drums for life, as well as ensure that it is gun-shy because the noise has caused pain.

Obviously it is important to see that introduction to gunfire is gradual, careful and associated with pleasure. It is also important that if the dog shows a fear or dislike of blanks, then they should not be used and one must resign oneself to the expense of cartridges. The sound of gunfire can be associated with feeding time and, providing it is at a sufficient distance, little or no notice will be taken. Later on, it can be associated with the pleasurable thought of a retrieve. This is the best way of overcoming any signs of nervousness when a shot is fired. Some dogs will also show timidity at the sight of a gun. This could have been caused by a variety of reasons but, in order to avoid it, it is important to get the dog used to the association with a gun. Carry one as often as possible, even if you have no intention of using it, or carry a hefty stick or crook which you can point skyward from time to time to stimulate the raising of a gun. It is also feasible to feed a dog with a gun lying beside his bowl on the floor.

Thus we have gun-nervousness, which can easily be overcome by gentle and careful handling; inherited gun-shyness, about which very little can be done with any degree of certainty; and man-made gun-shyness, which has been caused by fear or pain due to thoughtless and careless handling, again almost impossible to overcome other than by a long, slow process of re-education with no certainty of success in the end.

Hard Mouth

Just as with gun-shyness, a dog may inherit a hard mouth or have it thrust upon him. That hard mouth can be hereditary is an accepted fact, and anyone breeding from a dog that is known to have inherited this defect is very stupid indeed – unless you wish to live on paté all your life! A hard mouth in a gundog makes that dog a liability rather than an asset, not only as a field trial contender but also as a bag-filler. However, if a hard mouth in a dog has been caused by human error then there is no reason why that dog should not be bred from and produce useful puppies.

It is not possible to recognize an inherited hard mouth from a man-made one by sight. An enquiry into the dog's parenthood and junior education should prove the case. If it is known that either of the parents were rough on their game then, if the youngster also shows this fault, it would be sensible to presume it is inherited. If both parents have proven that they retrieve tenderly, then it can be assumed that the fault lies with the trainer or his family.

The best way to ensure that a dog becomes hard-mouthed is to send it for a lightly wounded cock bird early on in its retrieving career. A good gash with a spur and a peck around the eye is virtually a guarantee that the youngster will give that bird such a squeeze as to ensure that no further pain is inflicted on him. It can also, of course, cure the dog for life of any further wish to retrieve. A loose-feathered wood pigeon is also undesirable as a retrieve at an early age. Alternatively if the family is allowed to wrench or drag 'treasures' from the pup – albeit that they are favourite toys, hats or shoes – then this encourages a good hard grip in order to improve the odds of a fair tug-of-war. I have heard that bones encourage a hard mouth or, rather, I have been asked whether this is true – in my opinion it is not. Nor should the retrieval of any hard object necessarily be discouraged although I think it wise to ensure all dummies are well padded, as a soft mouthed dog not only means that he handles an object gently but also that his mouth is a soft and delicate orifice and should therefore be treated as such.

The cures for a hard mouth are various – extraction of the eye teeth being the most drastic I have heard of. Other 'cures' are winding barbed wire round a dummy or covering a dummy in gorse or other prickly substances so that when too firm a grip is taken pain is suffered. Of course this involves the co-operation of the dog in picking up that object which an intelligent dog is likely to jib at. Ordinary common sense is the most important asset for a gundog trainer. It is not difficult to assess the mouth of a young dog. Take careful note of how the pup handles an object, the pick up and the carry. It should be thoughtful, gentle and proud. A pup should be allowed to carry his treasure, whatever it may be, willingly and happily and encouraged to hand it over with confidence. But he should never be allowed to play with it or chew it. Reverence of a portable object both by dog and handler, be it a mouse or a pheasant, is essential. Care should be taken to ensure that dummies are attractive and retrieving exercises should neither be boring nor over-indulged in. Encouragement is often needed when progressing from the dummy to cold game to warm game, but sense and understanding by the trainer will ensure that the youngster understands that it is God's will that he should carry these objects and that, after all, is all the pup desires – to please and be pleased by his master.

And just a little more sense is needed again during the first season of work. Choose the retrieves a dog is allowed carefully, always dead birds, keeping a large cock pheasant until later in the season and retrieves from really tough, punishing cover until even later in the season. With birds coming to hand undamaged at this stage you should be set fair for many years of successful pot-filling. If not, find a happy retrieverless home for the dog and start again. The Kennel Club instructions to field trial judges concerning hard mouths is as follows:

All game should be examined for signs of hard mouth. A hard mouthed dog seldom gives visible evidence of hardness. He will simply crush in one or both sides of the ribs.

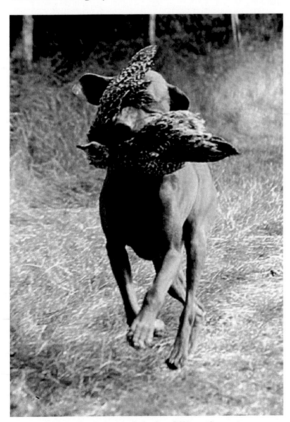

A youngster set fair for filling the pot.

Blowing up the feathers will not disclose the damage. Place the bird in the palm of the hand, breast upwards, head forward, and feel the ribs with finger and thumb. They should be round and firm. If they are caved in or flat, this is definite evidence of hard mouth. Be sure the bird reaches your co-judges for examination. There should be no hesitation or sentiment about hard mouth, the dog should be discarded. A certain indication of a good mouth is a dog bringing in a live bird whose head is up and eye bright. Superficial damage, if any, in this case can be ignored. At times the rump of a stronger runner may be gashed and look ugly. Care should be taken here, as it may be the result of a difficult capture or lack of experience in mastering a strong runner by a young dog. Judges should always satisfy themselves that any damage done has been caused by the dog, not by the shot or fall, and in cases of doubt, the benefit should be given to the dog. Handlers should be given the opportunity of inspecting the damaged game in the presence of the judges, but the decision of the judges is final.

TRAINING A YOUNG DOG

Having proved that your dog is suitable material, let battle commence. But always remember that the dog is an emotive issue and should not be allowed to overcome man's sense of humour and proportion.

Training Equipment

Training equipment can be simple or complicated but a light slip lead is the first requirement. In my opinion, choke chains should never be necessary. If you put a slip lead on a 12-week-old puppy and let him play with your hand as you walk along, within a week you will have that pup walking to heel on a lead.

A whistle is also essential if you are to control the dog at a distance. Man's voice is the last thing game likes to hear around the fields and the quieter you can be the

Learning manners; steady to hens. Photo: Petrie-Hay

A hen run can be invaluable for teaching a puppy not to run in. Photo: Petrie-Hay

more chance the dog will have of finding and producing fur or feather. I do not like the 'silent' whistle as I can never be sure that the dog has heard it. I would rather have an ordinary horn or bakelite type with a medium pitch which both dog and I can hear and understand. I also have at the ready a 'blaster' just in case things go wrong and I need to use surprise tactics. It is amazing how a really loud noise will affect a dog's behaviour if he is consciously doing wrong.

The third necessity is a dummy of one sort or another. It is best to have a variety in order to encourage the pup to get used to various sensations in his mouth. My first 'dummy' is usually a glove, cap or slipper that a 12-week-old pup can pick up and carry; I also use a duck or pheasant's wing at this period. Later, I make canvas dummies and use them plain or with a rabbit skin tied round, and another with feathers stitched on. It is also a good idea to have one that will float but also have some weight. An empty 'squeezy' bottle covered with canvas and with a little sand in it to give it weight is very adequate. Be prepared to lose them, so make some spares! And, finally, you need a gun and cartridges or blanks. You can go to the expense of buying a dummy launcher, which is very helpful but not essential. It is also handy to have a loft full of homing pigeons or a pen with quail in and also an enclosed area where you can keep rabbits. but these are all refinements and not essential to basic training. Some training classes will supply them and some trainers will allow you to use theirs. The use of a rabbit run is obvious but you must remember that a dog will quickly learn not to chase the rabbits in that run, but the wild rabbits up the fields are a whole new ball game. Treat them with respect and remember, however steady your pup is in the enclosure, he will need careful handling for the transition period to wild rabbits. Pigeons or quail can be used for pointing. Quail will behave like partridges; release the majority from the pen, leaving one or two call birds inside. The released birds will go off into the surrounding fields but will return in the evening when they hear their mates calling. In this way you can be sure that there is game in certain fields for the dog to point. The only snag is that quail would far rather run than fly and, if you wish to use them at the beginning of the year, then it is necessary to release some and take an older dog who will be prepared to chase and chivvy them around for 10 days in order to encourage them to fly. This works just as a good rousting does with the young pheasants at the beginning of the season.

The alternative is pigeons who will return to the loft after use. Take two or three pigeons in a cage into a field. You can then do one of three things with them:

1. Make a wire trap under which the bird can be placed. The trap must be strong enough to resist an impetuous snap and must have a cord attached to it which, when pulled, will tip up the trap and release the bird so that it can fly away.

2. Dig a small hole in the ground and place the bird into it, then put a tile on top to prevent escape. The tile can then be kicked away at the appropriate moment.

3. You can 'dizzy' the bird. This is quite simple and involves putting it to sleep for a short period. This is done by tucking the bird's head under one wing, holding it there and swinging the bird gently for a few seconds. On no account press the breast bone as this will kill the pigeon, which is **not** the object of this exercise! Now place the bird on the ground and it should remain motionless for a matter of minutes. If it is not asleep then you have not rocked it sufficiently and it will need a bit more. I have found the older the bird the more time is needed to hypnotize it. Once 'out', you can leave it on the ground with a little grass over it and a twig to mark the place. When the dog comes on point, you approach slowly and, if the bird does not awake when you are ready, simply tip it forward gently with one hand whilst with the other keep the dog at a safe distance. However, this is not normally necessary as the trance seldom lasts longer than 5–10 minutes.

Although almost all dogs will point quail, some do not react to pigeons. If this is the case, then it is possible to get a phial of concentrated scent of pheasant, partridge and so on, which you can apply to the pigeon thus making it more 'pointable'. However, I find these extras are not so much an aid for the exercise of pointing but to control the behaviour of the dog to flush. If you can produce a point when you want then you can be prepared to control the aftermath.

An area for training is necessary and also water for swimming. Not everyone has these on their doorsteps but it is always possible to persuade a friendly farmer to let you use his land if he appreciates that you are genuine.

Training Schedule

There follows a simplified general schedule for training your dog between the ages of 12 weeks and 18 months. It is not intended to be a full training guide or to replace the few good text books dealing with the subject. It will however answer the first questions a novice trainer usually has and, I hope, encourage the training of your dog.

It must be stressed that every puppy's mental ability varies, as does the trainer's time and patience. Make haste slowly, never force the pace and always ensure that the dog is happy and that you, the trainer, are in a kindly and relaxed mood during training sessions. Do not attempt to train a dog if you are in a hurry, irritated or if the weather is unsuitable. A high wind is never conducive to obedience, and both bleak and cold and hot, muggy weather adversely affects both dog and man.

Much basic training can be done in the house or garden and no pup should be allowed to run free on open ground where there is game until he is absolutely under control. One of the most important factors in training is to anticipate events to prevent wrong-doing rather than have to correct misbehaviour.

From three to six months

Come on command at all times.

Sit on command, both on the lead and when free; beside on the left, and in front of the trainer. Combined with word of command, use a hand signal and a whistle of your choice.

Heel on and off a lead. Start training on the lead. Next let the lead trail on the ground still attached to the collar, then remove the lead. Let the pup nuzzle your left hand and walk briskly. Use the word 'heel' frequently so that he associates the word with the action.

Combine **Come**, **Sit** and **Heel**. When walking to heel encourage him to sit each time you stand still.

Stay on command, either sitting or lying as you wish. Start by sitting the pup with lead on and in your hand. Walk slowly round him and make him stay sitting, then take one pace backwards. Repeat this with the lead on the ground, repeat again with no lead. Once this is perfect then increase the circle and distance you step back. Always return to the pup at this stage. Do not call him to you. Once he is relaxed and confident that you will return you can begin to walk about 20 paces away, stand still, then a few seconds later say 'come'. Alternate this with returning to him, but always encourage him to come in at a gallop when you call him and to sit in front of you on arrival. Maximum distance to be aimed at now is 36.5m (40yds). Do not go further than this and do not go out of sight.

Pointing It is difficult to say when your dog should start to point. Some pups at three months will point anything from a sparrow to the family cat, others show no inclination until they are much older. The important thing is to know what to do when he does begin to point. Watch him carefully, and when you notice him stiffening go quickly but quietly from the side (never from the rear), slip on his lead and stroke him, encouraging him to remain where he is for as long as possible. It matters not what he is indicating, but you should impress on him that he is doing the right thing and that you are pleased with him. Once he has remained steady for any time up to 5–10 minutes (provided the object he is pointing has not moved), go forward quietly and then flush the object yourself by a sudden movement. Sit the dog, allowing him to watch the departure of the 'pointed'. Do not let him follow it. This procedure can start from three months upwards. As time goes by you will find that he gets more discriminating in his choice of objects to point. During this period good lessons may be taught in steadiness both to point and flush, so that by a year he should be automatically dropping to flush and watching the direction in which you will eventually be shooting. At no point should he be encouraged to flush his own game, still less to chase it once it has gone. It is essential that no other dog is allowed to interfere on these occasions.

During this period take the puppy for frequent rides in the car so that he gets used to it and to prevent car sickness. Always go out just before a meal and have plenty of air in the car. Drive carefully so the pup is not swung about.

From six to nine months

Fetch a simple retrieve. Use dummy that weighs not less than 2.2kg (1lb) and is at least 0.3m (1ft long). Throw it where the pup can see it, and let him run to retrieve it. Do this in a confined area and encourage him to bring it back to you, either by bending right down to receive him or by running away. Do not take the dummy from him straight away, pat him and fuss him and let him hold it in his mouth. If he does not want to give it to you, slip his lead on and let him walk to heel carrying it. Then say 'sit' and remove it very gently from him. Once you know he will retrieve and bring it to you never throw the dummy so that it lands in sight of the pup. In this way he will learn to use his nose and not his eyes to find it. Directly he is retrieving happily to hand, restrain him from running in by holding him gently at first, then insisting that he 'sit' on a lead, and then off a lead. Vary the type of dummy and never overdo this exercise. Two or three retrieves well done are quite enough.

There are three main types of retrieve from land. 'Seen' is self evident. 'Memory' involves putting the dummy on the ground in sight of the pup,

Gottlieb's Rusetmantle Eagle retrieving a rabbit dummy aged 7 weeks.

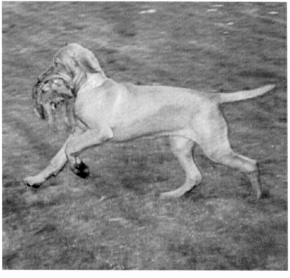

Harris' Szajani Damaszt retrieving a dummy aged 13 weeks.

251

walking away a short distance, then sending him back for it. Increase the distance as you progress. The third method is 'blind', which means that the pup does not see the dummy fall. This is best done by giving him an easy memory retrieve, then placing the dummy in exactly the same spot but without him seeing it. Send him for it just as you did for the memory and, preferably, close enough and up wind for him to scent it. In this way he will quickly learn that the word 'fetch' means to go and look for the dummy regardless of whether he has seen it fall or not. If possible, for every seen retrieve, give him two blind ones.

Shot Ensure that he has heard gunshot by this age. Ask a friend to fire a gun at least 90m (100yds) away from you whilst you are playing with the pup and watch his reaction. Providing he shows no fear, decrease the distance from the shot and combine it with playing or retrieving so that he is not in any way bothered by the sound. Once this is established, walk him to heel, sit him and fire a shot; repeat this but reverse the order to heel, shot and sit. When he will sit to shot, combine it with throwing a dummy. Do not let him retrieve the dummy, leave him sitting and fetch it yourself for at least a week. Once he understands that he must sit to shot and stay steady to falling dummies you can combine shot and retrieving.

Water Introduce your dog to water at an early age. Let him splash through brooks and streams or paddle in the sea or a pond. Only do this on a warm day so that he is not discouraged by cold water. Directly he will enter water willingly, encourage him to go deeper, either by sending in another dog as an example or, if necessary, going in yourself. Never let him be frightened by the water. Throw the dummy into the shallows to begin with, and then into deeper water. He will enjoy swimming for it. After you have achieved this, introduce steadiness, expecting him to sit and wait on the bank for the command to fetch.

The Drop It is absolutely essential that your dog should drop instantly when commanded. This is quickly taught provided that he understands your commands for sit, by whistle and hand as well as by word. Start by walking to heel and sitting him beside you. Then encourage him to move a little away from you but within arm's length and tell him to sit. Ensure he sits immediately where he is and does not come to sit beside you, if necessary push him down with your hand and step back. Continue to do this, increasing the distance only when you are certain that he understands that you wish him to sit away from you. At this stage, **never** call him to you and stop him half way. Always drop him as he is going away or playing, never after the command to come. Practise this drop by word when he is close by hand signal when he is looking at you, and by whistle when he is going away. Only after quite a period of time, when you are certain that he will drop at a distance on command, is it time to combine the commands of 'come' and 'sit'. At this stage, this means sitting beside or in front of you. Only when 'sit' also means sitting at a distance can you risk dropping him after having called him. Do not drop him too often on his way back to you or you will have a dog which comes in slowly expecting to be told to drop half way.

Once the drop is perfect then you can combine it with temptation, such as a falling dummy and a shot.

Nine months to a year

Quartering This is the term used for the systematic hunting for live game. I have left it until now as this is about the time when you will be beginning to control this instinct. Up until now, it was essential that there was no interference with the natural instincts of the pup when he set off to hunt for game. You were with him as a companion but not as a master. Some dogs need far more freedom and encouragement to hunt than others. There is only one taboo – never **ever** let a dog hunt for his own benefit and pleasure with no regard to his handler. This makes your dog a self-hunter, a fault which is almost impossible to correct once it has become established. The dog will be of no use as a shooting companion.

Your dog must discover for himself that only by quartering at a speed into the wind will his nose find scent. He may not point classically, he may chase, but he will show his instinctive ability as a hunter and pointer, and this you must foster and encourage. Once this is established, then you can introduce some discipline, but not before. This should take place on ground where there are birds but not ground game. The scent of birds is what he is learning to recognize and acknowledge at this stage. Try not to involve hares and rabbits; he can learn how to handle these at a later stage. Once you have established that he will hunt freely and point, introduce the discipline of dropping not only to flush but also to shot. Remember to do this or you will have a dog that associates the gun with retrieving only and, as a result, he will be inclined not to hunt when you carry a gun.

Once you have established that he is a natural hunter, it is time to control his quartering so that it is systematic and thorough. The easiest way to teach him to do this is to take him into a long narrow field of rough grass approximately 55–73m (60–80yds) wide with the wind blowing either up or down the field but not across it. Stand at the end with the wind blowing towards you and then start running to the further hedge calling the dog and waving him past you. Let him continue either as far as the other side or until he looks at you. At this moment start running in the other direction, calling him and again waving him past you. Repeat this over and over again until you have arrived at the top of the field. When teaching a youngster to quarter, always work him into the wind and very soon you will find that he will be zig-zagging in front of you naturally. You want to aim at walking in a straight line yourself with the dog working about 27m (30yds) either side of you and about 9–13m (10–15yds) ahead. If he diverts from this, use your stop whistle, call him in and start again. It is useful to have a special whistle for the turn when you are working ground that is not bounded by a natural stop. I suggest two slow blasts and, in the narrow field, blow them every time he turns. In this way he associates this whistle with changing direction. Initial quartering training should be done on ground where there is no game so that there are no distractions. Once he has got into a nice rhythmic pattern and you are certain that he is reliable on the drop, then you can take him where there is some game.

Over You can introduce jumping at any time during these sessions. Start over low objects which the pup can jump easily, and use the word 'over' every time he jumps. If you use wire or sheep netting of any kind, put a sack over it so that he can see it easily. Throw the dummy over it, send him for it and as he approaches the jump say

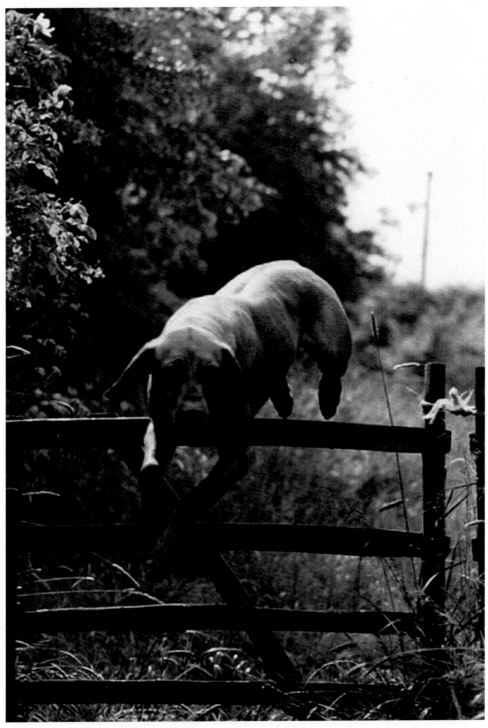

A fine jump by Petrie-Hay's Waidman Lulu on the command 'Over'.

'over'. Association of the word and action is important. Increase the height slowly and vary the obstacles.

Tracking This can be taught by trailing game down-wind. **Never** work up-wind when teaching a dog to track or he will use the air scent and not the ground scent. Get a friend to help you lay a trail by stringing a freshly-killed bird or rabbit between you and then dragging it along the ground. Your own foot prints must be far enough away for the puppy not to be able to follow them and, of course, this must be done out of sight of the dog. When the trail is ready, place a small bit of skin or fur at the start, put the dog on a shortish lead and take him to smell the flesh. Then encourage him to get his nose down on the trail and to follow the exact track which you made, making him go slowly and exactly. If he diverts, pull him back onto the line. As he improves you can lengthen the lead and increase the speed, but on no account let him raise his head or cut corners. It will be quite a while before you can leave him to follow a line free from your assistance. Have a separate command for this exercise. Use 'fetch' for a dead retrieve, and 'hie lost' for a runner which he must track. A young dog is puzzled when sent to retrieve a bird he has seen falling and has marked only to find that it has gone when he gets to the mark but, if you can encourage him to get his head down quickly and track the warm scent of the runner he will soon do this of his own accord.

One year to eighteen months

Quartering and pointing When he is about a year old, if all has gone to plan, you can start combining quartering with pointing. Take the dog onto ground where there is likely to be scent available for him to point. Allow him to quarter, point and drop to your flush of the game, then continue quartering. The next step is to introduce shot in combination with the flush. Provided that you have succeeded in your earlier lessons in keeping him rock steady to shot, no difficulties should arise, but still do not let him flush the game. Do not shoot to kill at this stage. Go slowly, step by step. Only once this is perfected comes the moment when you will have to ask a friend to accompany you to do the shooting. It is important that your concentration should be on the pup, not on hitting the game. The game can now be shot but not retrieved. Either pick it up yourself or go elsewhere for at least 10 minutes, then come back to the area and use it as a memory retrieve. It is important that the dog should not associate the point, shot and fall with retrieving at this time.

Flushing Now that he is steady to all facets of his pointing and retrieving job, it is time for him to flush his own game. Game in the open will generally flush as he approaches but in cover it will sit tight. Teach him by allowing him to go forward with you, and encourage him to 'get in' where you suspect the game to be. Do this by an excited movement of the hand and enthusiastic voice so that he bounces in – the sharper the flush the better chance of the bird rising for a sporting shot. If he has learned his lessons properly, as the game flushes he will drop. After half a dozen such flushes you can afford to shoot at a game provided that you can rely on his steadiness. Continue in this way for two or three months and resist the temptation to allow him to retrieve after the fall. It will pay dividends in the years to come. After this time, and provided all is as you would wish, then you can allow him to retrieve but after a reasonable wait at the drop. I do not consider that a young dog in his first year should be sent in for a runner.

General Hints and Tips

Take things carefully, keep the dog steady and do your best to think ahead so that you can avoid mistakes. In this way he will gain experience and give intense pleasure and satisfaction. Sensible owners treat their dogs like their children and expect the same respect and obedience from them. Given these conditions, a pup can grow up and mature in happiness and discipline to become a sound, steady worker. Stick to the rules – playing is for fun, work is for real.

It makes no real difference whether it is the man or woman of the house who does the training. A set training time and place should be arranged and only one person, one whistle and one dog should attend. All the rest of the day can be spent playing, sleeping and eating but when the slip lead is put on, the whistle comes out and the game-bag goes over the shoulder, that is school time and nothing and no-one should interfere or alter the routine. Stick to one trainer until the pup has gone right through his basic education. Once that is well accomplished, then it is the time to introduce the shooting.

Should the owner lack both the time and patience to train his own dog then a professional trainer may have to be used. Choose very carefully. Vizslas are not every man's cup of tea and, with the wrong handling, will be far worse than useless in the shooting field. If they are to be kennelled and trained by a stranger they will need much understanding and kindness. When is the best age for the dog to go away? Trainers, like prep school masters, appreciate youngsters whose brains are sufficiently developed to accept fairly intensive tuition and who have already had a modicum of the basic niceties – such as manners, cleanliness, and obedience to the normal requests demanded when living with a family. They do not welcome a wild, uncontrolled teenager with no knowledge of discipline. The usual age is around 8–9 months, providing the owners can ensure that until then the dog has not been allowed to chase and catch fur or feather.

Training Classes

Training classes and working tests begin in the spring. Vizslas are welcome to all the hunt, point, retrieve society sessions and it is far wiser to attend one of these than those organised purely for Retrievers or Spaniels. A letter to the secretary will produce full details of what is available in your area.

No sooner has the shooting season ended than the schools open, and keen owners and reluctant pupils can be heard gathering all over the country with whistles, dummies, launchers, rabbits on elastic and pigeons in cages. Societies for Retrievers, Spaniels and the retrieving Pointers all arrange suitable pieces of ground and trainers in attendance for the weekly or monthly influx of aspiring super-dog owners. Training courses are interrupted by working tests which supply progress reports and, finally, end-of-term exam results.

If the classes are well organised, and if the trainer is efficient, then they can be used

Wilks' Russetmantle Fennel retrieving happily to hand on the command 'Fetch'.

as a means to an end. Much responsibility lies on the shoulders of those who organize gundog classes and tests, as many of the students end up in field trials and, if the standard of field trial drops, where do you look for the reason? To the training and those who aided and abetted it.

Advantages and Disadvantages of Classes

Training classes have their advantages. The dogs become used to working in company, the owners realise they must take correction in public and a yard-stick is provided to judge progress against other dogs of the same age. For the hunt, point and retrieve breeds the classes try to cover three aspects of training – basic obedience, retrieving and hunting-and-pointing. Obedience is straightforward and the retrieving is similar to that taught in retriever classes, including waterwork if a suitable river or lake is on the ground. The advantage to the novice trainer is that the class provides not only instruction but also dummy throwers. A dummy launcher is limited in that the dummy is always going away from the dog whereas, with assistance, it can be thrown over a hedge towards the dog.

It is very much more difficult to provide suitable facilities for hunting and pointing. Do the Pointers or Setters have training classes or working tests? They do not, for the very reason that not only is the 'real thing' the best way to train a pointer, but to simulate it in training class conditions is impossible. Nevertheless, some help can be provided with pigeons and pheasants, or even rabbits, to provide steadiness to flush, shot and fall of game.

Some dogs will point handled game quite happily, some will learn to point even the string of the release trap when no bird is in the trap! This cannot be recognised as pointing but it can be used (when the bird is inside) for steadiness. First the trap is sprung by the handler and the dog drops as the bird rises. Once that becomes automatic then a shot can be introduced as the bird flushes and again the dog must remain down. Lastly the shot can include a dummy thrown in the direction of the parting bird, or a dummy can be launched. But let the bird get well away before launching the dummy to avoid an accident!

In this way training classes can certainly help in the retriever training and in the training for steadiness on point, dropping to flush and also in teaching a dog to 'back' the pointing dog. However, to train a dog to hunt and point there is no substitute for the effort you must make to find the real thing – suitable ground where there is a supply of birds and permission to use it. This is not impossible; in fact, it is essential if you want to train a Vizsla to work in its full role. If you are not willing to make this effort, then do not expect the dog to work as it should. Training classes can only help you as long as you accept their limitations.

Working Tests

Working tests are the inevitable outcome of training classes and, as such, are valuable in assessing the success or otherwise of the training. Puppy, novice and open tests are held and, if these are imaginatively laid out, they can give judges a fair appreciation of the stage of a dog's progress towards his debut on the shooting field.

Working tests should not be used to advertise a dog's potential as a worker. A proven worker must have a good nose and a soft mouth. Dummies give off a large amount of hand scent and are no proof of a nose for game, nor can a dog's mouth be judged by the manner in which it handles a dummy. Tests are an assessment only of the dog's ability to respond to commands (a very necessary part of the training) but no qualification for the inherent instincts necessary in a brood bitch or stud dog. Advertisements carrying the initials WTW (working test winner) are highly deceptive. The unsuspecting buyer accepts this as a prestigious field award. I would by no means denigrate the dog and handler who go through life entering and enjoying working tests (although I find this difficult to understand) but despise those who use the results as a genuine working qualification.

The working tests which take place at the Game Fair and other country events have a dual role; not only are they a competition but also act as a guide to the general public who wish to see the ability of various gundogs. This is a valuable shop window for all breeds and the demonstration put on by the hunt, point and retrieve breeds at all the recent Game Fairs south of the border have proved of great value in educating the public.

Wise Counsel from an Expert

Nigel Cox (Vallota) writes in 'Gundogs' in 1996

To get the best out of your Vizsla, you need to have a sense of humour and the ability to bend whilst never losing sight of your ultimate object, the finished article – a shooting dog, one that can deal with every eventuality.

Our first Vizsla came to change our way of life in 1973. For many years he was totally misunderstood in the hands of brand-new owners. We took him to Labrador training classes, which bored him witless, but he endured it all. It took years to understand what he wanted, which was to run free, point and then, on command, retrieve to hand.

First Steps that I Attempt

At around ten weeks of age, I throw a dead feral pigeon or a partridge and let the young dog run in and retrieve it. With a little encouragement they will bring it back to you. Do not snatch the retrieve from your young Vizsla. If it takes time to persuade the dog to let you have the retrieve, then this is time well spent. What is the point of this exercise, you may ask? The point is that I now know I have a retriever. This will never be forgotten, although it will be the only retrieve for the dog for a long time – until the hunting and pointing has been perfected.

Starting to Hunt

When you find your youngster is getting to be naughty, it is time to go to the field. Your first field trips should not be too long as young dogs find it hard to concentrate for any length of time – just like us when we were in the classroom on a sunny day looking out of the window with our young minds wandering! This sums up the young Vizsla to a tee! Take your dog out and walk into the wind with him; you will find he will naturally quarter. This means he will run with his nose at a 90 degree angle to the wind. It may not cover a lot of ground, but if you see he can naturally quarter let him do three or four of these and then praise him highly and finish for the day.

I find that little and often is the best way. Never overdo your work; keep it fun. Vizslas respond to your happiness and will naturally want to please you. If you are happy – so are they!

Let your dog discover game, preferably birds such as partridge and pheasant. Although you may well encounter ground game and get the dreaded chase, you must make nothing of these early chases. Pretend you didn't see it! It's all character building and they never catch them anyway.

As time goes on, your Vizsla will become stronger and, indeed, larger. This will enable him to have much more scope and now the real hunting can begin.

The Real Hunting

You need game at this stage – as mentioned previously, both partridge and pheasant. Game provides the reason to hunt. Hunting dogs, as Vizslas are, have an inbuilt instinct to find game. This is one of their special talents. Learn to understand what he is telling you. While hunting, he may have birds in front; if so he will go forward until he feels that he can move on no more and then come on point. Always go to him – but **never** from behind. Come in at a 90 degree angle so he can see you. Keep small, crouch on your approach, talk to him, calm him to avoid a full blooded chase. If you excite him, this will happen for sure.

Some people run their young dogs with a line stretching about thirty yards so that the dog can be steadied on point and prevented from chasing. It works for some, but I've never felt the need for this. My control is through thought and voice and in that order. You will still be getting unsteadiness on hares and low flying birds, but do not worry. When the Vizsla knows exactly what you desire, he will produce it.

I grouch a lot at young dogs when they chase. I bring them back to the exact spot where I told them to stop and make them stay for a few seconds, while asking them (in a deep tone of voice) what the hell they thought they were doing. After several such episodes they show less signs of chasing and this is to be praised highly. As time goes by, and with more trips out, they will become 95% steady – which is a great breakthrough.

Most are naturally talented pointers and, indeed, I've never owned a bad one yet. So this is an area of strength that can easily be worked on. Always praise when your dog has hunted out and pointed. It sounds elementary, but many people take it for granted. Praise them and they will do it better, at greater distance, next time if scent will allow. That's always the aim – better next time.

Full of Excitement

These days are full of excitement and are to be remembered. Have fun and enjoy what they are doing naturally for you. They are young dogs for only a short while.

Never hunt them for too long or they may learn to pace themselves. They don't look their best doing this. Remember, if you bore them they will bore others. Keep your sessions short and sweet.

Don't panic if your young dog is not doing as well as his litter sisters. Dogs do take longer to develop and will go on learning for much longer than a bitch. A bitch could finish her training and be very useful at two years of age; a dog may take another eighteen months. Bear this in mind! Training is not a race – take it at your Vizsla's own pace. There are no hard and fast rules – as they will demonstrate to you, while teaching you to understand what they are doing.

Retrieving

When you are happy with your Vizsla's hunting and pointing and you feel that the steadiness is good, then the next move is to retrieve and teach him hand signals. This is the easiest thing of all to teach as most Vizslas are natural retrievers and want to carry things about in their mouths to bring to you – so don't forget the praise when they have done so.

The thing to remember here is *never let them fail* and then they won't believe that it is possible to do so. Make your first retrieves seen and allow your youngster to run in. Encourage him to come back to you and, again, don't be in too big a hurry to take the retrieve from the dog. I give it back to him to walk round with for a while and then call him back and gently take it again. All the time praise the dog.

When they are happy to retrieve dummies to hand, I start to hold them on the lead for ten seconds longer each time before letting them run off to make the retrieve. This is introducing steadiness to the fall of game. Again, do not do too much at one session. Always leave while they want more. When they are steady we can introduce split retrieves and progress to blind retrieves.

The best way with the blind retrieve is to work the dog on a back wind to start with. That way they don't air scent the dummies and make a mockery of the lesson. Don't just put one dummy out – put five or six in an area of twenty yards. The dog is sure to find one – again, it's all about building confidence.

The Gun

Having complete your retrieving lessons, it's time to introduce the gun. You may well have been noisy with dinner bowls and banged them around at home. I find this good practice as the dog becomes accustomed to sharp bangs and becomes alert and interested. Again, I have never had a dog that has been remotely bothered by a gun; in fact, quite the opposite – they get keener when they see and hear them. Get a friend to shoot 200 yards away, down wind. Show your Vizsla the gun first; let it learn the smell of the gun; walk around with it so that it becomes a part of the pair of you. Tell him to look in the direction of the gun prior to the gun being discharged. They will love it. Within a week, your friend will be able to shoot as close as 40 yards from you and your dog.

Nearly There

Now is the time to throw a dummy and get your friend to shoot. This provides the dog with a real end product. When you can do all this, don't be tempted to shoot game over your own dog for the first shooting season or you will fall into the trap that I did many years ago of ruining all your steadiness work and teach him to run in. This can be rectified, but why risk it? Let others shoot so that you can concentrate on your youngster.

I have not touched on waterwork, as this is just another angle of retrieving, but the Hungarian Vizsla is a great water dog. Again, if you don't make a problem there won't be one.

With good luck and the right approach the sky is the limit – or it should be. You will have many years shooting over one of the better breeds of gundog. They can do it all if you will let them. They will also guard you with their life! What more could you possibly ask for in a gundog, friend and companion?

And finally, Gay Gottlieb Writes...

We all need encouragement to work our Vizslas. In the early days, Major George Wilkinson (Andesheim), David Layton (Midlander) and Louise Petrie-Hay (Waidman)

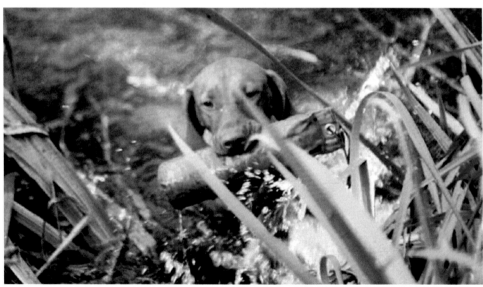

The Hungarian Vizsla is a great water dog. Photo: Chisholm

L to r: Vizsla enthusiasts at a Society tuition day in 1997. Photo: Ryan

were all instrumental in opening up a new world of activity and great enjoyment for me. Louise invited me to bring Russetmantle Troy picking up, and I was hooked. I ventured to trial him as I did Russetmantle Quiver; both achieved placings and both became champions, Troy with 12 CCs and Quiver with 20. When Sh Ch Russetmantle Paris (Troy's son who gained 18 CCs) was put to Sh Ch Russetmantle October (5 CCs), she produced: Russetmantle Fennel trialled successfully by Larry Wilks, Russetmantle Flake who followed in his sire's footsteps by winning a CC first time out at seven months, and Sh Ch Russetmantle Finch of Gunalt (13 CCs) who sired progeny with working and showing qualities. All three brothers worked on local shoots all their lives.

In spite of all the Vizslas I have trained and handled, my enthusiasm has never waned. To work out how handler and dog relate to one another takes time, and both have to find a balance of respect. For example, the Vizsla's powerful scenting ability is an instinct we cannot share with him. We can have no idea what he is scenting at his level, so if we do not read him right, unknowingly we may call him off the very scent we are asking him to find. What confusion must be caused in his mind! If the handler persistently misreads the dog's body language, then resistance sets in.

A Lesson I Never Forgot

One late, warm summer afternoon as the air was cooling, I took a youngster out to do some training. I asked him to retrieve a seen dummy, thrown at a distance at the end of a track. He sat, he went out on the command 'Fetch' like a bullet. He picked up the dummy, put it down and started to potter about. Thinking I had lost concentration, or he had, or both, I called him back and gave him the command again. Out he went, began to slow down, sniffed the dummy, nosed it and went to lift his leg on a nearby tree. By now, my patience was diminishing. My voice had changed pitch to a note of irritation. Drumming away in my head was my obedience training of years ago: 'If you give your dog a command, he must obey.' So out my dog went again; he was slinking, his tail between his legs – an unhappy dog. He was panting and so was I. Of course he did not pick up the dummy, he lay down beside it. My dilemma then was, what to do? We both went to sit in the sweet meadow grass beneath a shady tree and fell asleep together. Decision: no more retrieving for a week, different location, different time of day. He picked the dummy without question. What had gone wrong: too hot? did not feel well? dummy smelled foul? Maybe we were not in tune that day, maybe he had picked up stress from me but, whatever the reason, I did not read him right. But he taught me to give way and to respect an unknown factor, and the art of diversion.

This Vizsla worked all his days, he picked up partridge, woodcock, pheasant and duck and always with enthusiasm. His name was Russetmantle Quiver.

Training and handling Vizslas to a degree of competence in the field has given great satisfaction and enjoyment. I am not talking of the excellence required for field trialling necessarily, but of producing a reliable working gundog who can earn his keep acquitting himself out shooting, one who is capable of being part of the team on a driven shoot or walked up birds, in fact, a Vizsla who can fill the game bag. That is the ultimate aim.

chapter 14

As we have seen, a Vizsla is capable of doing many different types of work. He can be used for all purposes of shooting, stalking and falconry. The ideal however, where he is seen at his best and is most productive, is as a bag-filler is as a rough shooter's companion, where hunting hard for game and pointing it staunchly is the order of the day. One must be prepared to give up time and energy to his training and have suitable ground for him to work over.

Is he any better than the other breeds that hunt, point and retrieve? To those who know and love the breed he is. Why? Because in order to succeed in training a Vizsla, a very close relationship between man and dog is built up, and the character of the Vizsla makes this relationship more meaningful.

The work of the best Vizsla is equal to that of the best German Shorthaired Pointer. Both have superb noses, the softest of mouths and an urgent desire to hunt and find game. The difference between them lies in character and appearance. Anyone who has a good working Vizsla will never want to change to another breed.

Rigby & Gottlieb's Russetmantle Aspic. Anyone who has a good working Vizsla will never want to change to another breed. Photo: Rigby

Rough Shooting

As a rough-shooting companion, the Vizsla must hunt according to the conditions of the ground, fast and wide on moorland and stubbles, close and systematically in roots, and even closer in woodland where an out-of-sight point causes problems. His pointing ability will then hold game, giving the gun time to approach and position himself before the flush and, once game is shot, he must mark the fall and retrieve it dead or wounded from land or water. Hedgerows and ditches must be hunted, as must water meadows and marshy ground. Unlike Pointers and Setters, the Vizsla must hunt in all these conditions and adapt his pace and style accordingly; he must point fur as staunchly as feather. Once dog and owner have worked together for a while, the very

A Petrie-Hay youngster. Some say fur is indicated by the back leg. Photo: Petrie-Hay

stance of the dog will indicate to his owner what type of game he is pointing. Some say that it will be feather if the foreleg is up, and fur is indicated by the hindleg. I have not found this to be accurate – the dog raises the leg that happens to be spare at the time! It is more by a flick of the eye or twitch of the tail that you learn means partridge or hare. How high he holds his head will indicate the distance between him and his quarry, the higher the head the further the game. Scent can be carried 180–275m (200–300yds) when conditions pertain. The high head will indicate this, whereas weak scent clinging to the ground will not be located until the dog is almost on it and

Some say it will be feather if the foreleg is up. Photo: Petrie-Hay

Steady to flush. Col Craigie Halkett's 'Trick' on the grouse moor.

this will produce a very low headed point. When the shooter is ready the dog will go in and cause the bird to fly or rabbit to run and then remain steady so that a shot can be safely taken.

The difference between a Vizsla and a traditional English gundog such as a Pointer, Spaniel or Labrador as a rough shooting companion now becomes apparent. Instead of one dog for one job you have one dog that will take over the work of all three breeds.

On the Grouse Moor

No Vizsla can be more in his element than on the hill on August 12th. After an idle spring and summer it is very necessary to see that he is fit and hard before that day arrives. Muscles have to be toned up and feet must be hardened if he is not to suffer. Exercises should include galloping up and down steep slopes, perhaps after a ball, which will strengthen his muscles and his heart, and trotting behind a bicycle on hard roads for his feet. He will not want to be the dog that has to be left behind on the second day because he is too tired and stiff.

For Vizsla owners it does not matter whether the grouse are driven or walked up. However the game is played, your dog can take a leading role. Versatility is the slogan – grouse or pheasant, stands or walking up, duck or deer. A Vizsla is capable of making his presence appreciated whatever is asked of him. A pure British bird-dog is said to be spoilt if allowed to retrieve but I wonder why. Is it the training complications? This is a real teaser for anyone who has owned a good Vizsla. I can see and understand the other chap's arguments and yet I can prove them to be wrong. An English Pointer must hunt and point, a Hungarian Pointer must hunt, point and retrieve game. An English Pointer must not retrieve game, whereas a Hungarian must retrieve game. Undoubtedly it is an extra temptation for the Hungarian to know he will be asked to retrieve but that is overcome in basic training.

Walked-up grouse shooting is the best experience a young Vizsla can have. The

No Vizsla can be more in his element than on the hill on August 12th. Photo: Chisholm

scent of a grouse is strong and the terrain ideal for a long-legged, wide-ranging youngster full of enthusiasm and stamina. The hares are large and slow, just the temptation he needs to prove his steadiness to fur and the shot birds sometimes fall within sight of his keen eyes. What better conditions could you have to test your training ability and how exciting when your dog proves himself!

Perhaps a few hints on training might be helpful here. Hares are the meanest thing God made for the downfall of dog. There are two schools of thought on training dogs to be steady to hares – I have tried both, with success and failure. The first method,

The scent of a grouse is strong & the terrain ideal for a long-legged, wide ranging youngster full of enthusaim and stamina. Photo: Chisholm

267

A bag-filler, a rough shooter's companion retrieving a hare.

which is widely used on the Continent, necessitates a plentiful supply of hares. Take a young dog into an area where you can guarantee to see 15 or 20 hares in a morning, release him and encourage him to hunt. When a hare gets up let him chase it; having chased, call him in and make a fuss of him, on no account reprimand him at this stage. Repeat this exercise until his energies begin to flag. Now is the time to alter the reception committee.

On his weary return after about the tenth chase, thump him and thump him hard; a switch of some sort is the idea – hurt him but do not harm him. After this, walk him to heel, make friends again and then release him and encourage him to hunt. He may be unwilling, but insist until he flushes another hare.

According to the rules, this time, being both weary and sore not only will he not chase, but probably will drop to your whistle out of sheer exhaustion. Push on and, if possible, work him on another five or six hares. By this time the drop should be automatic and your worries are over. Familiarity and a stung backside does breed contempt and a lesson hard learnt is not quickly forgotten.

The second method is probably the more commonly used in this country as there are many areas where hares are scarce. In these conditions it is better that the dog is never allowed to chase. This is not difficult, but when working ground where there is a possibility of fur, it is essential that no other dog is present to encourage competition or give a bad example.

Almost invariably, when a pup encounters his first hare he does not chase it. The shock of such a large furry creature dashing away from him is quite sufficient to make him check, watch and wonder. Unfortunately this encourages the novice trainer to think he has a natural non-chasing dog. The dog will probably consider chasing the next hare he sees, so it is important not to take him on to hare ground until he is reliable on the stop whistle. Once this is achieved take him where there are likely to be hares.

Send him out quartering on a check cord and, when a hare gets up, drop him. If he should temporarily becomes deaf, you still have control with the check cord so use it sharply. I have found that most dogs chase hares because they are given the example of other dogs. If a dog is never allowed to chase, the problem need not arise. By taking him under control where there are hares and stopping him from the beginning, you will find that by preventing the pleasure of the chase, the wish to chase does not exist. This presumes that you can guarantee to find at least a limited supply of hares on your training ground. For the person who has to rely on a rabbit pen, then anything other than instant, automatic obedience will make life difficult. Do not take a dog which is unsteady to fur on the moors – he will be damned and you will be very unpopular.

Equally do not take a dog which is unsteady to fall of game. This is absolutely essential when walking-up and the dog is working 70–90m (80–100yds) away from you. His steadiness to point and flush will probably be trouble-free but, if game is shot and dropped within sight, a retrieve only on command is very important in case other birds are still to be flushed and shot. Shooting on ground other than moorland can make this aspect of training much simpler. Game shot over a pointing dog frequently falls the other side of a hedge or in a copse or down a valley. The temptation to run into fall of game is infinitely less under those conditions. The moment of greatest temptation is when the marked bird falls within sight and the handler, if not out of sight, is far enough away for threats to be impractical.

Therefore, if you want your Vizsla to be appreciated and invited to return, make certain that he is steady on point, steady to flush, shot and fall of game.

I remember one outstanding retrieve of a wounded bird which landed in rushes 180m (200yds) below us. The dog had marked it and set off at a gallop down the hill. His nose went down where the bird had landed and he set off on the trail. A rabbit dashed across but he worked on regardless following the blood scent; another rabbit bolted and then a roe deer appeared and trotted away, all ignored by the tracker. A hare could be seen directly in front of him getting up and galloping away. He continued to persevere and flushed another deer and pheasant. Then the rushes were too dense to see him but in another five minutes he was back up the hill with the wounded grouse in his mouth. That is the work of an experienced dog with the single-minded perseverance you would expect from a Vizsla. Great pleasure can be had from a visit to the moors and it gives the dog valuable experience for the rest of the shooting season.

Backing

For a one-dog man 'backing' can be a problem. However, if you have a number of dogs it is seldom necessary to teach them to 'back". At the time of year when larks are plentiful, starlings are feeding or even an old 'woodie' (who knows perfectly well that the stick I am carrying is not a gun) is sitting tight in an open field, one of the dogs will stiffen and point, either on scent or sight, it does not matter. A second dog will look up from whatever he is doing, see this dog on point and immediately freeze – then another will look at the second dog and freeze, and so on in succession. A number of dogs will all be pointing. None of them, apart than the first, are connecting with scent; they are automatically taking up a pointing stance which indicates that somewhere game is present. The 'backing' dogs have only 'backed' the sight of a pointing dog.

You can teach your dog to do this if you are a loner and have no companion dog. Run your dog with an experienced dog. When a point is achieved, slip your dog on a lead and take him slowly towards the pointing dog. Directly he is aware of the point, hold him steady and encourage him to remain thus until the game is flushed and away. After repeating this a number of times you will find it becomes a natural reaction. It is important that a dog should immediately 'back' a pointing dog because this avoids any interference when game is located. It also makes it much easier to train for steadiness when working in company.

Clothing

Clothing is an important consideration for any shooting day. Decisions are made easily later in the year when you can rely on it being both wet and cold, but in August it is different. There are four options: hot and dry, hot and wet, cold and dry or cold and wet. Such is the charm of our English summer. Upper clothing must be waterproof and removable, underneath must be decent and cool. It is quite *á la mode* to tie removables around your waist, so too much is preferable to too little.

Colour is all-important as for any type of shooting; it affects the presence of game just as noise does, and it is important that you should attempt to merge as closely as possible with the background.

The decision whether to wear shoes or wellingtons is not really a problem. I have found that walking long distances up and down moors can be rather exhausting if you are a Sassenach. Possibly one's feet suffer most and therefore it is very important that they should be as comfortable as possible. From choice I wear light, completely waterproof ankle boots – although these dear things do not really stand up to the Trades Description Act. I only have to put my foot down one of those rather strange holes that crop up on moors and my boot is filled with water. While watching my dogs, obviously I cannot keep both eyes on the ground, so one foot goes down into a hole and comes out very wet indeed. Now my feet, like my marriage vows, go on the principle 'in sickness and in health' or, rather, 'in dryness and in damp' and they prefer to go squelch, squelch in unison rather than alone. Therefore I find it necessary to lower the other foot into the wee burnie that I happened to have encountered five seconds earlier. No 'waterproof' shoes seem to be able to overcome the problem that when I immerse them in water they do not stay 'waterproof'.

The alternative is to wear wellingtons, which are waterproof – and if you do a silly thing like that the chances are you remain dry-footed and don't have to squelch around. Nevertheless, at the end of the day something very nasty happens when you remove these boots. Even the dogs recoil from the atrocious smell which cannot be avoided no matter what precautions are taken.

One further item, not to be worn but carried, is a stick or crook. Recently I was presented with a very beautiful crook by some friends. I am not normally addicted to walking with a stick but, after a few weeks, I discovered the joys of relaxing and resting my chin on both hands on the top of a crook. The old poem which says 'what is this life if full of care, we have no time to stand and stare' hit me sharply on the head and I realised the pleasure I had missed over many years. In fact, a crook on the moors can help you up things, down things, to stop things like rather fast dogs running past you when they should not be, catching things and, sometimes, walloping things on the head. A stick comes in very handy and, like lead and whistle, should be part of one's accoutrements.

End note

Finally let me say a word about cooking grouse. There are many ways of doing this and you only have to read a cook book to find out. Much depends on the age of the bird but I think I will tell you the fairest and finest way of allowing a grouse to leave this world. See that he is dressed correctly, baste him well with whisky, garnish him with heather then cook in a moderate oven until ready to serve. In what finer array could a true Scottish grouse wish to enter the gates of Heaven?

Picking Up

This is yet another outlet for a workaholic Vizsla. A good picking-up dog must not only be efficient at finding game and carrying it (good nose and soft mouth), but he must also be neither aggressive nor possessive. The back of a Land Rover stuffed with two or three pickers up and half a dozen mixed dogs is no place to be if there is a dog fight. Nor must he be a thief. It can be very embarrassing if you leave your dog with a brace of partridges to return and find only feathers.

I have two teams of dogs: the first XI and the second XI. On big days when I know there will be a great deal of work, the experienced older dogs come out, those who can be relied upon to get on with the job with the minimum of instructions and are safe to send after a runner into a covert with live birds. The second XI consists of one experienced dog and one or two youngsters. Young dogs have got to learn and, used in this way, birds are not lost and a fresh dog is preparing to take over from the old hand. My picking up career began 20 years ago and I quickly learnt my first lesson, which was to leave the work to the dogs. In my enthusiasm I would go bashing through the thickets with the dogs. The keeper asked me who was meant to be doing the retrieving! 'Stand still and send the dog – save your energy for commanding your forces,' he said. I use the dogs not only for retrieving but also walking up across the stubbles and sugar beet with the dogs working ahead. The guns thoroughly enjoy

Gottlieb & Winnock's dogs illustrating that a good picking up dog must not be aggressive towards others. Photo: Ryan

The author with Ch Russetmantle Troy, Waidman Brok, Che & Crumpet
on a frosty picking up day. Photo: Petrie-Hay

shooting over them as pointers. The dogs get a thorough experience of duck as many are reared and driven over the guns. The river is at the bottom of a steeply sloping wooded hillside and the wounded mallard take a lot of finding.

I learned the importance of watching my language. At the end of one morning I was asked by the Brigadier to look for a wounded partridge in some roots and also a dead bird seen to fall in a copse beyond. The dogs covered the roots from end to end, getting points on live birds but no sign of the runner. We worked the surrounding hedges and ditches with no success, so went on to the copse and almost immediately

Col Craigie Halkett's 'Trick' advancing to flush 'roading' on the moor.

found the dead cock pheasant. When I got back to the pub the guns were coming out and they asked whether I had found the birds. I reported that we had failed on the partridge but that I had found the Brigadier's cock! It took a long time to live that down.

We also came across woodcock. Not all dogs will retrieve these birds as they have a slightly sour taste, but I find that if the Viszlas are hesitant to pick them up, at least they will point them. Therefore, I keep closely in touch with them when there is a woodcock down and we seldom lose one. Over the years my eyes have become acclimatised to looking for them and I can now pick one out from amongst the camouflage of dead leaves.

A good picker up not only uses his dogs to find the birds but also uses his own eyes. I was inclined to watch and follow the working dogs and often the keeper would pick up a bird that I had actually walked over. When we went into the coverts after a drive to 'sweep up' I was watching the dogs working, while his eyes were on the ground. I learnt to let the dogs get on with their work of collecting the runners and the birds out of thick cover whilst I picked up the dead ones in front of me.

I also learnt the meaning and importance of 'Watch that bird'. If these words ring out from the line of beaters, I know that this is one bird that will make my day. It will be a pricked bird that possibly is not visible to the pickers up and likely to carry on for quite a distance. If I can see, mark and collect it, it will be a memorable retrieve for the dog. Brok was my star performer on this type of bird. When we were standing well behind the line of guns his instinct would tell him whether a bird was pricked or not and he would go and return with a bird that I could have sworn was untouched. At first I was cross with him, not only for going without command, but also for possibly catching a live bird. But every examination proved him correct with a pellet found in the thigh or wing, and it was not long before I appreciated that such behaviour, although not accepted in a field trial, was invaluable to a picker-up. Many such birds land and, given the chance, will go many miles only to die a lingering death. If a good dog is onto them quickly this is avoided which is the prime object of picking-up. There is much to learn about dogwork, game and guns which makes picking-up such a fascinating sport on its own.

I am lucky in that I get quite a bit of partridge picking-up at the beginning of the season and my experience here brought home to me the absolute necessity during the drives of either being in the line with the guns or 275–365m (300–400yds) behind. Anywhere in between spoils the shooting and is dangerous. Up in line one is in a good position for marking, but the dogs cannot be sent until the end of the drive. If well back, the dogs can get onto a wounded bird immediately. A lightly-pricked partridge recovers quickly and then is away and out of the working area of the dogs, leaving little or no scent.

I remember Crumpet chasing a low-flying bird across a large field, over a hedge, up a bank and into a spinney – in all a distance of at least 275m (300yds). She returned with the wounded bird. I know we would have lost that bird otherwise because, first, there was no ground scent unto the spinney and, second, I would not have considered hunting in that area because the bird was shot 180m (200yds) in front of us. This is an example of bad training for dogs but, some time or other, a picker-up must decide whether he wants to field trial his dogs or to let them earn their keep picking-up. There

*The bag filling pickers up: the author with Ch Russetmantle Troy, Waidman Brok,
Che & Crumpet. Photo: Petrie-Hay*

is a moderately happy medium between control and efficient picking-up. In the above situation, it was the dog who realised that the bird was wounded and that the situation was urgent. Most experienced pickers-up will agree that dogs have a sense beyond ours which recognises a wounded bird in the air. A dog will seldom bother to behave in this way on an untouched bird.

It is well to remember that, when working dogs in thick brambles, their feet will suffer unless you apply something that will help to harden the pads. I recommend a liberal quantity of iodine and balsam rubbed into the feet two or three times a week for some time before the shooting season starts. Repeat this dose during the season if the pads appear to be softening. However, for heaven's sake apply it before going out and not when bring the dog into the house or you will have a lot to answer for when the carpets start looking a funny colour.

I can strongly recommend picking-up as a winter occupation and, although the money does not go far, the fun and enjoyment to be had for oneself and one's dogs are beyond price.

There are two golden rules for pickers-up:

1. Never allow yourself or your dogs to distract the guns. Ensure they are aware of your position and, once there, do not move. Shooting someone is embarrassing and being shot is painful. Always check with any gun who has his own dog whether or not he would like your help. Some bring their dogs for the work and others, believe it or not, bring them along purely for the beer and are only too grateful if your dogs will do the work.

2. Prevention is always better than cure. A friend was badly bitten in the hand when he went to rescue his dog who was caught up on barbed wire. Pain will often make a dog automatically bite the hand that tries to help. **Never** attempt to lift a dog off wire until you have put a stick in its mouth which he can bite onto. Better still, prevent the dog jumping the wire until you have prepared it. I noticed one gun who had fixed a piece of split hose round the shank of his shooting stick. This was easily removed and placed over the top strand of barbed wire for the dog to jump over, then replaced around his stick. A 'puffer' antibiotic is always advisable to have in your pocket, as also is a needle and thread. One friend of mine owned a bitch who was a compulsive jumper; she only had to see a fence or gate and she was over it quite regardless of whether or not they were going that way. She was an excellent jumper but, nevertheless, did get caught up in wire from time to time. When this happened her owner could be seen sewing up the offending gash, having powdered it first. The bitch died a natural death at the age of 15.

Why Have Field Trials?

What is the purpose of field trials? To find the best shooting dog on that day. And for what purpose? One presumes to assist in selective breeding, although no mention is made of this, and to check that the winner is a good specimen of the breed, free from hereditary defects and of good temperament. The accent is on winning. A field trial is a competition, run under a set of rules and to a standard controlled by rules which the judge must adhere to. Under these conditions, is the dog which wins the trial necessarily the dog that should be used to improve and perpetuate the breed, or are we losing sight of this consideration? Is the winning dog the best shooting dog, or is he the best-trained dog, in which case should we not award the prize to the handler and breed from him!

Ch Russetmantle Troy indicating game.

Often I am not satisfied that the winning dog is the dog with the drive, initiative, perseverance and keenness that are the natural abilities I am looking for and that cannot be instilled into him or her if they are not inherited. The winner is the dog which works under the control of the handler and, if the handler is experienced, providing his dog has an average ability, then by the rules of the game he could win. The dog with the burning ambition to find game, the instinct to point steadily and the keenness to retrieve the bird as quickly as possible in order to hunt on, more often than not will slip up by breaking one of the rules, not because he is out of control or purposefully disobedient, but because his keenness can at times overrule his schooling. Biddability and controllability are important; a wild dog is worse than a useless dog, but a dog which has the courage to obey its instinct in the presence of game is a better game finder than the one which is fearful of stepping out of line.

Why do the Germans have the Derby and the Solms tests? These spring and autumn blood-line tests exist not only to test the natural working abilities of the young dogs but also their character and temperament, with a view to their future role in the

Ch Russetmantle Troy working onto a point.

shooting field, their potential as stud dogs or brood bitches and to assess the qualities inherited from their breeding. These dogs have only completed their basic training and it is possible to judge the truly natural qualities and capabilities of their work before these qualities are hidden by the final training. The classification of 'Excellent' can only be awarded if the judges consider the work of the dog is attributable to its inherited natural ability and not to the training.

Thus we can see that it is accepted that a higher degree of training can inhibit natural ability. Controllability can be seen by the natural desire of the dog to keep in touch with his handler and willingly to take instruction from him. Obedience is

The point.

instilled by training and is a vital part of a gundog's education. With this in mind, why am I and some of my co-judges not satisfied? The nitty-gritty of the matter lies in the fact that so often the best dogs must either be marked down or even eliminated by what I choose to consider is a minor indiscretion. The beginning of a chase on game, even though the dog is stopped, can prevent its name being put on the short list. A 'run-in', although not listed in the Guide under Eliminations (it is for Retrievers and Spaniels), is considered a major crime. Never have I known a dog that has run-in fail to be eliminated. This is surely an anomaly. A short case, if corrected, cannot be described as being 'out of control' which is, quite rightly, a reason for elimination – in fact, to be able to control such behaviour should surely be marked up. The man who resists temptation has a far stronger character than he who is not tempted. And a run-in must surely be related to conditions. A run-in should only be a crime if it interferes with the sport. Only the finest margin separates it from a quick retrieve.

When does a normally steady dog run-in? Probably on two occasions. If a bird is dropped within a few yards of him there is no way he can be blamed for picking it up. It will not interfere with the shooting nor will it disturb the other game. The dog could be said to be tidying up. If it is eliminated for this then, in all fairness, every other contender should be put in a similar situation and this is not possible in a trial. I maintain that it should be ignored. The other occasion when a useful shooting dog will commit a peccadillo is when a bird is seen to be winged, lands and then starts to run. In this case the dog may jump the gun. When out shooting how many of our dogs are not expected to collect that bird instantly? A pause of even a minute could make the difference between a quick death or a lingering one for the bird. On a poor scenting day that bird will leave little or no trail for even the best of dogs to follow unless he is close behind, and the best of dogs knows this from experience.

Surely the ultimate penalty should not be exacted in a trial when the dog is behaving as it would be asked to in the shooting field? This is the way a first-class shooting dog can be excluded from a field trial award and all that is associated with it. Are field trials achieving their objectives when it is possible for a brilliant dog to be eliminated on such flimsy grounds?

I do not pretend that this happens all the time, but it does happen under our present system of judging. Is it in the best interests of the breed that a dog with a mediocre nose but which is completely steady takes preference as the best shooting dog over a far superior natural worker whose keenness produces an error in steadiness? These dogs are not non-slip Retrievers nor are they close working Spaniels – they are wide, fast-ranging pointers which must work hard and fast to find game, hold it and then retrieve it speedily and tenderly. Many genuine, honest working dogs are not entered in the trials because their owners are discouraged by this form of judgement. Yet are not these shooting dogs the ones we want to see running in trials, showing the full potential of the breed and offering their services at stud to perpetuate the very qualities that are necessary to maintain and improve this group of multi-purpose pointer/retrievers?

If the objective of field trials is to produce the best shooting dog, then it is important that the result reflects the potential scope of the winner as best shooting dog rather than the best-trained dog.

How to Run in a Field Trial

When deciding to run in a field trial you must first be sure that your dog, be it a puppy or adult, is ready for competition. By that I do not mean that there can be no possible chance of it not winning, but that you have proved that it will hunt on strange ground in front of strange guns; that it will point and remain so, providing the game holds, and that it will actually pick up a warm bird or rabbit (if you have a puppy competing then you can refuse a fur retrieve if you so wish). Finally, you must be sure that he will swim not only in your own swimming pool or lake, but in a strange one. It is also necessary that the dog should be under control, reasonable control that is, in order that he does not spoil the conditions for the other competitors. If a dog does not drop to flush, but moves to mark the fall of game and then stops, that's all right. If he sees a hare or rabbit, just cannot resist beginning to follow but you have sufficient authority to stop him, that is all right too. If a bird is shot off the end of his nose and flaps in front of him, not many dogs will resist this ghastly temptation, and if he is tempted it is very bad luck. Luck, do not forget, is the one factor which the organisers are totally incapable of eliminating if a trial is to be conducted as nearly as possible to a shooting day, and any competitors must be sporting enough to accept this. Nevertheless, should this happen and your dog be eliminated, which it must under Kennel Club rules, it is quite possible for the judges to award a Certificate of Merit if they consider that in other respects the dog has worked well and proved that he can hunt, point and retrieve.

In a field trial a dog must also swim and, in a novice stake, where possible all the competitors are encouraged to do the water test. The last requirement, and possibly the most important from the breed point of view, is that the dog should be soft mouthed. If your dog has a mouth like a gin-trap and consistently mangles game, then do not enter him in a field trial, no matter how efficient a game finder he is – there is no use in game finding if you cannot eat the produce, and great harm can be done to the breed if such dogs run at trials.

After reading this, you will realise that any self-respecting Vizsla who is used for shooting is eligible to enter a trial. If you decide to enter your dog in a trial, the next step is to note the date and venue, to apply for an entry form, and read the regulations. Then you must remember to send off the entry form with the required fee by the required date; in fact as early as possible in order to make the work of the secretary as easy as possible. You should also write to the secretary of The Kennel Club and ask him to send you the Kennel Club Rules and Regulations for Field Trials, that is, J, JA and JB, in order that you will understand the procedure that governs all trials held on live game. This will include the *Guide to Field Trial Judges*, which will give you an insight into how the judges assess the performance of your dog.

Handlers and Handling

Handling is a special field trial word which describes the waving of arms, blowing of whistles, leaping around, falling over and the general apoplectic actions of a competitor at a field trial whilst attempting to control his dog. When out shooting with his dog you would describe him as a normal, sane, balanced person but, once in the line under the judges' orders, he becomes terrified and hysterical. His dog reacts just as one would expect an intelligent animal would do. Out shooting he knows his owner and his job and gets on with it accordingly – in a trial he becomes perplexed and excited. His owner, obviously temporarily insane, must be pandered to in the hopes that he will revert to his normal, healthy state of mind as soon as possible. This is an extreme example of field trial nerves which affects many handlers. With time and experience they usually get over this but, if not, it kills either them or their efforts to continue trialling. One could spend many happy days at trials never looking at the dogs, just watching the antics of the handlers. It has an amusing fascination all of its own. I recall one handler who imitated a policeman on traffic duty to perfection, another who was constantly winding and unwinding his arms in a sort of Cordon Bleu sauce-making exercise and yet another who never stopped blowing on his whistle till finally the pea got stuck and he was right up the proverbial gum tree, completely purple in the face.

A competitor must think about what the judges have seen when they have to consider their marks for handling and what they mean when they report that a dog was well handled, or over-handled or did not respond to handling. In a nutshell, handling is the final outcome of training and almost every mistake a dog makes can be attributed to bad handling, in other words, lack of training – all, that is, except a true hard mouth, and in this case the dog should not be entered in a trial anyway. The very best handler is seen and not heard, the worst is heard and seen to be totally ineffective.

There is no doubt that nerves, like luck, play a great part in trials and are difficult to overcome. Much good dogwork is spoilt by a nervous handler losing his confidence in front of the gallery, or by a handler who is under the mistaken impression that he has to prove his dog is obedient to every instruction, thus interfering with his natural working ability. In the judges' opinion, a good handler is the one who listens carefully to the instructions given regarding the beat, who checks the wind and ground conditions intelligently and who controls the dog with the minimum of noise and actions. Obviously this can only be achieved with a steady dog with good game-finding and retrieving abilities, and applies to an experienced handler and dog.

Help can be given to a novice if he considers the following points. The judges indicate clearly to the handler the ground to be covered by his dog and every effort is made to ensure that this will be upwind. The position of the guns should be noted and the dog then sent off in the direction which will give him the maximum benefit of any available scent. Handler and dog dictate the speed at which the line advances. At this stage it is most important to keep the dog working within his beat and this can be done by word, whistle or hand signals, obviously the quieter the better, and good marks will be given if the dog responds quickly. Directly the dog comes on a firm point, it is up to the handler to see that the judges are aware that a point is being claimed. A good handler knows better than the judges whether his dog is on a productive point and he must go quickly and quietly up to his dog to ensure there is no flush until the guns are in position and the judges tell him that he may send his dog in to flush the game.

Steadiness to flush, shot and fall of game is required and this is far easier to ensure if the handler is close to his dog. It may be necessary to steady or drop the dog on command and a handler will get good marks if this is done quietly and effectively. If the game is shot then the handler must wait until told by the judges to send his dog for the retrieve. At this stage good marking by the handler is helpful as at least then he knows where he should send his dog if the fall was blind to the dog.

Handling onto a blind retrieve is naturally necessary but the more quietly done the better. If the dog is in the area of the fall and is using his nose, do not interfere with him. Handling at the water retrieve should be kept to the minimum. Keep your dog sitting whilst the shot is fired and pigeon thrown then, when told by the judges, send the dog and wait quietly for him to return. If encouragement to enter water is needed, give it quietly and, once the dog is swimming, leave him alone to get on with the job. If the dog has been trained for the test then it should be quite unnecessary to whistle or call him in once he has the bird.

Over-handling is almost always the result of nerves and lack of confidence in the dog – try to relax and leave the dog to get on with the work as if it was an ordinary shooting day. Under-handling is the other extreme, where a dog blatantly works off his beat and the handler makes no effort to check this, or the handler stays rooted to the ground when a dog is pointing, neither claiming the point nor going forward to help ensure steadiness. Another example of under-handling is when a handler is given a retrieve and sends the dog in a vague fashion towards the fall, allowing it to gallop in all directions in the hope that he may be lucky and stumble across the bird. A good handler appears to be doing very little, but the little he does is effective. A final word – remember the one thing a handler may **not** do is handle (touch) his dog!

Guide for Handlers

All stakes organised for breeds which hunt, point and retrieve are run in accordance with Kennel Club Rules and Regulations, copies of which may be obtained from the field trial secretary of The Kennel Club. These comprise:

J   Kennel Club Field Trial Rules.
JA Regulations for the Various Breeds.
JB Guide to the Conduct of Field Trials

J and JA are mandatory; JB is a guide only. Judges are bound by J and JA just as much as handlers; whereas JB is only a guide to judges who may exercise discretion in their interpretation of the recommendations made therein.

The notes below are designed to convey the spirit of field trials rather than the chapter and verse of rules and regulations, which are found in the above and which should be read by all handlers prior to competing. Addenda in the July 1997 KC Rules and Regulations are now listed under J, JA and JB.

General Rules

- The essential thing to remember is that the handler and his dog along with the gun are a game finding team.
- The handler must consider the ground, wind direction and cover, and decide how best to work the dog.
- The dog must run across the wind to scent game, point game when winded, and remain on point until the gun is ready for the shot.

- On command, the dog should find and retrieve game shot.

These four points set out what is required of a handler and his dog in the shooting field or at a field trial.

The judge at a field trial only imposes himself upon the team by:

- Defining the area of ground for the dog and handler to work.
- By signalling when the dog can work out its point, having instructed the guns and made them ready for the shot.
- By signalling if and when the dog may retrieve.

This makes it clear that the handler of the dog is responsible for ground treatment once the judge has defined the area and the direction he requires the line to proceed. It is the handler's responsibility to read his dog and signal when it is pointing game.

Field trials should approximate as closely as possible to an ordinary shooting day, and handlers should therefore remember at all times that their main objective is to find and produce game.

Guns, both on a shooting day and at a field trial, do not want to stand about idle. In either event, therefore, an efficient handler and dog get on with the job and find game for them quickly. This is what the judges are looking for in field trials, and they should give the prize to the most efficient at this, provided that the dog behaves himself properly and in accordance with the rules.

On arrival at the field trial meeting place

Competitors are expected to arrive half an hour before the scheduled time of starting. They should immediately report to the steward, collect their number, find out where they can exercise their dog and learn what arrangements are being made for transport and lunch during the day.

Competitors are advised to take this opportunity to give their dogs as much exercise as possible, as they will have to be on the lead for the rest of the day, except when under the judges.

Before the start, one of the judges will introduce the host for the day, the guns and officials, and will brief the competitors on the task planned for the day.

On being called to perform

Competitors must be ready to come quickly into the line when called to do so by the steward.

They should immediately report to the judge, who will indicate to them the general direction of advance, the limits to which a dog may be allowed to quarter and any other general instructions or cautions, for example, the proximity of a road or railway. It is now up to the handler, within the scope of these instructions, to find game on the ground as quickly as possible. As soon as he is sure of these instructions, he should remove the collar and lead and command the dog to quarter in search of game. When his dog indicates game, he should signal by raising his hand. When the judges are ready, the game should be flushed but, if it is shot, the dog should not be sent to retrieve until the judges' permission has been given.

Handlers should be aware that pointers rely for pointing largely on air-borne scent, and that therefore the dog which quarters across the wind and into it is most likely to give itself the best chance of finding game. Judges will recognise this also and do not expect to see a dog conform slavishly to the line of guns regardless of the direction and vagaries of the wind. It is up to the handler to decide how to tackle the allotted ground and to control the pace of advance. This should be as fast as will allow the dog to cover the allotted ground adequately without the likelihood of missing the game.

Remember, the game will probably be running on quickly all the time away from the sight and sound of the line of guns. A very slow line will probably never catch up with it. On the other hand, on a bad scenting day, it is easy for an inexperienced dog to go too fast.

Note: It is generally accepted that when hares and rabbits are clapped tight in their form, they may not give off any scent. A dog failing to point a hare or rabbit in these circumstances cannot be regarded as having missed game.

At all times, handlers must be aware of the judges' problem of thoroughly testing 12 dogs during the course of a fairly short day and, therefore, they must not waste time.

The handler should expect to continue quartering his dog, even after a successful flush and retrieve, until told by the judges that they have seen enough for the moment. When told to put his dog on the lead, the handler should do so immediately.

Handlers can normally expect to have two 'runs' in the course of the day, as well as the water test, unless the dog is eliminated for any reason.

Water Test

The water test at field trials is semi-artificial, in that each dog is required to perform a set test by retrieving a previously shot bird.

In novice stakes, a shot is fired and a bird is thrown into the water in view of the dog. The dog should remain sitting and steady until given the command to retrieve. In all other stakes, a bird is concealed on the other side of a stretch of water. No shot is fired, and the dog is expected to swim across, find and retrieve the bird, re-entering the water with the bird on the return journey where practicable.

Handlers and dogs still to be tested are not permitted to watch the performances of previous dogs, and will be directed by the steward where to stand.

Queries and Complaints

Handlers must remember that judges are under considerable pressure, both to get through the day's programme during a short winter day and to produce a definite and fair result at the end of it. Nevertheless, judges should always be ready at the end of the day to discuss with the handler concerned any decision regarding his or her dog, or any other problems; they should not, of course, discuss the merits or demerits of other competitors' dogs.

Conclusion

At the end of the day, when the prizes have been awarded, it is customary for the winner to thank the judges.

Field Trial Judging

I read an article on field trial judging which said that if the handler is to train his dogs effectively, he must know and be aware of the judging factors involved.

The qualifications for a Pointer/Retriever judge are that he must be conversant with the Kennel Club Field Trial Rules and Regulations and must have gone through the procedure for judges, that is, taken a book at a field trial under two or three different judges. If well reported by those judges and they consider his assessment of the dogwork to be fair and reasonable, then he may be invited to judge a novice stake as a learner judge. Again if no adverse report is made either about his conduct or decision, then his name can be considered by The Kennel Club for addition to their Panel B of field trial judges. After this, when he has co-judged two Open or All-aged Stakes, his name may be presented to The Kennel Club for promotion to Panel A. Once a judge is qualified he must be prepared to stand by his decision and opinions and, as far as possible, ensure that during a trial he can see all things at all times.

A field trial judge is only one of us ordinary people who has accepted a judging appointment regardless of journeys and weather because he enjoys watching dogs work. A good judge should be impartial and friend to none; he is no good if he lacks the respect of officials or competitors. He should give no award unless, in his opinion, a proper standard of performance has been achieved. There is no way to tell how a judge comes up with the best dog on the day, because each judge has his own ideas and subjective opinion about the situations met at a field trial where conditions are constantly changing. Some mistakes by a dog can be overlooked because they are unseen. The judge is trying to evaluate the total work of the dog, not the individual performances of hunting, pointing and retrieving. A judge appreciates that neither handler nor dog are machines. It is possible at a trial that the best dog is not in the awards owing to the conditions of his particular run and that the winner was only the dog who did no wrong. Since judges too are human their judgement must be personalised. Judging calls for good personal and physical qualities, but it is a tough, thankless task. There can be only one winner and eleven losers, and the elements, availability of game and poor shooting can also be against the judge. Most judges use some form of judging system and certainly a memo book, but there are times when a judge is so cold, wet and miserable that the only thing on his mind is a roaring fire and a large drink.

A good judge will help the competitors to the best of his ability. He can do this by briefing them kindly and carefully at the beginning of their run, by remaining calm when things go wrong and by explaining his assessment of their dog in confidence at the end of the day. This will help to give the competitor confidence and an insight as to how the judge evaluated the good and the bad.

At every trial there are two judges. One of these must be a Panel A judge who takes responsibility for the trial and makes the final decision should there be any disagreement between them. Otherwise the two judges assess the dogs independently and both should see everything that occurs on the day. At the end of the morning they discuss their assessments and decide which dogs they wish to be brought into the line after lunch. At the end of the day they make their final decisions and place the dogs in order of merit, deciding then whether they consider the quality and standard of work merits the premier award. It is wise to remember that at times a first prize may not be given, not because the work of the dog placed first was unsatisfactory in any way, but because the situations pertaining to the availability of game and retrieves were too simple to test the dog's ability. The dogs must run in the order of the draw at the start of the trial and there is no way that the luck of the draw, ground and game can be eliminated.

Guide to Field Trial Judges issued by The Kennel Club Field Trials Committee

Breeds which Hunt, Point and Retrieve

1. Trials should be run as nearly as possible to an ordinary day's shooting. Judges are responsible for the proper conduct of the trial in accordance with The Kennel Club Regulations and with the schedule for the stake. They should co-operate with the host and the steward of the beat to achieve the best results in an atmosphere of friendliness and confidence. If conditions force them to depart from usual practice they should explain the reasons to handlers and spectators. Guns and handlers should be briefed at the start.

2. Judges at Open and All-aged Stakes should ask the guns to shoot everything, except directly over a dog out working. In other stakes judges should ask the guns to shoot only over the 'Point' and when the handler is beside the dog, unless otherwise directed.

3. The first round should be taken as drawn. For subsequent rounds, judges may call forward dogs at their discretion so that those showing merit will be thoroughly tested and given every opportunity in roughly comparable conditions of wind, scent and ground. Dogs which are not forward within 15 minutes of being called may be disqualified.

4. Judges should so position themselves that they can see every move of the dogs while in the line. They should regulate the pace of the line to the handler and dog to avoid game being flushed on a part of the beat not yet covered by the dog. Game so flushed should not be counted as missed by the dog.

5. Judges should accede to a request from the handler of a puppy in a Novice or Puppy Stake who asks to be excused from retrieving fur.

6. If a dog catches game and the judges are satisfied that the game was unwounded and undamaged, the dog should be eliminated. When it appears the game will not flush for the dog, the handler may ask permission to take up his dog, and should only be marked down for handling if subsequently shown to have been wrong.

7. Judges must confirm the arrangement for the collection of unretrieved and unwanted game.

8. Judges may discuss situations that arise and must agree that actual marks they

award as these represent their opinions and should be kept strictly to themselves. The marks should represent the work seen on the day, and should not be influenced by past performances.

9. The standard of work in Open and All-aged Stakes carrying field trial championship status should be higher than for other stakes. A prize should not be awarded unless the dog has had a productive point, a retrieve in the field and has completed the retrieve, whatever the conditions of the day. Other stakes may be judged more leniently, but a prize should not be given unless the dog has proved himself a pointer, and a retriever on land or at the water, and has swum. Certificates of Merit are not prizes and are awarded at the judges' discretion to dogs showing all-round qualities and that swim.

10. Judges should mark the following categories:
(i) **Ground treatment:** The dog has to hunt the allotted beat thoroughly, making good all ground, missing no game and using the wind correctly. A dog that deliberately runs into game up wind should be discarded, but if he drops to birds rising down wind of him, this is a credit.
(ii) **Pointing:** The dog should point game staunchly, and work out only on word of command. He must be steady to flush, shot and fall. Persistent false pointing should be severely penalised, but an unproductive point, where the dog indicated by nose down and wagging tail where departed game lay, should not be marked but may be credited as a 'point' for the award of Certificate of Merit. It is accepted that hares and rabbits in their forms may not give off scent for the dog to point. Judges should not penalise dogs for failing to point in such conditions.
(iii) **Retrieve:** The retrieve must be on command. If game is shot over the point and is marked, the dog should go straight into the fall and any diversion marked down. With blind retrieves, judges should indicate to the handler where the game fell. The dog should go directly as indicated by the handler and any diversion from that line, with consequent waste of time and risk of disturbance of game, should

Harris' Szajani Palinka indicating game ahead. Photo: Everrit Stewart

be marked down. On a long blind retrieve, the dog should be taken towards the fall. A handler should be allowed to position himself where he can see to direct the dog according to conditions, but he should be beside the judges for the delivery.

In the case of a strong runner, the judge should give the immediate order for a dog to be sent. Wounded game should be retrieved before dead game. The seen dead game lying in the open does not really test a good dog, so should not be highly marked and should be avoided except in stakes other than Open and All-aged. Not more than two dogs should be tried on the same bird. When a judge goes forward to locate the game, no further dog should be tried on it. If more than one bird is down, and the dog changes birds on the way back, he should be severely marked down.

The pick-up should be clean with a quick return and delivery to hand. A dog that puts game down to take a firmer grip should not be severely marked down as he may have had a gruelling stint quartering, but sloppy retrieving and finishing should be penalised.

All game should be examined for hard mouth. A hard-mouthed dog seldom gives evidence of hardness. He will simply crush in one or both sides of the bird. Blowing up the feathers will not disclose the damage. Place the bird on the palm of the hand, head forward, and feel the ribs with finger and thumb. They should be round and firm. If they are caved in or flat, this is definite evidence of hard mouth. Be sure the bird reaches your co-judge and the handler for examination. There should be no hesitation or sentiment with hard mouth – the dog should be eliminated. A certain indication of a good mouth is a dog bringing in a live bird whose head is up and eye bright. Superficial damage, if any, in this case can be ignored. At times the rump of a strong runner may be gashed and look ugly. Care should be taken here, as it may be the result of a difficult capture, or lack of experience in mastering a strong runner by a young dog, not by the shot or fall, and in cases of doubt the benefit should be given to the dog. Handlers should be given the opportunity of inspecting the damaged game in the presence of the judges, but the decision of the judges is final.

(iv) **Game finding ability:** This is of the highest importance. The judges will be looking for it throughout the dog's work by the manner in which he works his beat, finds his game and responds to scent generally, and by the degree of sense of purpose and drive that he displays.

(v) **Steadiness:** The dog must in all cases be steady to flush, shot and fall. He may move to mark the fall, and this may be a credit. A dog that runs in to retrieve and is stopped, and then retrieves on command should be marked down according to the extent of the break, but the dog that does not stop should be eliminated. Dogs should be steady to fur and feather going away.

(vi) **Facing cover:** There are occasions, such as on a grouse moor, when this category cannot be marked. Unless all dogs can be marked, none should be. In general, the dog should go boldly into reasonable cover when ordered, either to push out game or to retrieve it. The judges should agree what is reasonable.

(vii) **Style:** This embraces grace of movement, stylishness on point and of the retrieve, and the general appearance of keenness, competence and happiness in what the dog is doing.

(viii) **Handling:** Noisy, ineffective and over-handling should be severely marked down. Usually the best dogs seem to require the least handling, but the dog should be responsive to his handler's signals.

(ix) Water retrieve: This should be fully assessed, with special attention to direct, courageous but not suicidal entry, strong swimming, direct emergence and speedy delivery to hand. In Open and All-aged Stakes the water retrieve is blind across water and should be judged accordingly, including the re-entry into water carrying game.

Eliminations: Hard mouth, whining or barking, flushing upwind, out of control, running in or chasing, failure to hunt, missing game birds on the beat, refusal to retrieve or swim.

Major faults: Not making ground good, missing game on a beat, unsteadiness, sticking on point, persistent false pointing, not acknowledging game going away, failing to find dead or wounded game, catching unwounded game, disturbing ground, noisy handling, changing game whilst retrieving.

Kennel Club Schedule for Breeds which Hunt, Point and Retrieve

1. Dogs shall be run singly under two judges.
2. Dogs shall be required to quarter ground in search of game, to point game, to be steady to flush, shot and fall, and to retrieve on command.
3. Water retrieves: Dogs shall be required (1) in Puppy, Novice and Non-winner Stakes to retrieve from or across water a seen bird which has been thrown and shot at whilst in the air; (2) in all other stakes to make a blind retrieve of a bird from across water re-entering the water, where practicable, with the bird and with no shot fired.
4. Dogs must not wear any form of collar when under the orders of the judges. All dogs must be kept on a lead when not competing.
5. Any dog which in the opinion of the judge fails to hunt, point, retrieve tenderly, complete the water test, is gun-shy, or is out of control shall not receive any prize. Any dog in any stake must have been tried at least twice in the line, excluding the water retrieve, before receiving a prize.
6. Eliminations and major faults as amended in July 1997.

Various Competitions in the Field

Two organisations in this country foster and protect the interests of the breed, the Hungarian Vizsla Society and the Hungarian Vizsla Club. Both have run field trials over the years. The Vizsla Society organises regular get-togethers which include training sessions; also training days, field days and working tests, and they provide annual trophies which are awarded to the dogs which accumulate the highest points not only for working ability but also for conformation. Both the societies are represented on The Kennel Club Field Trial Council. Two representatives on The Kennel Club Field Trial Committee look after the interests of all the hunt, point, retrieve breeds.

In 1982 The Kennel Club authorised a Hunt, Point, Retrieve Field Trial Association on which both the Society and Club have two representatives. This Association runs an annual Field Trial Judges' seminar which is attended by all the panel A and B judges, learner judges, field trial secretaries and field trial stewards. The Association also organises the BHPR Championship Stake.

The *Shooting Times and Country Life Magazine* award annually a silver salver to the dog who has run in not less than three field trials and gained the highest marks. This covers all the hunt, point and retrieve breeds. It was first awarded at the game fair in 1977 for the 1976 season and has been won every year since by a German Shorthaired Pointer. Until 1982 Vizslas, although featuring in the awards and qualifying by running in three or more trials, were never placed in the final line up, but in 1982 this was broken and Mrs Sylvia Cox's Viszony of Vallota came second having run in nine trials and gained 50 marks, only two marks below the winning dog who ran in 10 trials and gained 52 marks.

BHPR are the initials for a Kennel Club gundog classification – Breeds which Hunt, Point and Retrieve. In February 1979 there was an opportunity to alter this from BHPR to P/R or Pointer/Retriever. The two words instead of six seemed a good idea, in saving of wind and paper. BHPR may sound attractive to some, to others it could be a drug or a trade union.So battle commenced on the pros and cons of an alternative umbrella title for such gundogs.

The title describes the variety of mid-European Pointers which, unlike English Pointers and Setters, are expected to retrieve from land and water, and also hunt in cover as well as in the open. Examples of dogs other than Vizslas are the German Shorthaired Pointer, German Wirehaired Pointer, Weimaraner and Large Munsterlander, the Drentse Partridge Dog, the Italian Spinone, the Brittany Spaniel, also the Wirehaired Vizsla. The only breed in this list which gives any indication as to its work is the German Pointer. In some ways this is to its detriment as many German Pointer breeders will agree. The most common question one has to answer is "Do they retrieve?" Yes, all these breeds retrieve and, if they wish to run in field trials, then The Kennel Club stipulates that in order to win an award, this group of gundogs must not only hunt for game, point game, retrieve fur and feather, but also complete a water retrieve either of a bird from the water with a shot fired in the novice stake, or of a bird from land across a stretch of water as a blind retrieve with no shot fired in the open and all-aged stakes.

Eliminating faults are hardmouth, whining or barking, running in and chasing, out of control, failing to enter water. Credits are game-finding ability, style on point, drive, good marking, speed and efficiency in gathering game, good water work and quiet handling. This is expected from all the breeds, and all these breeds are capable of completing such a schedule although the style of work differs slightly. The Weimaraner, which is a larger, heavier dog, is slower and possibly more methodical than the more lightly-built Hungarian Vizsla. The hairy Munsterlander is more inclined to forge through thickets, whilst the German Shorthaired Pointer air scents on approach and, if no scent of game is available, wastes no time in working through the scrub. They all vary in their style of pointing as do all Pointers. Much depends on the pointing situation – a classic point is produced by classic conditions, where scent of game ahead is carried high on the wind. Where little wind or scent is available, a tiny snatch of scent will spin a dog round producing an inelegant U-shaped point. When game is very close, the head will be low; the further the game, the higher the head, and more attractive the point. Style of retrieving varies more with the individuals than the breeds, and this also applies to their entry into water and style of swimming.

This is what the dogs described as breeds which hunt, point and retrieve must be capable of doing in the field. The argument for altering this title was basically a dislike of the unnecessary amount of words which encouraged the use of initials. The alternative suggestion was Pointer/Retrievers which adequately described this type of gundog and is brief and simple. Those against the alteration argued that the word 'hunt' was all-important since it emphasised the necessity for the dogs to search all types of terrain for the game they had to point, and they held that the use of initials was very popular in this modern age. Against this it was pointed out that all dogs must hunt before finding game. You would never expect to add the word 'hunt' to Pointers, Setters or Spaniels. Why should it then be necessary for the Continental breeds? A good reason is that to the Englishman Pointers, Setters and Spaniels are explanatory, and the most ignorant amongst us understand the work of these dogs. But 'Vizsla' or 'Weimaraner' gives no clue whatsoever until explained vividly and graphically as breeds which hunt, point and retrieve. By using the word 'hunt' it takes them out of the category of the Pointer/Setter group whose work is primarily on open stubble or moorland, and indicates the true use of BHPRs which is to hunt all types of ground: open, scrub, woodland, roots and marshes, anywhere in fact where game scent is available.

These were the pros and cons of the debate, and the final decision was that there should be no change. So, whether you like it or not, BHPR is the official classification for breeds which hunt, point and retrieve.

In conclusion, Gay Gottlieb Writes

Louise Petrie-Hay states: "The Vizsla's temperament is an anomaly, utterly contradictory. Happiness, confidence and a deep and sincere wish to please on one hand, sensitive, contrary, soft and strong-willed on the other."

It certainly does create a strange and difficult mixture for training and, added to a capacity for feeling bored and ashamed, it affects the Vizsla deeply if his owner appears displeased. His sense of humour and natural exuberance can save the day, but a continual diet of rigorous, disciplined training will create such resistance he will become an immovable force. Many of us have learned the hard way and, in some cases, Vizslas will have been ruined. But many of us have also learned to temper our training programmes to the individual dog, so that we work with him and not against him, seeking solutions and alternatives, adapting to his particular temperament. And, as LPH & Nigel Cox demonstrate, to get the best out of your Vizsla you need to have the ability to bend whilst never losing sight of your ultimate goal - 'a shooting dog' that can deal with every eventuality.

In the last two decades, it seems we have come to love and accept the Vizsla's character and that it is unique and different to other HPRs. His complex personality and way of working does need enlightened handling. He will not always conform to our terms. His wide repertoire takes time to develop and, if we are to make the best use of his all-round performance, he will pose a challenge. However, with dedicated support and informed awareness, it has been proved that his performance in the field can be the highest.

Conclusion

Whatever our ultimate aim is in working our Vizslas, whether field trialling, picking up, beating, or any other discipline for that matter, the end result should be that our Vizsla fulfills our needs, so it is always well worth tempering our methods to obtain a final result. The crux of the matter is that the right handler and the right dog can achieve all things. Each dog's temperament is so different, its talents so varied, excelling in one aspect perhaps more than another that, although the principles of training HPRs must be understood and valued, they must be honed and refined according to the individual's needs. A slight leeway should always be allowed and so, together, the giving and taking result in the sort of Vizsla you want. When properly nurtured and trained, and with due attention given to extending its gifts and talents, the owner is assured of a most endearing and capable companion. I hope the day never comes when the Vizsla is used solely as a competitive dog, an automaton in the show ring or in the field. Its elements are as a working gundog and a cherished member of the family, where all its qualities can enrich our lives.

Bibliography

Scott, John Paul, and Fuller, John L. *Genetics and the Social Behaviour of the Dog. University Press. USA. 1966.*
This book is an authoritative information on the behaviour of the dog based on nearly 20 years of research at the Jackson Laboratory where both authors were senior staff scientists at Bar Harbor, Maine.

Fox, Dr Michael, *Understanding Your Dog. Blond & Briggs. UK. 1975.*
Dr Fox is a recognised authority on canids and several scholarly studies on animal behaviour have won him wide acclaim in the scientific community. He owns a rare Telomian dog, several wolves, foxes, jackals and coyotes.

Pfaffenberger, Clarence, *The New Knowledge of Dog Behaviour. Howell Book House. USA. 10th Edition 1973.*
Clarence Pfaffenberger is a Member of the Board of Directors of Guide Dogs for the Blind. He was assigned the task of finding the ideal puppy which would become the ideal guide dog. He spent many years collaborating with those working at the Behaviour Research Laboratory at Hamilton Station, keeping valuable scientific records. Mr Pfaffenberger also contributed to the work at the pioneer institutions at Fortune Fields and the Seeing Eye.

Glossary

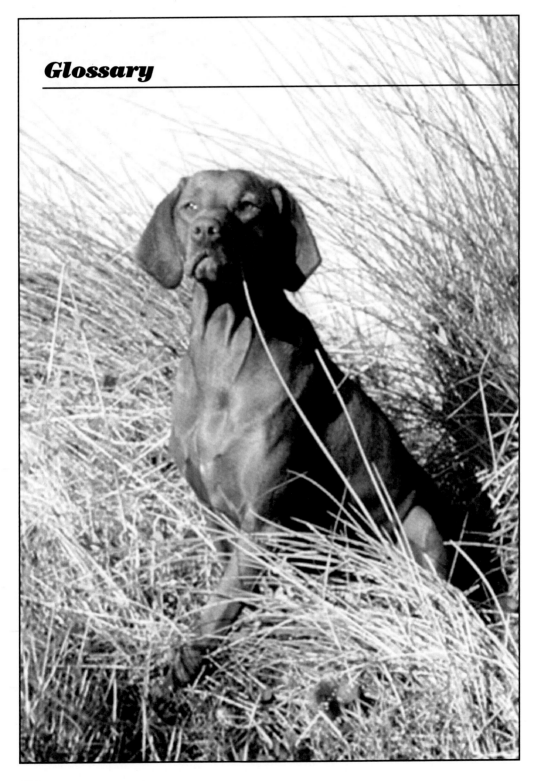

Angulation	Angles formed by the joints, specifically applied to the shoulder with the upper arm (front angulation). Also to the angles of the stifle and hock (rear angulation)
Back	The back is the portion of the topline commencing from the point just behind the withers and ending at the loin/croup junction: the thoracic and lumber vertebrae regions of the spine
Balance	Symmetry, no part too big or too small in relation to another part
Bite	The way the teeth meet when the jaw closes
Body length	The body length is usually taken as the distance from the point of the shoulder to the rearmost projection of the upper thigh
Bossy	Superfluous muscular development over the shoulder (fault)
Bow legged	Front or back legs curving outward (fault)
Brisket	The base of the rib section, lower part of the chest in front of and between the forelegs. Thus the term 'depth of chest or 'shallow'
Cannon bone	Section between the hock joint and the foot of the back legs
Cat-foot	Neat round arched compact foot
Clean head	A head devoid of extraneous muscular or bony lumps, free of wrinkles
Cloddy	Thick-set, lacking elegance (fault)
Chest	The front area of the body at the terminus of the breast-bone
Coarse head	Head broader than the ideal, excessive lumpy bone or muscle development (fault)
Conformation	Shape and form of the body
Coupling	Loin, connecting the forehand to the hindquarters
Cowhocks	Hocks pointing inward to one another (fault)
Covering the ground	The amount of ground covered by the spread between the front and back legs when moving, it means easy, economical action, with maximum stride length or reach compared to the height from the ground to brisket; question of measurements and ratio of the parts (when moving)
Crabbing	The dog moves diagonally, thus the hindlegs do not follow the track of the forefeet, and the back legs move sideways (fault)
Croup	Part of the backline above the pelvis, from loin to 'set on' of the tail
Daylight	The distance from the lowest point of the body to the floor, shows too much or not enough daylight
Dewclaw	The fifth claw on the inside of the foreleg
Dewlap	Loose pendulous skin, in folds, on the chin, throat and neck regions (fault)
Down in pastern	Showing an angle forward or sideways which is abnormal, due to faulty faulty bone structure, weak tendons or muscles (fault)
Drive	Impetus - 'to move with drive'. Hind quarter propulsion
Dudley nose	Liver coloured nose
Elbows in	In which the elbow is placed too firmly up against the chest. Thus restricts movement (faults)
Elbows out	In which both or one elbow are some distance from the chest wall, causes unsound movement, energy wasting and tiring gait
Ewe-neck	Concave topline of neck, resembling the neck of the ewe or camel (fault)
Fiddle front	Combination of curved forearm, elbows out, pasterns close together and turned out feet (fault)
Flank	Sides of the body below the loins
Flew	Pendulous lips and cheeks

293

Forearm	Section of front legs, between the elbow and pastern joint, composed of the radius and ulna
Front or forehand	The entire aspect of the dog except the head when seen from the front
Gait	Movement, action
Gay tail	Tail carried over the back (fault)
Gene	One of the many thousands of determinants concerned with the development in the offspring of hereditary characters and contributed in equal numbers by the parents
Goose rump	Steep croup, sloping more than 30 degrees to the ground (fault)
Hackney	To lift the forelegs high under the chin when moving (fault)
Hare-foot	Elongated foot, with long third digits (fault)
Hawk eye	A yellow eye (fault)
Hock	The joint between the second thigh and the pastern of the hindleg
Knuckling-over	Forelegs bent forward at the knee (fault)
Leathers	Ear flaps
Length of neck	The first seven vertebrae (cervical) of the spinal column, from head to withers
Level bite	When the teeth meet edge to edge
Level topline	An even backline from neck to tail
Light in eye	Eyes light in colour or yellowish (fault)
Light boned	Inadequate frame (fault)
Loaded Shoulder	The muscles under the top half of the shoulder blade have been over-developed so that the blade is pushed outward from the body and cannot occupy its natural position (fault)
Loin	The section between the rib and the croup
Long in the back	The total length of the back is too long compared to the height of the dog (fault)
Long in leg	Legs too long in proportion to the rest (fault)
Muzzle	The fore-face
Occiput	Protuberance at the middle and rear of the skull
Overshot	The upper incisors protrude beyond the lower teeth leaving a gap (fault)
Pace	A gait in which the legs move in lateral pairs (fault)
Paddling	Throwing the front feet sideways in action (fault)
Pastern	The bones between knee and foot (foreleg) and hock and foot (hindleg)
Pigeon toes	Toes point in (toeing in) (fault)
Pin toes	Toes pointing in (fault)
Plaiting	Placing one forefoot in line with the other (fault)
Quality	Denotes refinement, degree of excellence, a distinguishing characteristic
Quarters	The two hindlegs together
Rangy	Long and loose limbed (fault)
Reach	Distance covered with each stride. 'Plenty of reach'. Maximal stride length
Roach back	Excessive convex curve of back line from the eighth rib over the loin and the croup (fault)
Scissor bite	Upper incisors just overlap
Second thigh	Lower thigh, gaskin
Set of tail	Placement of tail

Shelly	Narrow, with little depth to chest (fault)
Short coupled	Short and strong in loins
Short in body	Total length of body being short compared to the height (fault)
Shoulder	Region created by the shoulder blade and supporting muscles
Sickle tail	Tail carried high in a semi-circle (fault)
Sickle hock	The hock joint is bent so that the cannon bone is at an angle rather than vertical to the ground creating a curve suggesting a sickle (fault)
Single tracking	As the speed increases the legs incline more and more under the body. The paws come to travel in a single line
Slab sided	Flat in the ribs (fault)
Snipey	Tapering face, narrow and shallow in muzzle (fault)
Sound	Free from malformation
Splay foot	A foot with toes spread wide apart and lacking arch (fault)
Spring of rib	Roundness of the ribs
Stifle	Joint between the upper and second thigh in backleg corresponds to the knee in man
Stilted	Short restricted stride (fault)
Stop	Depression between the forehead and eyes
Straight hocks	Hocks lacking angulation or bed at the joint (fault)
Straight	Pasterns with little or no slope to the bones between the joint and the foot Pasterns (fault)
Straight shoulder	Insufficient angulation between shoulder and upper arm (fault)
Straight stifle	Insufficient angulation of the joint (fault)
Stride	Distance from one padmark to the next of the same foot in any gait
Substance	Body weight, power
Swayback	Dipping back line (fault)
Trot	Two time movement, right front, left rear, and left front and right rear, when the foot is placed on the ground
Tendon	Band of elastic tissue joining the muscle to the bone
Terrier front	Normal shoulder angulation with short upper arm, showing little forechest (fault)
Throaty	Excessive loose skin under the throat (fault)
Tighten up	To develop more muscle
Topline	Profile of upper outline from the back of the skull to the tail
Tuck-up	Upward curve under belly - too much (fault), too little (fault)
Turn of stifle	Angle of the joint
Type	The sum of those parts that make the dog look a particular breed
Undershot	The lower teeth project beyond the upper ones (fault)
Unsound	If for any reason physical or mental, is incapable of carrying out the functions for which it was designed
Upright shoulders	Shoulders too nearly vertical (fault)
Weedy	Lacking in bone (fault)
Whelp	To give birth too; noun - a newly born puppy
Whelping	Giving birth to puppies
Withers	The highest point of the shoulder where the blades meet. The point from which the dog is measured
Wry mouth	The lower jaw does not line up with the upper jaw (fault)

Appendix A - VIZSLA SHOW CHAMPIONS

Owner	Name	DOB	Sire	Dam	Breeder
Amos-Jones	Sh Ch Hammerton Hold Court at Cassom	6.7.92	Sh Ch Russetmantle Finch of Gunalt	Glendun Dallas of Hammerton	D J Jones
Barlow & Woods	Sh Ch Pitswarren Sarah	25.5.94	Sh Ch Szolnoki Zacasher by Pitswarren	Pitswarren Prisca	Harper
Bicknell	Sh Ch Kencombe Delius	2.4.89	Sh Ch Szappanos Szeivacs of Abbeystag	Sondek Duchess	Winchcombe
Bicknell	Sh Ch Pitswarren Isaac of Szentendre	27.12.91	Ch Fandango in the Sun at Hookside	Sh Ch Pitswarren Leila	Harper
Boys	Sh Ch Windhover Ondine of Galfrid	9.7.70	Waidman Fules	Atalanta Lass of Zelten	Maxim
Boys	Sh Ch Galfrid Jade	12.2.73	Galfrid Gaspar	Matai Sari of Galfrid (Hun Imp)	Boys
Boys	Sh Ch Galfrid Mia	16.11.73	Galfrid Gaspar	Saline Coire of Galfrid	Boys
Boys	Sh Ch Galfrid Rosa	24.7.82	Galfrid Sean	Mocsarkereso Vac of Galfrid (Hung Imp)	Boys
Boys	Sh Ch Galfrid Whig	30.4.84	Galfrid Rudi	Galfrid Kerstin	Boys
Boys	Sh Ch Galfrid Bennet	7.4.85	Sh Ch Galfrid Whig	Sh Ch Galfrid Rosa	Boys
Boys	Sh Ch Galfrid Sidney	9.4.92	Sh Ch Galfrid Whig	Galfrid Marthe	Boys
Bradbrook	Sh Ch Russetmantle Bee	1.11.81	Sh Ch Russetmantle Crisp	Russetmantle Ash	Gottlieb
Chisholm	Ch Shooting Star of Vaternish	1.11.84	Pizzigato Polka of Nevedith	Nevedith Crumpet of Hildon	Birchall
Comybeare	Sh Ch Tragus Pennies from Heaven at Clantor	14.11.93	Captain Jeeves of Glendun	Glendun Blossom of Tragus	Upton
Coombe	Sh Ch Castlefield Rhapsody in Blue	8.10.82	Ch Abbeystag Emilo	Russetmantle Jan	Coombe
Coote	Sh Ch Glendun Dollar of Stregaya	12.12.87	Galfrid Wise of Vizvar	Stregaya Celebrity of Glendun	Winter
Coote	Sh Ch Stregaya Fleet	8.3.90	Stregaya Echo	Sh Ch Glendun Dollar of Stregaya	Coote
Dickinson	Sh Ch Calversham Braeville	7.7.77	Penkevil Zaube	Kenstaff Gay Sadie	Coupe
Digby	Sh Ch Hookside Sounds of Silence at Alsziv	21.3.89	Hookside Perseus	Sh Ch Hookside Braid (Exp USA)	Elliott
Digby	Ch Alsziv Pasque	13.4.91	Sh Ch Szappamos Szeivacs of Abbeystag	Sh Ch Hookside Sounds of Silence at Alsziv	Digby

Owner	Name	DOB	Sire	Dam	Breeder
Digby	Ch Nicaels Russe by Alsziv	5.6.95	Ch Alsziv Pasque	Sh Ch Russetmantle Ember	Wilks
Douglas-Redding	Sh Ch Wolfox Fabia	3.12.69	Wolfox Saline Attila	Wolfox Kinford Rica	Douglas-Redding
Douglas-Redding	Sh Ch Abbeystag Claudia of Wolfox	12.8.72	Sh Ch Futaki Lazslo (USA Imp)	Abbeystag Wolfox Flavia	Gray
Elliott	Ch Fandango in the Sun at Hookside	8.10.82	Ch Abbeystaq Emilo	Russetmantle Jan	Coombe
Fairlie	Sh Ch Russetmantle Qure of Tasairgid	14.5.84	Ch Abbeystag Emilo	Sh Ch Russetmantle Poppy	Gottlieb
Fairlie	Sh Ch Tasairgid Designer Genes	8.6.89	Sh Ch Galfrid Whig	Sh Ch Russetmantle Quire of Tasairgid	Fairlie
Finch	Dutch Lux Swiss & UK Sh Ch Prins (Dutch Imp)	8.6.75	Kamp Milo-Cinnamon V D Beulaker	Luizza	Middleton
Foster	Sh Ch Kinford Zsuzsi	17.4.68	Waidman Ficko	Kinford Vlada	Petrie-Hay
Fuszine-Szeqvari	Sh Ch Hookside Braid (Exp. USA)	21.4.87	Hookside Saturn	Hookside Minx	Elliott
Gottlieb	Sh Ch Waidman Remus	25.6.69	Waidman Fules	Kinford Viada	Petrie-Hay
Gottlieb	Sh Ch Galfrid Sofia of Russetmantle	2.10.75	Sh Ch Waidman Remus	Saline Coire of Galfrid	Boys
Gottlieb	Ch Russetmantle Troy	28.7.76	Galfrid Odo	Galfrid Leda of Russetmantle	Gottlieb
Gottlieb	Sh Ch Russetmantle Sage	8.2.79	Ch Russetmantle Troy	Sh Ch Galfrid Sofia of Russetmantle	Gottlieb
Gottlieb	Sh Ch Russetmantle Paris	21.12.80	Ch Russetmantle Troy	Sh Ch Galfrid Sofia of Russetmantle	Gottlieb
Gottlieb	Sh Ch Russetmantle Poppy	21.12.80	Ch Russetmantle Troy	Sh Ch Galfrid Sofia of Russetmantle	Gottlieb
Gottlieb	Ch Russetmantle Quiver	14.5.84	Ch Abbeystag Emilio	Sh Ch Russetmantle Poppy	Gottlieb
Gottlieb	Sh Ch Russetmantle Crisp	28.7.80	Ch Russetmantle Troy	Russetmantle Katcha	Gottlieb
Gottlieb	Sh Ch Russetmantle Ochre	21.11.85	Ch Abbeystag Emilio	Sh Ch Russetmantle Poppy	Gottlieb

Owner	Name	DOB	Sire	Dam	Breeder
Gottlieb	Sh Ch Russetmantle Finch of Gunalt	21.2.88	Sh Ch Russetmantle Paris	Sh Ch Russetmantle October	Gottlieb
Gottlieb	Sh Ch Russetmantle Mace	22.7.88	Sh Ch Russetmantle Paris	Sh Ch Russetmantle Ochre	Gottlieb
Gray	Sh Ch Abbeystag Wolfox Flora	3.12.69	Wolfox Saline Attila	Wolfox Kinford Rica	Douglas-Redding
Gray	Ch Abbeystag Bruna	12.8.72	Sh Ch Futaki Lazslo (USA Imp)	Sh Ch Abbeystag Wolfax Flora	Gray
Gray	Ch Abbeystag Emilio	19.2.74	Sh Ch Futaki Lazslo	Abbeystag Wolfox Flavia	Gray
Gray	Sh Ch Futaki Lazslo (USA Imp)	26.5.71	Dual Ch & Am Ft Ch Janos V W Come Lately	Ft Ch Futaki Lenke	Bela Hadik
Gray	Sh Ch Szappanos Szeivacs of Abbeystag	27.5.83	Ch Abbeystag Emilio	Huntley Beech	A M Jones
Hardy & Hallam	Sh Ch Bournehouse Red Rhapsody of Tokaji	17.4.93	Captain Jeeves of Glendun	Sh Ch Gardenway Height of Elegance at Bournehouse	Williams
Harper	Sh Ch Gardenway Rica of Pitswarren	25.6.85	Ch Russetmantle Grebe of Gardenway	Ch Gardenway Bula	Perkins
Harper	Sh Ch Pitswarren Levi	14.11.88	Pitswarren Zacchaeus	Sh Ch Gardenway Rica of Pitswarren	Harper
Harper	Sh Ch Pitswarren Tanzie	11.8.90	Sh Ch Pitswarren Levi	Russetmantle Dream of Pitswarren	Harper
Harper	Sh Ch Pitswarren Leila	14.11.88	Pitswarren Zacchaeus	Sh Ch Gardenway Rica of Pitswarren	Harper
Harper	Sh Ch Szolnoki Zacasher by Pitswarren	17.3.92	Pitswarren Zacchaeus	Alcsi Orsi (Hung Imp)	Knight
Harper	Sh Ch Szolnoki Zacanyja by Pitswarren	17.3.92	Pitswarren Zacchaeus	Alcsi Orsi (Hung Imp)	Knight
Hensey	Sh Ch Castlefield Mill Lane	15.10.87	Sh Ch Captain Quincey of Glendun in Blue	Sh Ch Castlefield Rhapsody	Coombe
Houghton	Sh Ch Swanside Zsigmond	10.10.72	Bingo Vom Wurmbrandpark (Austrian Imp)	Sh Ch Swanside Czarina	Simkin
Houghton	Ch Galfrid Tara	1.4.76	Galfrid Prej	Matai Sari of Galfrid (Imp)	Boys
Houghton	Ch Peckers Perchance	5.2.79	Sh Ch Swanside Zsigmond	Ch Galfrid Tara	Houghton
Houghton	Sh Ch Peckers Parody	27.4.81	Sh Ch Swanside Zsigmond	Ch Galfrid Tara	Houghton

Owner	Name	DOB	Sire	Dam	Breeder
How	Sh Ch Pipwell Golden October	7.10.85	Dutch Lux Swiss & UK Sh Ch Prins (Dutch Imp)	Hookside Dusk of Pipwell	How
Hurst	Sh Ch Russetmantle Bronze	1.11.81	Sh Ch Russetmantle Crisp	Russetmantle Ash	Gottlieb
Islip	Sh Ch Russetmantle Seth	8.2.79	Ch Russetmantle Troy	Sh Ch Galfrid Sofia of Russetmantle	Gottlieb
Kleinmann	Ch Valleyhunters Valhalla	2.7.92	Ch Valleyhunter Special Envoy (Isr Imp)	Valleyhunters Little Dream	Kleinman
Kleinmann Assaf	Ch Valleyhunter Special Envoy	16.6.90	Valleyhunters Challenge	Valleyhunters Matai (Whelped in Quarantine)	Countess
Lambert	Sh Ch Gryffe Opal	7.2.92	Gardenway Master Mariner	Gryffe Rittia	Plunkett
Lambert	Sh Ch Mystical Megan of Gesztenye	22.6.93	Ch Curzo Laski	Gryffe Rittia	Plunkett
Larner	Sh Ch Galfrid Hugo of Yelrehta	11.5.72	Matai Bitang Tucsok	Faradpusztai Charlotte of Galfrid (Hung Imp in whelp)	Boys
Larner	Sh Ch Yelrehta Gemini	31.7.73	Sh Ch Galfrid Hugo of Yelrehta	Halstock Fair Maid of Yelrehta	Larner
Leggett	Sh Ch Swallow Sunset	16.9.91	Sh Ch Russetmantle Finch of Gunalt	Castlefield Midnight Blue	Dimon
Lyne	Sh Ch Pirospont Topaz	7.12.83	Sh Ch Russetmantle Seth	Courthill Chloe	Islip
Marshall	Sh Ch Vaternish Bronze Star at Lowerdon	21.4.88	Sh Ch Galfrid Whig	Ch Shooting Star of Vaternish	Chisholm
Matmor	Sh Ch Hookside Artimis (Exp USA)	19.3.89	Ch Fandango in the Sun at Hookside	Piccadilly Pedra	Elliott
McCabe	Sh Ch Chantilly Jester (Exp Spain)	12.7.72	Saline Szeppataki Csaba (Hung Imp)	Saffron Flora	McCabe
McCabe	Sh Ch Russetmantle Kushba of Bohoc	5.1.78	Sh Ch Swanside Miklos	Sh Ch Galfrid Sofia of Russetmantle	Gottlieb
Mills de Hoog	Sh Ch Swanside Miklos	10.10.72	Bingo vom Wurmbrandpark (Austrian Imp)	Sh Ch Swanside Czarina	Simkin
Neill	Ch Saline Judi	6.4.81	Sh Ch Chantilly Jester (Exp Spain)	Saline Grote	Auchterlonie

Owner	Name	DOB	Sire	Dam	Breeder
O'Keefe	Sh Ch Magyar Quail.	25.2.93	Gardenway Harvest Moon	Horshams Primrose at Magyar	Evans
Packham	Sh Ch Kazval Krugerand	11.7.92	Sh Ch Vaternish Bronze Star at Lowerdon	Russetmantle Easter of Wyndsmoor	Whyte
Perkins	Ch Gardenway Bula	28.4.80	Galfrid Sean	Galfrid Erika	Perkins
Perkins	Ch Russetmantle Grebe of Gardenway	14.4.82	Ch Russetmantle Troy	Sh Ch Galfrid Sofia of Russetmantle	Gottlieb
Perkins	Ch Gardenway Charlotte	18.2.84	Ch Russelmantle Grebe of Gardenway	Ch Gardenway Bula	Perkins
Perkins	Ch Gardenway Dawn Run	10.5.87	Ch Russetmantle Grebe of Gardenway	Ch Gardenway Bula	Perkins
Perkins	Sh Ch Gardenway Drumlargen of Gardenway	10.5.87	Ch Russetmantle Grebe	Ch Gardenway Bula	Perkins
Perkins	Sh Ch Gardenway Dawn Breeze	2.1.95	Hung & Int Ch Kilato Teri Furge Mokany of Helmlake	Ch Gardenway Dawn Run	Perkins
Purkis	Sh Ch Chilsham Shropshire Lad	16.11.91	Pitswarren Zacchaeus	Gardenway Oriole of Chilsham	Purkis
Rankin	Sh Ch Artic of Zelten	28.10.67	Joram de la Creste (Fr Imp)	Kinford Lidi	Rankin
Rice	Sh Ch Gamelands Zorro	17.2.72	Sh Ch Waidman Remus	Sh Ch Kinford Zsuzsi	Foster
Rice	Sh Ch Gamelands Zeckie	8.1.71	Waidman Flook	Kinford Nora	Foste
Rice	S It Ch Swanside Czorna	15.2.75	Waidman Brok	Sh Ch Swanside Czarina	Simkin
Seward	Sh Ch Galfrid Anna of Annadale	16.7.77	Kenstall Xavier of Galfrid	Saline Coire of Galfrid	Boys
Simkin	Sh Ch Swanside Czarina	7.11.69	Waidman Flook	Bonni Robin	Maloney
Steele	Sh Ch Nicael Polestar of Streamhawk	13.9.93	Ch Alsziv Pasque	Sh Ch Russetmantle Ember	Wilks
Swindell	Sh Ch Czassa Calista	25.11.78	Dueke Larange	Golden Claret of Czassa	Swindell
Todd & McCormick	Sh Ch Tasairgid Pure Genius at Drevhamor	8.6.89	Sh Ch Galfrid Whig	Sh Ch Russetmantle Quire of Tasairgid	Fairlie
Townsend	Sh Ch Galfrid Kipps	27.6.89	Sh Ch Galfrid Whig	Auchinner Batina	Boys
Turtle	Sh Ch Russetmantle Swallow of Nantagrove	1.11.89	Sh Ch Russetmantle Paris	Sh Ch Russetmantle Ochre	Gottlieb
Tymczuk	Sh Ch Castlefield Windmill Girl	15.10.87	Sh Ch Captain Quincey of Glendun	Sh Ch Castlefield Rhapsody in Blue	Coombe
Upton	Sh Ch Wicked Lady of Tragus	7.8.92	Gardenway Red Admiral	Glendun Pippa	Marshall

Owner	Name	DOB	Sire	Dam	Breeder
Webster	Sh Ch Russetmantle Jake of Asquanne	16.6.79	Sh Ch Waidman Remus of Tragus	Galfrid Leda of Russetmantle	Gottlieb
Whiting	Sh Ch Stregaya Derringer of Cragvallie	1.3.87	Sh Ch Galfrid Whig	Russetmantle Ribbon of Stregaya	Coote
Wilks	Sh Ch Russetmantle October	20.11.85	Ch Abbeystag Emilo	Sh Ch Russetmantle Poppy	Gottlieb
Wilks	Sh Ch Russetmantle Ember	25.10.86	Ch Abbeystag Emilo	Sh Ch Russetmantle Poppy	Gottlieb
Williams	Sh Ch Gardenway Height of Elegance at Bournehouse	20.10.88	Ch Russetmantle Quiver	Ch Gardenway Charlotte	Perkins
Wilson	Ch Cuzco Laski	7.3.89	Oroshaza Alicante	Glenbreck Gerda	Pia
Winter	Sh Ch Captain Quincey of Glendun	13.9.83	Oroshaza Phara	Russetmantle Posy	Marlow

Complete up to LKA Championship Show 1997

Stop press: Show Champions made up in 1998
Bitches:
Barwick's Bequerelle Star Creation
Crook's Finnougric Maple Dancer
Lambert's Gesztenye Giselle

Dogs:
Le Mare's Int & Hung Ch Teri Furge Mokany of Helmlake
Perkins' Gardenway Dramatist
McCullough's Vereker Sparrowhawk
Wilks' Nicael Rully

Appendix B - CHAMPIONS & FIELD TRIAL CHAMPIONS

Owner	Name	DOB	Sire	Dam	Breeder
Chisholm	Ch Shooting Star of Vaternish (B)	1.11.84	Pizzigato Polka of Nevedith	Nevedith Crumpet of Hilldon	Birchall
Digby	Ch Alsziv Pasque (D)	13.4.91	Sh Ch Szappanos Szeivacs of Abbeystag	Sh Ch Hookside Sounds of Silence at Alsziv	Digby
Digby	Ch Nicaels Russe by Alsziv (D)	5.6.95	Ch Alsziv Pasque	Sh Ch Russetmantle Ember	Wilks
Elliott	Ch Fandango in the Sun at Hookside (D)	8.19 82	Ch Abbeystag Emilio	Russetmantle Jan	Coombe
Gottlieb	Ch Russetmantle Troy (D)	28.7.76	Galfrid Odo	Galfrid Leda of Russetmantle	Gottlieb
Gottlieb	Ch Russetmantle Quiver (D)	14.5.84	Ch Abbeystag Emilo	Sh Ch Russetmantle Poppy	Gottlieb
Gray	Ch Abbeystag Bruna (B)	12.8.72	Sh Ch Futaki Lazslo (USA Imp) Wolfox Flora	Sh Ch Abbeystag	Gray
Gray	Ch Abbeystag Emilio (D)	19.2.74	Sh Ch Futaki Lazslo (USA Imp)	Abbeystag Wolfox Flavia	Gray
Houghton	Ch Galfrid Tara (B)	1.4.76	Galfrid Pej	Matai Sari of Galfrid (Hung Imp)	Boys
Houghton	Ch Peckers Perchance (B)	5.2.79	Sh Ch Swanside Zsigmond	Ch Galfrid Tara	Houghton
Kleinmann	Ch Valleyhunters Valhalla (B)	2.7.92	Ch Valleyhunter Special Envoy	Valleyhunters Little Dream(Isr Imp)	Kleinmann
Kleinmann	Ch Valleyhunter Special Envoy (D)	2.7.92	Valleyhunters Challenge	Valleyhunters Matai Countess	Assaf
Neill	Ch Saline Judi (B)	6.4.81	Sh Ch Chantilly Jester (Exp Spain)	Saline Grote	Auchterlonie
Perkins	Ch Gardenway Bula (B)	28.4.80	Galfrid Sean	Galfrid Erika	Perkins
Perkins	Ch Russetmantle Grebe of Gardenway (D)	14.4.82	Ch Russetmantle Troy	Sh Ch Galfrid Sofia of Russetmantle	Gottlieb
Perkins	Ch Gardenway Charlotte (B)	18.2.84	Ch Russetmantle Grebe of Gardenway	Ch Gardenway Bula	Perkins
Perkins	Ch Gardenway Dawn Run (B)	10.5.87	Ch Russetmantle Grebe of Gardenway	Ch Gardenway Bula	Perkins
Wilson	Ch Cuzco Laski (D)	7.3.89	Oroshaza Alicante	Glenbrek Gerda	Pia
Cox	Ft Ch Viszony of Vallota (B)	16.8.80	Waidman Brok	Calversham Amber	Andrews
Petrie-Hay & Cox	Ft Ch Archenfield Crusty (B)	12.1.91	Vallota Varazs	Clare of Arkenfield	Gardner

Complete up to January 20th 1998

Appendix C - IMPORTS

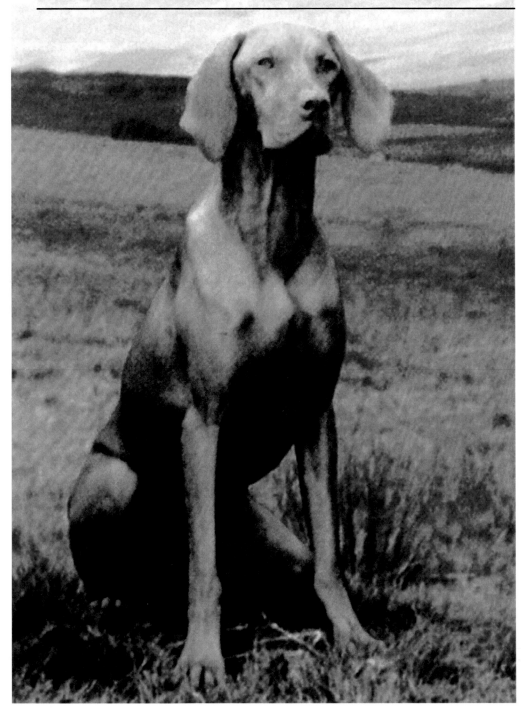

Name	DOB	Sire	Dam	Breeder	Owner	Origin
Adalyn Von Hunt 8/56 (B)	9.7.55	Morho Z Povazio	Asta Z Povazio	Mr/Mrs Hunt	Maj R H Petty	USA
Agnes 8/53 (B)	27.5.48	Puschi	Vlada	Drevenka Istvan	Mrs J Wyndham-Harris	Hung
Alcsi Orsi Q04 (B)	14.7.88	Csatarkai Cudar	Alcsi Gizi	Mr J Kiss	Mr/Mrs Knight	Hung
Bella Vom Wurmbrandpark (B)	21.5.69	Bodo von der Dopplehutte	Tornaspusztai Zsa Zsa	Dipl Ing Gunther Wanivenhaus	Mrs L Petrie-Hay	Aust
Bingo Vom Wurmbrandpark(D)	21.5.69	As above	As above	As above	As above	Aust
Bolnokai Nelli 5/74 (B)	21.8.68	Edenkerti Csibesz	Szilvasvaradi Ara	Dr Daniek Geza	Maj F H Griffiths	Germ
Cool Hand Luke at Castlefield J10 (D)	26.6.83	Am Ch Sascos Melto Mariner	Am Ch Firebrands Ziggy Stardust	Ms P Hartman	Mrs/Miss Coombe	USA
Dade of Kirbydeene Q02 (D)	27.12.88	Verocei Asa	Vixie	Cathelain	Mr/Mrs Downing	France
Derby of Kirbydeene Q02 (D)	27.12.88	As above	As above	As above	As above	France
Erneszt 8/53 (D)	27.5.48	Puschi	Vlada	Drevenka Istvan	Mrs J Wyndham-Harris	Hung
Faradpusztai Charlotte of Galfrid 10/72 (B)	17.3.69	Matai Legeny	Allatkerti Dorka	Ozv Sartay Janesne	Miss A Boys	Hung
Sh Ch Futaki Lazslo 4/72 (D)	26.5.71	Ch/Ft Ch Janos V W Come Lately	Ft Ch Futaki Lenke	Count Bella Hadik	Mrs S Gray	USA
Joram de la Creste 2/62 (D)	?	Schan von Trutzhoff	Kobra z Povaila	Countess de La Celle la Creste	Mrs J Matuszewska	France
Jozsalaki Poci WO1 (D)	24.3.95	Siomenti-Tornyai Virgonc	Jozsalaki Fruzsina	Dr P Bagladi	Mr M Butler	Hung.
Int & Hung Ch Kilato Teri	6.6.90	Vadaszfai Kozak	Kavai Pompas	Mr R Jozsefine	Mrs K Le Mare	Hung
Furge Mokany of Helmlake (D)						
Matal Akac (B)	10.11.70	Sibriktelepi Dani Viktor	Matai Piri	M Farkashazi	The Hon W E A Wilson	Hung
Matai Pirok (B)	1.6.73	Matai Lurko	Matai Panni II	As above	Mr J Parkes	Hung
Matai Sari of Galfrid (B)	25.2.70	Matai Bitang Tucsok	Matai Boske	As above	Miss A Boys	Hung
Matai Vica (B)	2.1.73	Helvecia Alfa	Matai Gerle	As above	Mr Heyman	Hung
Mocsarkereso Vac of Galfrid (B)	13.2.76	Mata Vadasz	Morcos Pusztai Bori	Mr J Kiss	Miss A Boys	Hung
Napkettei VadeszElod (D)	15.10.66	Ajax Olca	Miss Golden Firebird	Mr P A Wright	Mrs B Fitzroy	USA
Penlees Red Alert at Castlefield (D)	21.11.83	Am Ch Dirigo Gamblers Marker	Am Ch Firebrands Constant Comment	Mrs B Anderson	Mrs/Miss Coombe	USA

Name	DOB	Sire	Dam	Breeder	Owner	Origin
Pintyohazi Janka (B)	1.4.95	Hung Ch Vadaszfai Kontar Szorenyi	Pintyohazi Cifra	Ms E Pinterne	Mr M Butler	Hung
Pitypang Entri of Hookside (B)	21.1.92	Hung Ch Pitypang Taller	Huberlus Garas	Ms Z Fuzesine	Mr M Elliott	Hung
Dutch Lux Swiss & UK Sh Ch Prins (D)	8.6.75	Kamp-Milo Cinnamon Magyar V D Beulaker	Luizza	Mr S Middleton	Mr R M Finch	Dutch
Saline Szeppataki Csaba (D)	6.6.68	Kisufalui Dani	Arokparti Erzsok Ledi	Mr J Zoltan	Mrs K Auchterlonie	Hung
Sibriktelepi Tigi (D)	13.6.61	Edenkerti Csibesz	Sibriktelepi Maca	Mr J Farkas	Mr A McRae	Hung
Sir Toby Puck of Sleepy Hollow (D)	7.10.80	Am Ch Zachary of Sleepy Hollow	Pieces of April	Mr/Mrs Mather	Mr J Williams	USA
Sir Wigglesworth Witherspoon (D)	3.9.70	Jancsi Futaki	Vati Almos	Attila Stzanko	Mrs B Robinson	?USA
Starleypoint Komlosreti Arok(D)	7.12.69	Kevei Arom Csimbi	Hubertus Narcisz	Janos Kilner	Mrs P Jackson	Hung
Tardosi Gyongyi (B)	21.6.59	Betyar 674	Csikcsikoi Ari Nora	Mr Lajos Dudas	Mr A McRae	Hung
Trapp Cipra of Helmlake (B)	2.11.87	Hung Austrian Ch Matai Cseles	Anya	Dr T Jakkel	Mrs K Le Mare	Hung
Valleyhunters Little Dream (B)	10.9.87	Dirgo Marker Pd-N Full	Valleyhunters Legend	Ms J Assaf	Miss S Kleinmann	Israel
Valleyhunters Matai Countess(B)	?	Whelped in Quarantine then returned to Israel				
Vermilion Villarsia (D)	4.6.95	Peceli Don Bela	Vallota Vermilion	Mr A Pol-Boxtart	Mrs S Cox	Dutch
Warhorse Lwow (D)	8.4.66	Warhorse O'Jay	Am Ch Warhorse Bella	C Warholm & E Minde	Mrs B Henderson	USA
Zilfrim Buckhouse Bonnie (B)	15.6.95	Rainscote Risky Business	Tasairgid the Main Chance of Zitfrim	Mr/Mrs Kneebone	Miss B Bonnefin	Guern
Zufrim Chestermouse (D)	As above	As above	As above	As above	Mrs E Curnow	As above
Zilfrim Jacks Chance (D)	As above	As above	As above	As above	As above	As above
Zilfrim Kindred Spirit (B)	17.5.94	As above	As above	Mr M J Kneebone	Mrs Kneebone	As above
Zilfrim May Storm (B)	17.5.94	As above	As above	As above	Misses J Smith & S McCathie	As above

Complete up to LKA Championship Show 1997

Appendix D - IMPORT OFFSPRING AWARDS

Name	Title	Awards	Offspring Title	Awards	Sex
Alcsi Orsi (B)	None	None	Szolnoki Zacanyja By Pitswarren Sh Ch	6 CCs 11 Res CCs	Bitch
			Szolnoki Zacasher By Pitswarren Sh Ch	4 CCs 4 Res CCs	Dog
			Szolnoki Asvahviz	1CC 4 Res CCs	Bitch
			Szolnoki Kifli	1CC	Dog
Bella vom Wurmbrandpark (B)	None	1 CC 1 Res CC	Waidman Buda	2 CCs 2 Res CCs	Dog
Bingo vom Wurmbrandpark (D)	None	1 CC	Swanside Zsigmond Sh Ch	12 CCs 13 Res CCs	Dog
			Swanside Miklos Sh Ch	6 CCs 2 Res CCs	Dog
			Golden Claret of Czassa	2 CCs 7 Res CCs	Bitch
			Penkevil Zauber	1 Res CC	Dog
Dade of Kirbydeene (D)	None	None	Gardenway La Valliere of Shalback	1 CC	Bitch
			Gryffe Cumulus of Gesztenye	1 CC	Dog
Faradpusztai Charlotte of Galfrid (B)	None	None	Galfrid Hugo of Yelrehta Sh Ch	4 CCs 4 Res CCs	Dog
Futaki Lazslo Sh Ch (D)	Sh Ch	3 CCs 6 Res CCs	Abbeystag Emilio Ch	6 CCs 6 Res CCs	Dog
			Abbeystag Bruna Ch	6 CCs 1 Res CC	Bitch
			Abbeystag Claudia of Wolfox Sh Ch	3 CCs 2 Res CCs	Bitch
			Mindenday Zalda	1 CC 1 Res CC	Bitch
			Abbeystag Beren of Wolfox	1 CC	Dog
			Abbeystag Dominique of Zelten	1 Res CC	Bitch

Name	Title	Awards	Offspring, Title	Awards	Sex
Joram de la Creste (D)	None	None	Artic of Zelten Sh Ch	8 CCs 8 Res CCs	Dog
			Saline Achilles	1 CC 1 Res CC	Dog
			Fruin Reward	1 Res CC	Bitch
			Wolfox Topaz	1 Res CCBitch	
Kilato Teri Furge Mokany of Helmlake Int & Hung Ch (D)	Int & Hung Ch	2 CC 1 Res CC	Gardenway Dramatist	2 CCs 1 Res CC	Dog
			Gardenway Dawn Breeze Sh Ch	4 CC 1 Res CCBitch	
Matai Sari of Galfrid (B)	None	None	Galfrid Tara Ch	13 CCs 5 Res CCs	Bitch
			Galfrid Jade Sh Ch	3 CCs 3 Res CCs	Bitch
			Galfrid Gaspar	1 CC 2 Res CCsDog	
			Galfrid Rosa Sh Ch	3 CCs 2 Res CCs Bitch	
Mocsarkereso Vac of Galfrid (B)	None	2 CCs 5 Res CCs	Pipwell Golden October Sh Ch	5 CCs 3 Res CCsBitch	Dog
Dutch Lux Swiss & UK Sh Ch Prins (D)	Sh Ch	3 CCs 2 Res CCs	Mindenday Prins Xavier	1 CC	Dog
			Mindenday Prins Hal	1 Res CC	
			Hookside Whisper of Dhulea	1 Res CCBitch	
Saline Szeppataki Csaba (D)	None	None	Chantilly Jester Sh Ch	20 CCs 10 Res CCs	Dog
			Starleypoint Kati	1 Res CCBitch	
Starleypoint Komlosreti Arok (D)	None	None	Starleypoint Ulles	1 Res CCDog	
Valleyhunters Little Dream (B)	None	None	Valleyhunters Valhalla Ch	3 CCs 1 Res CCBitch	
Valleyhunters Matai Countess (B)	None	None	Valleyhunter Special Envoy Ch	3 CCs 3 Res CCsDog	
Warhorse Lwow (D)	None	None	Starbeater Phoenix of Galfrid	1 CC	Bitch

Complete up to LKA Championship Show 1997

Appendix E - CRUFTS WINNERS

Year / Judge / Award	Name of Dog / Bitch	Owner	Breeder
1971 Mrs V C Yates BCC + BoB DCC	Kinford Zsuzsi Waidman Remus	Mrs M Foster Mrs G Gottlieb	Mrs L Petrie-Hay Mrs L Petrie-Hay
1972 Mr W E Foster BCC + BoB DCC	Swanside Czarina Sh Ch Waidman Remus	Mr R Simkin Mrs G Gottlieb	Mrs Maloney Mrs L Petrie-Hay
1973 Mrs G Broadley BCC +BoB DCC	Sh Ch Kinford Zsuzsi Artic of Zelten	Mrs M Foster Miss P Rankin	Mrs L Petrie-Hay Miss P Rankin
1974 Maj J L Houghton BCC + BoB DCC	Sh Ch Swanside Czarina Gamelands Zorro	Mr R Simkin Mrs M D Rice	Mrs Maloney Mrs M Foster
1975 Mr R J Gadsden DCC + BoB BCC	Sh Ch Artic of Zelten Gamelands Zeckie	Miss P Rankin Mrs M Rice	Miss P Rankin Mrs M Foster
1976 Mr E Froggatt DCC + BoB BCC	Abbeystag Emillo Sh Ch Abbeystag Claudia of Wolfox	Mr & Mrs A J Gray Mrs B Douglas-Redding	Mr & Mrs A J Gray Mrs S Gray
1977 Mrs J De Casembroot DCC + BoB BCC	Sh Ch Chantilly Jester Sh Ch Swanside Czorna	Mrs H McCabe Mrs M Rice	Mrs H McCabe Mr R Simkin
1978 Mr D L Page DCC + BoB BCC	Galfrid Hugo of Yelrehta Sh Ch Swanside Czorna	Mr D Larner Mrs M Rice	Miss A Boys Mr R Simkin
1979 Miss L Turner DCC + BoB BCC	Russetmantle Troy Russetmantle Kushba of Bohoc	Mrs G Gottlieb Mrs H McCabe	Mrs G Gottlieb Mrs G Gottlieb
1980 Mr J Cartledge BCC + BoB DCC	Galfrid Sofia of Russetmantle Ch Russetmantle Troy	Mrs G Gottlieb Mrs G Gottlieb	Miss A Boys Mrs G Gottlieb
1981 Mr W Parkinson BCC + BoB DCC	Sh Ch Peckers Perchance Calversham Braeville	Mr R Houghton Mr J K Dickinson	Mr R Houghton Mr A Coupe

Year / Judge / Award	Name of Dog / Bitch	Owner	Breeder
1982 Mr R M W Finch			
DCC + BoB	Russetmantle Paris	Mrs G Gottlieb	Mrs G Gottlieb
BCC	Sh Ch Peckers Perchance	Mr R Houghton	Mr R Houghton
1983 Mr F G Waring			
DCC + BoB	Sh Ch Russetmantle Paris	Mrs G Gottlieb	Mrs G Gottlieb
BCC	Sh Ch Peckers Perchance (Ch Status) Nov 1983	Mr R Houghton	Mr R Houghton
1984 Mrs M Lyndesay Smith			
DCC + BoB	Sh Ch Russetmantle Bronze	Mr M Hurst	Mrs G Gottlieb
BCC	Galfrid Rosa	Miss A Boys	Miss A Boys
1985 Mrs M A Layton			
DCC + BoB	Sh Ch Russetmantle Paris	Mrs G Gottlieb	Mrs G Gottlieb
BCC	Russetmantle Poppy	Mrs G Gottlieb	Mrs G Gottlieb
1986 Mrs V Foss			
DCC + BoB	Sh Ch Captain Quincey of Glendun	Mrs J Winter	Mr & Mrs Marlow
BCC	Sh Ch Russetmantle Poppy	Mrs G Gottlieb	Mrs G Gottlieb
1987 Mrs J Allen			
DCC + BoB	Ch Russetmantle Grebe of Gardenway	Mrs J D Perkins	Mrs G Gottlieb
BCC	Gardenway Rica of Pitswarren	Mr & Mrs J P Harper	Mrs J D Perkins
1988 Mrs H Parkinson			
BCC + BoB	Ch Shooting Star of Vaternish	Mr & Mrs B Chisholm	Mrs Birchall
DCC	Ch Russetmantle Quiver	Mrs G Gottlieb	Mrs G Gottlieb
1989 Mr D L Page			
BCC + BoB	Ch Gardenway Charlotte	Mrs J D Perkins	Mrs J D Perkins
DCC	Sh Ch Captain Quincey of Glendun	Mrs J Winter	Mr & Mrs Marlow
1990 Mrs O Hampton			
BCC + BoB	Ch Gardenway Dawn Run	Mrs J D Perkins	Mrs J D Perkins
DCC	Ch Fandango in the Sun at Hookside	Mr M Elliott	Mrs / Miss Coombe

Year / Judge / Award	Name of Dog / Bitch	Owner	Breeder
1991 Mr G Waring			
DCC + BoB	Cuzco Laski	Mr B J Wilson	Mrs M A Pia
BCC	Sh Ch Glendun Dollar of Stregaya	Mrs S Coote	Mr & Mrs P Winter
1992 Mrs J Froggatt			
DCC + BoB	Stregaya Fleet	Mrs S Coote	Mrs S Coote
BCC	Sh Ch Hookside Braid	Mr M Elliott	Mr M Elliott
1993 Mrs M G Gottlieb			
DCC + BoB	Sh Ch Pitswarren Levi	Mr & Mrs P Harper	Mr & Mrs P Harper
BCC	Sh Ch Hookside Artimis	Mr M Elliott	Mr M Elliott
1994 Mr R Houghton			
DCC + BoB	Szolnoki Zacasher by Pitswarren	Mr & Mrs P Harper	Mr & Mrs O Knight
BCC	Magyar Quail	Mrs H O'Keefe	Mr D M J Evans
1995 Mrs M E Holmes			
DCC + BoB	Sh Ch Pitswarren Levi	Mr & Mrs P Harper	Mr & Mrs P Harper
BCC	Sh Ch Russetmantle Swallow of Nantsgrove	Dr & Mrs Turtle	Mrs G Gottlieb
1996 Mrs J D Perkins			
DCC + BoB	Pitswarren Isaac of Szentendre	Mr & Mrs S Bicknell	Mr & Mrs P Harper
BCC	Bequerelle Star Creation	Mrs G Barwick	Mrs G Barwick
1997 Mr D Layton			
DCC + BoB	Sh Ch Nicael Polestar of Streamhawk	Mrs P F Steele	Mrs M Wilks
BCC	Bequerelle Star Creation	Mrs G Barwick	Mrs G Barwick
Stop press:			
1998 Mrs S R Gray			
DCC + BoB	Digby's Ch Nicael Russe of Alzsiv		

Appendix F - PRE-POTENT VIZSLAS

Name of Dog/Bitch	Offspring : Dogs	Bitches
Dogs: Ch Abbeystag Emilio Owned & Bred by Mrs S Gray Sired 8 Sh Ch (2 Ch)	Ch Fandango in the Sun at Hookside Ch Russetmantle Quiver Sh Ch Szappanos Szeivacs of Abbeystag	Sh Ch Russetmantle Quire of Tasairgid Sh Ch Russetmantle October Sh Ch Castlefield Rhapsody in Blue Sh Ch Russetmantle Ochre Sh Ch Russetmantle Ember
Sh Ch Galfrid Whig Owned & Bred by Mrs A Boys Sired 7 Sh Ch	Sh Ch Galfrid Bennett Sh Ch Stregaya Derringer at Cragvallie Sh Ch Vaternish Bronze Star at Lowerdon Sh Ch Tasairgid Pure Genius at Drevhamor Sh Ch Galfrid Kipps Sh Ch Galfrid Sidney	Sh Ch Tasairgid Designer Genes
Ch Russetmantle Troy Owned & Bred by Mrs G Gottlieb Sired 5 Sh Ch (1 Ch)	Sh Ch Russetmantle Seth Sh Ch Russetmantle Paris Ch Russetmantle Grebe of Gardenway Sh Ch Russetmantle Crisp	Sh Ch Russetmantle Poppy
Pitswarren Zacchaeus Owned & Bred by Mr & Mrs P Harper Sired 5 Sh Ch	Sh Ch Pitswarren Levi Sh Ch Szolnoki Zacasher by Pitswarren Sh Ch Chilsham Shropshire Lad	Sh Ch Pitswarren Leila Sh Ch Szolnoki Zacanyja by Pitswarren
Ch Russetmantle Grebe of Gardenway Owned by Mrs J Perkins Bred by Mrs G Gottlieb Sired 4 Sh Ch (2 Ch)	Sh Ch Gardenway Drumlargen	Gardenway Charlotte Sh Ch Gardenway Rica of Pitswarren Ch Gardenway Dawn Run
Sh Ch Waidman Remus Owned by Mrs G Gottlieb Bred by Mrs L Petrie-Hay Sired 3 Sh Ch (2 Ch)	Sh Ch Gamelands Zorro Sh Ch Russetmantle Jake of Asquanne	Sh Ch Galfrid Sofia of Russetmantle
Sh Ch Futaki Lazslo (USA Imp) Owned by Mrs S Gray Bred by CNHT Bela Hadik Sired 3 Sh Ch (2 Ch)	Ch Abbeystag Emillo	Ch Abbeystag Bruna Sh Ch Abbeystag Claudia of Wolfox

Name of Dog	Offspring : Dogs	Bitches
Sh Ch Russetmantle Paris Owned & Bred by Mrs G Gottlieb Sired 3 Sh Ch	Sh Ch Russetmantle Finch of Gunalt Sh Ch Russetmantle Mace	Sh Ch Russetmantle Swallow of Nantagrove
Bitches: Sh Ch Galfrid Sofia of Russetmantle Owned by Mrs G Gottlieb Bred by Mrs A Boys Dam of 6 Sh Ch (1 Ch)	Sh Ch Russetmantle Seth Sh Ch Russetmantle Paris Ch Russetmantle Grebe of Gardenway	Sh Ch Russetmantle Kushba of Bohoc Sh Ch Russetmantle Sage Sh Ch Russetmantle Poppy
Sh Ch Russetmantle Poppy Owned & Bred by Mrs G Gottlieb Dam of 5 Sh Ch (1 Ch)	Ch Russetmantle Quiver Sh Ch Russetmantle October	Sh Ch Russetmantle Quire of Tasairgid Sh Ch Russetmantle Ochre Sh Ch Russetmantle Ember
Ch Gardenway Bula Owned & Bred by Mrs J Perkins Dam of 4 Sh Ch (2 Ch)	Sh Ch Gardenway Drumlargen	Ch Gardenway Charlotte Ch Gardenway Dawn Run Sh Ch Gardenway Rica of Pitswarren
Saline Coire of Galfrid Owned By Mrs A Boys Bred by Mrs K Auchterlonie Dam of 3 Sh Ch		Sh Ch Galfrid Mia Sh Ch Galfrid Sofia of Russetmantle Sh Ch Galfrid Anya of Annadale

The above are pre-potent Vizslas that have produced 3 or more Show Champions up to LKA Championship Show 1997

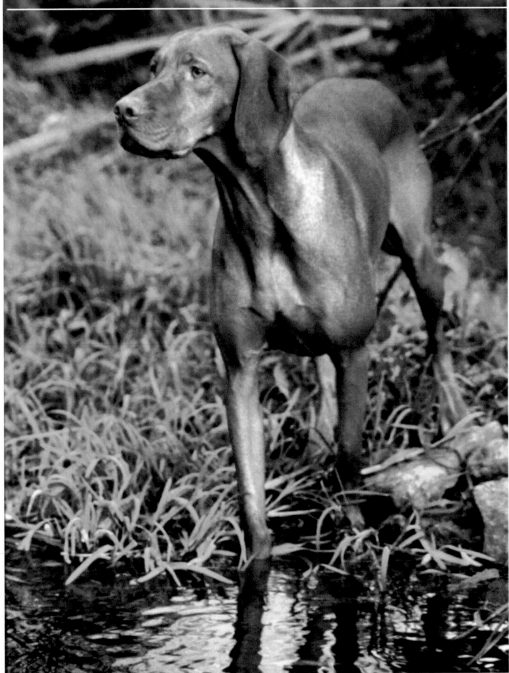

Appendix G
MAJOR WINS AT CHAMPIONSHIP SHOWS WITH CCs

Owner	Name of Dog	Championship Show	Year	Award
Mills de Hoog	Sh Ch Swanside Miklos	National Gundog	1975	Res. Best In Show
Bradbrook	Sh Ch Russetmantle Bee	SKC	1984	Gundog Group
Perkins	Ch Russetmantle Grebe of Gardenway	Bath	1986	Res. Gundog Group
Winter	Sh Ch Captain Quincey of Glendun	Merseyside	1986	Best In Show
Winter	Sh Ch Captain Quincey of Glendun	National Gundog	1988	Best In Show
Perkins	Ch Gardenway Dawn Run	Birmingham National	1989	Gundog Group
Perkins	Ch Gardenway Dawn Run	Paignton	1989	Gundog Group
Harper	Sh Ch Pitswarren Levi	Manchester Society	1993	Res. Gundog Group
Townsend	Rainscote Risky Business	Blackpool	1993	Gundog Group
Harper	Sh Ch Pitswarren Levi	East of England	1993	Res. Best In Show
Harper	Sh Ch Pitswarren Levi	Leeds	1993	Gundog Group
Digby	Ch Alsziv Pasque	LKA	1993	Gundog Group
Digby	Ch Alsziv Pasque	Manchester Society	1994	Gundog Group
Harper	Sh Ch Pitswarren Levi	Leeds	1994	Gundog Group
Coote	Sh Ch Stregaya Fleet	National Gundog	1994	Res. Best In Show
Leggett	Sh Ch Swallow Sunset	Birmingham City	1995	Res. Gundog Group
Coote	Sh Ch Stregaya Fleet	Richmond	1995	Gundog Group + Res. BIS
Upton	Sh Ch Wicked Lady of Tragus	Midland Counties	1996	Res. Gundog Group
Bicknell	Sh Ch Pitswarren Isaac of Szentendre	SKC	1997	Res. Gundog Group
McCullough	Vereker Sparrowhawk	Gundog Society of Wales	1998	Best In Show
McCullough	Vereker Sparrowhawk	Blackpool	1998	Group 1

Complete up to LKA Championship Show 1997

Appendix H - COMPARATIVE TABLES OF REGISTRATION

COMPARATIVE TABLES OF REGISTRATION FOR THE YEARS 1987 - 1997

1987	1988	1989	1990	1991	1992	1993	1994	1995	1996	1997
169	314	335	223	246	290	323	385	340	458	504

SHOW CHAMPIONS

In the 1970s 28 Show Champions were made up.

In the 1980s 32 Show Champions were made up.

In the 1990s (up to LKA Championship Show 1997) 43 Show Champions were made up.

By the end of 1997 (LKA) there were 103 Show Champions.

CHAMPIONS

In order to gain the title of 'Champion', a gundog has to have gained an award in a Field Trial or attained a show Gundog Working Certificate. The Gundog also has to have won a Challenge Certificate under three different Juges.

Currently (January 1998) there are 18 Champions and 2 Field Trial Champions in the breed.

In the 70s 4 Champions were made up.

In the 80s 9 Champions were made up.

In the 90s 5 Champions were made up.